REPATRIATING POLANYI

BY THE SAME AUTHOR

Tázlár: A Village in Hungary
A Village Without Solidarity: Polish Peasants in Years of Crisis
Market Economy and Civil Society in Hungary (ed.)
Tea and the Domestication of the Turkish State
Socialism: Ideals, Ideologies and Local Practice (ed.)
When History Accelerates (ed.)
The Skeleton at the Feast. Contributions to East European Anthropology
Civil Society: Challenging Western Models (ed. with E. Dunn)
Property Relations: Renewing the Anthropological Tradition (ed.)
Turkish Region (with I. Bellér-Hann)
Teach Yourself Social Anthropology
Postsocialism: Ideals, Ideologies and Practices in Eurasia (ed.)
The Postsocialist Agrarian Question (with the "Property Relations" Group)
Galicia: A Multicultured Land (ed. with P.R. Magocsi)
Studying Peoples in the People's Democracies (ed. with M. Sárkány and P. Skalník)
Not the Horse We Wanted! Postsocialism, Neoliberalism and Eurasia
The Postsocialist Religious Question (with the "Civil Religion" Group)
Market and Society: The Great Transformation Today (ed. with K. Hart)
Eastern Christians in Anthropological Perspective (ed. with H. Goltz)
Economic Anthropology: History, Ethnography, Critique (with K. Hart)
The Anthropological Field on the Margins of Europe, 1945–1991 (ed. with A. Bošković)
Economy and Ritual (ed. with S. Gudeman)
Oikos and Market (ed. with S. Gudeman)
Industrial Labor on the Margins of Capitalism (ed. with J. Parry)
Anthropology and Civilizational Analysis: Eurasian Explorations (ed. with J.P. Arnason)

REPATRIATING POLANYI

Market Society in the Visegrád States

CHRIS HANN

CEU PRESS

Central European University Press
Budapest–New York

Published in 2019 by

Central European University Press

Nádor utca 11, H-1051 Budapest, Hungary
Tel: +36-1-327-3138 or 327-3000
Fax: +36-1-327-3183
E-mail: ceupress@press.ceu.edu
Website: www.ceupress.com

224 West 57th Street, New York NY 10019, USA
Tel: +1-732-763-8816
E-mail: ceupress@press.ceu.edu

ISBN 978-963-386-287-2

Library of Congress Cataloging-in-Publication Data

Names: Hann, C. M., 1953- author.
Title: Repatriating Polanyi : market society in the Visegrád states / Chris Hann.
Description: Budapest ; New York : Central European University Press, 2019. | Includes bibliographical references and index.
Identifiers: LCCN 2019002066 (print) | LCCN 2019013848 (ebook) | ISBN 978-963-386-288-9 (Pdf) | ISBN 978-963-386-287-2 (hardcover : alk. paper)
Subjects: LCSH: Polanyi, Karl, 1886-1964. | Economists—Hungary—Biography. | Capitalism—Europe, Central.
Classification: LCC HB102.P64 (ebook) | LCC HB102.P64 H36 2019 (print) | DDC 330.15/42092 [B]—dc23
LC record available at https://lccn.loc.gov/2019002066

Printed in Hungary
Prime Rate Kft., Budapest

To the memory of Ernest Gellner, an inspirational Central European of a later generation than Karl Polanyi, but no more sympathetic to militant (neo)liberalism

Of course, most citizens of socialist countries were perfectly aware that propaganda was just that. Some responded by viewing the countries of the "class enemy" as virtual paradises of abundant consumer goods and freedom. The bitterness they felt after the collapse of socialism and the emergence of "predatory capitalism" which left them "the losers" of the transformation is perfectly captured in an East German joke about the socialist rulers and their propaganda that circulated in East Germany in the 1990s: "They had been lying to us for forty years. How could we have known that they told us the truth about capitalism, of all things?"

Carla Bethmann (2013, 250n202)

Table of Contents

List of Illustrations

Preface

Forwards (n)ever!

This book brings together selected products of decades of research in Central Europe. Most chapters present localized ethnographic data, but the goal is always to illuminate larger questions (in Cambridge, first as a student of Jack Goody and later as a junior colleague of Ernest Gellner, that is how I was trained). One persistent question is: what light can the small academic discipline of socio-cultural anthropology shed on the rise and fall of socialism, and comparable epochal moments in world history? While acknowledging the unity of Marxist-Leninist-Maoist socialism as a civilization, it is equally important to recognize the varieties of socialist experience. The two variants on which I concentrate are the locations of my own fieldwork in Hungary and Poland. These countries are near neighbors, whose alliance has been formalized since 1991 in the Visegrád cooperation (which also includes the Czech Republic and Slovakia). Yet the paths of Hungary and Poland remain distinct and defy reduction to a general model or ideal type.

A second set of questions, implicit throughout the book, is the obverse of the first: how can the study of socialism and postsocialism contribute to the development of theory in the human and social sciences, in particular socio-cultural anthropology? The heartlands of Marxist-Leninist-Maoist socialism in Eurasia are territories in which very few Western socio-cultural anthropologists have specialized (of course, these lands had many pertinent intellectual traditions of their own). The visibility of these social formations is high in social sciences such as political science and sociology, but empirical studies of socialism have not contributed significantly to the formulation of theory in anthropology. In the absence of such impact, it would seem that the anthropological study of socialist and postsocialist societies has simply reflected dominant intellectual paradigms formed elsewhere, such as totalitarian or postcolonial theory.

As the third decade of postsocialism draws to a close, it is high time to reconsider these questions. To clarify my own theoretical perspective, I have drawn repeatedly on the work of Karl Polanyi (1886–1964), profiting from several recent studies of his renewed relevance in the age of neoliberalism. Polanyi is in no need of physical repatriation: his ashes were returned from Canada to Budapest in 1986 to mark the centenary of his birth. Few would have guessed at the time, when socialist power holders cautiously permitted citizens to acquaint themselves with a voice largely silenced hitherto, that Karl Polanyi would come to be viewed as the most significant guide to the contradictions of a thoroughly globalized capitalism in the new century. I discuss his life and work in the Introduction and conclude in Chapter Eleven that his notions of "market society" and the "countermovement" that follows the pursuit of *laissez-faire* are indispensable for grasping the history of the Visegrád states in the last three decades.

The parenthetical (n) in the title of this Preface is an indication that some of my arguments are nuanced, even hesitant. Since 1997 I have lived in Germany, initially in West Berlin, and since 1999 in Halle in former East Germany. Although I have never carried out formal fieldwork in this city, the time I have spent here significantly exceeds the length of all my projects in Hungary and Poland since the 1970s. *Vorwärts* is a venerable concept in German social democracy. East Germans are more likely than West Germans to recognize the phrase *Vorwärts Immer, Rückwärts Nimmer*, and to associate it with their former leader Erich Honecker, who invoked it in a famous speech to mark the 40th anniversary of the German Democratic Republic. This turned out to be the last such celebration. "Forwards ever, Backwards never" has obscure origins in a nineteenth century military march, but the slogan encapsulates the progressivist vision of Marxism-Leninism. No matter that Lenin himself expressed a more realistic appraisal of political trajectories in his famous article "Two steps forward, one step back"; Honecker's rhetoric epitomized the basic linearity of the socialists' march toward an anti-capitalist utopia.

Today such a dogma seems ridiculous or absurd. The collapse of the Soviet bloc coincided with the rise of neoliberal economic policies and also with a diffuse paradigm shift in the human sciences, often characterized as "postmodernism" or the demise of "grand narratives." The latter trends have undoubtedly had an impact on the kind of research which socio-cultural anthropologists have undertaken in the former socialist countries after 1990, some of which had barely been accessible previously. We have become far too smart to fall for easy teleologies. Sociological discourses of "transition" and the "risk society" were made vividly immediate by events such as the collapse of the Russian Ruble in 1997, and by the financial turmoil on a global scale that began in 2007. The collapse of socialism in the context of neoliberal globalization has opened up new fields in which ethnographic attention to changing cultural meanings and social relations can augment the perspectives of larger social science disciplines. But (as I learned from Goody and Gellner long ago) ethnographic accounts, however rich, are never enough.

This book builds on intimate local knowledge dating back to the 1970s and 1980s. It is fueled by the conviction that close-up investigations of social change at the micro level of society (such as a village community) remain as vital as ever. But it is no less essential to address social relations at the macro level. In 1989 the citizens of Eastern Europe and the former Soviet Union were offered another version of utopian thinking. Distinguished scholars announced the "end of history." Some experts conceded that it might be necessary to apply some unpleasant medicine in the form of "shock therapy" to restore societies to what was posited as their natural condition, in which the market-based action of free individual agents would ensure rapid access to the promised land of economic prosperity. The German Federal Chancellor Helmut Kohl, in his famous 1990 speech in which he promised "blooming landscapes" in the new *Bundesländer* that replaced Honecker's socialist republic, acknowledged that there might be difficult moments ahead, and that not everyone would grow more prosperous at the same rate. But the universal validity of utopian teleology was the dominant refrain: citizens should be prepared to make sacrifices in an imperfect present, for the sake of a more perfect future.

The reality was that for many people the transition to market capitalism in Central and Eastern Europe turned out to be more of a dystopia—in terms of material livelihoods on the one hand, and of immaterial values and identities on the other. The two dimensions are, of course, interrelated, and both are investigated in this book. For its framework, I have drawn on an earlier publication. In the Easter term of 1988 in the Department of Social Anthropology at Cambridge, where I was a University Lecturer, I convened a series of seminars in which visiting speakers addressed the changes already under way at the time in Hungary. The pace of events exceeded all expectations. By the time the papers appeared in print in 1990 as a special issue of the *Journal of Communist Studies*, the title of that journal was already obsolete. But it seems to me that the title of that seminar series *Market Economy and Civil Society in Hungary* remains topical three decades later. In my contributions at the time, I expressed doubts about each of these fashionable slogans and especially their coupling. Both market economy and civil society are central to the present book. Alongside market economy I have paid particular attention to property, since the postsocialist years have demonstrated as clearly as any moment in history the centrality of property relations for the embedding of economy in society. In the context of (un)civil society I have repeatedly been struck by the salience of ethnicity, often in combination with religious affiliation, sometimes veering toward xenophobia and racism, in shaping postsocialist social relations.

The Visegrád states have not been smoothly integrated into a European Union of democratic polities, liberal civil societies, and efficient market economies in the last 25 years. In an inaugural lecture at the University of Kent at Canterbury in 1993 (published in Hann 1995a) I commented on a "new orientalism" characterizing Western attitudes toward the region. Such prejudices did not disappear following the major wave of European Union accession in 2004–2007. On the contrary, the ensuing mobility of some Eastern Europeans, notably when they entered the labor market in Britain, intensified othering processes. Subjected to negative stereotyping in Britain, citizens of the new member states in turn reaffirmed their disdain for others located still further east, and therefore presumed to be less developed or "civilized." As opinions between "old" and "new" EU continue to diverge, notably concerning how to deal with migrants and asylum seekers from outside Europe, and with Russia increasingly demonized in ways reminiscent of the Cold War, the disorder which the West has long associated with

Eastern Europe seems pervasive across the entire so-called continent. Meanwhile the global economy muddles through thanks to (among other factors) public bailouts and the financial policies of the People's Republic of China, whose leaders continue to pursue their own variant of utopia through an unprecedented combination of one-party rule and decentralized "socialist market economy." Unfortunately, there is mounting evidence that those high growth rates in East Asia have their own frightening dystopic consequences for the environment, while state indebtedness has risen to exceed Western levels. The economic interdependencies of the globe have become more intense and perhaps somewhat more transparent than they were in Karl Polanyi's time. In the Conclusion I ask whether *Eurasia,* Europe and Asia together, can transcend the ideological oppositions of the era of Marxist-Leninist-Maoist socialism, in order to fulfill its responsibilities for the sustainability of this planet.

Chris Hann
Halle (Saale), October 2017

Note

The chapters of this book were written at different times over almost three decades. Some are amalgamations of components previously published separately. I have resisted the temptation to engage in significant rewriting. To update the arguments thoroughly would in some cases have meant writing a new book. Though I have weeded out some repetition, each chapter can be read as a self-contained contribution. To change the tenses and correct for weaknesses of various kinds would have meant losing the documentary authenticity of the moment of writing, which was generally in the immediate wake of field research. I have therefore made only minimal revisions, mainly to ensure consistent vocabulary across the chapters and to update references. In the 1990s, for example, I was persuaded by several editors to use "communism" to describe the era which came to an end around 1990. This reflects preferences "on the ground" in some circles (particularly in Poland), but in this book I opt consistently for "socialism," the term officially espoused by the power holders of that era and used by most citizens and academic analysts alike. Consequently "postsocialist" is the term I use for recent decades. The words postsocialist and neoliberal have by now become robust enough to justify deleting the hyphens which I sometimes inserted in earlier publications. Chapters One, Eleven, and Twelve are new. Substantive changes in the other chapters (such as an important later reference) is marked with the use of italics and square brackets.

Acknowledgements

The gestation of this book has been long. It made most rapid progress during a Fellowship at the Institut d'Études Avancées at Nantes in 2013–2014, and I am grateful to everyone at that remarkable institution, especially its Directors Alain Supiot and Samuel Jubé. Just when I thought I was reaching the finishing line, the "migration crisis" of Summer 2015 took me by surprise at my main field site in Hungary. This led to a series of distractions, some of which have fed into the last chapters. For permission to make use of materials previously published I am grateful to a number of journals and presses (details are specified at the beginning of the chapters concerned). For long-term collaboration in Hungary I am indebted to Margit Feischmidt, László Kürti, Attila Melegh, Mihály Sárkány and Sándor Striker, as well as to countless friends in Tázlár and Kiskunhalas. In Poland I wish to thank Jacek Nowak in Kraków and Stanisław Stępień in Przemyśl. Others who have helped in various ways along the way include Johann Arnason, Gareth Dale, Keith Hart, Don Kalb, and Nigel Swain: my sincere thanks to all. Without the help of Anke Meyer in my office I would never have finished the task.

I have followed the history of the Central European University from its beginnings, initially through the eyes of Ernest Gellner and later with the help of many other friends who have worked there or been associated with the institution. Readers of this book will soon realize that I am critical of the concept of civil society. Indeed one of my main goals is to show that, while he is absolutely right to criticize "market fundamentalism," the social philosophy of George Soros, with "open society" at its core, is seriously flawed. The shameless attacks launched in 2017 by the Hungarian government on the university founded by Soros have only confirmed me in this view. But precisely because of the current pernicious hounding of the CEU, it gives me great pleasure that this book has been accepted by its publishing arm. My editors at the Press, first Szabolcs László and then József Litkei, have done a terrific job throughout the production process.

Like Karl Polanyi, my ultimate concern (beyond all local detail) is with the conditions—and the social relations—that enable human communities to flourish, in freedom. It is easy to succumb to pathos and dangerous illusions in the pursuit of this ancient goal. In this regard Marxist-Leninist-Maoist socialism and its immediate aftermath teach equally rich lessons. But the challenge is still there, more urgent than ever. To answer this challenge, I argue that it is critical to acknowledge Eurasian commonalities and connections. For Europe today, this means constructing an entirely new politics: a new version of the *Ostpolitik* of Willy Brandt, without illusions, but now on the scale of the landmass.

Again like Polanyi, my concern with the *social* and the *communal* is firmly grounded in a *personal* constellation. Although her concrete research interests lie elsewhere in Eurasia, Ildikó Bellér-Hann is familiar with most of the people, places and predicaments explored in this book. I thank her for her presence and support during four decades.

CHAPTER ONE

Introduction: Karl Polanyi and the Transformations of Socialism and Postsocialism

In the background of this book are large issues of social change and the place of Marxist-Leninist-Maoist socialism in world history. But I am a journeyman social anthropologist, not a global historian, let alone a philosopher. Since ethnographic methods have dominated my discipline for the last century, most of the chapters are based on micro-level analysis and observation in the particular places where I have carried out field research. In this Introduction and in the Conclusion, however, I concentrate on the bigger picture. Beyond the rise and fall of Marxist-Leninist-Maoist socialism in the twentieth century loom even larger agendas: understanding the relationship between economy and society in human history, and how it might be recalibrated to enable improvements to the present mechanisms of globalized neoliberal capitalism. I interpret the failures (the overall account is predominantly negative) of both socialism and the postsocialist transition in the light of ancient aspirations to embed institutions such as markets and property in a framework conducive to the flourishing of human communities.

The two national variants of socialism on which I concentrate are the locations of my fieldwork in East Central Europe: Hungary and Poland. The villages and towns in question fall within the Central European polity into which Karl Polanyi was born in 1886.[1] Polanyi

[1] I refer of course to the Austro-Hungarian Empire, also known as the Dual Monarchy. Polanyi self-identified as Hungarian. He was born in Vienna and fought in Austrian Galicia during the First World War, in territories which

made his scholarly reputation in England and North America following the publication of *The Great Transformation* in 1944. I shall argue that the conceptual approach put forward in this book and elaborated in later writings offers a helpful perspective on both socialist and postsocialist transformations of his homelands. It is time to repatriate Karl Polanyi: first to illuminate recent developments in his homeland, and secondly, on this basis, to bring Polanyi back home to economic anthropology, a field to which he made seminal contributions in the 1950s.

Of course, this task must be undertaken critically. Polanyi never did field research in East Central Europe. He never lived in a one-party socialist state, nor did he join a Communist Party. He was, however, for many years a "fellow traveler," who continued to defend the Soviet Union even after Stalin's abuses of power became widely known. He condemned Soviet repression of the 1956 revolution in Hungary. Yet in his final years, before his death in 1964 in Canada, he was cautiously optimistic that socialist power holders in both the USSR and Hungary might find new ways to build morally defensible communities, ways superior to those of the capitalist West. I argue that the Hungarian implementation of "market socialism" in the years after Polanyi's death was an original and relatively successful realization of these hopes. But ultimately this experiment failed. It was followed by the imposition of new, more doctrinaire ideologies of market and private property after 1990.

Karl Polanyi argued for a substantive definition of the human economy in terms of material livelihoods (Polanyi 1957, 1977). But he was equally concerned to understand how this economy was bound to society, to values and identities, to what Aristotle (one of his favorite writers) termed *eudaimonia*: "human flourishing" or simply "happiness." In *The Great Transformation* Polanyi drew attention to the "double movement," whereby British society in the nineteenth century sought to defend itself against the rise of the "self-regulating market." Polanyi recognized that the countermovement to the market ("self-protection") could breed conflict: in particular, trade protectionism

now form part of Poland. I thank Gareth Dale for sharing drafts of his excellent biography (Dale 2016a).

could lead to jingoism and eventually to Fascism. Contemporary models of free trade and populist reactions to them can be approached in a similar way. The accession of most states of Central and Eastern Europe to the European Union in 2004–2007 has accelerated their integration into a globalized economy, while exposing them to intensified dependence and class differentiation. Foreign investment has done little to slow out-migration. Unemployment rates have fallen compared to the 1990s, but wages are approximately one quarter or one third of those paid for the same work in countries of the "old EU." The end of four decades of socialist repression was supposed to open up these countries to new forms of liberal civil society, but economic insecurities have contributed to a widespread poisoning of the public sphere. The results include xenophobic resistance to asylum seekers and the victimization of long-established minority groups (notably the Roma). The pattern is illustrated in the materials which I present from southeast Poland in Chapter Nine, which present some tensions of the 1990s. If, in this particular case, the tensions have been alleviated in the new century, this is primarily because the brutal ethnic cleansing of the 1940s largely achieved its objective (Buzalka 2007; Hann 2009).

In short, the guiding thread of this book is a Polanyian interpretation of market society after socialism. Market society does not mean that social organization is now based on competitive markets as depicted in old-fashioned economics textbooks. Rather, as Polanyi explained in detail for the case of nineteenth century Britain, market principles are institutionalized through political and legal processes. Outcomes depend critically on the state. (Marxists would add class relations, but Polanyi was reluctant to embrace this terminology, which has proved difficult to operationalize.) This is thus a project grounded in economic anthropology, understood not as a narrow sub-discipline but as an expansive agenda based on a holistic materialist understanding of the embedded "human economy" (Hann and Hart 2011; Hart 2013; Hart, Laville, and Catani 2010). In the remainder of this Introduction I shall explain in more detail how Polanyi's ideas can illuminate such a perspective on his homeland.

Me and Mr Polanyi

More than fifty years after his death, Karl Polanyi's popularity owes more than a little to the financial crisis that began in 2007, which has caused social scientists to question whether the current institutions of global capitalism can remain compatible with free democratic societies (Levitt 2013; Block and Somers 2014; Streeck 2017). But Polanyi's star had been rising steadily long before the latest crisis, ever since the emergence in the 1980s of what has been termed neoliberalism. His reputation has been steadily consolidated through the conferences and publications generated by the Karl Polanyi Institute for Political Economy, established in 1988 at Concordia University, Montreal. Gareth Dale's recent publications (2016a, 2016b), building on his earlier introductory volume (Dale 2010) and his edition of the Hungarian writings (Polanyi 2016), will surely seal Karl Polanyi's place in the pantheon of twentieth century thinkers. In our present moment in history, his approach—above all as it was articulated in the sparkling prose of *The Great Transformation*—seems more timely than ever.

Though born in Vienna, Karl Polanyi was brought up in Budapest, the Hungarian capital, in the period of its most dynamic growth. While politics were dominated by the gentry and aristocracy, industry and commerce were strongly associated with Germans and Jews. The Pollacseks were Jews who chose the path of assimilation and adopted the Hungarian-sounding name of Polányi in Karl's childhood. He was baptized into Protestantism but classified socially as Jewish in the bourgeois circles in which his mother hosted a prestigious salon frequented by intellectuals of diverse backgrounds. Polanyi was educated privately and at an elite Gymnasium; he was a multilingual polymath from childhood. His main subject at university before the First World War was law, but he also studied economics and imbibed the positivist philosophy of Ernst Mach. So did many others in the twilight of the Empire: the work of Mach was the subject of the doctoral dissertation of the Kraków-born anthropologist Bronislaw Malinowski and a treatise by Lenin in the very same years. Politically, Polanyi was somewhere between the two. After years of liberal radicalism as a student activist, Polanyi was traumatized by military service for his Emperor. These were the years in which Malinowski (also a subject of Franz Joseph)

Figure 1. Karl Polanyi with his daughter Kari (1938, courtesy of Kari Polanyi Levitt)

was revolutionizing ethnographic fieldwork methods in Melanesia. Following the war and the defeat of the 1918 October revolution in Hungary, Polanyi left the country for exile in Vienna. For approximately a decade he made his living as an economics journalist. During these years he deepened his knowledge of Karl Marx and argued with the Austrian liberal economists Mises and Hayek in the "socialist calculation debate" (Bockman, Fischer and Woodruff 2016). While critical of the methodological individualism of his opponents, Polanyi nonetheless retained the core of their subjectivist theory of value (Dale 2010, 101–3). Yet he blended this value theory with the "guild socialist" ideas that also appealed to Marcel Mauss during the inter-war decades.

Both as a socialist and as a Jew, it was obvious by the early 1930s that Karl Polanyi had no future in Austria. Even before his move to England in February 1934, he had developed close relations with Christian Socialists in London and Oxford. Although his religious feelings waned in later life, during the 1930s he seems to have regarded socialism as a continuation of the most admirable strands of Christianity. In the "machine age," he argued, utilitarian or "scientific" individualism was tearing communities asunder. Socialism offered the best prospect for restoring Christian moral teachings (Rogan 2017). In the later 1930s, these convictions underpinned a detailed analysis of modern British economic history, embellished with a survey of recent ethnographic literature. The aim of *The Great Transformation,* the opus magnum finally published in 1944, was to show that the modern form of economy in the guise of "market society," pioneered in Britain, was historically unprecedented. In the past "the economy" had been embedded in a totality, not conceived as a separate domain or thing. During the years in which he worked on this book, Polanyi taught at colleges of the Workers' Educational Association in southern England. He also undertook grueling lecture tours in the United States and completed the writing while holding a short-term appointment at Bennington College, Vermont.

Even after publishing *The Great Transformation*, Polanyi failed to land an academic job in Britain. After toying with the idea of returning to Hungary, he eventually accepted an offer from Columbia University, New York, where he spearheaded an interdisciplinary project which led in 1957 to the co-edited volume *Trade and Market in the Early Empires*. Polanyi's own contributions to this volume refined the institutionalist theory of his earlier historical work. He emphasized that "reciprocity" and "redistribution" (concepts first introduced in *The Great Transformation*) were more important than market exchange in integrating the human economy throughout its history, until the rise of industrial capitalism. This book launched a fierce debate between Polanyi's "substantivist" followers and those, generally labelled "formalist," who insisted that the theories and methods of mainstream (neoclassical) economics were appropriate for the study of the economy everywhere in time and space. This debate continued beyond Polanyi's death in 1964, eventually petering out by the end of the decade. By the 1970s, when I began to study social anthropology, new paradigms were emerging. We were expected to be familiar with the toolkit of the substantivists, but the old textbooks now seemed stale. The exciting new ideas came from neo-Marxists such as Pierre-Philippe Rey and Maurice Godelier (see Seddon 1978 for an anthology). As a graduate student I found these Western Marxist approaches, with their focus on "mode of production," more convincing that the Polanyian perspective, with its focus on exchange.

It is more than a little embarrassing today to reflect back on why I made no use of Polanyi and substantivist economic anthropology in my dissertation, which was based on fieldwork in the country he grew up in. My main adviser in the mid-1970s at the Ethnographical Institute of the Hungarian Academy of Sciences was Mihály Sárkány, the country's leading authority in economic anthropology, who had translated several works of Polanyi into Hungarian; but I did not connect them to my own project. I warmed up to Polanyi for the first time in earnest in 1986, when there was some modest fanfare in Budapest to mark the centenary of his birth. Numerous early writings were re-published (English translations of the most significant texts can be found in Polanyi 2014, 2016), and some later works were published for the first time in Hungarian. I began to appreciate the Central European roots of a scholar whose entire life before the publication of *The Great Transformation* (when he was 58) was still shrouded in mystery in the Anglosphere. I found it particularly instructive to compare him to Malinowski, despite the fundamental differences in temperament and political orientation (Hann 1992a).

A few years later, socialism in Hungary and throughout Eastern Europe collapsed. It was replaced by rapid privatization and marketization, in accordance with the neoliberal orthodoxies of the age. Socialist welfare states were scaled back, employment guarantees were withdrawn, and millions of citizens were forced into poverty and migration. You would think that Polanyi's critique of market society would have provided the razor-sharp tools for incisive critique of this new order, more dramatically exposed in the East than in the sluggishly evolving Western capitalist world. Yet few scholars have applied the Polanyian approach to postsocialist Eastern Europe. Maurice Glasman's *Unnecessary Suffering* (1996) is a notable exception, but while this critique of the new wave of "market utopia" owes much to Polanyi, it is not grounded in empirical research. A lot of empirical work has been undertaken by sociologists and anthropologists, but few have drawn significantly on Karl Polanyi. In Budapest an interdisciplinary group at Corvinus University has recently established a *Karl Polanyi Center for Global Social Studies*; but to operationalize the approach and key concepts of a Jewish cosmopolitan, even one who was always deeply attached to his Hungarian identity, is a risky investment for a young scholar wishing to pursue a career in that country today. As for Western researchers, they have followed the fashions of their disciplines and in anthropology (unlike sociology) Polanyi remains unfashionable. Altogether, apart from token references to his best known title, and in spite of the international Polanyi revival, few scholars working on the Visegrád countries, whether natives or foreigners, have engaged closely with his ideas. This volume cannot remedy these decades of personal and collective neglect. With the perspective of hindsight, however, though I have not cited him as often as I should have, it seems to me that a good deal of my work over the last three decades, in Poland as well as in Hungary, has been shaped by the economic anthropology and social philosophy of Karl Polanyi.[2]

Polanyi's Substantivist Economic Anthropology

To outline the theory behind Polanyi's critique of economics and capitalist market society is no easy task, partly because Polanyi never produced major synthetic works of theory. Throughout the major works (Polanyi 1944; Polanyi, Arensberg and Pearson 1957; Polanyi 1966; and Polanyi 1977), theoretical propositions are entangled with empirical descriptions of historical societies, notably industrializing Britain, ancient Athens and the Dahomey of the slave trade. These works are broadly consistent in their approaches, but emphases shifted. In the works drafted after the Second World War, Polanyi sometimes acknowledged that the target of his venom in *The Great Transformation* was no longer so dangerous. The principle of the market, which had wrought such damage in the nineteenth century, had apparently

[2] Coming to anthropology after undergraduate studies of economics, it was taken for granted by my new teachers that I would specialise in economic anthropology. However, the formalist-substantivist debates had not had much resonance in the Department of Social Anthropology in Cambridge. Students were encouraged to develop their own orientations, which in my case meant continuing with the Western Marxist contributions which I had begun to explore in other disciplines when still an undergraduate. Years later I realised that Jack Goody did not hold Polanyi in high esteem, due to the Hungarian's downplaying of the role of markets in the *longue durée* of Eurasian history. Goody's successor Ernest Gellner was more sympathetically disposed to a Habsburg émigré, but lacked sympathy for Polanyi's politics. Later, when I was appointed to a Lectureship in Cambridge, I was surprised to discover that Raymond Firth, associated with the "other side" during the controversies between formalists and substantivists, had a deep respect for Polanyi. Firth attributed the major shortcomings of the substantivist position to the simplifications and distortions of George Dalton after Polanyi's death (Personal Communication, circa 1990).

been tamed by new forms of polity, both in the USSR and in the West. The "great transformation" was being accomplished, and the new challenge in the 1950s was to respond to the challenge of "machine civilization." Nonetheless, the main concepts of the earlier work reappear in the comparative historical economics of his later years.

Polanyi's project is fundamentally similar to that of Max Weber. He wants to understand the relationship between economy and society in their most general senses: in other words, the long-term significance of production, exchange and consumption for the formation of human communities. Though Polanyi admired much in Karl Marx's work, especially the early writings, which he read soon after their publication in 1932, he was repelled by what he saw as the economic determinism of historical materialism, which eliminated human agency or freedom. For this reason he usually described himself as a democratic socialist rather than a Marxist. He admired Weber's historical vision, but felt that the great German sociologist was too inclined to generalize from premises relevant only to the kind of highly rationalized society in which he lived. *The Great Transformation* moved at two levels. It documented the structural transformation of economy and society in nineteenth century Britain, but it also addressed the emergence in this same century of *laissez-faire* and *homo economicus* as expressions of liberal ideology. For Polanyi, Weber's individualist theory of social action showed that he was in thrall to the latter—to the "economistic fallacy," as he called it later.

Weberians might respond that their master's distinction between instrumental rationality (*Zweckrationalität*) and a substantive rationality concerning values (*Wertrationalität*) is rather similar to the binary adopted by Polanyi himself when distinguishing two different senses of the term "economic." The first sense of economy was that of *economizing*, the rational calculation of means in relation to ends, e.g. in the pursuit of profit, or more formally, "the maximisation of subjective utilities in conditions of scarcity." This gradually became the dominant standpoint in economic science in the wake of Adam Smith. The shift away from the old political economy towards marginal(ist) utility analysis took place concomitantly with the rise of market ideology in the era of free trade. It reached its climax in the 1870s with the almost simultaneous gestation of the "neoclassical synthesis" in Cambridge (William Jevons), Lausanne (Léon Walras) and Vienna (Carl Menger). Polanyi was particularly influenced by Menger.

Opposed to this "formalist" approach was the substantive, an understanding of economy in terms of "man's dependence for his living upon nature and his fellows" (Polanyi 1957, 243). This reached all the way back to the etymological origin of the word for economy, the *oikos* of Aristotle, the well-ordered, self-sufficient household or estate. Polanyi wrote most explicitly about the two meanings of economic in *Trade and Market*, which was a clarion call to reprioritize the substantive meaning by analyzing the diversity of economic institutions in human history. The example of ancient Athens showed that, although markets played an important role in the provisioning of the population, they were never dominant. The first democracy was ultimately regulated through its political institutions. The same applied in the various "primitive" economies reviewed in Chapter Four of *The Great Transformation*. Here, as in Athens, economy was *embedded* in society.[3] Polanyi quoted from early anthropologists (notably Richard Thurnwald and Bronislaw Malinowski) to argue that the profit motive was not universal, and that in human societies over the millennia goods were distributed primarily according to principles that were "non-economic" (in the narrower, formalist sense of economy). To generalize the assumptions of neoclassical economics to other societies in time and space was to be guilty of the economistic fallacy (discussed most fully in Polanyi 1977; see also Hann 2014a).

After these initial steps, Polanyi proffered a "special tool box" for capturing the mix of institutions found in different human societies. One important "form of integration" was reciprocity, which he considered to be exemplified in stateless societies. A second was redistribution, which was likely to be the dominant form of integration in any centralized polity from small chiefdoms to more complex states. Market exchange was a third principle, co-existing with the others but never dominant until very recent times. In *The Great Transformation* "householding" was specified as a fourth form of integration, but this was deleted in the reformulation of 1957. These terms were intended as a very general typology. Later Marxist critics complained that Polanyi did not engage closely with the sphere of production, and they had a point. Most of his work in the 1940s and 1950s was indeed focused on the sphere of

[3] For analysis of the later confusions surrounding the term embeddedness, which has been deployed in very different ways by economic sociologists, see Beckert 2009.

exchange and organized around the loose concept of "integration."[4] Polanyi repeatedly challenged the economists' assumption that money had evolved naturally in order to meet the needs of trade and market. Closer historical analysis (e.g. Polanyi 1966) showed that money, markets and trade had largely independent origins, and so the "catallactic triad" of modern economics had to be deconstructed. Long-distance trade "administered" by political controllers preceded the rise of price-forming markets, while fungible, multi-purpose money owed its origins to the rise of the state rather than to any functionalist utilitarian logic.

The concept of commoditization had been around for a long time and Polanyi was impressed by Marx's analysis of commodity fetishism. The *disembedding* of the economy from society with the onset of the industrial revolution led to the emergence of what he termed "fictitious commodities": land, labor and money. These were not produced as commodities, he argued, and the attempt to allocate them as if they were just another factor of production was a basic error, one that would certainly lead to disaster for the integrity of the community. The causal mechanism, diagnosed at length in *The Great Transformation*, was based on the axiom that no human society could tolerate radical disembedding, in particular the reduction of human beings and nature to commodity status. People would defend themselves against these monumental incursions, e.g. by claiming higher wages and rights before the law. The "countermovement" would threaten profits as well as political peace, leading to Fascist reaction that would bring economy and polity back together in a new, antidemocratic amalgam. This, in essence, is how Polanyi explained the collapse of European civilization in the first half of the twentieth century.

What is the status of this body of work today? It has an obvious pertinence to many phenomena of the contemporary world economy,

---

[4] Polanyi's terminology was not consistent. In *The Great Transformation*, he wrote of "principles of economic behaviour," but in Polanyi (1957) and Polanyi (1977) the usual term is "form of integration." He also used the term "patterns." The term "transactional mode" is not used by Polanyi, but became widespread among later substantivists (Dalton 1968). Jean-Michel Servet (2013) argues that this latter term is unfortunate in that it invites the neo-Marxist critique that Polanyi was concerned solely with phenomena of exchange. In fact, according to Servet, the typology was devised to provide a comprehensive classification of all economic domains, including production and consumption.

such as financialization, labor migration and landgrabbing by capitalist corporations. Yet the meticulous scholarship of Gareth Dale also draws attention to weaknesses. Polanyi exaggerated the absence of supply and demand in the ancient world. He used ethnographic sources in a similar selective manner, overlooking those passages in the ethnography of Malinowski which, on the face of it, would lend support to notions of individualism and even economistic behavior among the Trobriand Islanders.[5] Anthropologists have shown that general-purpose money does not necessarily corrode the core of community life in non-European societies, as the substantivists thought it must (Parry and Bloch 1989). They have even greater reservations when it comes to the study of contemporary complex economies. Polanyi sometimes comes close (notably in *The Livelihood of Man,* 1977) to suggesting that, once the market has been elevated to such a position of prominence, then society surely *will* be dominated by the economistic fallacy, and as a result, the axioms and methods of mainstream economics, rather than substantivist institutionalism, *will* be appropriate and sufficient after all. This demarcation, solidified by his student George Dalton after Polanyi's death, is unhelpful. It cordons off the countless ways in which even the most complex "anonymous" markets are mediated by human agency. Moreover, this division of labor, leaving capitalist economies to the economists and everything else to the historians and economic anthropologists, contradicted Polanyi's own view that the heyday of the market was over by the 1940s, and that new forms of re-embedding were already under way and in need of study.

These tensions are indicative of deeper inconsistencies, not to say confusion, in Polanyi's position, which continue to bedevil assessments of his work. He sometimes undermined his arguments by falling back on the very compartmentalization of economy and society that his own work called into question. In the words of Louis Dumont, "ayant critiqué l'économie comme idée, il a pensé à la conserver comme chose" (1983, 20). His work is an extraordinary cocktail: ancient history and ethnography, political economy and Christian theology, international relations and moral philosophy, are all mixed together. *The Great Trans-*

[5] Most Melanesianists reject such interpretations and attribute them to the individualist predilections of the Polish-British anthropologist himself.

formation is a rhetorically impressive contribution in the genre of *Kapitalismuskritik*, but it lacks the coherence of Marx's original because it focuses not on capitalist exploitation but on something that is harder to pin down, the ephemeral destructive flowering of "market society." Though Polanyi was clearly influenced by Ferdinand Tönnies, his vision lacks the parsimony and coherence of Tönnies' distinction between *Gemeinschaft* and *Gesellschaft*. Despite his criticism of the liberal and neoliberal economists, notably Mises and Hayek in the 1920s, his Christian "ethical individualism" inhibited him from embracing class in the Marxian sense. Polanyi took it for granted that the state would have to be the key actor in accomplishing the new socialist society, but he paid little attention to the myriad ways in which states (even those governed by democratically elected socialists) serve the interests of capital and capitalists. As a result, his theoretical conceptualization of market is sometimes simplistic, neglecting the rules and organizational forms on which markets depend (corporations as well as the state), even when this institutional embedding is richly described in his empirical work.

These are serious deficiencies. In spite of them all, what many continue to find inspiring in Polanyi is the moral and political exhortation to uphold the importance of community, and indeed to build it afresh, consciously, in an era of technological and economic alienation when it is under unprecedented attack. The "market situation," imagined as one of profit or utility maximization between anonymous atomized units, is not the original situation of the human economy and it should not be the gold standard of our contemporary theorizing. Instead of expanding the list of fictitious commodities by allowing the economistic fallacy to colonize ever greater domains of our life-worlds, we should be exploring new forms of embedding, of consolidating social citizenship and the *économie solidaire*.

Polanyi was a Central European intellectual of the twentieth century, whose publications and anti-market passion were strongly marked by the turbulent path of his life. The prospect of a "new West" along socialist lines, which he called for eloquently in the late 1950s, may look Eurocentric to a contemporary anthropologist. Yet at the end of his life Polanyi hailed decolonization and expressed the hope that the emergence of what we now call the global South could rejuvenate humanity and save it from the perversions of both market society and machine civilization. This makes him appealing to contemporary alter-globalization activists. Whatever the scholarly ambiguities and shortcomings, the writings of Karl Polanyi continue to inspire and to facilitate productive conversations across the trenches of academic disciplines.

A Polanyian Approach to Market Socialism

Polanyi can thus be hailed as a humanist and admired for prose which gives voice to his passionate moral vision. But if that is all that is left after the specialist critiques, why should we bother with his "special toolbox"? Why should we waste our time digesting his account of the Speenhamland system of poor relief in Britain 200 years ago, a major element of *The Great Transformation*, if it has long been superseded by economic historians? Why should anthropologists look to Polanyi to understand the embeddedness of the economy when that basic point was made earlier (and arguably more coherently) by Marcel Mauss (1925)? Contemporary critiques of the neoliberal world order are two a penny: do we need to go back to Polanyi's critique of the original economic liberalism?

My aim in this book is to apply Polanyi's historical vision and economic anthropological toolkit to his Central European homeland in order to understand better its passage through socialism and postsocialism. Polanyi himself did not focus on this part of the world professionally. His optic was directed elsewhere, primarily on the more advanced West. Like most intellectuals of his generation everywhere in Europe, he grew up with a strong evolutionist notion of progress. The Galileo Circle of freethinking intellectuals and the short-lived bourgeois radical party in which he was active on the eve of the First World War exemplified this view of the world. He was, of course, aware of the unevenness of capitalist development. His experiences in Austria and then later in England must have reinforced his perception of class divisions. Yet, like Marx, he took the emergence of a new form of society in nineteenth century Britain to herald a universal transformation. Polanyi hoped that, in spite of all the catastrophes of the early twentieth century, the next stage would be a re-embedding of economy in society in the framework of a democratic socialism. He did not live long enough to witness how the course of actually existing socialism would confound this philosophy of history.

The title of Polanyi's major work is potentially misleading. Some readers have supposed that *great transformation* refers to that moment in the late eighteenth century when market exchange first broke free of societal frameworks. His "disembedding" would then be analogous to the "big ditch" which Ernest Gellner postulated between "modernity" and all previous forms of "traditional society" (Gellner 1983). On this interpretation, Polanyi's terminology would be consistent with the dominant binary of classical sociology. But *great transformation* as he uses the phrase in the book refers not to this moment of *disembedding* but rather to drawn-out processes of *re-embedding* during and after the disastrous spirals of the early twentieth century. Fascism brought economy and polity back into a certain mutual interdependence, but one that was incompatible with democratic freedoms and ethically indefensible. The challenge after 1944 was to re-embed within new democratic frameworks.

Polanyi followed how the People's Democracies of Eastern Europe set about this task. He was aware of the abuses of Stalinism, but continued to sympathize with reformist elements within communist parties, including that of Hungary, where in November 1956 the Party was able to hold on to power only with the aid of Soviet tanks. It is reasonable to assume that Polanyi would have endorsed the measures taken in the 1960s to develop a variety of "market socialism," culminating in the introduction of the New Economic Mechanism on January 1, 1968. In abstract theoretical terms, he might have interpreted this as a reconciliation of the positions taken in the socialist accounting debates of the 1920s. The encompassing framework of economic activity had to be a socialist totality. But it was a mistake to imagine that central planners could ever command all the information needed to ensure smooth production flows, let alone divine the changing tastes of consumers. To meet citizens' needs, it was necessary to decentralize economic decision-making, to enhance the role of market signals, and thereby recognize the strengths of neoclassical economic analysis.

The Hungarian market socialist economy, like any other economy, can be described in terms of the four forms of integration identified by Karl Polanyi in 1944. In the middle of the twentieth century the socialist countries of Eastern Europe were still largely agricultural and the gap separating them from North-West Europe was huge.[6] The

[6] The major exceptions were the industrialised regions of Bohemia, Silesia, and East Germany.

socialists thought they could close this gap by relying on redistribution as their dominant form of integration. This implied what Polanyi termed "centricity": the power of the center to extract taxes or tribute, and at the same time to reorganize social relations and inter-sectoral relations according to the desired political goals. All socialist regimes relied heavily on this power but the ways in which they did so were far from uniform. For example, while the "commanding heights" of the economy in sectors such as heavy industry and mining were everywhere nationalized, the treatment of small, family-owned businesses varied from country to country. There was also variety in the provision of housing. Much of the urban housing stock was nationalized; shortages accentuated by rapid urbanization and industrialization made the allocation of apartments a key domain of contestation. In the countryside, however, housing remained overwhelmingly private.

Given the starting condition of backwardness, differences between town and country were considerable. Most socialist countries exercised their redistributive power by implementing mass collectivization, with the goal of replicating urban industrial models of production in the rural sector. For political reasons, this measure was not imposed in Poland or (outside the Soviet bloc) in Yugoslavia. (This did not mean that farmers prospered in these two countries, since here, too, it was impossible to consolidate private farms.) Strategies of collectivization varied greatly. In some countries, notably the USSR in the 1930s, the rural sector was made to pay for the accumulation of capital in urban industry. Hungary represented the opposite path. After the failure of early attempts to encourage farmers to join cooperatives voluntarily, collectivization was imposed more coercively in 1959–1961. Almost from the beginning, however, it was accompanied by generous funding of the mechanized collective sector and by investments in rural infrastructure. My dissertation documented how the village of Tázlár was transformed in little more than a decade from a settlement consisting largely of scattered farms to one dominated by a nuclear center in which households had access to electricity and piped water for the first time (Hann 1980a). In terms of the numbers of people drawn for the first time into state systems of life-long social security, this "socialist civilizing process" in the countryside was the most notable accomplishment of Marxist-Leninist redistribution (Hann 2015a).

The market form of integration was never entirely absent. Johanna Bockman (2011) has demonstrated how socialist planners were influenced by the market-dominated economic science of the West (to which some of them made noteworthy contributions). Their mistake was to suppose that centralized economies could approximate the solutions of the market, or even simulate them with mathematical precision. But from the 1960s they acknowledged the errors of over-centralization and introduced major concessions. Hungary was the most innovative of the socialist countries and its rural sector exemplified the new flexibility. Cooperative farms were given freedom to devise their own production and marketing strategies, and encouraged to establish sideline activities on a profit-making basis (Swain 1985). Consumers benefited from expanding supplies of agricultural produce. They also profited from improved services in many other domains of the economy as the state encouraged private business initiatives. Some markets were severely distorted. Cars were not produced in Hungary and had to be imported; the waiting period was long (many years), but some people found ways to speed things up. The authorities allowed investment in private housing to expand beyond "vacation cottages" and in this way the material incentives for hard work in market-oriented activities continued to expand in the 1970s–1980s. New patterns of social stratification ensued from these institutionalized processes, but they were quite different from those of the pre-war era, not least due to the dramatically altered status of the rural population. These new inequalities garnered resentment from those too poorly situated to benefit from them. Predictably, they were criticized by conservative factions within the ruling Communist Party. Yet hardly anyone alleged that the market form of integration was dominant, or that this socialist economy was on the road to becoming disembedded in the sense of Karl Polanyi.[7]

[7] The most influential critique of this era to draw on Polanyian concepts argued that, despite this opening to the market, "class power" was actually in the hands of the intelligentsia by virtue of its command of redistribution (Konrád and Szelényi 1979). This work, together with that of János Kornai, discussed below, helped shape the perspective of anthropologist Katherine Verdery, whose general model of socialism highlighted the rational accumulation of resources by state officials (Verdery 1996). This model differs from the Polanyian approach advanced here. It has been critiqued by Thelen (2011); see also Hann (2014a).

Polanyi's reasons for deleting "householding" from the revised set of forms of integration which he proposed in 1957 are not entirely clear (see Gregory 2009). The domestic group is a universal unit of human economy. Even in complex societies where members are far from equal and a male patriarch exercises power over other males as well as females, the household does not merely replicate the principle of redistribution at the micro level. It is a site of emotional commitments, of an intimate mutuality which was arguably peculiarly intense under socialism due to the repressive character of the public sphere and the inadequate functioning of markets. In the case of socialist Eastern Europe it is again important to attend to rural-urban differences. In both sectors, women entered the labor force and benefited from new institutional supports in childcare, though the greater share of domestic chores continued to rest with them. The major difference was the continued vitality of the rural household as a unit of production, both for subsistence and for commercial sale. In Hungary this was creatively harnessed by socialist cooperatives and crucial to the overall success of collectivization.

Operationalizing reciprocity, the last of Polanyi's four forms of integration (which he himself usually placed first), poses a challenge. This term first became prominent in the ethnographic works of Malinowski and Thurnwald in Melanesia. Polanyi thought that the moiety systems studied by the latter, in which there is no political center, exemplified the principle of reciprocity. Others have harked back to Mauss's analysis of *The Gift* (1925), which clearly formulates the obligation to return a gift with a counter gift. In this sense it is easy to find plentiful examples of reciprocity in socialist economies. The most conspicuous in the Hungarian countryside at the time of my fieldwork was the institution of *kaláka* in rural housebuilding. This was a work party to accomplish a major task, most commonly laying the foundations of a new building. Labor was typically lubricated throughout the day with beer or wine, and followed by a celebratory meal when the job was completed. If friends and neighbors helped you in this way, you and other members of your household were naturally expected to extend similar help when invited.

This institution was in decline well before the end of socialism in Hungary in 1989–90. As a result of the expansion of the market principle, major tasks such as housebuilding were increasingly undertaken by private entrepreneurs and the scope for *kaláka* was limited. Quite a lot of work was organized informally, in the "grey" economy where networks and "connections" were critical. Alena Ledeneva (1998) has popularized the Russian term *blat* and the concept of the "economy of favours." Even in Hungary, where shortages of consumer goods were less of a problem and bureaucratic rationalities more scrupulously observed, it was useful to possess *protekció*, the ability to call upon a state official for a favor, usually with the implication that one was ready to reciprocate with goods or services of one's own. This kind of integration is surely important in most, perhaps all, human economies. It is reasonable to assume that it was most prominent where socialist economies were least successful in the provisioning of goods and services through the other forms of integration. People adapted to these shortcomings by helping each other get by in everyday life, through behavior that might be both interested and disinterested, sometimes mutual and convivial but sometimes thoroughly alienating, sometimes promoting balanced, egalitarian relations, but sometimes reinforcing hierarchies. The socialist "economy of favours" took many forms, but it was everywhere conditioned by the dual imperfections of markets and bureaucracies.

But this is not how Polanyi used the term reciprocity. In his typology, it was positively charged and associated with the symmetry of tribal moieties. Perhaps the best way to reformulate it for the globalized world of today is to recall the original Greek meaning of symmetry, which referred to balance or equilibrium rather than the more formal symmetry of mathematics or moiety systems. The symmetry of reciprocity draws attention to the omnipresent ethical component of Polanyi's work. Reciprocity is *not* the economist's tit for tat, nor can it possibly be the extortion of favors in a political economy of shortage and repression. Rather, it consists of flows (or "prestations" in the terminology of Mauss) between human individuals and groups that are predicated not on selfish utilitarianism but on sympathy for and trust in others. Perhaps the best term to capture this quality is mutuality (Gudeman 2008). The precondition for this reciprocity or mutuality was theorized by Polanyi (1944) in terms of "responsibility" and "freedom in a complex society."

Reciprocity or mutuality in this sense differs from obligatory gift-giving. It is not the "primitive" antithesis of the advanced market economy. It is to be found in technologically complex, advanced economies in which producer and consumer enjoy symmetrical relations that are not dominated by short-term profit-maximizing. Jean-Michel Servet (2013) identifies such an expanded notion of reciprocity as the basis of the *économie solidaire*, an economy devoted to meeting human needs, "man's dependence on nature and his fellows." Servet follows Polanyi in stressing that this reciprocal form of integration always co-exists with other forms. Polanyi did not suppose that needs could be met through an anarchist rejection of centricity, or through an informal (or "second") economy flourishing in the grey interstices of the formal, legal economy. On the contrary, his human economy was predicated on a strong state charged with balancing the principles of redistribution, market and householding. Thus understood, it is not householding that is the odd-man-out in the set originally proposed by Polanyi in 1944. When it comes to understanding the complex economies of the machine age, reciprocity is the joker, an ineffable ethical dimension of all social relationships, inside households, markets and bureaucracies alike, and between them all. This elusive mutuality can only be achieved when one all-important political prerequisite is in place—freedom.

Precisely this condition was never met in the People's Democracies. I have suggested above that the Hungarian mix of forms of integration had much to commend it, especially from the point of view of the country's rural population. The former peasants, long excluded from the substantive entitlements of citizenship, were among the major beneficiaries of four decades of proletarian dictatorship. Yet they voted against the socialist party as soon as they were given an opportunity to do so, in 1990. They supported policies of propertization which, as I show in this book, soon proved highly detrimental to the material interests of the great majority, with consequences which continue to shape the political landscape of Hungary three decades later. More generally, I argue on the basis of my fieldwork that Hungarian market socialism opened up many spaces for a new mutuality, both within the planned economy and in the unplanned "second economy." But the climate was one in which these forms of integration were cast in oppositional rather than complementary terms. The extension of the market form of integration led all too frequently to short-term profit-seeking, rather than long-term relations of the kind imagined by Jean-Michel Servet. The implication is that no human economy with the spirit of reciprocity at its core can be built upon non-democratic political foundations. The main lesson of the Hungarian case is that it is all well and good to institutionalize an economic hybrid superior to that of any other socialist state, but unless it can be embedded in a democratic polity, this mix is worthless. Or, if not exactly worthless, it is at any rate too fragile to be consolidated politically. In the revolutions of 1989–90, the beneficiaries of socialism rejected their *ancien régime* unambiguously.

The reconciliation of town and countryside lay at the core of the Hungarian experience of socialism. Flexible collectivization provided the cornerstone for both accumulation in the countryside and successful provisioning in the cities. This Hungarian path differed from most other experiences of socialism. Opportunities for accumulation by rural households were always much more limited in the Soviet Union, which struggled to recover from the extreme violence with which a rapacious model of collectivization for the benefit of industry was imposed by Stalin. In Poland, collectivization was averted after the political disasters of 1956, but this was a pyrrhic victory. Where land was still in private ownership, socialist power holders were inhibited by their ideology from extending the market form of integration (Hann 1985). The upshot in Poland was a chronically inefficient agriculture, inadequate provisioning of the cities, and more generally a shortage economy that contributed massively to social unrest and ultimately to the collapse of the system.

Hungarian market socialism under János Kádár bears closer resemblance to the reformist socialism of China and Vietnam since the 1980s than to any other Soviet bloc state. Following the death of Mao Zedong in 1976, Beijing power holders from 1979 onwards worked out their own original combination of the four forms of integration. Redistribution declined, but not dramatically; the commanding heights were not privatized, and in recent years social security schemes have been extended to the countryside in ways reminiscent of town-country convergences in Hungary. The scope of markets has increased enormously, yet at multiple levels it is the political institutionalization of market processes that determines outcomes. Householding remains a vital principle, particularly in the countryside but also in the cities, which have experienced an efflorescence of family businesses. In East Asia, as in Eastern Europe, there is pervasive concern with corruption and the deteriorating quality of interpersonal relations: with the lack of reciprocity in the sense of mutuality and social solidarity. Perhaps it is not too late for China and Vietnam to learn from the mistakes made in Eastern and Central Europe, and find ways to introduce the democratic freedoms without which their societies will remain stunted.

A Polanyian Approach to the Confluence of Neoliberalism and Postsocialism

Neoliberalism, like the original liberalism as analyzed by Karl Polanyi, can be investigated at two levels: ideology and material reality. It is generally accepted that a pro-market ideology coupled with a minimalist conception of the role of the state played a significant role in the demise of the "embedded liberalism" that prevailed in the advanced capitalist countries after the Second World War. Margaret Thatcher famously drew inspiration from the works of Friedrich Hayek. But the actual institutions of governance remain remote from libertarian blueprints. States continue to play a decisive role alongside transnational corporations that bear little resemblance to the textbook world of market-based competition. The discrepancy between the doctrines and reality has led some scholars, in economic anthropology and other disciplines, to question the usefulness of the term "neoliberal." However, it remains the best short descriptor available to capture the dominant trends in global political economy over the last four decades, the leitmotiv of which is intensified marketization.[8] The postsocialist world exemplifies the pertinence of the term. No one can doubt that processes of transition in the Visegrád states would have been very different if they had been launched in the 1960s under the aegis of Keynesianism and the Marshall Plan, rather than in the 1990s, when militant neoliberalism was in the ascendant.

---

[8] Cf. Colin Crouch: "There are many branches and brands of neoliberalism, but behind them stands one dominant theme: that free markets in which individuals maximize their material interests provide the best means for satisfying human aspirations, and that markets are in particular to be preferred over states and politics, which are at best inefficient and at worst threats to freedom" (2011, vii).

As in the socialist era, it is important to acknowledge that neoliberal postsocialism had many variants. The Polish model of "shock therapy" was one of the more disruptive (though arguably one of the more successful when one considers economic growth rates in the present century). By contrast, the Hungarian transition to capitalist liberal democracy was, at least on the surface, one of the smoothest. Power changed hands repeatedly during the first postsocialist decades, but the country remained stable while privatization and foreign investment proceeded at a rapid pace. But, after the socialists in power between 2002 and 2010 were perceived to have led the country into moral as well as financial bankruptcy, Viktor Orbán proclaimed in 2010 that the time was finally ripe, under his leadership, to transcend the legacies of socialism. Where is the country now, almost three decades after the elation of the "system change" (*rendszerváltás*)? Social security benefits, notably unemployment, have been cut drastically. The rural symbiosis between household and cooperative was speedily destroyed and access to EU subsidies after 2004 has not offered an adequate replacement. Since 2010, Orbán's Fidesz-led governments have interfered blatantly in markets to a far greater extent than previous socialist-led governments, partly in order to appease elites through a new patronage system. In 2014 and again in 2018 Orbán held on to his two thirds majority in parliament, allowing him to alter the Constitution at will. Given the feeble and fragmented character of the opposition, it is hard to see how his Fidesz party will ever be dislodged—except perhaps by a more extreme, more xenophobic party of the right. Similar populist parties have gradually come to dominate politics in Poland and other countries of the region. I interpret this phenomenon in terms of a new "countermovement" in the sense of Polanyi (1944). Those who find the integrity of their lifeworlds threatened by capitalist market society need to salvage self-respect and identity, as a way of protecting themselves. In Central and Eastern Europe, the most readily available symbolic resources are those pertaining to the nation. For historical reasons, the associated emotions tend to be more virulently aggressive than the jingoism noted by Karl Polanyi in his analysis of the double movement of nineteenth century Britain.

The blanket Western verdict on the economies of the "actually existing socialism" of the Soviet bloc remains overwhelmingly negative. The same judgment is pronounced on Hungary, where the market form of integration was prominent, as on neighboring Romania, where it was largely suppressed in the 1980s in favor of increasingly dysfunctional forms of redistribution. Western gloating in the aftermath of the Cold War has been reinforced by influential economists such as János Kornai, who have long insisted that the mixed forms of Kádárism were contradictory (Kornai 1990, 1992). Kornai began his career as a member of the Communist Party, but he became aware earlier than most of the economic flaws of "over-centralization." Following the market reforms of 1968 and their later refinements, he concluded eventually that no experiments to deploy markets within a socialist framework could substitute the real thing. In works such as *The Road to a Free Economy*, he epitomized neoliberal prescriptions for the post-socialist world, above all private property rights as the basis for incentives and economic efficiency. Kornai was not averse to state measures to regulate market behavior; in sectors such as health care, far-reaching intervention is warranted to correct past abuses. Overall, however, he deplores the fact that the Hungarian market socialist state built up a system of entitlements and expectations which it could not afford. From the point of view of economics, social transfers to raise welfare standards and incorporate large sections of the population previously excluded from the benefits of social citizenship were "premature." Socialism, from this perspective, was a misconceived attempt to remedy historic backwardness on the periphery. The postsocialist countries must pay a high price today because they dared to pursue a different road, to implement a different mix of forms of integration. In short, according to János Kornai, the laws of economics proclaim the futility of such alternatives: the market must prevail.

It is not hard to imagine how Karl Polanyi would have reacted to this analysis. Critical of the economic determinism of Karl Marx, he would have been appalled by the turn of events that has led to falling living standards and heightened insecurities for large sections of the Hungarian population, and by the justifications for this decline proffered by Kornai.[9] By what logic was it mistaken to extend the benefits of citizenship to the historically excluded peasantry? I have argued

[9] See Kornai 2007 for his absorbing personal account.

in the preceding section that increased reliance on the market form of integration in cases such as Kádár's Hungary and today's China and Vietnam is consistent with a well-balanced human economy, provided that other forms of integration remain vital to the totality. By definition, the impulses behind impersonal market exchange are selfish in nature. But when balanced and countered by the forms of redistribution, householding and reciprocity, the unrivalled efficiency of the market as a system of information can be harnessed for the benefit of all.

This is not what has happened with neoliberal capitalism over the last half century. After roughly three decades of Keynesian stability following the Second World War, the 1970s saw a squeeze on profits and the rise of the neoliberal ideology which has dominated world governance in the last three decades (Streeck 2017). This "market fundamentalism" (Block and Somers 2014) is dangerous because it extends the logic of profit-making to realms in which no human communities have tolerated markets previously. The term disembedding is potentially misleading, because this process is only made possible by particular configurations of social and political institutions. As with nineteenth century *laissez-faire*, the human economy is *always* embedded, not only in political and legal frameworks but also in ethical norms and even cosmologies. But if these institutions are themselves saturated in the logic of the market, then economy threatens to destroy the very foundations of society. This domination threatens not only democracy but the future of capitalism itself, which paradoxically depends on some modicum of opposition to market logic in order to avert self-destruction (Streeck 2016).

Wolfgang Streeck pays little attention to the former socialist countries. He may be right that the main action is unfolding elsewhere, but it is nonetheless instructive to insert the Visegrád states into his account. These countries abandoned the holistic economies of socialism in favor of a capitalism which had already abandoned Keynesian pragmatism in favor of market fundamentalism. They were large enough to be of considerable interest to foreign companies (especially West German capital). The former socialist states were promptly compelled to participate in a "race to the bottom" to attract foreign investment. Long-simmering ideological grievances vis-à-vis socialist power holders made it easier for new local businessmen to justify sharp practice and ride roughshod over legislation protecting workers: after all, in the new conditions they were the sole source of wealth creation and jobs. Membership of the European Union has done little to alleviate conditions. On the contrary, while Brussels continues to promote the market form of integration that lay at the origin of the original Common Market, its commitment to redistribution ("social Europe") has become feeble (as is evident in the long-term problems of the Eurozone and the disintegration of the Greek economy over the last decade).

This is a very different configuration from that analyzed by Karl Polanyi. When the market broke free of society in early-industrial Great Britain, society fought back. Abolition of the Speenhamland system in 1834 marked a defeat, but from the 1860s onwards measures to protect the labor force, to curtail the allegedly free market, to promote unions and mass democracy, began to have a substantial impact. The tensions of the double movement led ineluctably to the world wars of the twentieth century. By contrast, in Central and Eastern Europe since 1990 the market form of integration has been imposed in a global context of neoliberalism on societies which had been introduced to industrial modernity via socialist institutions, with their social protection (excessive in the eyes of Kornai) built in from the start. Having rejected that socialist mix, the self-protection of society now has to be reformulated on an entirely new basis. That is the current predicament of countries such as Hungary. In the short term at least, the moral vacuum is devastating—more crushing than nineteenth century Britain, where the early socialists could theorize alternatives, but also more hopeless than contemporary Western Europe, where non-orthodox economists and their ilk can explore new forms of the *économie solidaire*. In postsocialist Central and Eastern Europe, everything which smacks of socialism and the *solidaire* is tainted. But could this very condition of hopelessness, resulting from the fusion of neoliberalism with postsocialism, make this region a crucible of further transformation?

Three decades after the collapse, local verdicts on socialism tend to be more nuanced than the external, expert verdicts. Of course, many postsocialist Eastern Europeans take pleasure and pride in their new freedoms, which have opened up vistas undreamed of under socialism. New middle classes have emerged, citizens have passports allowing them to travel wherever they like, whenever they like. It is unfortunate that, in practice, many do not have the means to travel, not even to find better opportunities to work. Then there are those who, thanks to socialist redistribution, used to receive vouchers for trade union recreational facilities, but who now enjoy no holiday at all. Some of those who find their way abroad take jobs well below those for which they are qualified. The chapters in this volume document some of the consequences of marketization and propertization since 1990. In general terms we can say, with Polanyi, that we are dealing with another aberrant utopia. The new version of market liberalism is obviously different from the old *laissez-faire*. Capitalism has become more globalized and financialized, and digital technologies have revolutionized business and consumption. But the root poison is evidently the same: a quasi-mystical faith in markets and an impoverished view of human nature, just as Karl Polanyi diagnosed in *The Great Transformation*. Polanyi assumed, in the last decades of his life, that the great transformation was well under way in two distinct forms, that of Keynesian social democracy in the West and socialism in the East. But now we are back in the nightmare of economic liberalism.

Socialism, for (neo)liberals such as Kornai, was a premature attempt to remedy historic backwardness on the periphery of capitalism. The postsocialist countries must suffer today because they dared to pursue a different road, to implement a different mix of forms of integration. Neoclassical economics proclaims the futility of such alternatives, as if they were contrary to human nature. But Polanyi shows us that this is false, that no economy can be severed from politics and society, and that the domination of the market form of integration undermines the reproduction of everything that matters most for human flourishing. He would not have shed many tears for the states of the Soviet bloc, because none of them came anywhere close to creating acceptable conditions for freedom in a complex society. But he would nonetheless have detected much that was positive in the balance of forms of integration in socialist Hungary, the country with which he identified most strongly.

This Book

The first half of this volume concentrates on economic transformations, especially privatization policies. The spotlight falls on the Hungarian village of Tázlár, which I have known and visited regularly since 1976. Chapter Two considers "market socialism" with reference to Karl

Polanyi and János Kornai. Empirically, it focuses on the impact of "the market" in Hungary in the early 1990s. In a postscript I outline how the expansion of small-scale, cross-border trade in southeast Poland, rather than fostering trust, was associated with the intensification of negative interethnic stereotyping.

Chapter Three focuses on land as private property in Tázlár and the transformations experienced in that community in the early 1990s. After the collapse of pragmatic socialist institutions, the principles of market economy were imposed dogmatically. Following Malinowski, I argue that a broad view of land tenure must move beyond legal categories to address social relations and even "mythological" foundations, which in this case means engaging with the traditional values of smallholder peasant economy. Following Marx, I argue that the ideology of free markets and private property mystifies the emerging social relations of postsocialism. Chapter Four extends the analysis to other studies of decollectivization carried out at the Max Planck Institute for Social Anthropology and to a broader range of property objects in postsocialist Eurasia and beyond. Diagnoses of propertization echo those of marketization, but in this chapter I point to ways and means of resisting these trends that can be theorized as benign forms of the countermovement.

Chapter Five considers social trends in the postsocialist countryside in the former Soviet Union as well as Hungary and Poland. I show (drawing on the work of Tommaso Trevisani) that the concept of class seems readily applicable in Uzbekistan, against a background of corruption and coercion, while in Central and Eastern Europe many descendants of the old peasantries continue to maintain a significant measure of autonomy from the market and thereby to defy the standard class categorizations of sociology. Karl Polanyi viewed labor as a "fictitious commodity," one that was incompatible with the moral embedding of community. Zooming in again on the village of Tázlár, it is suggested that workfare schemes, commonly criticized as a punitive instrument of neoliberal governance, are actually welcomed by most members of the community. At the same time, however, polarizing tendencies and the emergence of a new *precariat* following the decollectivization of agriculture, contribute to the most malign aspects of the double movement in the Visegrád states today, including populist intolerance towards minorities and immigrants.

The latter themes are then taken up in five chapters which engage with (un-)civil society and ethnicity. I have been suspicious of "civil society" ever since its appropriation by those I term "militant liberals" in the 1980s. The grounds for my "reactionary" view are outlined in Chapter Six, which begins in Tázlár and continues in the form of a dialogue with the late Ernest Gellner, who was a strong advocate of civil society (the concept and its concrete referent) in the early 1990s. The dissident intellectuals who argued that socialism had suppressed associational life were largely correct, but they were mistaken in viewing these liberal freedoms as a sufficient condition for a healthy society offering opportunities to all citizens. Civil society has become a well-established term in political anthropology, where it is nowadays commonly equated with the activities of non-governmental organizations. It is undoubtedly the case that many civil society activists do a terrific job on behalf of marginalized constituencies unable to articulate their interests except through these representatives. But this use of civil society is a far cry from the ideals of the European Enlightenment, where the concept originates, as well as from the East Central European radicals of the 1980s. Now, as under socialism, it is important that anthropologists reach beyond articulate political elites in capital cities to engage with larger populations. Most citizens are as disconnected from the new civil society organizations as they were from socialist power holders and their organizations in the past. We need to engage with the "society" that lies beyond today's impoverished notion of "civil society." Analyzing the many facets of this distinction, including a renewed cleft between countryside and town, is the essential first step to understanding many increasingly *uncivil* phenomena in recent years.

As a grass-roots slogan to mobilize populations for the future, civil society proved to be unsatisfactory. The futurist orientations of Marxist-Leninist-Maoist socialism have been replaced instead by a plethora of rituals oriented toward the past. Symbolic legitimation and "memory work" have been focused above all on the nation. In Hungary, this process was already well under way in the 1980s, as I showed in an analysis of Saint Stephen's Day rituals (Chapter Seven). The twentieth of August has retained its status as the premier national holiday, though I show in concluding this chapter how the nature of the celebrations and the meanings associated with Saint/King Stephen have changed under postsocialist conditions.

The main focus of the next three chapters is southeast Poland, nowadays the eastern boundary of the Schengen Zone and "Fortress Europe." My first test case for the proclaimed democratic civil society is the Lemko-Ukrainian ethnic minority in the Carpathian Mountains (Chapter Eight). In Chapter Nine I document the ethno-religious contestation of the 1990s in the city of Przemyśl, close to the Ukrainian border, in a framework provided by Ernest Gellner's theories of nationalism. Chapter Ten extends the analysis of the vulnerable situation in which the Ukrainian, Greek Catholic minority of this region found itself in the aftermath of socialism. These chapters note, on the one hand, the negative consequences of the new market economy, and on the other the incivility which follows when, in the new, more open political climate, "culture" and even "civilization" are invoked by a local majority to denigrate others. In the first decade after the Cold War, ideas put forward by political scientist Samuel Huntington concerning a "clash of civilizations" enjoyed considerable popularity. The hybridity of the Greek Catholic Church, straddling east and west in the heart of Europe, provides the basis for an anthropological response to the "closed" vision of the political scientist.

Chapter Eleven is a synthesis that draws on my most recent field trips in the 2010s. It begins by reviewing a number of efforts by socio-cultural anthropologists to explore the contours of neoliberal market society in the Visegrád states (including Slovakia and the Czech Republic), and recent reactions that might be classified as perverse forms of societal "self-protection." In an era in which some academic analysts have abandoned the concept of *society* in favor of a focus on the *self*, the evidence gathered by anthropologists suggests the need to probe behind discourses of individual initiative and personal responsibility. I illustrate the argument from ongoing field research in the small Great Plain town of Kiskunhalas. The "migration crisis" of summer 2015 was experienced dramatically—albeit vicariously—by the inhabitants of this economically depressed region. Negative attitudes toward strangers were quickly instrumentalized by populist politicians, but they need to be grasped in the context of the wider crisis of European and global capitalism. The tools offered by Polanyi enable a theorization in terms of the double movement. When the Gods of consumerism fail to deliver and society adopts a fierce nationalism as its new transcendent value, the social philosophy of Polanyi warns that a descent into Fascism may be imminent. But the inhabitants of Tázlár and Kiskunhalas who vote for parties such as Fidesz or Jobbik are not inherently Fascist. I submit that current postures would change very quickly if the European Union were capable of rediscovering principles of redistributive solidarity and responsibility in Polanyi's sense.

The Conclusion considers the era of neoliberal postsocialism in three frameworks of increasing time depth: first, the disorderly condition of the post-Brexit European Union; second, industrialization, a European breakthrough that is now well over two hundred years old; third, the emergence of complex stratified societies, a Eurasian innovation of the Bronze Age. I argue that the future of human economies and *eudaimonia* depends on a reassertion of Eurasian commonalities, above all in countering the market form of integration by means of effective redistribution.

CHAPTER TWO

Market Principle, Marketplace and the Transition in Eastern Europe

(1992, 1998)

Introduction: Market Socialism and Economic Anthropology[1]

In this chapter I explore images and understandings of "market" in Hungary in 1990. Long before the recent revolutions, Hungary was widely perceived to be on the front line of the insidious spread of a "market principle" in Eastern Europe. I begin by asking how we can best grasp the path followed by Hungary in the Kádár period (1956–1988), with a particular focus on the concept of "market socialism." This concept has generated a large literature in twentieth-century economic thought, with major contributions coming both internally (i.e. from theorists working within socialist countries) and from Western authors (e.g. Le Grand and Estrin 1989). The concept can be plausibly applied to Hungary after the introduction of the New Economic Mechanism in 1968. I have regularly used it as shorthand for indicating Hungary's significant divergence from standard models of centrally planned economies (Hann 1980a, 45; Hann 1990a, 1). The Hungarian reforms included a significant measure of devolution to enterprise man-

[1] *The main sections of this chapter were prepared in December 1990 for a conference at the University of St Andrews convened by Roy Dilley. The paper was published as Hann 1992c. Data were gathered during field research in July-August 1990 and from the mass media, which I followed throughout the year, in particular* Népszabadság *("People's Freedom"—the former Communist Party daily, which was transformed into a limited company in 1990 and succeeded in expanding its circulation under foreign ownership, before eventually being closed down in dubious political circumstances in 2016) and* Heti Világgazdaság *("World Economy Weekly"—a lively news magazine specializing in economic affairs both at home and abroad, which flourishes to the present day).*

agers. They are conventionally summarized as an attempt to achieve an optimal combination of plan and market, leading to the establishment of what is variously termed a "regulated," "guided" or "simulated" market (Berend 1990).

The economic reforms in Hungary were periodically contested and renewed. They are widely regarded as having led to an impasse by the late 1980s (Swain 1992). Certainly the country had economic difficulties in this period, but it is perhaps too simple to blame "market socialism." Hungary would not have abandoned its course in favor of a headlong rush towards capitalism were it not for external political developments in 1989–90. Today the gradualist aspirations of socialist reformers have been jettisoned and the stage is dominated by neoliberal politicians and economists who see "the market" as incompatible with any definition of socialism. János Kornai, an economist whose reputation is perhaps even higher in the West than in his native Hungary, was active as a public intellectual, such that some of the technical terms with which he analyzed "economies of shortage" circulated very widely. He argued that piecemeal reforms of the post-1968 type were necessarily insufficient to tackle the structural problems of a socialist economy (Kornai 1990). Enterprises remained subject to interference from the central authorities, budget constraints were always "soft," and capital markets hardly functioned at all. For Kornai, all talk of "simulating" a market in order to improve economic co-ordination, whilst leaving ultimate power in the hands of the politicians and planners, was based on a contradiction. For him there was only one possible route, namely the creation of a "genuine market economy," without simulation. In accordance with most expert and lay opinion, this true market can be conceived only in terms of capitalism and private property as developed in the West. After all, no alternative has a proven record, nothing else can offer Hungarians the living conditions they see in neighboring Austria and Germany. Socialist economies are represented as artificial and distorted, whilst capitalist market economies are seen as "natural." For example, when discussing the process of privatization in Hungary Kornai argues that "it is indispensable to thoroughly analyze the concentration structure of genuine market economies, where competition has resulted in a kind of natural selection (Hungarian: *természetes szelekció*)" (1990, 83).

Locating himself explicitly in the tradition of Ludwig von Mises and F.A. Hayek, Kornai gives considerable prominence to the dimension of property relations. The most fundamental problem of state ownership is that in practice such property belongs to no one. His own definition of a free economy runs as follows:

> A free economy is, of course, a market economy, but the concept is richer and refers not only to the fact that the main coordinator of economic activities is a specific mechanism, namely the market. A free economy is one that allows unhampered entry, exit, and fair competition in the market. The notion of a free economy also implies a certain configuration of property rights and a certain institutional and political structure. The system promotes the free establishment and preservation of private property and encourages the private sector to produce the great bulk of output. It is a system that encourages individual initiative and entrepreneurship, liberates this initiative from excessive state intervention, and protects it by the rule of law. A free economy is embedded in a democratic political order, characterised by the free competition of political forces and ideas. Given my own value system, the guarantee of these liberties has a high intrinsic value and should therefore enjoy top priority in economic policy-making. (Kornai 1990, 22–23)

I shall return to some of these themes below in the context of fieldwork data. Here I wish simply to note the triumphant emergence in Hungary of a current of opinion, promoted vigorously by the country's leading economist, which wished to do away once and for all with half measures, tinkering and simulation, by introducing into Hungary the "hard," authentic version of a "market economy." This version was widely perceived to be both natural and scientifically verified: after all, Kornai has the enhanced legitimacy that is conferred by a university chair in Boston, as readers of the semi-popular work from which I have quoted above are reminded in its blurb. His proviso—"given my own value system"—is overlooked, and the Kornai recipe is taken to be indispensable for the efficient organization of all industrial societies. Any other recipe, such as aspirations to ground a market economy in a hierarchical structure of property rights that would transcend the public-private dichotomy, is rejected by Kornai as naïve wishful thinking, a chimera which would be sure to disappoint the Hungarian people in practice.[2]

Kornai's liberalism underestimates the role played by the state in the evolution of modern economies. His line of argument is deeply colored by antipathy towards the values of the socialist party, as implemented during its long hold on power. Yet there is a curious affinity between the conceptual apparatus of Kornai and the arguments of a great compatriot of an earlier generation who was highly critical of liberal capitalism and sympathetic to reformist variants of socialism. Karl Polanyi argued that the industrial revolution had ushered in an era in which, for the first time, "market exchange" provided the dominant form of integration, i.e. the manner in which the economy was embedded in society (Polanyi 1944; see also Polanyi, Arensberg and Pearson 1957; Levitt 1990; Hann 1992a). Polanyi viewed this development as dangerous and dehumanizing. It allowed selfish maximizing impulses to escape from the social controls previously exercised through other forms of integration, notably those of "reciprocity" (fundamentally egalitarian) and "redistribution" (fundamentally hierarchical). The notion of an all-corrupting "market principle" was further developed by anthropologists working in the substantivist school which Polanyi established. In their introduction to the collection *Markets in Africa*, Paul Bohannan and George Dalton (1961) elaborated the dis-

---

2 Kornai was by no means the most extreme or unrealistic commentator. He spoke out against a rapid privatization which would dispose of state assets too cheaply, favoring what he called an "organic" transition in which the ratio of private property would be gradually increased. The simplest and crudest representation of "market economy" which I found in the Hungarian press in 1990 came in an interview in a mass-circulation daily with a distinguished academic economist from my own institution: D. M. Newbery, Chair of the Faculty of Economics, Cambridge University:

"Professor, what would you teach us East Europeans?"

"It's as clear as two times two: the most important thing is to be competitive. . . . In order to create the market an entirely new way of thinking is needed. It is not enough to encourage market economy in the abstract, whilst holding back from risk-taking. It is not possible to liberalize an economy in half measures, just as it's not possible to make love and retain one's virginity. . . . I tell you again, basic modes of thought have to be adjusted towards the market economy." (*Népszabadság*, May 5, 1990, 6)

tinction between the market principle and marketplaces as anthropologists had studied them in pre-capitalist "tribal" and "peasant" societies. They pointed to the paradox whereby the extension of the market principle typically led to the extinction of earlier forms of marketplace, with the loss of those integrating social aspects that were just as important as their economic functions. Modern market systems are presented as lacking any comparable integrative function, as devoid of any social or cultural dimension, or "disembedded."

This substantivist project exercised some influence upon social science theorizing about socialist Eastern Europe. In an argument that is constructed upon explicitly Polanyian foundations, György Konrád and Iván Szelényi (1979) suggested that the socialist states were governed by a principle of "rational redistribution." Recent anthropological work on the region reflects the continued influence of the substantivist approach. Katherine Verdery has argued that socialist systems suppressed free markets "precisely because they move goods laterally rather than vertically towards the center—as all redistributive systems require." Like other commentators, she too postulates "the market" as an agent in the present wave of reforms.[3]

There is a congruence here between the substantivist tradition in anthropology, with its postulate of a (hidden) market principle, and the contemporary economist's reliance upon essentially the same concept in his critique of "market socialist" experiments in the Kádár period. Of course the values at stake are directly opposed: Polanyi deplored the influence of the market principle, whilst Kornai sees it as the only road to salvation. Neither theorized the term "market socialism." Unwilling to sully the concept of the market, Kornai prefers to describe Hungarian policies after 1968 in terms of a consumerist orientation which in his view did nothing to alter the defective structures of control. The fact that many marketplaces in Hungary were well provisioned (and even efficient and competitive) in this period can thus be dismissed.

---

3 Verdery sums up recent changes in Eastern Europe as based on "the intention to decentralize economic and political decision making, as well as to allow a much increased integrative role to the market" (1991b, 432). [I took up this theme again and deepened my comparison of Kornai and Polanyi in Hann 2014a]

These markets are "peripheral" (to use the substantivist terminology) phenomena, subordinated to the dominant principle of centralized distribution, which is exemplified in other, less visible markets (such as industrial raw materials). The concept of "peripheral markets" is dismissed by the purists on both sides. Both its neoliberal proponents in Eastern Europe and its radical opponents in the west continue to need a strong concept of the "market principle" for their differing ideological projects. The convenience of such a concept is obvious. But if economic anthropology is to shed light on concrete phenomena of exchange, it has to develop more nuanced approaches, explore exactly how different kinds of market are institutionalized, and take account of the symbolism and moral discourses surrounding them.

Markets in Hungary in 1990: Representations and Realities

Having just edited an academic volume about "market economy and civil society" (Hann 1990c), I was pleased to find in the summer of 1990 that the theme of "market economy" (*piacgazdaság*) was still prominent in public discourse.[4] Television news programs highlighted social problems that were projected as somehow associated with a wave of uncontrolled petty trading, prostitution and pornography, and new protection rackets. There was footage at peak viewing times of chaotic marketplace scenes, including interviews with concerned council officials, and long-suffering local residents bemoaning the lack of any effective regulation by the council. Allegations highlighted moral issues, such as traffic in young children, allegedly being routinely sold by their Gypsy parents. Another television program featured counterfeit currency disseminated on some of the larger marketplaces of southern Hungary by powerful gangs originating in Yugoslavia and Bulgaria. Newspapers carried detailed analyses of violent disputes between Syrian and Algerian gangs for control of the money-changing business

[4] *Piacgazdaság* is a compound made up of *piac*, meaning market (related to the Italian *piazza)*, and *gazdaság*, meaning economy. *Gazdaság* can refer not only to a national economy but to a single farm; it is derived from *gazda*, which can also mean "owner" and is the standard Hungarian term (though of Slav origin) for farmer.

on the streets of central Budapest. Soon after arriving in Budapest, I came across media allegations that Soviet soldiers were selling potentially lethal shells and rockets to local scrap metal dealers in a district I knew well from my earlier fieldwork. There was also a long-running story concerning the market sale of foodstuffs that were dangerous to health. The supplies were associated with a serious outbreak of swine fever in countries bordering on Romania and "tourists" from that country became the prime suspects. It was suggested that at least some of the tinned food unofficially imported from that country stemmed from supplies dispatched there as aid after the revolution which overthrew Ceaușescu.

Without performing any sophisticated content analysis, it was obvious that these stories had some common themes. Those guilty of treating family members as alienable property, those who accosted tourists on the streets to change money, and those who converted gifts of food into illicit commodities, could not possibly be ordinary respectable Hungarians. The ethnic and racial prejudices involved were complex. The main culprits as far as the new unregulated marketplaces were concerned were the Polish dealers, conspicuous throughout the country in every large town by the end of the 1980s. Even when Poles were not in fact the most numerous group in the local market, people tended to refer to it as the "Polish market." However, I had the impression that the media showed less hostility towards these northerners than they displayed towards "Balkan" neighbors and the principal internal other, the Gypsies. Hungarians who frequented such markets might argue that Poles deserved sympathy: they were to be found wheeling and dealing only because they had no other options open to them, given the chaos of the Polish economy.[5]

These marketplaces were also referred to as the "Little Comecon," an ironic allusion to the international trading bloc that worked so

[5] A fuller explanation of the phenomenon which has seen Polish traders establish powerful networks from Stockholm to Istanbul, and from West Berlin to Beijing, is not possible here. It was enabled by the fact that by the late 1970s many Poles were able to obtain passports that allowed them to travel much more freely than other East Europeans. They relied on petty commerce to gain access to convertible currencies.

Figure 2. An informal "Little Comecon" marketplace in Budapest, 1990 (source: 76176:Fortepan/Erdei Katalin)

imperfectly.[6] The basic currency in these markets was the Hungarian forint, but barter was also common and by 1990 western currencies (above all the Deutschmark) were increasingly influential. Most of the items supplied were for domestic consumption: Hungarians could be confident of getting towels from Poland at better prices than in Hungarian state shops; likewise shoes from Czechoslovakia, and various tools and automobile accessories from Romania and the USSR. I also heard of teenagers who travelled to Hungary from East Germany and Czechoslovakia in order to buy denims supposedly originating in Istanbul from Polish middlemen. Others would go to these markets in search of some vital component for their car, a part not available in any country through the official channels. Major players, as in the "second economy" generally, were those with good information networks (often through relatives in neighboring countries) and the capital to enable them to exploit these characteristic shortages. Nevertheless, I have the impression that these marketplaces have always been dominated by small dealers. Even if by 1990 there was no limit to what amenable customs officials were prepared to allow through for the appropriate bribe, there is a limit to the capacity of a Polski Fiat and trailer.

6 [Two decades after the collapse of the trading bloc itself, the abbreviation "little Comecon" remained a common way to refer to diverse branches of informal economy. See Czakó, Giczi and Sik (2010).]

At the extreme of this petty trading were the efforts of ethnic Hungarians from the USSR to secure a few forints for local purchases when that frontier was opened to tourists and private visitors in 1990 (for the first time in forty years, and even then under very strict controls). All they could bring with them were one or two bottles of vodka or cheap wine, so they would set out their stall, complete with a single glass, to provide market-goers with a tipple. Unfortunately, this is one sector of the economy in Eastern Europe where competitive principles are reasonably effective, so business was tough.[7]

These marketplaces were the scenes of occasional skirmishes with the police and local authorities in the 1980s. Even in 1990 permission to undertake a research project might not have been readily granted. In general, tolerance increased over the decade, and (as in Poland in 1990) efforts were made to bring all forms of open-air trading under local council controls. At Lake Balaton (Hungary's main tourist center) the council allocated a suitable field on the outskirts of a major resort, put up notices in Polish, and attempted to collect relatively small sums from traders as a daily levy. They did not go so far as to provide any sanitation, as the press was quick to point out, even though this site served many visitors as a caravan park and holiday home for much of the summer. At Balaton as elsewhere, traders had little difficulty in resisting attempts to control their activities: markets could easily disperse and new ones emerge overnight.

Overall it seemed to me that the Hungarian media in the summer of 1990 were rather successful in fostering a sense of principled hostility towards everything that smacked of Polanyi's uncontrolled, "disembedded" market. There was perhaps less concern in Hungary with "negative egalitarianism" than in other socialist societies (Potter and Potter 1990; Holy 1992). But the situation was one in which vital

[7] Hungarian citizens also benefited from the trading opportunities created by the opening of this Soviet border in 1990. The queues to cross were many miles long on both sides, and the days of waiting produced ugly scenes (as elsewhere on East European borders in 1990). When the Soviet authorities moved to restrict traffic across this border they justified their action with reference to adverse economic effects, but there were complaints in the Hungarian press that restricting cross-border movements by Hungarian and Soviet citizens would simply strengthen the trading power of the Poles throughout the area.

moral principles were at issue: ordinary Hungarians were being demeaned and exploited by every kind of mafia (this word was much used and discussed) and this was closely associated with the growing prominence of new marketplaces and the extension of market practices into wholly inappropriate areas of social life. There was, of course, a close connection between this morality and the official ethos of the socialist period, with its roots in pre-socialist peasant Hungary, all of which emphasized mistrust of the marketplace and sought to erect value systems outside it (cf. Stewart 1990). There was, however, no question of hackneyed socialist rhetoric condemning the private sector and "speculators." The public-sphere moralizing under the new regime of 1990 was all the more effective because it was not made in the old political terms. By this time, all the leading Hungarian political parties (including the ex-Communist Party, now renamed the Hungarian Socialist Party) were in fundamental agreement on the need to encourage the growth of a "real market economy."

The Village of Tázlár

The village of Tázlár lies on the Great Plain, about eighty miles southeast of Budapest. It has no regular marketplace, and very few foreigners are seen here. It was a significant event in 1990 when a Polish car (apparently containing genuine tourists rather than traders) had a breakdown on the main road that passes through the scattered farms of this community. Over the last few decades Tázlár has had a dynamic agricultural economy. In common with most of the communities of this region its poor quality, sandy soils are compatible with some high-value branches of production, particularly vineyards. Many of these communities have been allowed to develop distinct forms of collective farm which I call specialist cooperatives (Hungarian: *szakszövetkezet*); but before considering these it is necessary to sketch the pre-collectivization history of this area.

The community took shape on previously uninhabited *puszta* towards the end of the nineteenth century (Hann 1979). It was remote from major market centers, and few farmers produced any significant surplus. Tázlár remained poor and there were pronounced inequalities. Some of the poorest families sent their children to work as servants (*cseléd*) on the farms of the rich landowners, and others worked as day laborers on large estates further afield. During this period many other Hungarian villages experienced similar tendencies, as inequalities in property-holding increased and lands formerly held and used on a communal basis were "fragmented into exactly measured and independently used parcels of private property" (Fél and Hofer 1969, 52). Tázlár was unusual in that, as a late settlement, its lands were from the outset held and used as private property; there was therefore a more active market in land here than in more traditional communities. Nevertheless, the diverse immigrant groups which made up the new population managed their farms in the usual family-centered ways. They migrated to Tázlár as a result of the uneven impact of capitalist development, which forced many other peasants in Hungary at the same period to move to Budapest, or some other city, or abroad. But it would be wrong to imply (as I fear I did in early formulations) that the settlers were all equally in flight from capitalism. Late in the nineteenth century, for example, Ferenc Nacsa bought and farmed a large tract of land on a promising site in Tázlár, whilst retaining a perfectly adequate patrimony in his natal community sixty miles away. This enterprising family emerged as one of the prosperous upper stratum in the first half of the twentieth century, with close links to traders in nearby market centers.

In the jargon of the substantivist tradition in economic anthropology, Tázlár owed its modern genesis to the impact of the "market principle" upon Hungary. In this context, "market principle" was not concomitant with industrialization and intensified participation in national and international divisions of labor, but it did mean increased commodification of land and labor within the rural sector. Clearly many people were uprooted ("disembedded") from their earlier communities. The scattered farms of Tázlár lacked the cohesion of villages with a long history of continuous settlement, and the immigrants were slow to develop integrating institutions. They were relatively remote from major market centers. It is unlikely that they would have perceived any connection between the marketplace at the neighboring village of Soltvadkert, their main point of articulation with the national economy, and some abstract "market principle."

Between the end of the 1940s and the mid-1960s, this abstraction was ideologically condemned and markets were systematically repressed, though never entirely extinguished. In agriculture a system of compulsory deliveries was imposed, there were formidable campaigns against the so-called rich peasants (*kulák*) to strip them of their holdings (the descendants of Ferenc Nacsa experienced this fate), and mass agitation to persuade the peasantry as a whole to enter new cooperatives. After very poor results with such policies in the early 1950s, the Kádár government after 1956 set about renewing the mass collectivization program in a less dogmatic spirit. In Tázlár the impact of collectivization was felt at the level of ideology and property arrangements rather than at the level of technique and farm management. This was due to the distinctive features of the specialist cooperative.[8]

The essence of the *szakszövetkezet* was that the cooperative did not take the bulk of the land into collective cultivation (the norm for the Soviet *kolkhoz* or collective farm) but left the member and his family to carry on in the customary way. The farmer obtained remuneration in cash for the produce which he generated, subject to a 10 per cent deduction for sales made through the cooperative. There was no recourse to a collectivist payments system (such as the Soviet "work-points" scheme). Although the cooperative did farm significant areas collectively (much of which had formerly belonged to the richer private owners), there was no obligation upon cooperative members to work for the collective at all. This work was undertaken by newly hired employees. Most members remained independent family farmers, though they maintained significant links with the cooperative for marketing, fodder supplies, tractor services, and transportation.

The origins of this variant of cooperative, which falls in certain respects closer to western agricultural cooperatives than to the *kolkhoz*, are not clear. Substantial economic losses would have followed from adherence to the standard model in an area of scattered vineyards. It is likely that Communist Party officials who were natives of the region

---

[8] To be strictly accurate, the specialist cooperatives were not formally constituted in Tázlár until 1968. Between 1960 and 1968 villagers joined "production cooperative groups," which in practice functioned in the same way. Fertő et al. (1988) suggest that the delay in formal recognition was related to the village's relative backwardness when compared with neighboring communities, where farmers were able to join a specialist cooperative from the beginning. See also Gyenis (1971).

played a key role in arguing for concessions (Simó 1987). Whatever its precise origins, for the next quarter of a century this type of cooperative remained suspect ideologically. It was periodically asserted that they were "lower forms" of property, which would eventually make way for the more "progressive" forms. In fact these policies were not implemented consistently, and in the 1980s the gap widened further. I see this form of cooperative as containing the germ of a new system of property rights, one that is still capable of further development in the spirit of "market socialism," if it is not destroyed in the present wave of reaction (see Hann 1993b).

The economic success of this type of cooperative has been widely attested and a number of villages very close to Tázlár (above all Soltvadkert—see Fertő et al. 1990) have become well known throughout the country for their high levels of income and capital accumulation. Tázlár itself is not quite in the same league, but a lot of new wealth was evident in the mid-1970s: for example in newly constructed houses in the village center, and in the purchase of cars and other status symbols. This is the period in which Hungary acquired its reputation as a consumerist island in Eastern Europe, and there was much in this village to justify this image. This wealth had nothing to do with a local marketplace. For the citizens of a small community like Tázlár, the new consumer culture was built around shopping trips which took them as far as Budapest or Yugoslavia, and it involved the usual sort of networking skills as well as much patience (particularly in the queue to obtain a private car).

Relatively few Tázlár farmers participated regularly in agricultural markets. It was more convenient to sell their produce through the cooperative, which negotiated contracts with state enterprises. The prices were effectively determined by the state. Part of my research in the 1970s was devoted to showing that farmers responded elastically to these "price signals," contrary to conventional models of the peasant economy. Thus, when prices were lowered in the mid-1970s, in a brief phase of hard-line socialist propaganda responding to concern over increasing wealth differentials, there was a drop in production in the small-farm sector. Since the entire edifice of Kádár's Hungary rested upon a social compromise in which abundant affordable food supplies were a crucial component, policies were quickly altered (in line with the recommendations of the "agrarian lobby" that existed at the highest levels of the Party and the state). Farmers responded promptly to increased prices by stepping up production. In this sense, one may identify a market mechanism at work in Hungary in the mid-1970s. Prices were controlled by the government, but when supplies fell the price had to be increased in order to provide small farmers with effective incentives to supply the commodities the country needed. This pattern contrasted sharply with other collectivized countries.[9] One might even say that, in the later decades of socialism, Hungarian farmers constituted an effective pressure group on the basis of their market power. Behind the ostensibly totalitarian politics of this era, a covert pluralism could be detected.

I carried out my first fieldwork in 1976–77 at a comparatively favorable moment. The social compromise of the Kádár era dictated support for small farmers. This prosperity continued until well into the 1980s. By 1990, however, that era was over. I found that many farmers were seriously worried about stagnant price levels for their products (while costs had risen massively) and insecure markets. Soon after my arrival in the village in mid-August 1990 I called at the headquarters of the Peace Specialist Cooperative (unlike many others that year, with names like Lenin or Red Star, no one had suggested a change of name). The chairman seemed pleased to enter into a discussion about the progress of the farm since he had assumed the main leadership role in 1984. He came from a peasant family in the neighboring village. Despite his professional training as an agronomist and reaching a very senior position when still in his thirties, he had always managed to avoid joining the Communist Party. His strategy for the cooperative was eclectic. Soon after taking up his office, he had initiated the privatization of virtually all the cooperative's machinery. Tractors were sold off very cheaply, according to critics, to their drivers, whose contracts were terminated. Surplus labor was shed in other divisions too. Land was made readily available to those who wanted it, on a basis of long leases. The chairman consciously sought new ways to generate joint investment and production schemes between the cooperative and

[9] My own research concentrated on the contrast with Poland, where in spite of the persistence of private property rights in a *formal* sense, peasants were much worse off because, in the absence of an effective mechanism to link public and private sectors, they lacked *substantive* rights (Hann 1985).

its members, within a fully democratic framework. He was particularly proud of collaborative schemes for establishing new vineyards, in which certain productive tasks were still carried out by members' families in the traditional labor-intensive ways, while the cooperative provided mechanical assistance to relieve them of a significant part of the burden. The chairman was reluctant to countenance the demise of the cooperative, though he knew only too well that this was the target of some villagers, particularly those associated by 1990 with the Independent Smallholders Party. He argued that the cooperative was needed to provide basic resources at low cost to weaker members, not to mention its organization of various sideline activities, which provided the main source of wage-labor for women in the village.

In sum, the Tázlár specialist cooperative had an honorable record, claimed the chairman. In 1990 he had particularly enjoyed the irony of *kolkhoz* chairmen coming to the village from other parts of the country on fact-finding missions: the lower form of socialist property was now seen as worthy of emulation by the leaders of what had previously been considered the higher forms! Survival could not be taken for granted. For many cooperatives, including some of the *kolkhoz* type, everything would depend above all upon the persistence of a subsidy paid to farms handicapped by unfavorable ecological conditions. Unexpectedly, these subsidies had been drastically cut by the new government, with its commitment to *piacgazdaság*. The chairman likened this move in his end-of-the-year report to a "natural disaster" (*természeti csapás*). He conceded that such subsidies contradicted the logic of a pure market economy, but could I name anywhere else in Europe, he asked me, where governments dealt with agriculture according to "pure-market relations"?

I heard other points of view from cooperative members during the next few days. The leaders of the Smallholders Party favored moving within a few years to the abolition of the cooperative and the redistribution of all its lands. They were committed to their party's national manifesto, which promised full restitution of property rights on the basis of the 1947 situation (that is after the Land Reform and before the impact of socialist levelling and collectivization). This platform had strong emotive appeal, but the practical problems in this region were numerous. Even the activists themselves could sense an injustice in reallocating a vineyard planted and worked by a family for a generation to some city-dweller (or even foreign emigrant), just because the latter's father or grandfather had owned that land in 1947. It was suggested that in such cases, that is when the land had been improved and was in use as part of a family farm, the original owners should be offered compensation elsewhere. But a few owners were not satisfied with this proposed compromise; they insisted that they were only interested in reclaiming their original fields.

When the new political activists in the Smallholders Party talk about adopting the principles of a western market economy, as they frequently do, what they actually have in mind is not the removal of state subsidies through the application of a pure "market principle," but a vision of private property rights as elaborated in bourgeois political theory through the ages. Even the cooperative chairman agreed that it might be desirable to strengthen these private property rights. The worst scenario of all, he told me, would be a long period of uncertainty in which no one had compelling incentives to improve and invest. However, I suspect that most active farmers take a less ideological stance. They are interested not so much in freehold possession as in good prices for their products (and expectations remain comparatively high after the prosperity which they knew in the 1970s) and above all in a secure market. Unfortunately, the evolution of the wine trade in this region of Hungary led in the socialist decades to high dependence on large orders from undiscriminating buyers in East Germany and the USSR (where it was rumored that a low-quality Hungarian product had "socialist value added" to emerge as champagne!). These markets were near collapse by 1990. With prices already declining in real terms over the preceding five years, many farmers were bitter. Some said that they wanted to dispose of the vineyard plots which they had established jointly with the cooperative, but could not find a buyer at any price. These people tended to be unimpressed by the campaign for restoration of private property rights—certainly not before they knew what their new tax liabilities on such land would be. Few were willing to gamble on an embourgeoisement strategy in the prevailing conditions. Perhaps some had an inkling that one consequence of the elimination of the cooperative and the revival of a "pure" land market would be pre-war patterns of polarization on the labor market.

In the winter of 1989–90, one leading activist of the Smallholders' Party (not himself a farmer, but a private motor mechanic) had canvassed support throughout the village for an attack on the cooperative leadership before its annual general meeting. In ones and twos, he had amassed what he thought would be an irresistible movement. However, when it came to the meeting no one was willing to join him in his public denunciation of the cooperative and its leaders. The activist was chastened by this experience, attributing it to Tázlár's lack of cohesion in the past and an irrational resentment that a native of the village should assume a prominent leadership role. But it is also possible that this public reticence on the part of the villagers was based on a shrewd perception of where the unconditional endorsement of private property rights and a *piacgazdaság* would leave the greater part of the local population; and on a value system which was very different from that of Kornai and the new intellectual elites in the capital.

Cowboys and Comrades

Perhaps the most salient "market" in contemporary rural Hungary concerns not the land but housing construction. In contrast to the cities, where the redistributive state played a significant (though never monopolistic) role for most of the socialist period, in the countryside housing was always a key area for private enterprise (as well as for diffuse networks of reciprocity). Small building firms flourished in the 1970s and 1980s and Tázlár possessed several. Size (some employed large numbers of laborers, others very few) and a reputation for quality tended to be inversely related, but I think the elements of competition and choice were widely appreciated throughout the community. I was therefore interested to hear criticisms of this market in 1990, particularly from some well-established entrepreneurs. Their reasons were set out as follows in an article in a newspaper published in Soltvadkert. The article was entitled "The Small Businessman's Situation":

> In our large community at present 133 small businessmen are operating; in 98 cases it is their main occupation, whilst 25 are active alongside a waged-labor job, and 10 are officially pensioners. . . . The number of licensed small builders is 25, among them 8 qualified bricklayers. These respectable tax-paying small businessmen are justifiably incensed by the fact that at least

> 25–30 "cowboys" [*kontár*] have been working for years on a full-time basis without authorization. Because demand is dropping these are all the time representing stiffer competition and the established businesses are unable to compete effectively. Whilst an illegal operator rakes in profits, the honest businessman has to pay rates, national insurance, tax, etc. and after all this he's lucky if 15–20 per cent is left of his takings. The small businessmen can only campaign against this phenomenon through the organization which has represented them collectively in the past, with the aid and effective action of the tax inspectors. . . . Today it is open to everyone to become an entrepreneur, but for market competition it is also essential to make sure they are subject to fair, equal conditions . . . [10]

There is clearly no shortage of entrepreneurial talent in rural Hungary. The phenomenon analyzed by Szelényi (1988) was obvious enough in Tázlár in the mid-1970s and has remained conspicuous since. A good example is Jani (b.1949), great-grandson of Ferenc Nacsa, the *kulák* mentioned above. Jani had inherited some land, but only in the form of vineyards since his family's large holdings had all been appropriated in the 1950s. In any case Jani was more interested in machines than in the soil. After completing secondary education he took a vocational course and within a few years (still in his twenties) he was the proud owner of a private tractor. When I first met him in 1976 he was competing successfully with the cooperative to provide mechanical services to farmers; the additional purchase of a combine harvester a few years later enabled him to offer a full range of services. Jani himself preferred to work mainly on the maintenance side (the machines were usually old models, scrapped from some State Farm or *kolkhoz*, and spare parts were always a problem) whilst assistants carried out the work in the fields. Without any significant advantage in terms of inherited land (but

[10] *Vadkerti Újság*, 1990, 2 (5): 7–8. The word *kontár*, which I have translated as "cowboy" in this passage, is given in the dictionary as "amateur"—usually in the sense of "bungler." It is possibly related to the English counterfeit, and it was formerly used in Hungary to identify craftsmen who worked outside the framework of the guild. (See *Magyar Történelmi és Etimológiai Szótár*, vol. 2, Budapest: Akadémiai, 1970, 553–54.)

with the very significant assistance of his wife, who generated substantial income through small-scale farming in addition to holding a wage-labor job in the village and bringing up the children), Jani succeeded within a few years in re-establishing his family at a level of material superiority comparable to that enjoyed previously by his forefathers. At no stage did he have anything to do with the Communist Party. This new wealth was not achieved without some cost. Both Jani and his wife worked extremely hard, especially in the summer months. A few years ago he was briefly hospitalized and he tries now to work less and to follow a healthier diet. He has also had to put up with a certain amount of mockery and teasing precisely because he has done so well financially; he has a nickname which suggests a person who is excessively calculating, always with an eye on material advantage.

By 1990 Jani and his family had moved into an imposing new dwelling on the outskirts of the village, where in the yard he had added a fodder supply shop to his impressive array of agricultural machines Business was satisfactory. He had retail outlets in neighboring villages as well, and was looking ahead to the possibility of establishing the community's very first petrol station. He himself was now driving a brand-new BMW—paid for in forints, handed over to a Hungarian émigré who returns frequently to the region, who then dispatched the vehicle to Jani from Switzerland as a "gift."

Conversation was not easy on my first visit to Jani in August 1990, mainly because the phone kept ringing throughout the evening with news of important potential deals (mostly agricultural equipment and the motor trade). Later we were entertained when two drunks staggered into the fodder shop. Only one of these disheveled characters was in any state to talk at all, which he did with very limited vocabulary and what I took to be an alcohol-induced slur. The other occupied himself in front of a mirror, moaning gently as he prodded his mouth with a number of small implements. Whatever he had consumed that evening, it had not been enough to deaden the pain of ferocious toothache.

As I listened to a stream of banter over the next hour or so, the reason for this visitation became clear. These men were Soviet army officers, stationed at the barracks of Kiskunhalas about seven miles away. They had run up a very large bill at a restaurant in the town that afternoon, whilst bidding farewell to a colleague. Now they needed cash to pay their debt. To my surprise, when he had finally tired of teasing them, Jani took out his cash box and handed over the sum required. In the next few days I saw soldiers in the village on a number of occasions—all in civilian dress, though sometimes travelling in military vehicles. In the 1970s I had never seen a soldier in Tázlár—only the tracks of tanks in the forests. Occasionally I had been woken by the rumble of a convoy on a night exercise, but otherwise there was little to remind villagers of the proximity of a large Soviet base. Uniformed soldiers had been an occasional forlorn sight on the streets and in the coffee-bars of Kiskunhalas. I had heard rumors in the 1970s that some astute local traders had bartered alcohol for Soviet diesel fuel, but I had never found evidence for this. In short, I ignored the presence of the Soviet military in my monograph because they seemed to have no detectable impact on village life.

By summer 1990 it had been decided that these soldiers were to return to the USSR, most of them before the year's end. The villagers seemed rather sorry for them, for it was anticipated that they would have to spend the coming winter in tents. Meanwhile, of course, there were substantial material assets at bases all over Hungary, many of which could not be transported home. Hence the scope for an entrepreneur such as Jani; it turned out that his dealings with the Soviets were already well known in the village. The joke was that sooner or later he would purchase a tank (I heard from a number of sources, in all seriousness, that small arms had already been purchased in large quantities). Jani had already acquired a military jeep, but that particular deal had almost ended in disaster. Apparently higher-ranking officers had for once refused to accept the fiction that a piece of equipment had been written off in an accident. When the jeep was discovered on the outlying family homestead (where Jani's father still resided), substantial bribes had to be paid very quickly to avoid serious trouble.

On a more mundane level, Jani had managed to furnish his new holiday-home at a nearby beauty spot by drawing on the unwanted stocks of the officers' mess in the Soviet base. Through his contacts, he had also recruited private soldiers to work as day laborers in his vineyards. Apparently they were only too keen to undertake such work, a change from their routine. They did not need to be paid as much as Hungarian day laborers; all the employer had to do was ensure a good alcohol supply. While ordinary soldiers were content with booze, for the officers contact with Jani offered them a chance to accumulate wealth (for example enough forints to purchase a second-hand Volga car) that might really make a difference after the return home to the USSR (marrying a Hungarian girl was an alternative strategy, but this was rare).

In the course of a short visit, it was not possible for me to assess the strength of Jani's links with the Soviet suppliers, and I can hardly present this as a paradigmatic "market" situation. I am not aware of any other Tázlár villagers with similar contacts. But I am quite sure that, despite Jani's image as a somewhat devious character who never looks beyond the short-term benefits of the transactions in which he is engaged, he had established strong trust with his Soviet partners. This had already widened into a network that extended to other bases across the county. Enduring friendships had been formed, and I was told that Jani had taken his whole family as tourists to the Ukraine in the previous year, where they had been guests of the comrade with the toothache.

I tackled Jani about the rockets story which I had heard on television and read about in the press, since it was allegedly at the Kiskunhalas barracks that this particular violation of moral propriety had been committed. He said that in his view the whole story was a fabrication, a myth put about in the new, more open media to discredit the Soviets. Perhaps he wanted to imply that if anyone had put up some rockets for sale, he would certainly have known and been offered first option! It is possible that Jani's market information was not as good as he supposed. In any case, it is plausible to suggest that this and other stories received the publicity they did in Hungary in summer 1990 because powerful interests wished to alter public perceptions of "market exchange."

But we may ask in concluding: "what is this abstraction called market exchange?" While concrete markets vary enormously (for example according to the objects exchanged, the location of the market, and the nature of public regulation), analysts of very different political persuasion have found it convenient to oppose an ideal-type "market" to "the plan," or to "redistribution." Karl Polanyi (1944) classified (market) exchange and redistribution as different "principles of economic behavior." Although the impact of Polanyi's mature scholarship on his native country has been negligible, his moral sensibility to the domination of the "market principle" is relevant to the present transition, not least because a similar concept of the "market principle" has been strongly advocated since the mid-1980s by economists of a very different persuasion, keen to reject the redistributive compromises of "market socialism" and implement "the market" in some purer form [Bockman 2011]. The campaigns against foreigners who sell off unsuitable, ideally inalienable objects in informal or illegal circumstances can be seen as minor skirmishes within the discourse of a gigantic political struggle throughout Eastern Europe. At least in the case of Hungary I suspect that for many years to come, and long after the Soviet troops have gone home, it will be easy to incite public opinion against "the market."

Postscript: Trade and Trust in Southeast Poland[11]

As a result of new state borders and the ethnic cleansing of the 1940s, the People's Republic of Poland became one of the most ethnically homogenous "nation-states" in Europe. The government recognized minorities and supported certain forms of cultural expression that it was able to control, such as the Ukrainian Socio-Cultural Association it established in 1956. The policy was successful, at least insofar as minorities ceased to pose the kind of political problem they had posed in Poland before the Second World War. Of course, the official claim that 98.7 per cent of the People's Republic's citizens were ethnic Poles, virtually all of them Roman Catholics (Wiatr 1977, 137), disguised a reality that was still in many regions a good deal more complicated. Polish social scientists showed that, despite the precept of socialist internationalism, many Poles continued to hold extremely negative images of Ukrainians (Chlewiński 1980).

The southeastern corner of the People's Republic, where I carried out field research in 1979–1981, was devastated when the great majority of its indigenous Ukrainian population (including members of the

[11] *The postscript to this chapter is adapted from Hann 1998f. I am grateful to Dr Stanisław Stępień, Director of the South East Scientific Institute in Przemyśl, for his cooperation in a research grant awarded by the Economic and Social Research Council (R 236071, "The Politics of Religious Identity: the Greek Catholics of Central Europe,"1995–97). For invaluable initial guidance I also thank Father Serge Keleher and Grace Davie. Keith Sword and Stanisław Wiater were generous with information and comments; the 1998 paper was dedicated to their memories.*

Lemko ethnographic group, some of whom did not consider themselves to be Ukrainian at all) were deported on suspicion of offering support to terrorists. To avoid deportation, some Ukrainians converted from Greek Catholicism to Roman Catholicism and eventually assimilated fully into Polish society (Babiński 1997, 276). Others were able to continue practicing the eastern rites under the protection of the dominant Roman Catholic Church. This was the case in the city of Przemyśl, close to the Ukrainian border, which became the *de facto* center of the Greek Catholic Church in Poland (see Chapters Nine and Ten).

Poland elected a non-communist government in 1989 several months before the dramatic changes that engulfed the rest of Eastern Europe later that year and in 1990. By the end of 1990 Lech Wałęsa had been elected president of the new republic, while at local level the candidates of the Citizens' Committees, generally organized by Solidarity activists, swept away the old communist councilors. Under the "Balcerowicz plan," influenced by the Harvard economist Jeffrey Sachs and usually summed up in the phrase "shock therapy," the country embarked upon a rapid program of marketization and privatization. The Roman Catholic Church claimed its share of the credit for toppling the ancien regime, and sought promptly to claim its due reward in the form of new policies of religious education and abortion law reform. At the same time, in Przemyśl and elsewhere members of the Greek Catholic, Ukrainian minority expected their legitimate claims to be acknowledged after decades of repression.

Among early analysts of this momentous transition, sociologist Piotr Sztompka highlighted a pervasive "culture of mistrust" and suggested some general ways in which this "syndrome" needed to be changed (Sztompka 1996). He cited survey data indicating that Poles placed higher valuations on foreign-made goods than on local products "of comparable quality," and interpreted this as the "externalisation of trust" (1996, 49). Later in the article it was stated that strong externalized trust applied only to the West, and that there was "traditional external distrust towards Russia and other eastern neighbours" (1996, 53). According to classical liberal theories of civil society, social trust is generated through the "natural" proliferation of "free" economic actions. Although Sztompka commented extensively on attitudes to new forms of market economy, finding that a general climate of cynicism and mistrust continued to impede progress, he did not address

Figure 3. The Ukrainian bazaar in Przemyśl, (photo by Chris Hann, 1994)

these issues concretely. He overlooked the forms of petty marketing that have enabled millions of Poles to survive the dislocation brought by "shock therapy" after 1989. Much of this activity involved contact with foreigners and movement across the country's borders, which became much easier than before, in all directions. Polish men have long travelled westwards, e.g. to work as agricultural laborers (nowadays in Britain rather than Prussia), while women have entered domestic service (for example nowadays in Italy); others have attracted notoriety in the sex trade in Germany and Holland. On a more mundane level, and therefore less likely to attract media publicity, it has been estimated that the "suitcase trade" across the border with Germany brought in as much as 10 per cent of Poland's Gross Domestic Production 1995.[12]

These flows raise the question of how new economic forms impact upon interethnic relations and changing constructions of "Polishness." However, the theme of interethnic trust in post-communist conditions is not addressed by Sztompka in the above-mentioned paper, either internally or in relation to the unprecedented levels of petty trading across state borders. Although the value of the economic flows was no doubt much greater along the western border, Poland's eastern bor-

[12] This estimate is given by the Instytut Badań nad Gospodarką Rynkową, cited in K. Grzegrzółka, "Na zakupy do Polski," *Rzeczpospolita*, April 22–23, 1995.

ders too suddenly became porous. The forms of trade with Ukrainians differed radically from the patterns with Germany, but with the collapse of the old socialist enterprises these markets became of great economic significance to the residents of cities such as Przemyśl. It was said locally that this small town close to the Ukrainian border hosted the country's second largest "Russian bazar" (after the capital's). It spread beyond the established *targ* to colonize a sports stadium next door.[13] Traders arrived mostly by train and bus from adjacent parts of Ukraine, though some came from much further afield. The summer months were the most crowded, when whole families made the trip, often sleeping on their buses or in their old Ladas to save a little money. The main aim of most visitors in the first years after 1989, when travel restrictions were eased, was to sell anything they could and take some hard currency home with them. Though Poland was undergoing severe economic dislocation in those years, conditions almost everywhere in the former USSR were far worse. By this time Poland had a convertible currency. Increasingly, local traders in Przemyśl began to see opportunities for profitable exports to the east, and new business partnerships were formed with Ukrainians. However, the numbers of Poles moving eastwards to trade remained small in comparison to the numbers of Ukrainians entering Poland for this purpose.

Attitudes to the new commerce varied considerably. Apart from those who made their main living from the marketplaces, many consumers were grateful for the opportunity to gain access to cheap ex-socialist merchandise (which did not prevent them from speaking with contempt about its quality). Some shopkeepers protested that they had lost custom as a result of the new inflow of goods. Some criticized the authorities for tolerating those who offered their own labor for sale (mainly for very low rates of pay in agriculture and the building industry), at a time when many Poles themselves were out of work. Some were critical of the physical dirt that these temporary migrants invariably leave behind them, not just at the market but at the train and bus stations, the municipal camping site and the street corners where goods were sold illegally. Some residents put the emphasis on moral dirt, of

[13] The club is said to have used its share of the market taxes to sign foreign basketball stars and compete more effectively in the national league.

which there were several varieties. It was alleged (without evidence, so far as I could judge in Przemyśl) that some of the visitors extended informal economic activities to include prostitution. More seriously from the point of view of minority-majority relations, some Poles saw a moral peril in the very fact that the streets of Przemyśl were now once again full of people speaking Ukrainian (see Chapters Nine and Ten). The activities of Polish veterans' associations in Przemyśl exemplified virulent nationalist sentiment at the border of the nation-state. Their leaders (many said to be former communists) created a climate of opinion in which the majority of Polish inhabitants came to view any expression of Ukrainian identity as a threat and an affront. Survey data suggest that Polish attitudes to Ukrainians have remained highly negative. While the particular circumstances of Przemyśl are unique, the problem of cultural recognition and prejudice is widespread. In Przemyśl itself, sociologist Jerzy Jestal found that the most entrenched stereotype of Ukrainian was "dirty trader." Negative stereotyping was especially prevalent among young people in the city (Jestal 1994).

So, do these new forms of trade have the potential to contribute to interethnic trust and more tolerance of cultural difference? In one of the few monographs published on socialist Eastern Europe by Western anthropologists, the American William Lockwood documented the social integration that was achieved in the course of interaction on the marketplaces of Bosnia in the 1970s (Lockwood 1975). Muslims, Serbs and Croats came together for economic purposes and offered their goods to the members of other groups at the same prices at which they would sell to members of their own. But Lockwood argued that this was no more than a limited, "functional" integration: the economic interaction did not break down perceptions of group difference and did not lead to increased intermarriage. The integration that has been achieved through the rather different sorts of marketplace that have proliferated along Poland's eastern border in the 1990s seems to be similarly limited. The city of Przemyśl has been functionally dependent on this cross-border trade, and the local Polish nationalists do not oppose it as such. However, intensive interaction on the bazar, though it may create some new relationships of trust between individuals, is by no means inconsistent with the persistence of derogatory stereotypes about groups. Nationalist leaders appeal to the negative connotations of commerce when mobilizing groups for action.

Finally, it should be noted that current patterns of petty trading are likely to change drastically in the near future when Poland becomes a full member of the European Union. Poland is likely to come under pressure to police the border of the new "Fortress Europe" with great care. Some of the people who currently make their living through petty trade, and in future their children, may turn instead to make their living as border guards. Polish nationalists would feel comfortable with such a role, reviving as it would the glorious old myths of the *Antemurale*—Poland as the bulwark of European civilization, defined once more as congruent with the boundary of Latin Christianity. But this scenario is unlikely to raise the trust quantum in this part of Central Europe.

CHAPTER THREE

From Production to Property: Land Tenure and Citizenship in Rural Hungary

(1993, 1996)

Introduction: The Concept of Property in Anthropology[1]

The concept of property has long occupied a central place in Western political and economic theory, but it has had a chequered history in social anthropology, and has not figured strongly in recent work in the discipline. This chapter concentrates on a specific type of property right, the ownership of agricultural land. Although the wider economic climate is increasingly unfavorable to agriculture, postsocialist power holders are committed to the restoration of capitalist property relations, in the countryside and more generally. According to a distinguished Canadian political theorist, Western concepts of property underwent radical changes with the emergence of modern, market-driven economies (Macpherson 1962). Tracing these changes to the age of Hobbes and Locke, before the industrial revolution, Macpherson identifies a crucial link between new conceptions of property rights and ensuing processes of capitalist accumulation. Property rights were no longer embedded in a matrix of social relations, but were conceived in terms

[1] *This chapter is an amalgam of two papers, Hann 1993a and Hann 1996c. The first was written in 1991 and was awarded the Curl Prize of the Royal Anthropological Institute for that year. The published version benefited from the comments of Leo Howe, Hastings Donnan and anonymous readers for* Man. *I was indebted to the University of Cambridge for a travel grant which supported my visit to Tázlár in 1991. I continued to visit the village in the following years and extended the analysis in a paper written for a Workshop convened in Cambridge in September 1993 by Ray Abrahams. I thank him and other participants for much useful discussion. For a further updating of developments pertaining to property in Tázlár, see Hann 2006.*

of the "absolute" claims of private individual owners over the material objects in their possession. The Western intellectual tradition which accompanies this capitalist development reaches its rigorous denouement in utilitarian economic theory, in which the predominance of private property rights is the indispensable mechanism for the generation of incentives to invest, and hence of efficient production and growth (Ryan 1984).

Macpherson's work is consistent with that of Marx and Engels, who posited a similar close connection between the emergence of capitalism as a productive system and new forms of property. They countered liberal arguments in defense of private property with a revolutionary alternative, but this socialist alternative was still envisaged within the Western tradition. Late in their lives, both Marx and Engels were stimulated by reading contemporary accounts of "pre-class" societies outside the modern West, in which private property was absent (Engels 1972; Morgan 1877; see Krader 1972). The proposition that communal property rights had prevailed at the start of human evolution resonated well with their analysis of class conflict in later stages and with their prediction of a communist future for industrial societies.

Anthropologists and colonial civil servants alike found it difficult to think outside the terms of the dichotomy "either private/individualist or communal," predicated upon the modern Western understanding of exclusive ownership, even when the indigenous property systems they encountered were much too complex to squeeze into this framework. Having sought in vain in the early nineteenth century to identify landlords of an English (or Irish) sort in India, in order to secure the benefits which they assumed would flow from the institutions of private property and the free market, the imperial authorities spent much of the next century backtracking and qualifying those ownership rights. Some were tempted to replace concepts of private ownership with communal ownership, in the form of the "corporate village community." This idea persisted until, in the mid-twentieth century, a postcolonial government appropriated land from private landlords, and placed it under the "communal" ownership of the state (Neale 1962).

In this context, as in many others, the generation of Malinowski achieved a breakthrough. In the early 1920s W.H.R. Rivers was still preoccupied with "individualism and communism in respect of property" (1924, 103). The quality of Malinowski's Melanesian ethnography undermined such simplistic dichotomies. Although his analysis of land tenure is hardly the best-known component of his oeuvre and on the face of it seems pertinent only to certain types of preindustrial society, I argue that it can offer insight into the contemporary transformation of rural Eastern Europe. Malinowski was himself an Eastern European intellectual, and the full importance of his Polish origins for his later anthropology is still being uncovered (Ellen et al. 1988; Thornton and Skalník 1993). His liberal-conservative individualist values gave him a powerful aversion to anything smacking of communism, an aversion he shared with the Eastern European peasants who had collectivization imposed upon them. "There is no more jejune and fruitless distinction in primitive sociology than that between individualism and Communism," argued Malinowski, adding that:

> Almost to spite the anthropological theorists, the Trobriander insists on having his own plot associated with his personal name. This old, opposition is a vicious and unintelligent short-cut, because throughout this discussion the real problem before us was not the either-or of individualism and Communism but the relation of collective and personal claims. (Malinowski 1966 [1935], 380)

I shall show that this rejection of the "either-or of Communism or individualism" can be extended beyond the range of societies addressed by Malinowski himself. It is important to look beyond the political rhetoric of our age and examine instead the realities of changing collective and personal claims before, during, and after the socialist period.

The final two chapters of the first volume of *Coral Gardens and Their Magic* (1935) are the culmination of Malinowski's ethnographic writings about the Trobriand Islanders. As Edmund Leach points out in his Introduction to the second edition, they are "a most brilliant demonstration of what Malinowski meant by functional integration" (Malinowski 1966, xii). Malinowski argues that a full appreciation of land tenure requires detailed understanding of the entirety of what the next generation of anthropologists was to call the "social structure." He first gives a restricted definition of land tenure as "the body of rules which govern the practice of cultivation and apportionment of produce" (1966, 376). However, it is essential to locate these practices in a wider context of economic activities, legal titles and also "mythological foundations." Land tenure, in Malinowski's hands, turns out to be far removed from the dry, arcane topic that generations of colonial lawyer-anthropologists made it out to be. Since land was the key resource in preindustrial societies, the study of land tenure entails investigating the full complexity of the social arrangements for meeting the claims and entitlements of citizens.

For Lewis Henry Morgan, the story of human evolution was a story that began with "primitive Communism" and proceeded through the divisions of different kinds of "class society" as the encroachments of private property grew ever greater. Morgan, like the orthodox Marxist tradition to which he contributed so much, was convinced that such "individualist" trends in contemporary society must be reversed. In contrast, Malinowski's "functionalist" anthropology left no room for evolutionist arguments. Since it was not possible to obtain reliable information about the origins of human societies, in place of speculation and conjecture it was preferable to trace detailed links between different social institutions synchronically. Fieldwork revealed that the Trobrianders practiced a subtle blending of the communal and the individual. Thus, the sub-clan could be represented, according to Malinowski, by an individual, and although almost all work was done by cooperative groups (notably the "gardening team"), "individual titles exist and the land is subdivided, as it were, almost in deference to the desire for individual distinctions" (1966, 378). Hence his rejection of the "vicious" opposition of individualism and communism.

The rejection, however, applies to primitive society only. In the final paragraph of the book Malinowski associates both communism and Fascism with "the advent of the machine." The publications of his final years show a nostalgic, rather romantic, European liberal, committed to the superiority of capitalist individualism over the rival collectivist ideologies of his age (Mucha 1988). These values vitiate his overall analysis of Trobriand social relations. Malinowski persistently describes Melanesians in terms more appropriate to Western individuals. He fails to see, for example, that a district headman's relation to other villagers cannot be adequately explained in terms of western concepts of the person. Even so, critics have continued to find Malinowski's materials stimulating, often for purposes quite different from those he himself envisaged. In the context of decollectivization in Eastern

Europe, his invitation to consider "the relation of collective and personal claims" remains a valuable starting point. So too is his insistent advice to explore land tenure in the broader sense, "beyond the legal point of view."

Following Malinowski's lead, Max Gluckman, an Africanist who had been trained in the common law, developed a subtle and sophisticated theoretical framework for understanding land tenure in tribal societies (1943, 1965). Gluckman showed more clearly than his predecessors how property rights were tied to social and political status, thereby forming a hierarchy of "estates of administration." He further showed how this terminology could be applied to acephalous as well as to more centralized groups, and in situations where land was relatively abundant as well as where it was scarce and more directly subjected to social and political controls. Gluckman located "estates of production" at the bottom of the hierarchy, where rights to cultivate specific plots were vested in families, households or in specific persons. He thereby disposed of the still strongly lingering assumption that most tribal production was somehow "communal." In short, Gluckman refined Malinowski's position that land was held and used in ways that could not adequately be labelled either "communal" or "individualist"; for both of them, property rights could be understood only through a careful understanding of the entire social system.

Gluckman's stance did not imply an extreme relativism, with the prescription to jettison property as yet another ethnocentric Western concept unsuited to comparative analytical deployment. His basic argument—that property relations are intrinsically social and political relations—corresponds to mainstream thinking about property rights in Europe prior to the seventeenth century. The framework developed by Gluckman proved useful in other non-capitalist contexts, quite different from those for which it was originally devised (Humphrey 1983). It corresponds well to the expanded concept of property which Macpherson and other critics recommend for industrial capitalist economies, in order to present more realistic accounts of how these economies really work.

As the colonial tradition of land tenure studies faded, the concept of property began to figure in new ways in anthropological analysis. In Cambridge, Jack Goody explored the implications of property transmission mechanisms for the structure of kin groups and social organization generally (Goody 1962, 1976). Edmund Leach amassed data from a Sri Lankan village to argue, contra Meyer Fortes, that property was theoretically prior to kinship (Leach 1961). Leach seemed to critics to be (uncharacteristically) promoting some sort of economic determinism, but his claims did not impress anthropologists of a neo-Marxist orientation who rose to prominence in the discipline in the 1970s. For Maurice Bloch (1975), when Leach discussed property relations he was in fact merely probing another area of ideological "superstructure." He was thus no more successful than Fortes in grasping the underlying mode of production. Bloch conceded that in tribal economies such as that of the Zafimaniry of Madagascar it was impossible to distinguish property relations from the relations of production, and that both of these would be rooted in kinship. But among peoples with more complex economies, such as the rice-growing Merina and Leach's Sinhalese, property relations belonged to the realm of superstructure, as in capitalist societies. The property ideology mystifies the true character of social relations between persons, substituting representations of exclusive rights over material objects.[2]

Social anthropologists have not played a leading role in the study of property in "peasant societies," where the issue of "communalism versus individualism" presents itself in different forms. Teodor Shanin has argued that peasant landholding differs from the individual private property rights of modern capitalism. Property rights are vested not in individuals but in the family as a corporation, and sentimental attachments to family land run deep. Drawing on anthropologist Paul Bohannan, Shanin writes:

> Peasant political economy closely links the network of social relations with land tenure, a crucial determinant of the peasant's well-

[2] The trajectory of "property" in social anthropology continued beyond the neo-Marxist phase. A decade later Marilyn Strathern (1988) criticized the "proprietorial assumption" of Western accounts when proposing alternative notions of personhood and agency in Melanesia. Her emphatic opposition between the commodity economies of the West and the gift economies of Melanesia could be viewed as a postmodern reformulation of the nineteenth century binary that Malinowski had sought to displace.

> being and the family's social standing. The peasant land tenure represents a map of human relations rather than of impersonal slices of real estate along "Western" lines. This map of social relations is structured by diverse hierarchies of societal control. Land rights do not appear as clear-cut, absolute and exclusive divisions of legal ownership: a variety of rights with different degrees of formalization intermingle. (1990, 112–13; see also 24–25)

Alan Macfarlane has placed these characteristics of peasant property rights at the center of an ideal-type of peasantry, as a prelude to arguing that English villagers, as far back as records allow one to judge, were quite unlike peasants elsewhere (1978). According to Macfarlane, the English evidence suggests that, by the sixteenth century, land in England was owned very much like modern real estate, i.e. as an "absolute" right vested in an individual rather than in any family group or corporation. It could be bought and sold like other commodities, unhindered by the owners' emotional loyalties and identifications. This contradicts the picture painted by Marx and Macpherson, who had assumed the predominance of something closer to the picture painted by Bohannan. Macfarlane's provocative work has drawn little response from anthropologists, though many of his contentions, such as the postulate of a strong sentimental attachment to the land among peasant families and the patriarchal character of their property rights, are suitable subjects for ethnographic investigation. His ideal-type of peasantry has a further source of interest for East Europeanists, since it is largely constructed from accounts of historical peasantries in that region.[3] I now turn to consider Eastern Europe, following the remarkable changes that have occurred since the demise of socialist regimes in 1989–1991, changes nowhere more dramatic than in the new patterns of land tenure.

---

3 Macfarlane chose Eastern Europe to construct his model very deliberately: it was not quite western, and yet it was close enough to facilitate a series of comparisons with England. He later conceded that the East Europeanist sources on which he relied might not be perfectly accurate, but he did not consider that this undermined his project to construct a peasant ideal type (1987, 220).

Rural Transformations in Eastern Europe

Although the number of people living in the countryside remains high in comparison with other parts of Europe, rural society in Eastern Europe has been transformed almost beyond recognition in the course of the twentieth century. Many areas had experienced a gradual shift away from "feudal" patterns by the early decades of the century, as 3-field crop rotation and collective pasture associations made way for more "individualist" forms of ownership and land use (Fél and Hofer 1969). "Land hunger" was prevalent across much of the region, particularly during the Depression years. "Private" landholding was the key not only to economic security but also to social status and political power in the countryside (Warriner 1939; Fél and Hofer 1969). However, the human-land relationship was subjected to further, more drastic reformulation in the middle of the century with the imposition of collectivization. The elimination of a specific land-family link, together with increasing mechanization, are often taken to signal the demise of the traditional peasantry (Figes 1987; Shanin 1990). Nevertheless, anthropologists have continued to use the term peasant, not only in areas where collectivization was not pursued and technological change was slow (Hann 1985), but also in countries where full collectivization induced rapid and visible changes. For example, in Romania John Cole (1976) was among the first to study peasant-workers under socialism, and David Kideckel (1993) has analyzed the persistence of a "residual peasant mode of production" alongside the dominant socialist mode under Ceauşescu.

Across most of Eastern Europe, striking elements of continuity centered on the rural household as it (collectively) deployed the labor of its members. Usually, at least one household member would join the collective farm, to ensure that the household benefited from rights such as access to a "private plot." Another (or possibly the same person) would hold a regular wage-labor job, to provide income security, and to gain additional welfare and pension entitlements. But when required, all household labor resources were available for small-scale agricultural production. This might take place on a private plot, but it did not necessarily require any land base at all (e.g. where so-called "vertical integration" allowed farmers to purchase fodder from a socialist institution more cheaply than they would have been able to produce it for themselves, and then raise animals in their back yards). Such rural households could be seen, in Chayanovian terms, as practicing "self-exploitation" to produce goods more cheaply than they could be provided through either socialist or capitalist wage-labor alternatives.[4]

Some characteristics of rural Eastern Europe, such as the extensive incidence of commuting to industrial jobs and the prominence of part-time farmers in the more labor-intensive branches of production, are also found in other European regions (Franklin 1969). In general, however, the methods used to implement agricultural change in Eastern Europe, particularly at the moment of collectivization, introduced a more radical break in the history of rural society than is found elsewhere in Europe, where the evolution of peasants into farmers has been a more protracted, but generally smoother process. There is, of course, tremendous diversity within Eastern Europe. As in other parts of the continent, local outcomes have been greatly affected by very significant political differences at state level during the socialist period, which there is no space to explore here.

The most important distinguishing feature of the East European countryside, and the root of major differences from the rest of Europe in labor organization and farm management, was property relations. By 1962 most rural families had had their land removed from their direct control, though the timing and the political and legal conditions under which this took place varied greatly between countries, and even within countries. In Hungary, for example, after a decade of intermittent attempts, full collectivization was accomplished between 1959 and 1961 (Swain 1985). Villagers themselves had little say in the matter. They experienced collectivization as the appropriation of their property, the culmination of an on-going, politically motivated onslaught directed by socialist power holders against the independent peasantry. When Hungarian villagers recall these events, they do so in terms of the modern dichotomy discussed above. The land that was taken into the cooperatives had previously been theirs; it was private property (*magántulajdon*). The Malinowskian anthropologist will treat this claim with

---

4 For further discussions of Hungarian rural households under socialism, see Hann 1980a; Hollos and Maday 1983; Bell 1984; Vasary 1987. A useful guide to the work of A. V. Chayanov can be found in Shanin 1990, 319–40.

some caution and want to look more closely at how property rights were actually constrained by familial obligations. Mass collectivization did not in fact divest Hungarian villagers of their formal, legal property rights. Land belonged nominally to the individual previously registered as the owner—usually male, although women could also inherit land and act as effective heads of households. Land could still be inherited, and in certain circumstances it could even be alienated. This owner received rental payment from the collective farm which used the land, regardless of whether or not the owner was a member of this cooperative, and he might also be liable to pay property taxes. Despite all these complicating factors, it is fair to say that Eastern European villagers experienced a crucial and unwelcome change in the quality of their property rights at the time of collectivization.

By the time I began fieldwork in Hungary in 1976 property relations were not much discussed, either in official policy pronouncements or by villagers. The emphasis had shifted away from the primarily political goals of the 1950s, when the proprietors of above-average farms had been branded *kulák* and subjected to every kind of intimidation and humiliation. From the mid-1960s onwards greater attention was paid to economic goals, which in practice meant the maximization of production. Hungarian rural households were encouraged to produce the foods and beverages demanded by consumers, at home and abroad. The new socialist farms met part of this demand themselves, but a large proportion of agricultural production depended upon households. Socialist farm managers assisted the post-peasants with marketing and technical services, and with inputs that could be more efficiently produced through mechanized techniques on larger acreages. In some sectors complex forms of integration developed, e.g. a "putting-out" relationship according to which piglets born in the collective would be farmed out to household sties before returning to the socialist institution for eventual sale. Cooperatives began to relax the requirement that members needed to work in the collective sector: if it were conducive to raising overall output, members were allowed to work full-time, unsupervised, on their own plots, or in their homes and yards. Cooperatives and state-owned farms were often willing to lease additional land to their members, or indeed to any villager who applied. On the other hand, sometimes even the "private plot," to which every member was entitled, was not allocated physically. It could be commuted instead to a cash payment, or to a benefit in kind (such as a specified quantity of fodder). Meanwhile, the agricultural sector as a whole benefited from favorable state purchasing policies. The overall result was that many rural households were able to achieve high levels of commodity production and to improve their material living conditions dramatically. They also acquired new rights, unknown in the countryside before, such as rights to employment and to free health care. Policymakers and local agricultural officials emphasized not ideological precept but the pragmatic need to integrate small and large, "private" and "socialist," in order to maximize production and income levels. The formal-legal ownership of land shifted from being the most important of all social indicators to being almost an irrelevance.[5]

The "symbiosis" of small- and large-scale sectors was the key to the overall success of Hungarian collectivization (Swain 1985). The later expansion of part-time farming has been interpreted as "tacit decollectivization" by Elek (1991), and the integration of competing peasant and socialist "paradigms" at household level has been thoroughly studied by Vasary (1987). Szelényi and his associates, relying mainly upon statistical evidence, have shown that the new rural entrepreneurs were likely to be descendants of those whose "embourgeoisement trajectory" was interrupted in the early decades of socialist power, when "politics" was in command (1988). Somehow it seemed that these families had been able to retain their competitive edge: although unable to transmit significant material resources through the inheritance of property rights, they could nonetheless make sure that their values and "cultural capital" were passed on to the next generation.

By the mid-1980s sociologists were beginning to pay attention to a number of developments in property relations outside agriculture, which together amounted to a substantial modification of orthodox socialist principles. New forms of small cooperatives and "economic work partnerships" emerged to supplement the relatively small private

[5] Of course, other property objects became highly important at this time. The desire to acquire new cars and televisions, new houses, or at least a new bathroom, provided the consumer incentives which fuelled the small farm production boom in the 1970s. In addition, it gradually became possible to acquire exclusive property rights in the sphere of production: in the early 1970s it was still impossible to own a private tractor, but by the end of the decade even combine-harvesters could be found in private ownership.

sector. These functioned as the urban equivalents of the private plot in agriculture. There was a trend towards a diversity of property forms, the main purpose being, as in agriculture, to promote a principle of complementarity, in the interests of overall economic integration and higher levels of output, including service provision. In intellectual and political circles there was renewed discussion at this time of an old East European populist theme, the search for a "third way," between capitalism and socialism (Stark 1989; Hann 1990a).

These reformist currents in Hungary were overtaken by revolutionary developments elsewhere in Eastern Europe in 1989, which caused all hints of a "third way" to be aborted and left the field open to the hegemony of the "free market."[6] It was assumed by the new elites that the free market and private property rights would establish the twin conditions for "rejoining Europe." In the agricultural sector tacit decollectivization has been replaced on the agenda of most postsocialist governments by full-scale privatization of farmland. Again, there is a great deal of diversity between and within countries (Pryor 1991). My discussion will focus on the case of Hungary, where the Independent Smallholders' Party was relaunched in 1989 by surviving members of the political party which had been the most popular in the country in the last democratic elections of the 1940s. The main program of this party was the restoration of land ownership to the conditions of 1947.[7] In the spring of 1990 this party became a coalition partner in Hungary's first postsocialist government. However, most other politicians, including the Smallholders' coalition partners, had grave doubts concerning its policy of land restitution. Although it fitted well with the prevailing emphasis upon private property rights, there was an obvious danger that, in dismantling existing state-owned and collective farms, the sector would lose economies of scale, and levels of food production might be jeopardized. The government was committed to redressing the iniquities of the socialist period, but it could not afford to ignore economic

---

6 In Hungary, the work of János Kornai was particularly influential (see Chapter Two). Stark 1990 doubted whether privatization policies would in fact lead to the desired marketization.

7 1947 was selected as a benchmark because it followed the implementation of an egalitarian post-war Land Reform package and preceded the impact of socialist pressures from the late 1940s onwards.

outcomes. At the same time, many feared the creation of new iniquities—if, for example, former owners who had long left the village, or the country, were to receive windfall gifts of good arable land, and then fail to ensure that this land was efficiently cultivated. Many months passed before a series of comprehensive Compensation Laws were hammered out by parliamentarians in 1991–92.

Implementation of these laws has been fraught with difficulties. Two separate ideological strands can be identified, which merge superficially in their common support for "private property." On the one hand, the Smallholders and other "populist" voices insisted on the restitution of 1947 property rights, whilst on the other free market economists called for an efficient new capitalist agrarian structure, and doubted whether the fragmentation that would follow from redistribution to original owners was the best way to proceed. The law enabled former private owners and their direct descendants to claim compensation for the land lost by their families. Successful claimants receive a coupon, the value of which takes into account both the quality and the quantity of this land. It is possible to use this coupon to purchase assets other than farmland, but in this case its value is significantly reduced. It is also possible to alienate coupons for cash, in which case their value is likely to be lower still. In order to avoid fragmentation of plots, existing cooperatives must designate precise areas in which land is to be available for redistribution. It follows that there can be no guarantee that the original private owner (or heir) will be able to recover the patrimony. Claimants must use their coupons to bid for land in competitive auctions, the first of which were held experimentally in August 1992. It is theoretically conceivable that, even if one's family land is available in the auction, a higher bid from another villager might prevent one's regaining possession. Policymakers had very little idea of the level of demand for land, and other details, notably the value of the social security annuities to be made available as an alternative to land ownership, were similarly imprecise.

Such was the general state of play when I revisited Hungary in the summers of 1991 and 1992. But before I turn to consider the ethnographic evidence from the village of Tázlár, one further element of contextualization is important. The general economic climate in agriculture, as in the rest of the economy, has deteriorated since the boom years of the 1970s. Hungary produces far more food than Hungarians

Figure 4. Typical flat landscape near the center of Tázlár (photo by Chris Hann, 2001)

can consume, but the disintegration of the Soviet Union and East Germany has undermined export markets, and protectionist policies by the European Community make it difficult for Hungary to send its surplus westwards. The specialist cooperative in Tázlár was not alone in being unable to market its sheep, and villagers had the greatest difficulty in finding buyers for their pigs, even at prices offering barely any remuneration for their labor. The prices received for grapes and wine had fallen sharply in real terms since the 1970s, while the costs of essential inputs had continued to rise; in this sector, too, the biggest problem was that of finding a buyer. In short, the conjuncture and general prospects for farming—on whatever scale—were bleak.[8]

The Settlement of Tázlár

Tázlár is not, on the face of it, the most promising setting in which to bring Malinowski back to Central Europe. This settlement, introduced in the previous chapter, exemplified the uneven character of

[8] According to the assessments of international experts, rural incomes are likely to be further squeezed in years to come, and this must be accepted as a natural adjustment, since the levels of the 1970s were too high by international standards (in relation to urban incomes when compared with other countries at a similar level of development) and cannot be sustained (Newbery 1991, 7).

capitalist development in Eastern Europe. Farmland was parceled out from the 1870s onwards as a rather pure form of private property. The population grew from a few hundred in 1880 to over three thousand in the generation before 1950, before falling back to the present figure of around two thousand (see Hann 1980a, 6; cf. Juhász 1990). Probably most immigrants aspired to establish autonomous family farms, i.e. to own their land as private property and to farm it using exclusively familial labor. Some bought large areas and relied on extensive methods of farming. Many later arrivals had only small acreages, on which they sought from the beginning to make a living from intensive gardening and viticulture. In all categories, the immigrants generally built their farms on their plots. Consequently, there was very little consolidation of a nuclear center. The quality of the soil varies considerably. While "Church Hill" (thought to be the site of a medieval settlement, close to the center of modern village) had fertile dark soil that obtained a high Gold Crown valuation from the state's land surveyors, the soils of many of the peripheral parcels were of low value and a grave disappointment to their new owners.

It was not long before this settlement too experienced land hunger. A document drawn up by a Budapest lawyer in 1924 on behalf of Count Vigyázó, at the time one of the largest landowners in the country, shows that poor peasants demanded more land after the First World War. The Count resisted proposals to redistribute some of his lands by having his lawyer address the following text to the National Committee supervising the implementation of the Land Reforms:

> To make the relevant problem and the correctness of my point of view understood I must direct the attention of the Honored Tribunal to the soil conditions in the area in question, to the distinctive features of the situation in the vicinity of Tázlár. This is an incredibly barren world. One only has to leave the path of the railway to enter a real desert. The rough tracks wind their way between sand dunes as high as houses, even in late autumn the cartwheel sinks down completely into the sand. There is no sign whatsoever of any vegetation on these dunes, and the bleak and desolate spaces can barely support even a few weak thorn-apple bushes and spurge. Even the lightest breeze sets these dunes in motion and when they start to move they threaten to engulf the

> entire area. After an hour's cart ride in this sandy wilderness one gets the unavoidable impression that one is exploring not Hungary but some wild African landscape.
>
> Those who know the area of Kötöny *puszta* [then part of Tázlár, now attached to a neighboring community] will assure you that these descriptions of mine are not too strong or exaggerated. . . . The very best fields of this area would, in other regions, be classified as land unsuitable for the purposes of the Land Reform measures.[9]

The lawyer proceeded to argue that it was in the public interest not to inflict any of this appalling land onto the poor claimants, but to respect the integrity of the Count's property. His estate was primarily forest, which the Hungarian state at the time was generally encouraging. The lawyer argued that trees were especially important in this area to prevent further widespread movement of the sand dunes. As for the areas of pasture and ploughland owned by the Count, these were secondary to the estate but nevertheless essential to the functioning and financing of his forests. The lawyer strenuously rejected allegations from the government's inspector that the estate had kept too many animals on too small an area, and had, in effect, pursued a policy of ruthless short-term exploitation (*rablógazdálkodás*). On the contrary, argued the lawyer, even more animals were needed to help fertilize this dreadful soil! Therefore, the text concludes, Count Vigyázó should be left to manage the heritage of his family in his own way, since there was no doubt that "his private interest coincided with the public." To allocate sections of the estate to small peasants would be to split up key sections of forest, an "absurd result." Finally, the lawyer cast doubt on whether the claimants from this very poor village actually possessed the animals to warrant the proposed increase—at the Count's expense—in the area of collective pasture.[10]

---

[9] This document was discovered in the County Archive in Kecskemét by local historian Pál Szabadi, whom I thank for allowing me to cite it.

[10] Throughout this period some land was communally administered as pasture. All residents were able to gain access to this land through payment of the appropriate fee to the Pasture Association. The outcome of the Vigázó case is unclear, but there is no record, either in the archives or in popular

The economic developments of the pre-socialist period in Tázlár might be considered as a kind of "involution" (Geertz 1963). Ever greater numbers of people sought to intensify their agricultural activities, but the supply of land was limited, there was no technological breakthrough, and very little capital accumulation. The result was that people had to work ever harder in order to maintain the same low standard of living. In contrast to Geertz's—perhaps sanitized—analysis of "shared poverty" in Indonesia, in Tázlár social differentiation became even more marked. The very top layer consisted of rich and powerful landowners like Count Vigyázó, who probably never even visited their properties.[11] Much more numerous was the category of middle and rich peasants, people who relied on the labor of other, poorer though not necessarily landless families to operate their farms. The links between households took various forms, among the most common of which was the institution known as *cselédség*. The *cseléd* was generally a young boy from a poor family who would join a more prosperous household and work for it in the fields as well as on the farmstead up to the time of his military service. In addition to a small money payment, his parents would receive occasional gifts in kind, and the relationship frequently became a long-term "patron-client" bond. The patterns of economic cooperation were no doubt less intricate than those identified by Malinowski in the Trobriands. Even so, with some women in richer families not participating in field work, and some men in poorer families commuting long distances to seek supplementary income, the overall picture was clearly much more complex than the ideal type of autonomous family farming to which most peasants aspired, and which had impelled them to migrate to Tázlár in the first place.

---

memory, of the Count's estate having been broken up at this time. The area in question was not settled and farmed by peasants. After the Count's death it apparently passed to the Hungarian Academy of Sciences, before being taken over by the Forestry Commission in the socialist period. It is still known locally as the Vigyázó forest.

[11] It is alleged in the contemporary village that large tracts of the worst quality land were regularly bought and sold in the pre-socialist period by commissioned army officers, who were required to prove that they held estates above a certain size to qualify for membership of the Budapest Casino.

Living conditions in this community during the inter-war decades were desperately poor (Szabadi 1997). It is doubtful whether further redistribution of poor quality sandy soils would have made much difference. The sociographical works of the young Ferenc Erdei show that the inhabitants of this part of the Great Plain, known as the Danube-Tisza Interfluve, were in effect excluded from Hungary's stymied semi-feudal society (Erdei 1977; see Hann 1995a). Even the more prosperous residents of a village like Tázlár were "peasants," and a great gulf separated them from the citizens of the capital just eighty miles away. I find the concept of citizenship to be a useful one here. The citizens of Tázlár certainly had economic rights: the market in land remained very active throughout the pre-socialist period. By the inter-war decades a rather undemocratic style of citizenship was entrenched in the political sphere: Hungarian nationalist tendencies were so strong that the country's large Slovak and German communities were obliged to give up not only their languages but even their surnames (usually replaced by a similar sounding Hungarian name). Meanwhile, for the residents of villages like Tázlár, the civic and social dimensions of citizenship were barely developed at all.[12]

After the Second World War cooperatives were formed, initially on a voluntary basis. Tázlár farmers experienced the same crude levelling pressures as villagers elsewhere. Many were brought to financial ruin in circumstances of grave personal harassment and humiliation. At least one peasant alleged to be a *kulák* was driven to suicide. The acreage defining a *kulák* was determined nationally, irrespective of local ecological conditions. Many of the peasants thus classified in Tázlár were very far from wealthy. Some were barely able to produce for the market at all. During these years peasants were instructed by the new authorities to grow crops that were quite unsuited to the sandy soils; several

[12] The term "citizenship" is of course related to "city": both derive from Latin *civitas* (the state). The word has a long history in Western philosophy but Malinowski found it useful for elucidating the broader understanding of property rights in the Trobriand Islands, as did Gluckman (1965) for the Barotse. The classic sociological work outlining the various dimensions of citizenship remains Marshall (1977). The concept has generated renewed interest of late: for a stimulating introduction to recent debates see Andrews (1991), and for innovative anthropological usage Minnich (1992).

major investments in orchards by the new cooperatives proved to be ignominious failures. Many families migrated permanently to the cities in the 1950s.

As described in the previous chapter, Tázlár's experience of mass collectivization was unusual. The specialist cooperative (*szakszövetkezet*) was designed to ensure that past investments in high value, labor-intensive crops would not be lost. The chief such assets in the Danube-Tisza Interfluve were vineyards and, to a lesser extent, orchards. Members of the new specialist cooperatives were allowed to retain their vineyards as their private property. They were also able to continue farming their arable land more or less as before, with minimal obligation to work on other lands which were held and used collectively. Most land remained nominally in private ownership. Unlike vineyards, however, arable plots were liable to be expropriated in accordance with long-term plans to build up the cooperative's collective sector. Whenever this happened, the member was offered alternative land elsewhere for continued private use. In other words, although private ownership rights were seriously weakened following the establishment of the specialist cooperative, the member's rights to use the land, indeed as much land as he or she wanted to use, were not violated.

I have always viewed this type of cooperative as an exemplar of pragmatic market socialism, epitomizing the willingness of Hungarian policymakers to modify standard models of central planning in the interests of economic efficiency, for the benefit of the whole of society and of rural petty commodity producers in particular. Certainly this very flexible framework allowed villagers in places such as Tázlár, through their own hard work, to achieve high levels of material prosperity in the last decades of socialism. Unfavorable comparisons with the neighboring village of Soltvadkert, where socialist entrepreneurs were even more conspicuous, led many members to view the Tázlár cooperative as a socialist imposition and a hindrance to private farmers, even by those who benefited from its services. The "symbiosis" of private and collective can be understood in Malinowskian terms as "functional integration."

Some Tázlár villagers did their utmost to avoid the new cooperatives; they carried on farming in traditional ways and, if they resented having ten percent of the sale price of their product deducted by the cooperative, they usually had no great difficulty in finding alternative private marketing channels. At the other extreme, a few farmers became totally dependent on the cooperative for large quantities of inputs, including additional leasing of land. Most villagers were somewhere in between. Very few were enamored of the Peace Specialist Cooperative, which was dogged by leadership instability and incompetent management. But the social services it provided to disadvantaged members, particularly the elderly, were appreciated. While the official term was now *kistermelő* ("small producer," see Kovách 1988) and one very anti-communist man ostentatiously described himself as *magángazdálkodó* ("private farmer") on his visiting card, the topos of a return to independent peasant farming was very common. For those who had grown up under socialism, the term was now pejorative and the antithesis of any vision of progress. In the 1970s I found that it was commonly used humorously, with mild self-deprecation, in households which were reactivating old skills to exploit the attractive opportunities for small-scale farming: "*elkezdtünk újra parasztizálni*!'" ("we've started to become peasants again!").

Land ownership did not play a significant role in this conjuncture. In Tázlár, unlike the Trobriands, there is no split between the productive and the ownership aspects of land. Legal title normally remained with the original owners. However, when land was appropriated for the consolidation of the collective sector, alternatives were offered for use, but without title. The actual pattern of land attachments thus became very complex. In the later socialist decades the ownership aspect was demoted almost to the point of irrelevance, while all effort went to increasing production. Certainly the size of acreage ceased to be a significant social indicator, for in the new situation hardly anyone was interested in expanding their arable holdings to anywhere near the former *kulák* threshold. Long established vineyards were the most important assets in enabling families to take maximum advantage of the new economic opportunities. Some were able to expand and intensify their production to levels at which they once again became dependent on hired labor to supplement (or even completely to replace) family labor. However, most labor transfers between households were based on direct and indirect reciprocity; there was less recruitment of non-family labor than had occurred in the pre-socialist period.

From the point of view of citizenship, it is important to emphasize the general social and political trends of the socialist period. The civic rights of individuals were accorded no more respect in the 1950s than were private property rights in land. There was generally less opportunity for free expression in the machinery of local government than in the agricultural cooperatives. The long-serving council chairman in Tázlár was an unpopular Communist Party member of the socialist party who had no local family connections. He was removed from office following corruption charges in the early 1980s, but the council, though it commanded more trust from villagers thereafter, never became an open and democratic organ. No agencies operated effectively in the public sphere, least of all the Communist Party, which was the only sanctioned political association.

The picture is more positive, however, if one considers the social improvements of the socialist period. Public investments in roads, parks, cultural and educational facilities in the village were significant. Bringing these villagers effectively within the scope of a national health care system (through the crucial establishment of a doctor's surgery in the village) and within the scope of an education system that offered all children a thorough eight years of primary schooling, followed in the great majority of cases by secondary education, were major achievements. The guarantee of local employment which almost all men enjoyed throughout the socialist period was not quite equally available to women; but the Peace cooperative built up a number of sideline activities that created job opportunities in the village for those rural women unable to take jobs elsewhere. Almost everyone who wanted a job outside the family farm was able to find one without too much trouble. These were the major benefits of socialist citizenship. They were experienced much more positively in the later decades of socialist government than they were at the beginning, when complemented by the expanded opportunities for private accumulation of wealth noted above.

According to the Marshallian tradition, in Western democracies the accumulation of civic and welfare rights compensates citizens for the inequalities of capitalist class structures. In contrast, in this socialist case a radical attack on the old class structure was accompanied by a decline in civic and political rights (though in the Hungarian case these were only feebly developed in the pre-socialist period). This period was then followed by an expansion of entitlements in the social and economic dimensions of citizenship. Some analysts suspected that such a path would necessarily lead to a new structure of class inequal-

Figure 5. A street in the village center developed under socialism (photo by Chris Hann, 2013)

ity, perhaps resembling that of the past. The experiment was terminated before definitive answers could be given. One conclusion is certain: the legal ownership of land lost the social prestige that it had entailed in the pre-socialist era.

The Collapse of the Socialist Synthesis in the Early 1990s

In spite of the instructions they sometimes received (particularly in 1975, shortly before my first fieldwork) to expand the area of collective production and make progress towards "higher forms" of landholding, officials of the Peace cooperative in the socialist era were generally concerned with playing down questions pertaining to property rights. Instead they concentrated on the maximization of production. This policy was summed up by the Tázlár cooperative chairman in 1990 as "production-centered" (*termelés-centrikus*). What mattered was land use, not land ownership. When villagers talked about "their" land, it was not always clear which of these two they had in mind. For example, an individual might be in receipt of a nominal rent from the cooperative for land which he had registered as his when he originally joined, and which was later converted into a large field for collective use. This individual might simultaneously pay rent (usually at a similarly low level) to the cooperative for the use of other fields that might have come into cooperative ownership by various routes, e.g. when a family had emigrated without leaving any local heirs, or when land was transferred from a neighboring state-owned farm.

A year later in 1991, the same chairman recognized, with some reluctance, that the world had moved on. By now he was busy working out a new "property-centered" (*tulajdon-centrikus*) approach. A comprehensive "naming" (*nevesítés*) process covering all assets apart from land was accomplished in 1990. Shares (*vagyonjegyek*, literally "wealth tickets") were distributed to all those deemed to have contributed to the assets of the cooperative, whether through land taken into collective use, produce sold through the cooperative in the preceding twelve years, or labor carried out for wages or salaries. The formula used to determine these allocations was approved at a general meeting of the members. Because of its complexity, few villagers understood its implications. Some were retrospectively highly critical of the large share allocations made to senior leaders, which followed automatically from their high salaries. Most were puzzled by the whole exercise, which left them with pieces of paper that they could not readily convert into any other form of asset. It was theoretically possible to dispose of shares to other members, or to the cooperative itself, but few availed themselves of this possibility. Those who did so made use of their allocation to acquire some machine assets when these were sold off by the cooperative in 1992. The vast majority held on to their shares, which were expected to pay an annual dividend depending on the farm's performance.

Land was excluded from this initial privatization, but the chairman agreed to an experimental concession with a number of individuals who had come forward to claim land that had formerly belonged to them, on the edge of the village. He was anxious that, whenever possible, claimants should be able to regain full ownership rights over the plots associated with their families. However, he also talked about the difficulties this might entail. For example, if a claimant did not utilize the parcel allocated to him, it would then have to revert to the collective sector. In addition to the obvious problems of scale, it might become impossible to deploy machines at all if other successful land claimants in the vicinity were to interfere with rights of access. The chairman was therefore pleased when the Compensation Laws passed by parliament in Budapest allowed him the discretion he needed to ensure there would be some rationality in the land privatization program. At the same time, he recognized that many farmers would not be content with the eventual outcomes, notably those whose lands had been incorporated into large fields that would not be scheduled for redistribution. The chairman was also concerned that the public auctions could create much bad blood between villagers. Other village officials too, including the new mayoress (see Chapter Six), expressed their concern about possible conflicts of interest. They feared that the socialist institution would give preferential treatment to comparatively small numbers of persons in full-time employment at the cooperative headquarters or associated with its various committees.

This specialist cooperative was already in the middle of a major restructuring before the land question was addressed. The chairman insisted that the institution would maintain its cooperative character, and that everyone would still have an equal vote at the general meetings, regardless of the value of his or her shares. These changes and debates were symptomatic of the privatization campaigns proceeding elsewhere in Hungary at this time (OECD 1991; Stark 1990). The most interesting question for villagers in the early postsocialist years, one which they themselves constantly raised in conversation, was the desire—or lack of desire—for land itself. The question of how seriously villagers would pursue the restitution of 1947 land rights obviously had critical practical implications for the future, and not just in the agricultural sector. In Tázlár I found that a strong desire to re-establish private ownership rights was almost entirely restricted to elderly members of families who had been of at least well-to-do standing in the past, or who had a background as artisans or shopkeepers.[13] But few in this

[13] The trips I made in 1990–92 were brief, and the villagers with whom I discussed these matters were not a satisfactory sample. I am aware of the danger of bias toward a few "key informants" and their families, mostly "intellectuals" and former middle or rich peasants. This may not be such a problem if one bears in mind that few other villagers are in any position even to contemplate a future as private farmers. During these years many persons were still very unclear about the details of the Compensation Laws. They often did not know until I told them that a former owner reclaiming his or her land was be obliged to ensure that it would be cultivated for a period of five years––a serious qualification of "absolute" private property rights.

category were capable of farming land themselves, and they had largely failed to excite any interest in farming among the younger members of their families, many of whom have been well educated and are now established in urban careers. Meanwhile younger villagers, including some who had proven entrepreneurial abilities but no significant experience in family farming, showed little desire to become family-farmers, even when potentially in a position to claim back family land. By no means all successful younger entrepreneurs were descendants of middle or rich peasant families with entitlements to claim substantial compensation. In general, irrespective of background and the value of their compensation coupons, these entrepreneurs showed no willingness to invest in farming. This lack of interest was clearly influenced by their assessment of economic returns; but another very significant factor, emphasized particularly by women, was distaste for the lifestyle associated with farming (having to get up very early in the mornings, put up with smelly yards, etc.).

The safeguards introduced to ensure that large-scale socialist farms were not split up in too haphazard a manner necessarily made it harder for policymakers to meet their other prime objective, that of offering satisfying compensation to families who were victims of socialist land confiscations. Those victims who were still alive and wanted to reclaim land were anxious to regain the plots to which they remained emotionally linked, but they faced many problems in doing so. For example, my landlady (b. 1905, daughter of Ferenc Nacsa, mentioned in Chapter Two) belonged to a family classified as *kulák* and deprived of most of its landholdings in the 1950s. She wanted very much to regain full private ownership rights over one small parcel of land, used by her family for the best part of a century until the 1970s. However, her descendants, including her grandson Jani, who lives close by and who has become a highly successful entrepreneur (see Chapter Two), showed no interest. In adjudicating between the competing claims of original owners and current users, the compensation laws awarded priority to farmers who have used a given plot of land for more than five years. Most villagers in Tázlár agreed that, morally, the claims of former owners should be stronger. But in the context of a specialist cooperative, very difficult cases arose. For example, where a cooperative member had had his original land appropriated for consolidation into a large field, and he had invested in new vines on the land allocated to him instead of his original plots: should the original owner be entitled to the full fruits of those investments? Villagers themselves were divided in their views on such cases; many felt that, since the national legislation did not offer adequate guidelines, it should be the task of the local cooperative to facilitate equitable outcomes through mediation.

The case of another elderly villager (b. 1908) who hailed from a family of small shopkeepers raised further sensitive issues. This family had acquired land of very poor quality, in a remote part of Tázlár, in the inter-war years. When they too were classified as *kulák* in the early 1950s, this estate was neglected, and the land had little or no value by the early 1990s. In the 1970s, this villager was able to take advantage of the favorable conditions for small-scale farming by renting a number of plots from the cooperative. They were of good quality, and much more conveniently located than his original land. Nevertheless, when I talked to him in 1990 and 1991, this man insisted that he was interested only in regaining his patrimony, the land which his father had purchased and tilled more than half a century before. Though his wife was strongly supportive, other members of his family had no interest in this land. His sons had migrated to industrial jobs and had no intention of returning to the village. Nevertheless, this elderly man expressed a determination to regain his land, even if it meant a financial loss for the family (which might end up having to pay land taxes on property that was entirely useless to them). In 1990–91, there was no doubting the strength of his emotional commitment to the land. However, when we talked again in 1992, at which point he still had not received his compensation coupons, his position was shifting. His health was failing rapidly, he was now unable to work in the fields himself, and he was coming under pressure from one of his sons to explore the possibility of seeking ownership rights over some of the more valuable land he had been using in the recent past, even if this was sure to lead to a quarrel with the original owner.

For most villagers, including those recently made unemployed by the cooperative and local factories, the option of farming as a full-time occupation was not realistic. They lacked not only family farming experience, but also basic capital resources. Offering them land, whether or not it was represented as compensation for past wrongs, was a futile exercise in the absence of a massive new extension program to assist farmers. Far from experiencing the benefits of new private property rights, many of the villagers I spoke with in the early 1990s felt threatened by the loss of the rights they had come to take for granted in the socialist period, in particular the rights to employment and to free health care.

It is important to note the continuities with the peasant economy of the past. In Tázlár, despite the vicissitudes of land tenure, successful small-scale farming always depended upon close cooperation between household members. All aspects of the peasant economy, both before socialism and after the emergence of the cooperatives, were matters of familial and household concern. For the earlier period, scrutiny of the land archives reveals extensive buying and selling of land held as private property, but this can hardly be taken as conclusive evidence of "individualistic" attitudes or behavior. It would be a mistake to see the legal owner as the sole decision-taker, just as it would be wrong to approach the family as a conflict-free unity of collective interests. Outcomes are determined by interaction between persons, usually close kin, who have varying goals and resources at their disposal. The prevailing legal code is but one variable which may or may not have a decisive impact: in the case of current land claims in Hungary, conflicts deriving from generation and gender, together with the prevailing economic circumstances, seem to be of greater importance.

As the break-up of the Peace cooperative continued steadily in the course of the 1990s, villagers found themselves with a confusing array of paper "currencies." In addition to the *vagyonjegyek* of the cooperative, vouchers (*kárpótlási jegyek*) issued after the adjudication of Compensation Law claims could be realized for a variety of ends or sold for cash. These could be advertised and traded in the towns, but there was no sign of a market in Tázlár. Some villagers would not, for reasons of principle, consider using their vouchers for anything other than the acquisition of land. In 1992 it was necessary in Tázlár to undertake a third major distribution of cooperative assets, this time covering all of the cooperative's land that was not already owned by individuals or scheduled for individual ownership through auctions as provided for in the compensation legislation. By now the cooperative had decided to abandon collective sector production. The unit for the distribution of these lands was the Gold Crown (*aranykorona*), the same quality measure that underpinned land distribution under the compensation legislation. The area involved was considerable, and the formula adopted was the same as that for other cooperative assets two years earlier. Like the property shares distributed earlier, those land shares cannot be alienated outside the community.

The situation in these years was extremely fluid. If Hungary as a whole, because of the decision not to implement full and direct compensation, presents a more complex picture than other countries of the region, the specialist cooperative, with its peculiar blend of family and collective farming, represents the extreme of messiness within Hungary. In spite of the best efforts of both cooperative officials and the new democratic village council to disseminate accurate information, there was considerable confusion among villagers. Many families acquired new types of paper asset annually and had the impression that the goalposts were being constantly moved. The villager described above who was in conflict with his sons over whether he should use his compensation vouchers to claim back his patrimony (remote and economically marginal) or some other land that he had been using more recently with a lease from the cooperative (nearby and economically attractive), discovered in 1992 that he would not be able to use his vouchers for either, as neither plot fell in the area scheduled for the auctions. However, he was able to regain his original plots from the cooperative immediately. He was angry again in 1993 because, although he lived in the center of the village, he did not find out about the first auction until it had already taken place: there was a small parcel of land in the area sold off for which he would have liked to bid, because it had been associated in the past with his wife's family.

Many difficult cases arose because, as with the classification of *kulák* in the 1950s, legislation passed at the national level was inappropriate at the level of ecologically and socially diverse communities. The compensation legislation required more documentation than most villagers could readily provide, and they were not used to hiring lawyers to conduct the necessary searches. In theory it was possible to make claims for compensation without submitting all the specified documents if witnesses could be found to testify to the precise assets confiscated. However, Tázlár is located over thirty miles away from the county town of Kecskemét where the Compensation Office is located, and it was often impractical for villagers to pursue matters. They were referred instead to the local Land Distribution Committee, which is composed for the most part of persons of middle peasant background, and generally takes the line that wherever possible the claims of the original owners should have priority.[14] However this cannot be reasonably upheld in all cases. Some of the most awkward cases have been those where farmers have not been able to produce all the documentation to submit a claim under the compensation legislation, but the Gold Crown allocation to them in 1992 by the cooperative was not sufficient to enable them to obtain title to land they have actually been using for decades (if they have planted vines a very high Gold Crown valuation would apply, whereas their allocation from the cooperative would reflect the lower valuation of their original arable plots when these were absorbed into the cooperative's collective sector).

Questions of ideology, and even "mythological foundations" in the sense of Malinowski, entered strongly into the debates. In spite of the evidence for integration and symbiosis in the practice of the later socialist period, the individual/collective dichotomy had never been dislodged from common ways of thinking. In the recent transformations, powerful forces have sought to bring the world of practice back into line with the polarities of this ideology. Thus, the Independent Smallholders' Party in some ways mimics the mythologies of the high Stalinist period. It has based its political strategy on sanctifying the property relations of the immediate pre-socialist period (property relations being understood solely with reference to legal title). This was the most popular political party in Tázlár in the free national elections of 1990, and it is well represented on the Land Distribution Committee. In this party's representations of socialism the abuses of the early 1950s are held to exemplify the entire period. Its members dismiss the socialist period as one of neglect or short-term overexploitation of the environment (*rablógazdálkodás*), and deny that the specialist cooperative was an institution that, for all its imperfections, brought many benefits to its members. Smallholders organized a petition to the cooperative in 1990 for the restitution of the Church Hill lands (the

[14] As a consequence of this principle, cooperative members in effect have two distinct kinds of Gold Crowns following the 1992 distribution: Gold Crowns issued in relation to one's original land always trump Gold Crowns issued in relation to the other elements of the formula (produce sold or wages/salaries earned).

high-quality lands drawn into the collective sector in the mid-1970s). When the chairman initially prevaricated, they took direct action to parcel out these fields according to the original private boundaries. The cooperative later acquiesced in this intervention "from below," shortly before confirming its complete withdrawal from collective agricultural activities.

Who are the winners and losers of the transition in Tázlár? There was a widespread suspicion that the management of the asset distribution process enabled cooperative officials to come out on top—even though the leading "green barons" lived outside Tázlár and had no interest in acquiring land within the community.[15] Local smallholders formed a second, much more diverse group. The children and grandchildren of the former *kulák* have for the most part moved away: they have invested in urban housing and in education, and are unlikely to return to the mixed farming practiced by their forebears. For younger people who remain, land has become an impersonal commodity. This commodification is exemplified by the large-scale vineyards, which have physically obliterated the distinguishing features of the landscape. The scale of the technology is revolutionary and alienating; when people talk now about buying and selling parcels of these fields they do so without sentiment, without reference to the precise location of their rows within the plantation. A third group consists of cooperative members and employees of poor peasant background who, as a result of the privatization process, may receive an opportunity to acquire better quality land than that previously owned by their families. Some of these villagers have retained practical farming skills that have been lost in families that have invested more in education. They may be better placed in terms of their human capital to make a success of family farming, even in unfavorable postsocialist conditions. It is likely that they will have to lease land from owners who belong to the other groups. Thus the "productive aspect" will again diverge from legal ownership, and the Malinowskian invitation to probe beyond the latter will remain compelling.

[15] The phrase "green baron" was a popular designation for collective farm leaders in the years of transition. See Swain 1992. [See also Swain 2013.]

Figure 6. A street built in the 1990s.
The simple multi-purpose vehicle known as a csettegő *is often said to exemplify the ingenuity of the rural population in the socialist era (photo by Chris Hann, 2015)*

These groups and scenarios are ideal types and the realities will be more complex. Owing to the breakdown of the old class distinctions, in which land ownership played such an important part, there are no clearly bounded groups in contemporary, postsocialist Tázlár. Some men of poor peasant origin have married into families with a good land base and can now look forward to profiting from their *kárpótlási jegyek* and their *vagyonjegyek*. When conflicts arise, legitimating claims are seldom based on legal title alone. The more powerful claims tend to be those based on work, though on very different types of work, and the age factor is at least as important as social class. For most elderly villagers, it is the sweat of their forefathers that justifies their single-minded attempts to regain ownership rights over the plots associated with their family names (including matrilineal legacies). They are scornful of arguments that such principles may not be economically rational in a radically new situation. In fact, though upholding the principle of private property, they are contemptuous of those who prosper through "turning money" (*pénzt forgatni*) rather than through honest labor. Meanwhile younger members of the cooperative are more likely to emphasize the manual work they have put in over many years in justifying their claim to a generous share of the resources now being distributed. Least persuasive in the eyes of most villagers are the claims of the leaders of the cooperative that depend upon recognition of the productive value of their own white-collar contributions.[16]

The first and third groups identified above are the products of the socialist period. Together they can out-maneuver the second group, the local smallholders, including former *kulák* and their descendants. The cooperative chairman has followed just such a course throughout the transition. He has astutely presented himself as a leader genuinely concerned with the collective interests of all the residents of the village, while deflecting anti-socialist sentiment toward his deputy, the chief agronomist, who is perceived to be concerned only with his personal aggrandizement. At general meetings of the membership the leadership is augmented by lawyers who generally say that, given the constraints of the law, only the chairman's proposals are feasible (Hann 1993c). Voting is decisively influenced by the blocks formed by the cooperative's own work force, who can be relied upon to support the chairman who has given them their jobs. The very survival of this cooperative, when so many others have disintegrated, may be taken as evidence that many people value the security and entitlements that it continues to provide.[17] The more doctrinaire smallholders dismiss the communitarian rhetoric used by the cooperative leadership as subterfuge,

16 Longstanding peasant evaluations of work have a certain congruence with the Marxist ideology of the socialist period [see Lampland 1995]. These values were invoked to criticize the cooperative in the early 1990s when it began to scale down its agricultural activities and behave as a more rational market-oriented organization. The decision in 1992 to abandon arable production provoked negative comments locally, which were reflected in an article in the county newspaper. How could a distinctively agricultural community abandon its heritage in this way? The previous cooperative had, after all, managed to continue the territory's bread-producing function throughout the socialist period. Fields that had been well-managed for generations were reverting to the kind of landscapes graphically described in the 1920s by the lawyer quoted earlier in this chapter, and this was deplorable.

17 Previously known as the Peace Agricultural Cooperative, unlike many other socialist organizations it did not need to change the first term. However, when a new Constitution was approved in 1992, it was agreed to drop the word agricultural, in line with its transformed economic profile. Most of the cooperative's income is now obtained through two "industrial" sidelines, making plastic bags and the upper parts of shoes. [The cooperative was finally liquidated in the new century—see Hann 2006.]

designed to disguise the private ambitions of a few non-local individuals. It is commonly anticipated that these leaders will use their paper assets to obtain some of the most valuable forest land. They will then immediately realize their profits, exemplifying the pattern of postsocialist *rablógazdálkodás*. Critics also point out that the resources distributed by the cooperative to its members in recent years are in a very real sense not the products of local labor at all, but of the vast resources that the state poured in to agriculture, notably in regions classified as having an unfavorable endowment. They are angry at the prospect that the fruits of such public subsidies should now flow into private pockets.

Throughout these years the land itself has remained the focus of strong moral sentiments that appear to transcend group divisions, and even, up to a point, generational differences. Some villagers were prepared to concede cooperative officials their share of collective property (the assets distributed in 1990), but they did not consider it acceptable to divide the land itself according to a formula that included non-locals. Even where land was not a valuable asset in the present market conditions, in a community of relatively recent settlement where it had always been a commodity, there was strong support for the view (endorsed by several of the political parties) that land should not in any circumstances be made available for purchase to foreigners.[18] While committed to these values, villagers recognized that the new forms of "market economy" would continue to depend upon what sociologist Endre Sik (1994) terms "cultural" and "network" capital, as had been the case throughout the socialist period. In a relatively remote village like Tázlár, having the right connections in the towns to facilitate the sale of one's product was more important than ever, now that the supports from the cooperative have been drastically cut back.

[18] It is not thought likely that the soils of Tázlár will prove attractive to any outside investors, but people resent what they can hear through the media about developments elsewhere. I heard strong criticism of decisions to pay compensation to Jews now domiciled in Israel, even though it was acknowledged that the likelihood of such people wishing to become landowners again in Hungary was minimal. Perhaps this antagonism toward new "others" is to be expected now that the socialist state is no longer available as a scapegoat for all perceived injustice.

It follows that the new pattern of legal ownership is only one dimension of the emerging land tenure system. When analyzed in Malinowski's broader sense, it is clear that the future policies of the state will be decisive. State action will determine whether the new owners of land have supporting facilities available to them to assist them in their production and marketing. So far the evidence is extremely discouraging: the ecologically determined subsidies have been eliminated and support for the agricultural sector as a whole has effectively been abandoned in the name of "market economy." Together with private property and the image of family-farming, these are the mythological slogans that underpin the current reworking of the land tenure system in Tázlár. State action will also determine whether the many aspects of citizenship that developed in a positive direction under late socialism continue to develop, or wither and atrophy. In some areas there has already been a significant loss of entitlements. Young people cannot find work, and many have lost their rights to free health care. These are signs that the postsocialist state is again widening the gulf between peripheral villagers and the mainstream of the national society, a gulf which was effectively bridged for the first time in the last decades of socialism.

Conclusion: Synthesizing Malinowski and Marx

It is generally agreed among the legions of external advisers who have flocked to Eastern Europe in the last few years that the course of economic adjustment towards "'full-fledged market economies" depends vitally on "the social and political cohesion to see the process through" (OECD 1991, 4). At village level, this cohesion is difficult to sustain as those with claims based upon former *ownership* come into conflict with those who base rival claims on long years of *use*. The government's compromise on land privatization risks alienating its populist constituency. At the same time, it also runs the risk of serious economic dislocation if significant areas of land are transferred to persons whose heirs have neither the emotional commitment nor the economic incentives to consider family farming as a career. The authorities have tried to balance the contradictory pulls of two distinct ideologies of property rights: that of peasant economy, in which the land is held by the family as a corporation and is a source of enduring emotional identification, and that of free-market economists, for whom land is just another commodity to be placed in the hands of profit-maximizing entrepreneurs. The trade-off may lead to a less efficient rural economy than that which emerged in the later decades of socialism, when ownership rights over land were in practice systematically played down. Empirical observations show a significant gap between the assumptions of politicians and macroeconomists, and the realities of the Hungarian countryside. The emergence of a new stratum of entrepreneurial family farmers in present rural conditions looks extremely unlikely. If this is the case in a village which, thanks to the institution of the specialist cooperative, has allowed the persistence of a greater degree of economic independence and stronger continuities with the traditional farming economy than can be found in most other villages, then the overall prospects for economically successful decollectivization seem bleak.

In addition to exploring the micro-social foundations, anthropologists need to scrutinize the basic concepts of policymakers. Dilley (1992) has initiated such a critique in the case of "market." I have argued that "property" needs similar reappraisal. Economists and lawyers familiar only with Western assumptions of exclusive ownership can learn from anthropological studies of pre-capitalist societies. When property relations are approached in terms of social relations, rather than as claims over particular property objects, it is unhelpful to restrict an account of collectivization and decollectivization to the question of rights over land. The peasants who, under socialism, lost rights over their privately-owned land, gained both rights and obligations in other contexts, such as wage-labor employment, the schooling of their children, and medical provision. For many persons and families in Hungary today the current rhetoric about widening choice and extending property rights is a sick joke: even if they have some compensation vouchers, they cannot become entrepreneurial farmers because they lack the basic capital resources, and their social rights are being whittled away all the time.

I have emphasized the persistence of elements of peasant economy in the socialist period. The transition to decollectivization shows that, at least for many elderly people, attachments to particular plots remain extremely strong. A few strong-willed individuals may decide to pursue compensation claims accordingly, even if this is to the financial disadvantage of their families, asserting that they do this to re-establish identities and conserve family bonds. But most families will deliberate very carefully before claims are pursued by individual members, and the older generation will have to take account of the views of others. Those who grew up in socialist conditions show little evidence of sentimental attachments to family land, and a greater concern with a specific economic rationality. Those who are in a position to make choices, i.e. those who have accumulated sufficient capital in the socialist period, will ask "what are the prospects for farming in relation to other possible avenues for entrepreneurial investment?" In Tázlár, everyone is agreed that the answer is "extremely gloomy."

In these circumstances, a hypothetical historical anthropologist who, many years from now, investigates the archives of Hungary's post-socialist Compensation Office, may find it difficult to make inferences about "individualistic" or "familistic" actions. Most claims—though formally pursued by individuals—will follow protracted discussions within families. Even if the legal system provides scope for "individualism," the anthropologist needs to consider power relationships within families, age and gender ideologies, and the importance of occupation and class allegiances. When interpreting the patterns of compensation claims, this hypothetical future researcher will need to be sensitive both to the economic circumstances of particular families, and to the overall economic conjuncture. The lack of enthusiasm on the part of the younger generation is shaped by prevailing economic conditions and local assessments of the prospects for agriculture in this ecologically poor environment. Many more might have wished to become landowners, and agreed with their parents and grandparents to claim back specific family plots, if they thought that family farming might again become as economically attractive as it had been in the 1970s. A sharp dichotomy between "individualist" and "familistic" is unlikely to be more helpful than similar sharp dichotomies characteristic of the earlier anthropological literature on property relations.[19]

---

[19] Alan Macfarlane, in his work on England (1978), interprets the sale of land as evidence of "individualism" and a weak family-land tie. However, a fieldworker in sixteenth century England might have been able to show that families always discussed their options carefully, but were on occasion reluctantly compelled into such actions by specific economic circumstances.

It is probably premature to attempt to revive neo-Marxist approaches in anthropology, and it might seem particularly inappropriate to apply them to a region which has just repudiated socialism rather convincingly. Some orthodox Marxists might interpret capitalist restoration in Eastern Europe as the necessary resumption of an evolutionary development interrupted by a socialist revolution that was premature, in that it occurred before an adequate material infrastructure had developed. Such Marxists share common ground with bourgeois economists who criticize the premature welfare states of market socialism (see Chapter Two) and insist that only a market economy based upon "strong" private property rights can promote successful industrial development. However, it is very doubtful whether new property relations will be conducive to improving the economic performance of Hungarian agriculture. Collectivization, the forcible destruction of the old property rights system in the countryside, was followed not by rigid adherence to socialist property rights conceptions but by pragmatism and the general downgrading of rights over land as all citizens were forced to embrace an entirely new constellation of property rights. This led eventually not only to a rather successful expansion of production but also to considerable socio-economic progress, which recent attempts to restore the predominance of private property rights may jeopardize. In other Eastern European countries efforts to implement socialist property law were more dogmatically pursued; one might say that this law formed part of socialist "superstructure." Socialism in Hungary sought other kinds of ideological justification in its final decades: in the realms of production and consumption, rather than prop-

---

Sreenivasan (1991) has looked again at the records for Earls Colne, as published by Macfarlane, to suggest that some farmers later tried to regain plots they had lost in this way. This would seem to indicate a rather strong family-land tie, the opposite of Macfarlane's conclusion. (I am grateful to John Hatcher for drawing my attention to this rich article.)

The dichotomy may equally be challenged from the perspective of the modern capitalist family farmer, who may not behave so very differently from his peasant forerunners. I have heard owner-occupier farmers at the heart of British agribusiness in East Anglia express the view that they are merely "stewards" of land which has been in the family for generations. They identify with that land, and they do not feel free to alienate it, even though they have the legal right to do so.

erty in this narrower sense. Now, however, in Hungary too, property rights have to be specified more rigorously, and they are accordingly prominent in the new capitalist "superstructure."

Of course, many anthropologists are uncomfortable with such neo-Marxist terminology.[20] Perry Anderson develops the more subtle argument that property systems lie at "the nodal intersection between law and economy" (1979, 404). He goes on to argue that "juridical property can never be separated either from economic production or politico-ideological power: its absolutely central position within any mode of production derives from its linkage of the two, which in pre-capitalist social formations becomes an outright and official fusion" (1979, 405). This seems entirely compatible with Bloch (1975). In abstract terms, one might say that Hungarian market socialism developed a "fusion" comparable to that of Bloch's Zafimaniry, since ideas concerning property ceased to play any significant mystifying role in "superstructure." However, the analogy cannot be pushed too far. The last decades of Hungarian socialism saw a suppression of the official socialist property ideology and the tacit tolerance of creative and flexible alternatives, rather than any integration or fusion. Although this pragmatism was conducive to high levels of production among small-scale farmers, there remains general agreement among economists and political scientists that an efficient modern industrial economy is incompatible with a regime of weak or fuzzy property rights. In other words, the consensus is that meticulous juridical consolidation of property law is essential, and the question is whether this must necessarily occur in the realm of superstructure, in ways which will mystify social relations. The answer is surely no, for there is no reason in principle why more rigorous juridical concepts cannot be developed in a new framework of *social ownership*.[21] This would allow property relations to remain "embedded" (to use Richard Thurnwald's term, later popular-

[20] Among them Macfarlane. Specifically concerning the domain of law, he writes of "the borderland between superstructure and infrastructure, that artificial distinction out of which Weber breaks." (1987, 226).

[21] See Comisso 1991 and, for criticism, Hann 1993b. The reasons why so little was done in Eastern Europe to pursue the sort of "market socialist" model recommended by Comisso are too complex to pursue in this chapter.

ized by the substantivist school) and render base/superstructure dichotomies redundant.

Meanwhile property rights throughout Eastern Europe are presently being consolidated on the basis of a narrow vision of the private, rather than any form of social ownership. In these circumstances, neo-Marxist diagnoses of mystification may still be appropriate. It is not a question of postulating simple causal relationships between base and superstructure, or between material realities and cultural ideas. Ideas concerning private property rights proved to be extremely resilient in all socialist societies and must be taken seriously in anthropological investigations of both socialist and postsocialist economies. I have pointed to the confluence and confusion in the contemporary countryside of two quite distinct threads, that associated with "peasant economy" and that associated with modern economics. The latter is in the ascendant, but in going some way towards appeasing those still emotionally committed to the former, the present authorities in Hungary may be impeding the emergence of a new capitalist agrarian structure, for which the prospects are in any case gloomy due to the general economic conjuncture. A neo-Marxist hypothesis might interpret government policies as an astute political move, designed to ensure that the new capitalist order as a whole obtains some enhanced legitimacy through an association (in reality largely spurious) with older, populist conceptions of property rights. To what extent this connection is actually made by many Hungarian citizens must remain a subject for further empirical investigation. But when property rights are understood in the broader sense suggested in this article, we see that villagers are by and large under few illusions about the entitlements they have lost in the last few years. The new/old ideology is *not* doing its job; villagers are discontented and fearful for the future.

Malinowski concluded the first volume of *Coral Gardens and Their Magic* with the statement that he saw no need "to apologise for having enlarged upon citizenship side by side with land tenure" (1966, 376). In this chapter I have pursued a broad approach to property, especially land tenure, in twentieth century Tázlár. In understanding the transformations that have occurred it is important not to fall back into the rhetorical dichotomies that were first critically exposed by Malinowski himself (even if he himself was never fully able to transcend them). We still need, as Malinowski urged, to go beyond the legal point of view. Adapting his broad approach to the contemporary East European context it is clear that, following decades of rapid improvement, the majority of villagers have suffered a significant diminution in their entitlements with the demise of socialism. Rural people as a whole are the losers. Some individuals will, one assumes, in the fullness of time, emerge as relative and perhaps even absolute winners of the current transition, but it is too early at present to identify them sociologically. From the evidence of Tázlár so far they will not be simply the carriers of the "cultural capital" of a pre-socialist *kulák* class, nor the beneficiaries of the "political capital" of a socialist dominant class. Each of these elements may be important, and indeed they are not mutually exclusive. But before we welcome the arrival of a new class of postsocialist "family farmers" in place of the "small producers" characteristic of the socialist period, we can expect to see in Hungary the revival of something like the old class of "poor peasants": a rural underclass of second-class citizens. This is likely to threaten the relative cohesion and functional integration established during the later years of socialism.

CHAPTER FOUR

A New Double Movement? Anthropological Perspectives on Property in the Age of Neoliberalism

(2007)

Introduction[1]

Traditional liberal approaches to property have generally called for a high degree of private ownership, first as a guarantee of political liberty and later as the sine qua non of economic efficiency (Ryan 1984). Such models have been regularly reshaped and reasserted ideologically, recently under the banner of neoliberalism ("Washington Consensus," etc.). The collapse of the Soviet bloc is commonly interpreted as proof that there can be no alternative to private property as the most basic organizing principle of human economy, or at least of those economies which have reached a high degree of complexity and technological sophistication. The more or less simultaneous launch of a wave of privatizations in numerous Western capitalist countries, together with the emergence of numerous new property objects, above all in the field of intellectual property, leads the editors of the latest anthropological contribution to these debates to open their Introduction with the simple observation "Property is in"; they go on to develop a powerful critique of "the fetishization of private property rights" (von Benda-Beckmann, von Benda-Beckmann, and Wiber 2006a, 1 and 10). Similarly, the historian Hannes Siegrist has traced the emergence of intellectual property since the seventeenth century. Although "propertization" is nothing new, he argues that its most recent instances constitute a radicalization. Notions of property, by which he refers primarily to the *Leitidee*

---

[1] *This chapter originated as a review article commissioned by the editors of the journal* Socio-Economic Review, *where it was published in 2007.*

of exclusive private ownership, are penetrating more and more spheres of human social existence (2003, 2006). At the same time, Siegrist acknowledges tendencies in the opposite direction. For example, Jeremy Rifkin (2001) has emphasized the increasing importance of "access" rather than ownership, and Christoph Engel (2002) speaks of the "thinning out" (*Verdünnung*) of property rights due to the increasing constraints imposed upon owners by the state and other regulatory bodies.

This chapter will concentrate on what socio-cultural anthropologists have to contribute to these fundamental debates, taking most of its examples from recent investigations at the Max Planck Institute for Social Anthropology into postsocialist property relations, and then looking more cursorily at a wider body of literature. I adapt my framework from the classic study of another historian, Karl Polanyi's *The Great Transformation* (1944). Polanyi's opus magnum was an indictment of classical liberalism, responsible for so much human misery as industrialization proceeded in the nineteenth century, and for Fascism and two World Wars in the twentieth. The chief culprit was "the market," or more precisely, as Polanyi spelled out in later seminal contributions (1957), the idea that the self-regulating market could serve as the dominant "form of integration," free from the constraints of society. In the course of this process land, labor and money were transformed into "fictitious commodities." Polanyi's nightmare vision of the totally "disembedded economy" was of course an ideal type, one which sparked decades of polemics in economic anthropology. Even a cursory reading of *The Great Transformation* shows that its author was well aware of the role of the state in creating the prior conditions for the spread of liberal dominance. Polanyi also created the concept of the "double movement" to capture the way in which "Society" responded to this unprecedented threat. Thus labor, one of the three new fictitious commodities, achieved increasing protection through the rise of trades unions to defend the interests of the workers—society refused to allow human work to be denigrated as just another impersonal market commodity. It is evident from Polanyi's analysis (which owes much to Marx, though Polanyi is a less rigorous economist) that the rise of liberal markets and the rise of private property are closely related. I shall suggest that the current phase of neoliberalism can be viewed through Polanyi's spectacles. Markets and private property have expanded, and some interesting new fictional commodities have appeared on the scene, notably knowledge and culture. Anthropologists have been among the sharpest critics of these new instances of commoditization. But we need also to be aware of the ambiguities and counter-tendencies, which Hannes Siegrist terms "depropertization." I suggest that this complex can be approached in terms of a new double movement.

Even when addressing matters of contemporary political, economic and social significance through fresh case studies, anthropologists can draw on a long tradition of theorizing about property relations across the full range of human societies, both in time and in space (Hann 1998a). This intellectual tradition has reflected changes both in the world economy and in the conditions of anthropological research practice. The recent surge of studies reflects changes in ways of dealing with property and its many new forms but also new styles and theories in anthropology. Before turning to the work of the last two decades it is useful to begin with a brief presentation of anthropological approaches and their history.

The most basic element in the anthropologist's approach to property (and to other key concepts) is to question whether the understanding that has emerged in Western intellectual traditions can provide an adequate base for understanding the whole of humanity. The English term "property," in technical, legal, and academic as well as in "folk" understandings, is closely tied to the enclosure movement and the emergence of capitalism. How, then, can the patterns of access and use characteristic of precapitalist land tenure be described in terms of property relations? Moreover, the currently dominant understanding may be a highly distorted representation of how contemporary Euro-American property systems actually function. Even those committed in principle to the comparative analysis of social institutions may hesitate to make use of a concept which cannot readily be translated even into a closely related language such as German (where *Vermögen* often seems more appropriate than the standard *Eigentum*, while many German scholars prefer to use the composite term *Besitz und Eigentum* as their general designation of the field). The problems of translation into more remote contexts, a Polynesian island for example, are of course more formidable (Firth 1965 [1939]). Pauline Peters (1998, 370) is one of numerous scholars who have proposed abandoning the term. But her suggestion to replace property with the "the old language of 'rights'" would seem open to similar objections.

Despite the difficulties, the von Benda-Beckmanns and Wiber (2006a, 2006b) make a strong case for persevering with property. They argue that the term's surplus ideological "freight" can be offloaded and a rigorous conceptual model developed in its place. This model, which I shall discuss in more detail below, takes property to be a "cover term" for how human beings regulate their relations to the things which they value. All human societies have a property system comprising three elements: "first, the social units (individuals, groups lineages, corporations, states) that can hold property rights and obligations; second, the construction of valuables as property objects; and third, the different sets of rights and obligations social units can have with respect to such objects" (2006a, 15). In economic anthropology, Robert Hunt has issued similar calls for conceptual precision (e.g. Hunt 1998), but the von Benda-Beckmanns and Wiber insist that property is too significant for the functioning and reproduction of social systems to be confined to the domain of economy. While their own particular interest lies in legal pluralism they point out that property regimes "cannot easily be captured in one-dimensional political, economic or legal models." (2006a, 2). Earlier, drawing on the work of the historian Perry Anderson, I argued that this was precisely the fascination and challenge of property, which always linked economy (base) to the jural-ideological domain of superstructure (Hann 1998a; see also Chapter Three).

The most influential Western theorizing about property is underpinned by what I call the "standard liberal model." This can be traced back to the "possessive individualism" which developed in England well before the onset of Polanyi's "great transformation," above all in the work of John Locke (Macpherson 1962). But anthropologists have shown that the social significance of property is much broader than the liberal tradition recognizes, and that the political, economic and social functions of property are in continuous flux. In the twenty-first century the ownership of a certain amount of private property is no longer a precondition for political citizenship, as it was in numerous European countries in the nineteenth. The ownership of land and other means of production no longer has the same decisive social or economic significance in mature industrial societies that it had in the age of Locke and Marx. As James Burnham and many others pointed out long ago, managerial power and access to information are in some respects more critical than ownership per se, and the broader approach to property relations must take account of such factors. Entitlements to welfare benefits and social security may be considered as a new form of property, held in common by all citizens. In short, anthropologists have critiqued the narrow view of property and established its inadequacy even for the societies in which this reflects a dominant "folk model." Together with numerous scholars in socio-legal studies, they have argued for a wider compass.

The Anthropological Research Tradition

The anthropological perspective on property does not differ essentially from that of the sociologist and has from the beginning drawn heavily on legal traditions. In particular, the metaphor of a "bundle of rights," first used by Henry Maine in *Ancient Law* (1861), has influenced numerous later writers. It has been used primarily to draw attention to the very common circumstance that different persons or groups may hold different kinds or levels of rights over the same thing. Ownership, defined as the greatest possible combination of rights over a valuable object recognized in law, does not preclude the long-term allocation of use rights to another party and it need not include the right to alienate. It is thus a more specific term than property, but it too is potentially available for use in cross-cultural analysis.

Early theorists of property in anthropology, notably Lewis Henry Morgan (1877) and, following him, Friedrich Engels (1972 [1884]) were primarily concerned with explaining the evolution of human societies, culminating in the highly individualized private ownership characteristic of modern capitalism. This remains the impulse behind Marcel Mauss's analysis of *The Gift* (1990 [1925]), in which changing forms of exchange were shown to be predicated upon transformations in the ways in which people relate to each other through things, i.e. upon property. Like his predecessors, Mauss took as unproblematic the basic distinction between rights in things and the rights in persons that people held by virtue of belonging to specific social groups and political communities. Meanwhile the European colonial authorities were struggling to reconcile native systems of land tenure with their Western categories. For example, as Walter Neale (a colleague and disciple of Polanyi) showed for India, the British vacillated between recognizing the communal rights of village communities (later the basis of an allegedly stagnant "Asiatic mode of production" in some Marxist theorizing) and treating the powerful *zamindar* as if he were an English landlord (1962). Dutch officials classified apparently unused land in Indonesia as "wasteland" in order to transfer it into the ownership of the colonial power and eliminate the customary rights of indigenous groups (von Benda-Beckmann and von Benda-Beckmann 2006).

From the beginning much anthropological work was bedeviled by the misleading simplicity of "communal versus individual," an either-or dichotomy sustained by a combination of persistent Western folk beliefs and Cold War ideologies, long after the fieldwork revolution should have consigned it to oblivion. Malinowski devoted the last of his monographs on the Trobriand Islanders (1935; see discussion in Chapter Three) to a study of their gardening practices. It was essential, he contended, to probe behind the "legal façade" to grasp the underlying principles by which land was held and used. The ultimate basis was to be found in their matrilineal kinship organization rather than in any principle of economic rationality. Malinowski's student and successor Raymond Firth offered a comparable analysis of the property system of the inhabitants of Tikopia (1965 [1939]). He showed the coexistence of principles of individual ownership (and as a corollary the social recognition of theft) with principles of joint ownership by a kin group, or by a chief as its head. Land and important items such as sacred canoes were excluded from individual ownership.

Max Gluckman developed another influential property metaphor with his concept of "estates of administration" (1965), which grew out of his fieldwork in southern Africa in the late colonial period (especially in Barotseland, part of today's Zambia). While the notion of a "bundle of rights" was inherently static and did not address how the various rights were interconnected, Gluckman's contribution emphasized the delegation of rights in a political hierarchy. Thus, land might be "ultimately" owned by a king (as it is in Great Britain), but the typical African king delegated rights to regional chiefs, who in turn delegated to village headmen. The headman allocated plots to the households of the settlement. Each wife might receive her own plot to cultivate, which Gluckman referred to as an "estate of production." It is futile to look in the "hierarchy of estates of administration" for an exact equivalent to a modern European private owner. Land tenure was neither perfectly collective nor individual, but mirrored the social structure of the group.

In the case of an acephalous group, rights over any land that fell out of use reverted upwards to the group as a whole. The most basic principle in sub-Saharan Africa, where land was not generally scarce, was that the political authorities were obliged to provide citizens with as much land as they needed for their subsistence.

Gluckman's analysis was designed in part to correct the errors and abuses of British colonial administrators, who eventually began to show more flexibility in their recognition of native principles (Meek 1946). With the end of the colonial era, interest in land tenure and property in general declined. Of course there were exceptions. Franz von Benda-Beckmann demonstrated the centrality of the mechanisms for inheriting multiple forms of property in maintaining community cohesion in Minangkabau, Indonesia (1979). Numerous anthropologists investigated the consequences of property rights for ecology and environmental conservation (McCay and Acheson 1987). The impact of feminism led some scholars to consider the role of gender in the ownership and transmission of property and to rediscover Engels' arguments concerning the evolutionary origins of women's subordination (Hirschon 1984). Jack Goody (1976) analyzed the "women's property complex" in Eurasian societies and showed how this "diverging devolution" differed from the dominant mode of property transfer in egalitarian sub-Saharan Africa, where the abundance of land caused rights over persons to be much more important than rights over things. But very few twentieth-century anthropologists drew comparisons on this scale; the majority abandoned historical and evolutionary questions to a small minority of their colleagues and to archaeologists (see Hunt and Gilman 1998).

In short, a long history of anthropological engagement with property issues rather fizzled out in the postcolonial decades. These were precisely the years in which scholars in other disciplines, notably economics, were laying the foundations for a dogmatic revival of the standard liberal model. Garret Hardin (1968) highlighted the need for well-defined property rights to avert the "tragedy of the commons" and Harold Demsetz (1967) drew on ethnographic materials to explain the origins of property in terms of a cost-benefit analysis. Douglass North (1981) extended the economist's rationality assumptions to a vast range of institutions and postulated the centrality of property rules in historical change, thereby staking a claim on behalf of the "new institutional economics" to a field that was previously in the domain of the anthropologists.

Real Property: The Political and Moral Economy of Decollectivization

The most conspicuous features of contemporary propertization are intellectual properties and the continuous generation of new forms of property through new technologies. These have attracted a good deal of attention from anthropologists. However, such innovative forms should not blind us to the continued importance of "real property," i.e. the land.[2] On two occasions in the course of the twentieth century the basic "ground rules" of property for most of the inhabitants of the Eurasian landmass were subjected to a radical rupture. First, to use the language of communist ideology, the peasantry entered into an alliance with the working class. Through the institutions of the collective farm and the State Farm, rural living conditions were radically transformed and in many respects the gulf between town and countryside narrowed. Later, the abandonment of socialist property forms around 1990 called this long-term trend into question. Some anthropologists have suggested that, at least in some parts of the former Soviet bloc, features of the pre-industrial peasantry have again become prominent (Leonard and Kaneff 2002). Between 2000 and 2005 my research group at the Max Planck Institute (MPI) for Social Anthropology set out to investigate the dismantling of socialist property relations through a set of linked projects involving participant observation at community level. The larger question in the background of these studies was the extent to which postsocialist privatization has replicated earlier colonial processes, in the sense that the standard liberal understandings of land, emphasizing individual ownership and alienability, have been imposed upon the complex lived practices of other societies.[3]

---

[2] Land has always enjoyed a privileged status in property theorizing as well as in the subdiscipline of economic anthropology. This status derives straightforwardly from the fact that land has been a major factor of production and of reproduction in most human societies.

[3] For fuller discussion of the topics covered in this section see Hann (2005b, 2006) and Hann et al. (2003). We were by no means the first anthropologists to address these issues: in addition to Leonard and Kaneff (2002), valuable foundations are to be found in Kideckel (1995), Abrahams (1996), Creed (1998), and in numerous works of Katherine Verdery (e.g. 1999, 2003).

The MPI projects investigated not only the political economy of rural transformation but also more subjective factors, such as emotional attachment to the land, and issues of morality and justice, always a central component of debates about property (see Chapter Three). Many Hungarian villagers were angry when their government implemented a complex scheme of restitution that did not guarantee the return of the land that once belonged to their ancestors, but instead sought a compromise between this principle of elementary justice and the desirability of maintaining viable production units and avoiding massively complicated legal procedures. Neighboring Romania opted for restitution according to historic boundaries, and paid a heavy economic price for doing so (Cartwright 2001; Verdery 2003).

While the formal principle of private land ownership was well established in Hungary and Romania before the imposition of collectivization, this was by no means the case throughout the bloc, particularly in the Soviet Union itself. The uniformity brought by the imposition of socialist institutions was deceptive: even within countries there was usually considerable variation. While Hungary was exceptional in its pursuit of a "market socialist" model, some space for private initiative persisted everywhere in the form of the private plot and informal mechanisms within collective institutions (see Eidson 2006 for the East German case). Caroline Humphrey (1983) emphasized such factors in the only anthropological study we have of a Soviet collective farm, suggesting that land was held in a system of "estates of administration," the concept developed by Max Gluckman in the context of colonial Africa. She has also drawn attention to the continued importance of the personal ownership of valuables under socialism (2002b). In short, to view the socialist property regime as a vacuum, or as an evolutionary aberration that only a massive extension of private ownership could correct, is to ignore the complexity and authenticity of alternative ways of relating to the land and other valued goods.

The socialist rural economies varied greatly in their economic efficiency, but all took far-reaching measures to integrate their agricultural and industrial sectors. Most invested heavily in the material infrastructure of the countryside and made substantial transfers, e.g. to support social and cultural services. These supports contracted rapidly with the switch to "market economy," which in many cases destroyed the channels of marketing that had emerged under socialism (both formal and informal) without providing any adequate substitute. These problems were aggravated by the depressed conditions of agricultural markets worldwide. Many postsocialist farmers in Eastern Europe were well informed of high levels of subsidy to the agricultural sector in Western Europe and North America. Their view of their own new governments' policies was accordingly jaundiced.

Under these conditions it was inevitable that the property changes would have varying consequences for social stratification. Tatjana Thelen (2003a, 2003b) identified a renewal of patriarchy in the Hungarian village she studied, as newly empowered landowners imposed their will over females and junior males in their households. The descendants of the more prosperous farmers of the previous generation are prominent among the "winners" of the decollectivization process, at least in this case study. (Such continuities had been noticed by sociologists even before the property reforms gave the children and grandchildren of the *kuláks*, stigmatized at the time of collectivization, the best cards in terms of claims to re-establish their previous dominance; see Szelenyi, 1988.) The emergence in some privileged locations of successful independent farmers and other private entrepreneurs is one aspect of a new pattern of stratification, but the hierarchies established under socialism did not disappear overnight. In some parts of Eastern Europe they mutated into informal networks that provided essential "social capital" for the new owners (Lampland 2002). In the former Soviet Union, where disruption and economic shortages had been more severe, socialist institutions continued de facto to play a decisive role, despite their formal abolition (Ventsel 2005; see also Visser 2003, 2006).

These were some of the messy realities of the postsocialist countryside in the 1990s when Western advisers such as USAID officials stipulated a neoliberal approach. The economic theory behind private property is unchanged from that of classical liberalism: through obtaining a high degree of exclusive power over things, it is postulated that agents will exercise greater care over them, invest appropriately, and generally act such that the promotion of their selfish interests will be fully consistent with the collective welfare function of their society.[4] In the language of the new institutional economics, the advantages are phrased in terms of lowering transactions costs. However, widespread fragmentation of land ownership brought with it costs that, from the perspective of a villager in Tázlár, far exceeded the administrative costs of land allocation and use as these had evolved in the last decades of socialism. Even where there was continuity in the unit of production (i.e. large fields were still cultivated as single units), it became necessary for the farmer to negotiate with large numbers of owners, many of whom did not live in the countryside at all. The measurement and division of land was a contested, time-consuming and expensive process (for the case of Tázlár see Hann 2006; this volume, Chapter Three). While legal institutions had been largely irrelevant for most villagers under socialism, postsocialist regimes had great difficulty in creating efficient mechanisms for documenting and adjudicating claims, and then issuing title documents. In other words, some of the basic conditions for the neoliberal property paradigm have not been fulfilled and many villagers continued to recognize informal entitlements and "custom" (Cartwright 2003).

But the anthropological objections to propertization as a blanket prescription go deeper than this. Even if more of the "technical" prerequisites for neoliberalism to work were put in place, if legal machinery worked well and "corruption" could be eradicated overnight, it is still necessary to enquire more closely into the ways in which property is embedded in social relationships and expresses the norms and values of the community. The alignment of property rights with a morally acceptable distribution of power and wealth tends to create

[4] Some economists introduce psychological assumptions, namely that humans have a strong disposition to form attachments to specific things, and human communities to recognize that at least some of these attachments should be held exclusively (Schlicht 1998). That some villagers in Tázlár could form strong emotional attachments to particular plots of land confirms such assumptions. However, these attachments to land are by no means universal: Mihály Sárkány found no such sentimental attachments in the village he studied in Northern Hungary (Hann and Sárkány 2003). Even in Tázlár, more than a decade after a complex redistribution was set in motion it is clear that the great majority of farmers now approach land ownership entirely in pragmatic terms, as one resource among others (Hann 2006).

dilemmas in all societies (Widlok 2001). Following the historian E.P. Thompson, several members of the MPI research group adapted the concept of the moral economy and explored its intimate relations to the changing political economy. Our guiding assumption was that at least some moral norms are resistant to rapid change. They may "harden" as they become objects of explicit reflection when threatening changes occur in the political economy.

Our projects provided no support for radical-romantic contentions that notions of private property are inherently antithetical to human nature and therefore not to be found in non-capitalist communities. The Siberian hunters studied by Aimar Ventsel (2005) formed definite links to particular territories, which often led to a personal naming of this land. It was necessary to request permission from the "owner" in order to extract resources from this land, but this permission was always granted. Still, this is a far cry from neoliberal models of private property and, although much land has been theoretically allocated to individuals in the remote region of Sakha studied by Ventsel, principles of reciprocity remain the dominant form of integration. In his work among the hunters of Taimyr, John Ziker (2002, 2003) noted a stronger emphasis on sharing and informal entitlements as strategies to cope with postsocialist dislocation. These practices are strongly bound up with a cosmology that emphasizes close identities with the natural environment and expresses a distinctive moral economy.

The Russian villagers in the Volga region studied by Patrick Heady (2005; see also Gambold Miller and Heady 2003) display comparable forms of collective sentiment in very different economic conditions. At the time that land was formally allocated to individuals following presidential decrees in 1991, few villagers had any recollection of independent farming conditions, and few had the skills and capital needed to begin commercial farming. Land was distributed without regard to what had been owned before collectivization. For most Russian villagers, becoming a nominal landowner brought no change in attitude or in practice. Gambold Miller and Heady highlight the "loneliness of *fermer*-hood" (2003, 287) experienced by the exceptions, those who choose to take their land out of the pool used by the organizational successor to the collective farm. Envy plays a significant role in the moral economy. Most villagers continue to look to their local farm leaders to provide them with jobs and a minimal level of subsistence in return for using their land, while continuing to farm their individual plots intensively. Traditions of community solidarity have been by and large enforced. Patricia Gray (2003) reports similarly from Marii El that local opinion disapproved of these who split away from the socialist successor organization. Among Bulgarian speakers in southwestern Ukraine, however, Deema Kaneff found that the higher income levels of an independent farmer could be legitimated through a reputation for honesty and hard work. In the Azerbaijani communities studied by late Yalçın-Heckmann, collective institutions were eliminated altogether. In the absence of any large-scale successor farm, everyone is compelled to behave more individualistically. Without any organizational vehicle, the moral economy finds expression in informal comments, gossip and similar unofficial sanctions. There is no objection in principle to land moving into exclusive private ownership, but resentment does arise when income and wealth inequalities are not perceived to be legitimate (Kaneff and Yalçın-Heckmann 2003). The line between high levels of interpersonal trust and high levels of corruption has remained fuzzy, as it was under socialism. The revolution in property relations has not brought the hoped-for clarity but only deeper cynicism, often phrased as "they pretended to give us ownership rights, but owning land brings only responsibilities, and wealth is now generated elsewhere, where we are excluded." In such conditions it is interesting to find, as Davide Torsello has noted in Slovakia, that even those new owners who speak critically of the large institution that replaced their collective farm tend to trust this organization more than they do their fellow individual owners (Torsello 2003a, 2003b).

In Susanne Brandtstädter's Chinese case study the cosmology emphasizes lineage ancestors and the moral economy has a formal expression in the temple association, which deploys the funds supplied by wealthy emigrants to celebrate the community itself (2003; see also Brandtstädter 2001). There is also lavish expenditure on household life-cycle rituals, with levels of giving that might appear "wasteful" to the outsider, but which Brandstädter describes as a highly rational investment in personal relations, which count for a lifetime. The Chinese case is of particular interest, since the country remains officially socialist and property rights are indistinct in many fields, including land ownership. Yet, as in late socialist Hungary, the decentralization of rights and effective market incentives have sufficed to generate unparalleled economic growth. Brandtstädter's case study (admittedly exceptional in that the prosperity of the coastal regions of Fujian is massively enhanced by overseas transfer income) shows the two sides of the coin of moral economy in a state of harmony and good order: the collective side is represented by the temple association, and the interpersonal side by the efflorescence of gifts on ritual occasions. But it would be misleading to label these two aspects of the moral economy public and private. Another agent stands outside the moral economy—the state itself and its local apparatus. The Chinese state claims to be the ultimate owner of most land throughout the country, but according to Brandtstädter the villagers do not trust their state, which even in its post-Maoist, reformist phase has not been able to "create new binding rules to re-embed social relations" (2003, 436).

While the principle of private ownership is strongly associated with capitalism and that of collective (cooperative) or state ownership with socialism, anthropological case studies show that, at the community level, creative combinations are not only possible but desirable. Socialist property systems were complex combinations, by no means reducible to the stereotype of "open access." Contrary to the fears expressed by Hardin (1968), many scholars have shown that forms of common property can generate solutions that are both efficient and equitable (Ostrom 1990). However, in the contemporary world common property can seldom substitute entirely for markets and the state. Communities often hold contradictory ideas and they are prone to taking short-sighted decisions, e.g. concerning environmental sustainability. A market mechanism of some sort is essential for the efficient linkage of the communities, and state control of some sort is essential if market freedoms are not to be abused. Optimal property rules are likely therefore to be pragmatic combinations that have the flexibility to take account of particular property objects and local ecological conditions.

Among the MPI projects Barbara Cellarius's study of a densely forested zone in the Rhodope Mountains, Bulgaria, provided a fine example (2003, 2004). It took the postsocialist authorities almost a decade to get around to forest privatization, following the swift decision in 1991 to return agricultural land to private ownership within the old boundaries. It was difficult enough to create viable farm units, but individual management of forest holdings posed still more formidable problems. Bulgaria had a strong cooperative tradition in presocialist times, and in this case (unlike agricultural land) the new powerholders eventually agreed to allow the reconstitution of forest cooperatives, in which the owners were allocated shares proportional to their original holdings. The democratic management of these cooperatives poses another challenge, but the early signs seem encouraging. In other words, unlike the socialist period cooperatives in Bulgaria, modelled on the Soviet collective farm (which in theory placed all property in the hands of a local collectivity, but in reality left local people with little control of any kind), the new forest cooperatives seem to provide an efficient solution based on a high degree of self-management, which at the same time redresses a historical injustice.

Unfortunately the bad odor of socialist cooperatives has made it even more difficult to promote such solutions in contemporary Eurasia than in other parts of the world. One hopeful initiative to be found in recent years is the emergence of new forms of *obshchina* in thinly populated regions of Siberia. This ancient Russian term for community has been adapted to designate a new and loosely specified form of association for the "small peoples" of Siberia, some of whom have come forward with alacrity to register a claim on the basis of a historic "clan" tie to the land. The details vary considerably from region to region, and depend heavily on whether this legal status brings advantages in terms of raising credit, obtaining supplies, or marketing produce. In some areas of the Russian north, such as Yamal, studied by Florian Stammler, markets work well for indigenous reindeer herders and economic prosperity seems to have rendered the *obshchina* option superfluous (2005). However, in Sakha and in Chukotka the formation of *obshchiny* has been facilitated by the authorities and widely taken up (Stammler and Ventsel 2003; Gray 2001, 2005). So far at least, the granting of this privileged form of ownership to those eligible on the basis of ethnicity does not seem to have created friction with other residents, notably immigrant Russians who cannot claim this special historical relationship to the land. This is partly due to the fact that the entire land tenure situation throughout Siberia remains confused and fluid. Land is still generally abundant and remains far from becoming just another commodity available through a market. In these circumstances the devolution of property rights to *obshchiny* may work well for some indigenous people, but of course it cannot be a general panacea for the current problems of Siberia's population. The work of Alexander King among urban dwellers in Kamchatka highlights the negative consequences of the withdrawal of state subsidies and loss of public sector employment (2003). While communal land tenure can be part of a solution, a comprehensive new property regime must also include the private and collective ownership forms necessary for markets to function efficiently and an effective state.

If the latter elements can be put in place, there are compelling arguments for allowing and even insisting upon some form of local collective management and even ownership of land, and possibly some other key resources as well. Private ownership is likely to be a dominant form across a wide range of objects, from combine harvesters to snowmobiles. The state is essential as the provider of key services, notably health and education. But there are good reasons for treating land, lakes and marine resources as a common good, which may be allocated to households or individuals for use, but whose ownership is vested in the local community. In this way the moral economy would expand beyond the two facets identified by Brandtstädter. The era of the locally autonomous kin-based *obshchina* is over and the inhabitants of postsocialist rural communities need to be integrated into a state as well as organized through some sort of local association or cooperative. They need also to be integrated into market systems and to enjoy the freedom to cultivate close interpersonal relations. The state cannot be excluded from the moral economy, since it is by definition the expression of the larger political community. But it must always be supplemented by local forms of the kind explored by the MPI research team. Markets are usually perceived as a realm of impersonal maximizing activity that is by definition incompatible with the moral economy. Yet instrumentalist, profit-oriented activity may also receive moral approval. This was certainly the case for late socialist Hungary, when market incentives provided a successful mechanism for accumulation. Even in a more orthodox socialist rural economy like that of East Germany, Eidson and Milligan (2003) documented the persistence of entrepreneurial activity within the collective farm, to the general approval of those who benefited from such flexibility. Of course the market is also a sphere of division, in which benefits are seldom equally distributed. Both the market and private property remain partially distinct. They are drawn into the moral economy not only to the extent that they receive general approbation but also in the sense that most property and market relations depend heavily on relations of trust between persons. Yet in another sense the moral economy keeps up a constant pressure on the private owner, which constrains the possibilities for "rational" impersonal maximization. Just as contracts can never specify all the conditions of their fulfilment, so deeds of ownership can never exhaust the social complexity of property relations.

Taken together the results of anthropological work on decollectivization show the need for locally specific solutions in which state, markets and community resource management can all play a part. The general contrast between the ex-Soviet case studies and the Eastern European case studies shows the necessity for historical grounding. The private ownership of land became widespread in Russia only in the early twentieth century. Feudal restrictions were abolished earlier in Eastern Europe and peasants here had made a faster transition to private ownership. Although many villagers in Hungary still operated collective field management well into the twentieth century (Fél and Hofer 1969), by the time of collectivization a strong ethos of landownership had developed in most regions, such that the size of a peasant's holding was the prime indicator of his status or class. In Russia, where most farms were collectivized in the early 1930s, there was no serious discussion of returning land to former owners. Instead it was privatized according to principles of equality (though in some cases with differential treatment according to previous employment history—see Kaneff and Yalçın-Heckmann 2003). By contrast, in most of Eastern Europe collectivization occurred a generation later, and at the time of the regime change many villagers still had vivid recollections of the traumas they experienced in the 1950s and early 1960s. It is not surprising that land privatization was generally pushed through more promptly in these countries, and that there was widespread support for the principle that individuals—or their heirs—should as far as possible be given back exactly what had been taken from them.

In Russia it was not possible to refer back to a historical baseline as it was in Eastern Europe. Policies were shaped primarily by present-day considerations, and egalitarian principles remained influential in practice. In Eastern Europe, by contrast, there was often heated discussion over the baseline. Ownership had in many cases changed dramatically in the decades preceding collectivization: why, some people asked, should the victims of socialism be awarded their land back, or at least compensation, when the victims of earlier "democratic" land reforms and the casualties of ethnic deportations were awarded little or nothing of their property assets? In purely agro-economic terms it might well have been more rational to allocate land in large units to aristocratic families from whom it was taken in 1945 rather than in small fragments to those from whom it was taken in 1960. Political considerations rather than any noble commitment to justice dictated that the latter claims were recognized, despite the dislocation and high transaction costs created by the new pattern of ownership.

The MPI projects and other anthropological investigations of the demise of socialist forms of "real property" have demonstrated not the evolutionary superiority of private property but rather the limitations of liberal theories.[5] Privatization has been generally associated with dislocation, widening social inequalities, and declines in output and productivity. In some cases there have also been negative environmental consequences (Sneath 2000; Humphrey and Sneath 1999), while in Tázlár and many other parts of the postsocialist world a great deal of land has been taken out of production. At the same time, the anthropological studies have shown the need to submit multiple qualifications to the thesis of "propertization." Just as the private plot ensured continuity when collectivization was imposed, successor cooperatives have in many places smoothed the processes of decollectivization. Both collectivization and decollectivization come in many varieties, but overall there has been a lot of continuity in social security provision and no return to the conditions of the traditional peasantry. The new private property owners have their rights constrained on many fronts: by the informal norms of the community as well as by the formal legal framework of the state or of the European Union. This

[5] [One sophisticated liberal response to the manifest problems of the postsocialist dismemberment of the earlier property system was to insist on the necessity of creating effective private "property bundles." Michael Heller (a lawyer) identified a "tragedy of the anticommons" in urban Russia in the 1990s, where allocations of property rights to too many "stakeholders" led to an underutilization of resources (Heller 1998). By contrast, I maintain that the "tragedy of the privates" was by far the greater source of inefficiency—see Hann 2015d.]

calls to mind Polanyi's concept of the "double movement," devised to capture an earlier but essentially similar dialectic in the nineteenth century, as the scope of the market and private property first expanded, before being qualified and reined in through the agency of the victims of this expansion.

Non-Real Property: New Fictitious Commodities and Anthropological Theory

Though there is no doubting the world-historical importance of the collapse of Soviet socialism, the rural projects described above are in some ways untypical of recent anthropological work on property. They certainly do not reflect the range of this work. In this section I shall provide a necessarily more concise outline of recent contributions in other fields. It will be seen that the anthropological tradition of property research is again flourishing, and that part of that tradition continues to involve questioning the concept of property itself.

Although a high proportion of the postsocialist studies have focused on land, some have examined other property objects. Carolin Leutloff-Grandits (a member of the MPI team) concentrated on rights and emotional attachments to houses in her recent study of Knin (2006). This area of southern Croatia was populated mainly by Serbs until their violent eviction in the mid-1990s; strong pressures from international NGOs as well as the EU have not succeeded in creating conditions in which significant numbers of Serbs feel able to return to their homeland and reclaim their property rights. Catherine Alexander has investigated factory privatization in Kazakhstan and reported devastation similar to that documented by others in the post-Soviet countryside (2004). Caroline Humphrey has explored concomitant changes in consumer property, such as the villas of the new urban elites, and the emergence of new forms of "subjecthood" among those who continue to live in their previous apartments on housing estates, but who are now the responsible owners of their property (2002a, 2007 [cf. Fehérváry 2013]).

Recent studies of land tenure outside the former socialist world have raised very similar issues, e.g. when privatization policies fail to consider the wider context of implementation and "embeddedness" (James 2006; Peters 2006). Questions of sustainability have remained prominent in this literature. Most environmental anthropologists hold that the criterion of formal ownership in itself tells us little or nothing about the impact on conservation. Everything depends upon how resources are managed, which depends in turn on power relationships and the entire context of embeddedness noted above. Maritime anthropology continues to attract a lot of attention, though certain economic aspects differ in this context (McCay 2001). Since it is impossible to erect fences and to control the movement of fish, economic actors who depend on fishing for their livelihood are typically exposed to uncertainties greater than those faced by agriculturalists or pastoralists. Their property arrangements reflect their efforts to reduce uncertainty, for example owning boats collectively through cooperatives. Rapid changes in technology have led to over-fishing in many parts of the world and to novel attempts to avert a tragedy of the maritime commons. Canada, for example, has introduced a new form of property object, the "individual transferable quota" (similar principles have been implemented over a longer period in the European Union's "common agricultural policy," notably with respect to milk quotas). Studies of this institution in the Maritime Provinces have revealed numerous problems, including the concentration of the industry into highly capitalized boats, which squeeze out the smaller fishermen (Wiber 2000).

In this Canadian example, as in many other parts of the world, local people have increasingly resisted the juggernaut of privatization by asserting claims to property rights based on their indigenous knowledge, or simply on the fact that they are the autochthonous inhabitants and practitioners of a specific mode of economy. Activist movements have developed, and the idea of possessing a uniquely authentic culture is instrumentalized to promote local interests against outsiders (Kasten 2004b). Some anthropologists have been critical of the tendency to assert claims to property, material and intellectual, on the basis of group rights that exclude those residents who happen not to belong to the dominant ethnicity. It may well be difficult to reach agreement on the criteria for group membership and the well-intentioned attribution of rights to a native group can sometimes be highly discriminatory, as Toon van Meijl (2006) has shown in the case of the allocation of fishing rights to Maori in New Zealand. Other anthropologists have argued that, in spite of the difficulties, recognition of indigenous property rights is often the only practical way to further the interests of marginal populations which have long been exploited by external powers. It is seldom possible to restore those rights in anything like their original form, but numerous anthropologists have worked to support native title claims in order to remedy historic wrongs and to secure economic benefits for indigenous groups (see Kuper 2003 and the ensuing critical forum).

It may seem obvious that a pharmaceutical company which makes vast profits through the exploitation of a plant whose properties have previously been known and utilized by an Amazonian tribe should transfer some of those profits to the tribe. The same logic can be applied in various artistic fields, but there are almost always grave difficulties. In the field of music, for example, folk tunes are surely the property of the creators, and if recordings make money, then royalties should be paid (Seeger 2004). But how far can this principle be pushed in the age of "world music"? Paul Simon made South African rhythms famous all over the world with his album "Graceland"—and resurrected his own career in doing so. Should he have done more than he did to credit the native musicians and their communities? (Erlmann 1999). Major problems arise when particular contributions, though falling within an acknowledged cultural repertoire, may be claimed as individual creations. How is one to allocate royalties in such cases? In such circumstances the anthropologist may be called in to support the lawyer, who can only make the property rights effective if he has a precise definition of the property object. But most anthropologists are suspicious of pinning down what is or is not "culturally authentic," since for them culture is by definition dynamic and subverts such precision.

The propertization of culture has attracted increasing attention in recent years, notably in response to demands for the repatriation of museum artifacts and also thanks to the activities of UNESCO in designating sites of "world cultural heritage" (Brown 2003; Wiber 2006). A principle of open access to cultural knowledge has been boldly advocated by Erich Kasten with respect to the indigenous populations of Siberia, and he extends this principle to the ownership of the knowledge produced by anthropologists themselves in the course of their fieldwork and analyses (2004a). However, as with the principle of open access to scientific knowledge (for which the Max Planck Society has been a leading campaigner in recent years), the practical difficulties are immense. Some indigenous groups may not wish details of their social worlds to be made available to the world through the internet, and anthropologists will be obliged to respect those wishes. Progress in the natural sciences raises different issues: it is galling that the results of research in a state-funded laboratory regularly become the property of a private publishing enterprise. Should researchers be able to take out a patent before disclosing their results to the scientific community if this is the only way to ensure that their results are not appropriated without acknowledgment? The lesson from a great deal of anthropological work on the regulation of the commons is that open access is unlikely to be viable and it is necessary to work out new forms of community control if the quality of the pasture is to be preserved.

These are but a few of the property issues addressed recently by anthropologists. Space does not permit me to discuss how they have responded to the challenge of many other forms of intellectual property. From the angle of political economy, Keith Hart (n.d.) has argued that IP regulation is the key to understanding the evolution of capitalism since the onset of the machine age. Hart views the US as a poacher long turned gamekeeper: its present efforts to defend digital monopolies against intensifying competition from the likes of China and India are crucial to the future of world society. From the "culturalist" perspective that dominates contemporary anthropology there is widespread interest in how property is constructed, both by elite expert communities and among the wider public, and through the interaction of the two; the work of Rosemary Coombe (1998) has been especially influential. This work builds on earlier interests in the "social life of things" (Appadurai 1986). The significance of trademarks and "branding" for social identities has been widely taken up by specialists in consumption (Miller 1996). One message of these studies is that consumers are not passive victims. Trademarks are constantly subverted as citizens resist branding manipulation and set new limits to property rights through their creative appropriations, in some cases through organized opposition to capitalist management strategies.

Numerous anthropologists have taken an interest in new medical technologies, notably in the field of human reproduction and the commoditization of body parts (Parry 2004). Behind the materiality of these new property objects lies another vast realm of rapidly expanding intellectual property. For example, Pálsson and Harðardóttir (2002) have shown how the latest developments in genetic knowledge generate contestation over ownership at multiple levels in the unique case of Iceland. As in the land tenure studies described in the previous section, ethical conflicts pertaining to the moral economy, such as "ownership" claims over children born to surrogate mothers, need to be investigated in conjunction with conflicts of interest in the international political economy in which this new market is establishing itself. In all these fields the intensification of propertization often appears overwhelming. Yet it is also possible to recognize counter-trends. Anthony Seeger (2004) has pointed out that recent attempts by powerful interests to prevent the downloading of music on the internet resemble the fears expressed in the industry decades earlier over the spread of simple tape recorders, and indeed since the very beginnings of the "mechanical reproduction" of sound. Legal copyright restrictions depend on precision, but in practice the line between the authentic and the forged, the genuine article and a plagiarism, often remains fuzzy; this indeterminacy creates space for subversive agency. Despite the overwhelming evidence that privatization is on the rise, even in the internet, Keith Hart (2000) has argued that the new information technologies offer citizens unprecedented democratic possibilities, e.g. to exchange property objects directly and informally, circumventing the evolved institutions of both market and state.

The attention devoted to new technologies, and in particular the new "fictitious commodities" of knowledge and culture, has meant that some established fields of anthropological enquiry have received less attention in recent years. For example, the implications of property transmission mechanisms for family and household structure, and for social inequality in general, have been neglected (but see Grandits and Heady 2003; Brunnbauer 2003; Layton 2000).

Many of the anthropologists mentioned in this brief survey have sought to link their analyses of particular property objects to the development of theory. The on-going expansion in the scope of property poses an old issue in sharper form. If virtually all rights or entitlements are to be considered as forms of property, how is one to separate the study of "property relations" from that of social relations in general? I had little hesitation in accepting this slippage in my own work in rural Hungary, both because the property changes after socialism were central to general social restructuring and because villagers themselves made the connection by bringing other entitlements into a common calculus with the privatization of "real property." It is valid for analytic purposes to draw distinctions between property objects, as Tatjana Thelen (2003a, 2003b) does when exploring the effects of Hungary's new pattern of land ownership on gender and social structure. But is there any harm in retaining property as a cover term and accepting what follows, namely that property relations are indeed increasingly conterminous with social relations in general?

Some scholars have suggested that the way forward lies in a renewed focus on the concept of value (Verdery 2003; Graeber 2001). Some have articulated a radical critique of the basic Western concepts of property, sometimes grounded in the nature of new technologies and financial markets in Western societies (Maurer 1999) and sometimes in the local concepts of non-Western peoples (Povinelli 2004; Strathern 1988). Marilyn Strathern has argued that the inhabitants of the New Guinea Highlands do not understand the world in terms of a Western subject-object dichotomy. With new medical technologies undermining Western notions of the integrity of the human body, she suggests that the Melanesian world view now offers a more appropriate basis for thinking about property and ownership in general (1999).

Stephen Gudeman has been similarly sensitive to "local models" in all his contributions to economic anthropology. His recent work (2001, 2006, 2008) develops a general approach that constitutes the fullest riposte to date to the dominant models of economics, both neoclassical and "new institutionalist." "Calculating reason" of the kind exemplified by impersonal transactions in a market, Gudeman argues, has come to occupy an ever greater space in modern societies, but it can never fully obliterate the realm of community, where principles of solidarity and "mutuality" assume priority. Even the most "individualist" of modern capitalist societies is constructed on a "base" of human sociality that can never be captured through concepts such as utility maximization and transactions costs. With respect to the institution of property, Gudeman (2008) has developed a scathing critique of the widely cited attempt by Demsetz (1967) to apply an economic perspective to the emergence of private property among native Americans. The economist who considers only rational maximizing behavior is blind to the relationships and values which underpin property and hold society together.

As I noted at the beginning of this chapter, a systematic alternative analytic framework for understanding property regimes to that offered by the economists has recently been put forward by Franz and Keebet von Benda-Beckmann and Melanie Wiber (2006a; see also von Benda-Beckmann and von Benda-Beckmann 1999). Their model distinguishes four layers. The most general consists in the norms and values of a cultural tradition (they also use the term "ideology"). Layer two consists of political and legal regulations, often in a plurality of registers, concerned to specify, for example, the form in which objects are to be held and whether or not they can be alienated. This is the layer typically privileged in the economists' models. Layer three consists of the social relations of property, for example particular land use or inheritance patterns and the way that these may be tied to particular forms of kinship, and the implications for stratification and class differences. Finally, at the layer of "practices" the actors may reinforce the patterns of the other layers or they may initiate changes. In its rigor, this framework is an advance on the loose notion of embeddedness. Property must be analyzed at all four layers: to concentrate on legal categories, or to limit oneself to a simple contrast between norms and practice, is inadequate and distorting. Economic models that postulate the general superiority of private property to the other main types (open access, state and communal) are faulted for introducing false comparisons, by taking these forms out of social context.

This model is not ethnocentric. The von Benda-Beckmanns and Wiber warn against Western "state-centric" approaches that ignore other levels of jural regulation. They reject the general application of a simple dichotomy between public and private, and instead suggest that the analysis of modern Western property systems recognize multiple "relative publics." They also offer a systematic reinterpretation of the classical metaphor of the "bundle of rights" (2006a, 15–22). It can be usefully deployed in several quite different ways; first, as a way to express the totality of property rights and obligations; second, with regard to the rights which together constitute a "master category bundle," such as private ownership; third, with regard to particular property objects, such as land; fourth, with regard to the different valuable resources held by one and the same person or social unit. The results of the investigations into the partial demise of socialist rural property described in the first part of this review can be conveniently expressed in terms of this comprehensive framework. The rights and obligations associated with land, the key factor of production, and with concepts of ownership, both collective and private, can be unpacked with the help of the "bundle" metaphor. Property reforms at layer two have often failed because they were contradicted or resisted at the other layers. It follows that theoreticians and policymakers must incorporate these additional layers into their analyses and abandon the seductive reductionism of the standard liberal model.

The authors stress that theirs is a general framework for studying property rather than a specific theory. It will disappoint those looking to identify general laws of causality. No such laws appear within reach: sometimes the legal form may remain constant while massive changes proceed at the layer of actual social relationships, while in other cases property practices may sustain existing patterns of social relationships such that the transformation of legal categories has little wider impact. In short, change proceeds at differential rates at the different layers, and it may be difficult to reach agreement on when precisely a global "transformation of the property regime" has taken place. It follows that this approach is unlikely to appeal to those who, following in the footsteps of Jack Goody and Lewis Henry Morgan, seek to attribute a central role in human social evolution to a unified institution called property.

Conclusions

In this chapter I have sketched an anthropological tradition of engagement with the subject of property, especially land tenure, which dates back to the beginnings of the discipline in the nineteenth century. In the course of the twentieth century, I suggested, theoretical and historical work atrophied. With few exceptions anthropologists came, as a result of the "fieldwork revolution," to focus on the complex embeddedness of property in concrete local contexts; ethnography brought its own gains, but intellectual ground was ceded to other disciplines. Towards the end of the century, however, the demise of Soviet socialism and the emergence of many new property objects across the globe have led to a resurgence of interest in property, theoretical as well as empirical.

Few ruptures in the history of human land tenure have matched the disruption caused by collectivization and decollectivization. The former was a catastrophic act of total social engineering, but it did not obliterate all continuities, especially concerning personal property. The latter posed not only economic dilemmas but also the dilemma of how far continuities with the socialist era (e.g. through "successor cooperatives") could be tolerated and how far to go in attempting to reassert continuity with the presocialist era. The precise paths followed have varied. But everywhere property relations are of necessity lived in the present, and for many people the postsocialist present has been a disenchanting struggle for survival. Some of those who aspired for moral and emotional reasons to regain their private property came to experience the neoliberalism of the 1990s very negatively, as earlier generations of villagers had experienced the Stalinism of the 1930s and 1950s. The conclusions I drew from projects at the Max Planck Institute for Social Anthropology suggest that alternatives can be sought in pragmatic combinations of property ground rules, in which there is room for community control alongside markets and the state. The backwards-looking call for "historical justice" has no monopoly of virtue in the transformation of property regimes. There are also good moral grounds for pragmatism, for paying attention to the present and the future as well as to property claims grounded in the past.

Anthropologists have also contributed insights into a range of problems posed by new property objects against the backdrop of globalization. Some have attempted to contribute to theory by "deconstructing" concepts, including the concept of property itself, and highlighting the dangers of Eurocentric thinking. Anthropologists have not come forward with a new grand theory of their own. Rather, I have emphasized how the micro-level, ethnographic perspective, emphasizing concrete social relationships rather than formal legal categories and disembedded individual agents, exposes the hubris of the dominant property paradigms of recent decades. The analytic framework recently put forward by Franz and Keebet von Benda-Beckmann and Melanie Wiber develops the metaphor of the "bundle of rights" as a means to address the complex systemic character of the "property infrastructure nexus" (2006a, 10). This approach offers no insights into long-term historical changes nor does it provide ready guidelines for policymakers; but their framework is well designed to facilitate rigorous investigation of how changes in one aspect of the nexus affect other aspects and social relations generally, and thereby to elucidate the reasons for the widespread failure of policies based on the obsession with private ownership.

Finally (and I confess that this is more my own speculative, perhaps over-optimistic interpretation rather than an established consensus in the literature), I have argued that we should not exaggerate the impact of the present fetishization of private property. The trend to propertization, in the sense of extending individual ownership and converting more and more "non-real" objects into market or quasi-market commodities, often appears unilineal and irresistible. Many anthropologists have emphasized the deleterious consequences for the cohesion of communities, for what Stephen Gudeman (2001) terms "mutuality." But they have also drawn attention to resistance to the promulgation of new legal codes, which are modified and re-socialized "from below" as people struggle to adapt new property rules to the norms of their moral economy and their ongoing social relationships. Processes of modification can be observed at multiple levels, from the members of a post-Soviet *kolkhoz* who resist its fragmentation into parcels of private property to the diverse groups which participate in worldwide anti-globalization movements. The intensification of global economic interconnectedness is incontestable, but anthropologists have demonstrated that even products such as McDonald's hamburgers are subject to local appropriation (Watson 1997). All components of the "bundles of rights" that constitute property are subject to public regulation by the state and supra-state bodies such as the European Union. These controls, though they vary greatly in their effectiveness, can be interpreted as the continuous reassertion of Society, ultimately on a global level. There are no grounds for complacency (hence the question mark in my title) but at least some trends in the age of neoliberalism may contain the seeds of a Polanyian countermovement.

CHAPTER FIVE

Awkward Classes in Rural Eurasia

(2010, 2013, 2016)

Introduction: Rural Transformation and Class[1]

As the second decade of postsocialism draws to a close, explanations and evaluations of "the transition" differ greatly, both among those directly affected and among social scientists who have studied these processes. Among the latter, early diagnoses of an imminent "end of history" proved illusory, but many political scientists and sociologists have obstinately held on to the teleology implicit in the vocabulary they have been using from the start. For example, political scientist Everhard Holtmann finds it useful to distinguish an initial phase of chaotic *transition* from the phase of programmatic *transformation* which set in later in the 1990s. Recently, according to to Holtmann, we have entered the phase of "*post-transformation*," which means a return to a basic condition of stability. This new phase of "consolidation" comes in two variants, successful and unsuccessful; but even in the former cases, such as Germany's *neue Bundesländer* (perhaps especially here), postsocialist citizens remain fundamentally critical and distance themselves from their present governments (Holtmann 2009).

By contrast, anthropologists have been critical of the very vocabulary. Christian Giordano has argued powerfully that the phase of postsocialist transition is over "because it never started" (2005). In his view,

---

[1] *This chapter is a composite of Hann 2010a, which appeared in a Festschrift for Christian Giordano, Hann 2013b, a paper commissioned by a Polish internet journal of the radical left, and Hann 2016b, which was a contribution to a Karl Polanyi special issue of the new Budapest journal* Intersections. *I thank Tommaso Trevisani for detailed discussion of his Khorezm data and also Sasha Nikulin for much useful advice and permission to draw on materials which have not yet been published in English. For data pertaining to Hungary and Poland I thank Mihály Sárkány (Budapest), Rafał Smoczyński (Warsaw) and Mikołaj Szołtysek (Halle) for pointing me to sources.*

terms such as "transition," "transformation" and "system change" are all inadequate "because they implicitly or explicitly suggest a convergence hypothesis . . . in the last instance Westernization, i.e. the passive imitation of the liberal model of Anglo-Saxon provenance" (2005, 19). Giordano argues that all social change is transitional and that it is thoroughly ethnocentric to impose the categories of the "core" on the "periphery." The collapse of socialism came at a time when "monist models" of modernization had clearly failed in the Third World, but it was assumed that eastern Europeans so close to the core would prove culturally "more receptive" (2005, 16). This had proven wrong in the case of Italy, and it turned out to be even more wrong in cases such as Bulgaria, with their very different histories and "social capital" resources. Giordano pleads instead for recognition of multiple modernities, including the socialist project itself (where he follows Shmuel Eisenstadt and Johann Arnason). The next challenge is to specify the core criterion of modernity: it cannot be the consolidation of rational-legal authority in Max Weber's sense, since this has patently not been accomplished anywhere (Giordano and Kostova 2002).

The concept of class is more strongly associated with Marxist than with Weberian theory, though it is important in both. Marxist-Leninist regimes claimed that they had succeeded in abolishing antagonistic classes, while their critics detected the emergence of a new ruling class. My concern in this chapter is limited to the specific context of the postsocialist countryside, where Christian Giordano himself has made seminal contributions. I shall note the reasons why anthropologists have by and large been cautious in applying any concept of class to rural communities. Other social scientists have also become shy of class in recent years, opting instead for stratification or merely "identities." Many specialists in postsocialist transformation have preferred to speak of winners and losers, without insinuating that the members of these groups have solidified into new classes. Recently, however, Stephen K. Wegren and his co-authors (2006) have produced an impressive diagnosis of rural class relations in a postsocialist country. Their study concerns the largest and historically most interesting case, since rural differentiation in Russia was the subject of intellectual debate and political intervention even before the October Revolution. The authors note these antecedents, and that inter-regional equality was a priority of policymakers in the later Soviet era. Overall a high degree of equality was achieved. Collective farms and State Farms exhibited complex divisions of labor, but their hierarchies could hardly be described in terms of class differences. In the 1990s, however, as in the towns but to a lesser degree, new processes of differentiation set in. Wegren et al. argue that in recent years there has been a shift from stratification to class. They support this argument with a statistical analysis of survey data gathered in various locations over several years. The authors concentrate on the wealthiest and poorest segments and report a widening of inequalities with respect to income, land holdings, and capital stock.[2] Statistical evidence indicates that villagers are now forming classes "for themselves": members of the rich and poor segments have a consciousness of being winners and losers of the transition respectively, and those who have prospered are less likely to be critical of the government's reforms. Compared to the poor, they have a higher evaluation of their "personal efficacy" (p. 392), in particular of their ability to improve their situation through work. The poor are more fatalist, and many would apparently welcome a return to the old Soviet system.

Extrapolating social class from village statistical data has a long history in Russia. Lenin used data from *zemstvo* studies to support his Marxist claim that capitalist classes were already present in the Russian countryside (1977). This diagnosis was flawed, or perhaps merely premature, since the reforms later initiated by Prime Minister Stolypin did indeed promote significant differentiation among the peasantry. However, the agrarian economist A. V. Chayanov drew on the *zemstvo* data to make a very different argument (1986). He held that much of the statistical inequality in landholdings was a consequence not of class inequality but of differences in the availability of labor within the rural household, in the course of what anthropologists came later to call the "developmental cycle of the domestic group" (Goody 1958). This is the key idea on which Chayanov built his general theory of peasant economy (later adapted for even wider use by Marshall Sahlins as the "domestic mode of production"; see Sahlins 1972).

---

2 The phenomenon of urban oligarchs who invest in the countryside and in some cases come to dominate entire communities is not considered, but this increasingly prevalent new external element provides further support for the authors' general argument concerning new class relations.

The evidence considered by Wegren et al. (2006) does not suffice to refute an alternative, Chayanovian interpretation. Indeed, the authors explicitly point out that changing labor supply is bound to shape the future development of what they present as a class system *in statu nascendi*. They offer no insights into the living conditions of the majority of the rural population, which falls between the two extremes on which they concentrate, or into the interaction between different social groups or classes. The closest they come to such a dynamic account is when they note that the newly rich are no longer necessarily the objects of envy and sanctions, as they were in the first postsocialist years. They are not excluded from the community so long as they continue to participate in village activities. Indeed, those farming more land have above-average participation rates (388), which suggests that they may be seeking in compensatory fashion to legitimate their new wealth. To support their interpretations the authors cite anthropologist Margaret Paxson (2005), who found that demonstrative generosity on the part of those who could afford it was important if they were to avoid social criticism. But how far does such redistribution re-establish equality and homogeneity in rural society. Is it better understood as a purely symbolic gesturing to defuse resistance? Such questions can hardly be answered on the basis of positivist statistical analysis.

Social anthropologists specialize in uncovering realities that are not visible in the aggregate statistics which absorb the attention of other social scientists. Paxson's work is consistent with a large body of literature on redistribution and levelling devices in so-called peasant communities. Foreign anthropologists who carried out case-studies in more or less peripheral European villages after the Second World War knew that these places could not be seen as microcosms, that they were part of larger societies, and that peasantries were in their "final phase" (Franklin 1969). Yet there was a sense in which these communities still remained partly autonomous; they constituted distinctive social worlds, with forms of hierarchy and legitimation differing from those found in the "modern" urban sector. Half a century later, in most parts of Europe, the proportion of the population living in the countryside has declined. Few anthropologists spend a full year living in a face-to-face village community, as they once did. However, in Europe and world-wide, significant numbers of people do still reside in rural areas, most of them producing agricultural goods for their own subsistence as well as for the market. Large sections of urban populations continue to maintain rural links. Quite a few of these urbanites contrive somehow to produce significant income flows, including some of the food they consume, through mobilizing rural household resources. The globalization of agribusiness has by no means eliminated older interdependencies between cash-cropping and subsistence-oriented production.

Some anthropologists have begun to revisit the concept of the peasant, for instance through investigations of "post-peasant populism" in Central Europe (Buzalka 2007) or by linking "post-peasant futures" to new theoretical agendas concerning identity and value on a global scale (Kearney 1996). Yet socio-cultural anthropologists, who previously gravitated instinctively to the pre-industrial countryside, seem increasingly content to leave these futures to be investigated by rural sociologists, human geographers, political economists, and other specialists. This shift is conspicuous in Europe. The discipline that has traditionally specialized in studying the exotic "Other" no longer finds the European countryside very interesting. After almost half a century of the Common Agricultural Policy and a decade after the major eastern expansion of the European Union, the rural sector has surely been comprehensively modernized across most of the European continent. Perhaps the waning interest of social anthropologists is conclusive evidence of the demise of European peasantry?[3]

The title of this chapter borrows from a classic study of Russian peasants by Teodor Shanin, who wrote in the tradition of Chayanov (Shanin 1972). The peasant "awkward class" posed a problem for

---

[3] Numerous important studies of rural Eastern Europe have been published since 1990—but Gerald Creed, David Kideckel, Martha Lampland, Carol Nagengast, Frances Pine, and Katherine Verdery all draw heavily on their earlier community studies carried out in the socialist era. With few exceptions, the newcomers tend to gravitate to other locations and to avoid this genre. As for the "native ethnographers," my impression is that they, too, have increasingly focused their attention elsewhere. A recent collection presenting "anthropological perspectives from home" does include some village studies, but these are outnumbered by contributions addressing multinational enterprises, the military, punk subculture, the gay-lesbian movement, and transnational migration (Kürti and Skalník 2009). It seems to me an incontrovertible fact that the countryside receives less attention than used to be the case [but see Gudeman and Hann 2015a, 2015b].

Marxist theories because, although dominated and exploited by rapacious elites, smallholders in Russia and elsewhere generally had secure rights (sometimes full legal ownership) over the land they tilled and ancillary means of production. The word peasant was already being called into question by the time I began research in 1970s Hungary. In the interdisciplinary "peasant studies" literature of the time, inspired by sociologists such as Shanin and Bogusław Gałęski (1972), neo-Marxists tended to prefer labels such as "petty commodity producer." In Hungary the old term *paraszt* had emphatic negative connotations in the post-collectivization years (Hann 1980a). Villagers themselves preferred to use official categories such as *kistermelő* (small producer).

To my surprise, when I went to Poland a few years later to launch a new research project, I found that the traditional Polish word for peasant, *chłop*, was still very much alive, albeit in tandem with a more official census category *rolnik*, which is generally translated into English as farmer (Hann 1985). The sociolinguistic differences between these two socialist states evidently had something to do with the fact that, unlike Hungary, Poland had not implemented mass collectivization. I found that family-farming, much of it still primarily oriented to meeting household subsistence needs, dominated the Polish countryside. I was also rather surprised to find that the peasants I lived with in the Beskid Hills had very little sympathy with the Solidarity movement, which erupted soon after I had begun my fieldwork. The alliance of intellectual "dissidents," blue-collar workers, and the Roman Catholic Church, about which I had read a great deal in the preparation of my project, did not impress my village interlocutors at all. To my surprise, even the Church was sometimes criticized, for anticlericalism ran deep; only the newly elevated Pope, formerly Archbishop Karol Wojtyła, was a genuinely unifying figure in this remote peasant community.

Clans and Moral Economy

Though some have noted both the salience of class ideology and the existence of an "awkward class" of peasants in Polish history (Conte and Giordano 1995), most anthropologists have hesitated to demarcate lines of class cleavage in the postsocialist present. Among the exceptions, Michał Buchowski (1997) had no qualms in identifying both an agricultural and a non-agricultural rural proletariat in his Polish case study.[4] But this was a highly distinctive setting due to the particular problems faced by former State Farm workers when these institutions were abolished. Other studies of more representative settlements, in which the rural household was the basic unit of production, indicated the emergence of a "rural business class" before the end of socialism (Smigielska 1995). Differentiation has undoubtedly increased in post-socialist years. However, a recent study suggests that no class boundary separates entrepreneurs taking full advantage of EU subsidies from their "hobby gardener" neighbors (Pilichowska 2008).

Social inequality was a central theme of Tatjana Thelen's study in Hungary (2003a, 2003b). She found that the descendants of the former *kuláks*, those stigmatized as rich farmers under socialism, were successful in regaining their land; but she emphasizes elements of patriarchy, i.e. male control of female labor in the family, rather than the reappearance of class cleavages in the community. Other anthropologists have explained the new inequalities in rural Hungary not in terms of measurable differences in the ownership of land and productive capital, but rather in terms of political factors and social capital. Thus Martha Lampland argued, adapting concepts from Pierre Bourdieu, that the informal networks and expertise of the "green barons" of the socialist era helped them to emerge as winners of the Hungarian transformation (Lampland 2002; [cf. Swain 2013]).

Giordano and Kostova (2002) showed how the persons known as *arendatori* were able to profit from land redistribution in the Dobrudzha region of Bulgaria. The new individual owners of land were in no position to start autonomous farming operations. This enabled rural entrepreneurs (many of them formerly loyal socialist apparatchiks) and urban speculators to take advantage of the collapse of the older economic structures and the precarious legitimacy of the new state and its legal institutions to pursue their private agendas. Postsocialist cronyism is not fundamentally new: the gap between legality and legitimacy was wide under socialism, but local mistrust of the state in this region dates back much further, to the Ottoman era.

4 See also his more recent work on the middle class, Buchowski 2008.

A tendency to identify "clans" rather than class differences has been widely documented, irrespective of whether or not the land has been fully privatized and whether it is now farmed by households rather than a large enterprise. As Alexander Nikulin has pointed out for the Russian case, villagers are often reluctant to talk about such delicate matters. Their new dependencies will be concealed from visiting social scientists, just as the moneylending activities of the original Russian *kulaki* were likely to be concealed from the *zemstvo* researchers. Even if anonymity is guaranteed by today's researchers, villagers may worry that in a situation in which "the family clan of the chief farm engineer controls the machinery and spare parts, the clan of the chief zootechnician controls fodder, etc.," to divulge details about how the local rural economy really works might jeopardize their already precarious existences. Yet according to Nikulin, "the reason for this was not only the sense of fear, but also the sense of morality. Humanly, it is hard to speak about it. As one of the respondents asked in a fit of temper, summing up the informal characteristics of his family household: 'But why does our state create such conditions, which force us to steal?!'" (Nikulin 2011, 214–15).

If the "social production of mistrust" (Giordano and Kostova 2002) is one key concept for grasping postsocialist rural transformation, E. P. Thompson's notion of the moral economy was a more attractive pendant. Both themes figured prominently in our teamwork on decollectivization at the Max Planck Institute for Social Anthropology in Halle between 2000 and 2005 (Hann et al. 2003, Hann 2005b). We documented some of the enormous variation across the former Soviet bloc in terms of political economy and the legal changes of the 1990s. In most of the former Soviet Union distribution followed an egalitarian principle. There was great variation in the institutional context: only rural eastern Germany was incorporated at once into the mechanisms of the European Union, though other countries have followed since. Patterns have also varied within countries according to regional endowments and crop-specific production factors. Some branches are more vulnerable than others to global market trends.

Our projects sought also to probe the softer variables of the moral economy. We were concerned with how perceptions and attitudes of the kind described above interacted with the variables of the political economy in shaping reform outcomes. For example, Gambold Miller and Heady (2003) confirmed that, in the Russian case, deeply held values and emotions of envy inhibited the emergence of independent *fermery*. This moral economy took different forms. In many parts of Eastern Europe there was a deeply held moral conviction that collective institutions were parasitic on peasant households, and that all land should be returned to the families which had owned it in the past.[5] This had consequences for the political economy. In the Romanian case, for example, it meant that the postsocialist state could transfer two major "liabilities," namely land and social welfare, to small-scale producers who were hardly in a position to bear this burden (Verdery 2003). Verdery offers an extensive discussion of social capital. In her account, class formation is assumed, but postponed indefinitely into the future. In Bulgaria, Cellarius found that private ownership was the dominant moral principle concerning agricultural land, yet there was also strong local support for the cooperative management of forests (Cellarius 2003). In the case of Azerbaijan, Yalçın-Heckmann (2010) reported that the dismantled socialist institutions were not the focus of any collective moral nostalgia. To succeed in farming it was important to be able to mobilize the extended family, and there was a strong aversion to the use of wage-labor within the community; many preferred to seek the cash they needed to meet moral obligations (such as generous gifting at weddings) through labor migration.

In a particularly strong version of the moral economy argument, political scientist Olivier Roy argued that the persistence of the *kolkhoz* in Central Asia could be understood as the survival of a neo-tribal solidarity group. He went so far as to argue that this institution had been transformed from its Soviet functions to become an embryonic form of a new civil society (1999). Like the arguments about an embryonic class structure, Roy's civil society optimism needs ethnographic testing.

---

5 [This was the dominant opinion in Tázlár, a fact I have noted elsewhere in arguing against popular usage of "moral economy" that confines it to anti-capitalist, or at any rate anti-market sentiment. See Hann 2010b. In more recent work in the village, however, I have found a certain nostalgia for the compromises of the socialist era, shared by individuals of differing class background and contrasting biographies during and after socialism. On the basis of these accounts, I have characterized the postsocialist condition as being one of "moral dispossession" (see Hann 2011; 2015c).]

Tommaso Trevisani's case study, based on fieldwork in 2003–4 in the cotton-producing district of Khorezm, Uzbekistan, emphasizes long-term socio-cultural continuities (Trevisani 2010). Soviet sources for this region stressed intra-household exploitation rather than class differences. The latter were evidently not acknowledged locally, although rural society was certainly highly unequal. The Uzbek case exemplifies a gradualist path of agrarian transformation. A system of *pudrat* (family sharecropping) was initiated in the 1980s and it persisted after the formal conversion of collectives into a new form of association (*shirkat*) in the 1990s. Cotton procurement continued de facto, and the former collective farm chairman and brigadier retained much of their power. Trevisani also traces the emergence of a laboring class (*yollanma ishchilar*), villagers who are compelled to work for the new private farmers. However, unlike their Russian counterparts, the latter have not become private owners of the land they farm. They are highly dependent on the whims of officials, especially their district governor, who has replaced the collective farm chairman as the key patron or "boss" (*yoshulli*). The allocation of land for private farming was shaped more by political criteria than by economic factors. Trevisani documented a case in which a former *kolkhoz* chairman, the descendant of an elite family of the pre-socialist era, succeeded in securing the best land for himself thanks to his links to the governor.

The new private farmers are extremely vulnerable. They face a dilemma between growing cotton according to their officially approved "business plan," which has the advantage of security (at least concerning input supplies), and growing rice, which is more profitable but politically risky, since land can no longer be "hidden" as it was under the lax regimes of the *kolkhoz* and the *shirkat*. Much of the labor force for the new enterprises is recruited from the extended family, though non-kin workers are also mobilized. Trevisani diagnoses significant "repatriarchalization" (cf. Thelen 2003b), but his analysis concentrates on the new class relations. Distinctions can also be drawn *within* the ranks of the private farmers: *katta* farmers are an elite who are able to use their state connections ("bureaucratic capital") to manipulate political factors to their advantage; some have urban "sponsors"; some continue to hold a job in the state sector, not so much for the salary, which is nominal, but in order to maintain their networks. In another telling example, Trevisani shows how the fortunes of a rural entrepreneur improve after he deploys his legal qualifications by, in effect, working for the governor as a spy.

Within the new laboring class, few question privatization per se. There is resentment over corrupt procedures, but Trevisani characterizes the weapons of the weak as "fairly blunt." A colleague working in the same region undertook a more detailed investigation of both laborers and private farmers in this regard. He concluded that their "non-compliance" is generally better understood as an individualist rational choice strategy, which ultimately "serves to cement the position of the state plan" and the entire oppressive status quo (Wall 2007, 237). Yet Trevisani makes it clear that the old collective institutions have not vanished completely: all private farmers are still subject to residual *corvée* obligations to support local public institutions. The corrupt patronage of the new powerholders is still modified by some observance of the norms of an older moral economy. This is particularly clear in the continued priority given to household plot (*tomorqa*) allocations, which enable even the weakest households to produce most of what they need for their subsistence.

This case-study illustrates both the changes and continuities of recent rural transformation. Uzbekistan is a good example of a country where "transition" was never properly launched. In the current phase of "post-transformation" it would presumably qualify as *dekonsolidiert* in the terminology of political scientist Everhard Holtmann (2009), since, as in the case of Belarus, the path of democratization has effectively been reversed. Trevisani, however, emphasizes the successful consolidation of state power in recent years. He depicts the Soviet *kolkhoz* as a "straightforward system of patronage" in which the persistence of a "traditionalist ethos" enabled a significant rise in living standards in the later decades of socialism (partly on the basis of falsified statistics of cotton production, though for Trevisani this activity does not qualify as resistance). By contrast, the current system is better seen as an "open" market of political protection. The new private farmers can be characterized in terms of Weber's ideal-type of the "political entrepreneur." Group relations have become more transparently conflictual, and the constraints on cotton producers, nowadays nominally free producers for the market economy, are in some ways even greater than they were under socialist collective planning. The clientelism that served in the late socialist era to justify local and regional elites vis-à-vis

Moscow has now become a more cutthroat individualist activity. The new elites lack legitimacy, in part perhaps because the surplus (rent) that can be extracted from this overpopulated and degraded environment has been substantially reduced. Yet overt contestation of the new class and gender relations remains muted. The state seems able to instrumentalize elements of the old moral economy in support of these hierarchies. Contrary to the optimistic prognosis of Olivier Roy (1999), there is no sign of a civil society in any liberal, plural sense.

From Peasants to Farmers: Questioning Modernization and Neoliberalism

As Trevisani has shown for Central Asia and Giordano and Kosteva for the Balkans, to grasp recent changes in the postsocialist countryside it is often instructive to attend to long-term historical developments. In Central and Eastern Europe this means first and foremost considering the uneven impact of industrialization. Western social theory has emphasized the impact of new factories and the stark contrast between the owners of capital and those who own nothing but their labor power. The relationship between factory owners and their workers clearly differs from the archetypal relationship of a feudal estate. Even in Eastern Europe, serfdom was abolished in the course of the nineteenth century. Rural districts were still characterized by considerable inequalities, but the great estates of the past were generally on the wane by the beginning of the twentieth century. The rural population of Europe, not only dispossessed "rural proletarians" but also the children of smallholders unable to establish viable economic units of their own, left the countryside to seek work in the new factories. Millions migrated overseas, because opportunities were lacking at home. In some countries (notably some parts of Britain), an unambiguously proletarian class emerged within the countryside, but this was the exception. More common was the situation in which the village household retained at least some access to the means of production. Some were able to increase their capital stock (tractors, combine harvesters etc.). They also expanded their acreage at the expense of the less successful, whose members eventually departed for the towns. The overall picture in Western Europe is one of *gradual* urbanization accompanying industrialization. The size of the agricultural population falls in line with the declining contribution of this sector to national income. Eventually, the rural population stabilizes. It may even increase in certain favorably located areas, when urban elites start to relocate to villages to enjoy a higher quality of life as daily commuters; in some especially attractive rural areas there is the phenomenon of the dacha and the second home.

What makes these rural transformations problematic ("awkward") for social theorists is the continued significance in many countries of the family as the key unit of production as well as consumption (see Chayanov 1986). Instead of exploiting the labor of dispossessed neighbors, the farmers of Western Europe expanded their capital equipment while continuing to rely on the labor of family and close kin, as in the traditional, subsistence-oriented peasant household. Moreover, countering the harsh Marxist language of exploitation we have also to recognize the persistence of traditional values and national heritage. The countryside has always been a fertile source for the pastoral mythologizing of community (Creed 2006). It is occasionally suggested that Western farmers are not really concerned to maximize their profits. Rather, as stewards of family-owned land, in these discourses they selflessly devote themselves to taking care of the environment and making it available as a consumption good for stressed urbanites.

An equivalent general sketch of the socialist path to industrial modernity necessarily diverges from such Western European stereotypes. The exodus from the over-populated countryside to the new industrial factories took place more abruptly in Eastern Europe due to collectivization, which was a much more comprehensive and dramatic intervention than any burst of enclosure in the West. In contrast to capitalist modernization, the socialist variant aspired to replicate industrial divisions of labor within the countryside. Especially in the form known as the State Farm (Russian: *sovkhoz*; in Poland the PGR), but also in the more widespread collective or cooperative farm (*kolkhoz*; *spółdzielnia rolnicza*), complex new hierarchies were imposed. It generally took some time before the members of agricultural cooperatives came to enjoy wages and pensions comparable to those of urban factory workers. In the interim, they were remunerated according to "work points," supplemented by the allocation of a "household plot" for subsistence gardening.

Compared with the more gradual nature of most capitalist development, the break-neck pace of socialist industrialization did not allow for the urban housing stock and associated infrastructure to keep pace with the expansion of the factories. The resulting "underurbanization" (Szelenyi 1983) meant that many of the new factory workers had little choice but to leave their families at home in villages. Both long-distance commuters and the "worker-peasants" who travelled to the factory on a daily basis continued to regard the village as their real home and to participate in agricultural work on a part-time basis. Rural-urban links persisted in Western Europe as well. But they lasted longer and had more important consequences in socialist countries, partly because of the structural problems of underurbanization, and partly thanks to the opportunities offered by socialist rural institutions, to which I turn below.

Neither the capitalist nor the socialist path quite fits the ideal type according to which urban industrialization is characterized by the dispossession of smallholder producers in the countryside, a severance of rural-urban links and the dominance of wage-labor in both sectors. The distinctive, recalcitrant features of the countryside have not been eradicated in the decades of neoliberalism. Recent years have brought massive changes in the technologies and social relations of food production, as in all other sectors of the economy. All over the world, more and more peasants have been dispossessed through what has come to be known as "landgrabbing"; the power of multinational agribusiness is greater than it has ever been. Yet, smallholders still remain a force to be reckoned with. China, the world's most populous state, has implemented radical market-oriented reforms, leading hundreds of millions to seek better lives through work in the cities; but most of these migrants still have rights over land in their natal communities—they have *not* been dispossessed. In Europe, cut-throat competition characterizes all markets including those for agricultural products. However, to a greater extent than in any other sector, market outcomes are mitigated by state policies, above all by the policies of the European Union. Capitalized family-farmers leave their fields fallow and their machines idle when it is in their interest to do so, due to the payment of EU subsidies. They keep their hedges neat and preserve the "cultural landscape" not because of an altruistic concern with the aesthetic tastes of urban tourists, but because these activities, too, are subsidized by Brussels. In short, the world which the rural populations of postsocialist Central Europe joined when admitted to the EU in 2004–2007 is, despite the prevailing ideology of neoliberalism, to a considerable degree a non-market world. Before looking more closely at recent adaptations in Hungary and Poland, let me briefly review the historical background of socialist modernization processes.

Collective Farms Which Worked and Peasant Farms Which Did Not

Comparisons between Hungary and Poland have fascinated many scholars. The two historic Christian kingdoms of Central Europe have followed very different paths in recent centuries. Whereas the Polish state disappeared with the partitions of the late eighteenth century, Hungary rose to share imperial grandeur with Austria in the last half-century of the Habsburg Empire. The rebirth of the Polish state coincided with a national humiliation for Hungary, which lost most of its territory at the Treaty of Trianon (1920). In terms of their social structures, during the inter-war decades both states remained predominantly rural in character, with resilient aristocratic and gentry elites more prominent than representatives of the new industrial capitalism. The peasantry, comprising well over half the population, was commonly perceived as the most urgent socio-political issue. Attempts to ameliorate poverty through distributive land reform in the 1920s had little impact here or anywhere else in Eastern Europe. Following the Second World War, the peasants were still the most numerous social class, socially immobile and barely integrated into the entitlements of citizenship. Further measures of egalitarian land reform were again largely unsuccessful, because few newly established smallholders had the human or capital resources to manage viable family farms. The peasant parties were the strongest political forces in the last democratic elections, but they were eventually eliminated by communist parties that had a clear agenda to industrialize and to collectivize agriculture as rapidly as possible.

As a result of socialist policies the proportion of the rural population, and more precisely that of the agricultural labor force, began to decline from previous levels, though it fell more slowly than might have been expected on the basis of Western precedents. After four decades of the People's Republics, agriculture's contribution to GDP was still relatively high in both Hungary and Poland: around 8%. However, statistical similarities concealed quite different paths of socialist modernization in the two states. The divergence began in 1956, a year of political crisis in both Hungary and Poland. Whereas the former recovered to complete mass collectivization in the years 1959–1961, the Polish socialist authorities were never strong enough to implement such drastic measures. In contrast to Hungary, the *rolnictwo* sector remained dominated by smallholders, who owned the plots which they farmed; but published statistics of ownership and production were not a reliable guide to what was really going on in the two countries.

The distinctive features of the household sector in the Hungarian village of Tázlár have been outlined earlier in this volume (Chapters Two and Three). This version of "market socialism," productively combining familial enterprise with socialist institutions, allowed considerable continuity with the old peasant economy. At the same time it enabled a great improvement in rural living standards, most visible in the modernization of the housing stock. Here, too, there was a symbiosis between public and private: the local state initiated electrification, piped water and general infrastructural improvements, while residents themselves took responsibility for improving their accommodation, e.g. through relocating to the village center and installing modern bathrooms and kitchens. Some built separate houses for their children. The historic "civilizational" gap between countryside and town narrowed, especially when the members of agricultural cooperatives began to receive pensions comparable to those paid to industrial workers. Some urban residents were envious of the opportunities for accumulation that were available in small-scale farming; they too engaged in small-scale farming in their spare time, either in "auxiliary plots" close to the city or in their natal village, if this was not too far away. It has been estimated that household-based production was responsible for up to half of Hungary's total agricultural output in the last decades of socialism (see Swain 1985). These products were highly competitive on international markets and brought in significant amounts of hard currency. During this period, about 60% of all Hungarian households were involved in some form of farming; about one third of these restricted their work to self-provisioning, while the remaining two thirds, i.e. 40% of all Hungarian households, produced agricultural commodities for sale on the market (Harcsa and Kovách 1996). Agriculture's share in GDP and the size of the rural population both declined, as was to be expected in the course of industrialization. However, the declines were very gradual because so many industrial workers still lived in the countryside and engaged in agricultural activities, for subsistence but also for the market.

After my doctoral project in Hungary, I chose to work in Poland because the northern neighbor presented so many striking contrasts (Hann 1980b). Following the failure to collectivize, socialist policies to privilege heavy industry and inhibit private enterprise in all sectors brought stagnation to the countryside. Limited measures to encourage "agricultural circles" and later (under Edward Gierek in the 1970s) to modernize the agrarian structure by promoting "specialist" farmers did little to improve productivity or even to ensure adequate supplies of food to an expanding urban population. Because of underurbanization, worker-peasants were just as conspicuous as in Hungary (Kolankiewicz 1980); but unlike Hungary, there were few spinoffs in terms of agricultural commodities. The ensuing market shortages, in comparison to the abundant provisions available in Hungary, played a major role in successive political explosions in Poland, hastening the eventual collapse of the socialist political economy. Socialist ideology inhibited private investment in production, but it was more tolerant in the sphere of consumption: millions of peasants therefore invested what cash they earned (or in fortunate cases the remittances they received from the USA) in new housing. Far from being dispossessed, they made long-term investments in their village homes, endowing their children by adding another story or erecting a new dwelling, since the housing market in the city was effectively closed to them. This bore a superficial resemblance to the accumulation strategies of their Hungarian counterparts, but the circumstances were very different, since in Poland there were few synergies with the local state.

The bleak scenario for Polish consumers and economic planners was in some ways a marvelous opportunity for the foreign anthropologist, who was presented with a laboratory for investigating peasant traditions that stretched back to the era of the partitions. Serendipity led me to the Lower Beskids (adjacent to the fuzzy boundary with Bieszczady), to a community called Wisłok Wielki, close to the Slo-

Figure 7. Threshing wheat in Wisłok Wielki (photo by Chris Hann, 1981)

vakian border. This settlement had an ethnic and religious history that diverged greatly from the mainstream. It was also untypical in that its remoteness rendered daily commuting to industrial jobs difficult (although some residents in the 1970s did travel to work at the socialist sawmills in Rzepedź, only ten miles away; in previous decades they had migrated as far as Silesia to work in the mines). Despite these specificities, I argued that the ways in which the Polish colonists of this section of the Carpathians had recreated peasant economy since the 1950s bore faithful witness to the general contradictions of socialist rural political economy in Poland (Hann 1985). In some respects, including the integrating role played by the Roman Catholic parish, the world documented by Thomas and Znaniecki (1918–19), had not been fundamentally disturbed. As elsewhere in Poland (especially in the more remote areas of the east), the majority of farms were small and poorly capitalized. Wisłok Wielki had a State Farm and a large state forestry, but there was no fruitful symbiosis of the kind that had evolved in Hungarian socialism. The inhabitants were hardly integrated into the national society. Both geographical mobility (in terms of rural-urban migration) and social mobility (e.g. via access to higher education) were significantly lower compared to the Hungarian countryside. However, even in this remote settlement a few villagers were constructing large modern houses, in some cases even before they had acquired a tractor. The proportion of the population living in the countryside and engaging in agriculture was even higher than in Hungary and among the highest in Europe, but productivity was low. Polish households had retained stronger property rights, at least superficially. They owned slightly more productive capital (tractors, etc.) than their Hungarian counterparts. I nonetheless concluded that Hungary had embarked on a rather successful socialist modernization of its quasi-feudal social structure, whereas in Poland, in the absence of a strong socialist sector, the ensuing stagnation of agriculture was disastrous for all concerned—except for the visiting anthropologist, curious about the persistence of "tradition."

After Socialism: Agribusiness and Marginalization

The last two decades have brought great changes to both Hungary and Poland. There has been a certain convergence after the very different policies pursued under socialism, but it is also possible to detect new differences. In Poland, neoliberalism in the form of "shock therapy" had less initial impact on the countryside than it had on the industrial sector (with the exception of the terrain farmed by cooperatives and State Farms). The Hungarian success story in agriculture came to a sudden end with the loss of important markets in other countries of the ex-Soviet bloc, and above all with the measures to decollectivize land and break up collective farms. The flexible forms of cooperation in the region of my fieldwork experienced the same fate as other regions (see Chapter Three). A small minority benefited, in particular former officials of the collective farms who were well placed to acquire land as private property and build up farms that would be viable in new conditions (Swain 2013). The majority of households which managed to produce agricultural commodities in the framework of socialist policies lacked the capital to develop in this way. Sharp processes of differentiation ensued in which "farms with peasant characteristics" (*paraszti jellegű gazdaságok*) dominated (Harcsa and Kovách 1996, 120). Similar processes took place in Poland. In terms of class formation, the consequences were most transparent where cooperatives and State Farms were privatized (Buchowski 2009). In both countries, the strengthening of an embryonic elite capable of practicing capitalist agribusiness and competing on Western markets was accompanied by the emergence of a much larger group of persons and households who felt themselves marginalized in the new divisions of labor and in effect pushed (back) into the condition of the peasant. Institutional transformations and changes in the statistical classifications, including recognition for the first time of the rural unemployed, make comparisons with the socialist era difficult. But it is clear that in both countries the numbers of persons working in agriculture declined, and that agriculture's contribution to the national economy fell sharply.[6]

The decline in the agricultural labor force and in the contribution of agriculture to GDP did not necessarily mean a decline in rural population. The chaos of the postsocialist decades has induced significant migration from town to countryside, reversing the familiar trend of modernization under both capitalism and socialism. In Poland, the share of the rural population continued to rise after its entry into the EU. However, the national figure of almost 39% disguises considerable regional variation. In the southeast the proportion is almost 60%, whereas in Silesia it barely exceeds 20%. Within each province, significant migration has taken place to periurban villages that provide commuting access to major cities. Although tourism compensates in certain locations, in general the more remote settlements have continued to stagnate.

Maria Halamska, after drawing attention to these trends, analyses "the development of a new model of agriculture" in Poland (2011, 43–47). On the one hand, the number of truly tiny farms is decreasing.

[6] According to Maria Halamska (2011), the share of agriculture in Poland's GNP fell from 7.2% in 1992 to 3.1% in 2002, before stabilizing at around 4% after Poland joined the European Union (2004). In Hungary the share has fallen steadily to reach a record low of 3.1% in 2012. Measuring "deagrarianization" is complicated. In Poland it is still the case that almost one third of the working population contributes something to farm production, while 7.2% "glean the majority of their income from current work in agriculture" (Halamska 2011, 40). These figures are considerably higher than EU averages and can be attributed to Poland's conspicuous failure to modernize agriculture in the socialist decades. As for Hungary, official figures indicate a decline in the agricultural labor force from 15.5% of the total in 1990 to just 5.5% in 2001 (Központi Statisztikai Hivatal 2005). However, these figures do not include those whose main occupation is outside agriculture or who are unemployed, but who still undertake some agricultural work "part time."

EU subsidies have improved the situation of full-time family farmers, some of whom began to invest in their farms when designated as "specialists" by socialist officials in the 1970s. The overall trajectory of those in this group resembles that of the capitalized farmers of other European countries. On the other hand, Poland continues to have a much larger number of subsistence-oriented, "quasi-peasant" farms than any other country in Europe. More than 40% of farming households "produce only for the farmers' own needs" (Halamska 2011, 45). They are able to detach themselves from the market in this way because one or more members of the household enjoy earnings outside agriculture. In the postsocialist decades, older patterns of the worker-peasant or *pluriactivité* have taken new forms. In addition to allowing access to Brussels farming subsidies, EU membership also opened up Western European labor markets to migrants from Central Europe. The response has been staggering. Relationships between these migrants and their families at home are not so different from those analyzed by Thomas and Znaniecki a century ago.[7] The remittances they send enable relatives at home to keep going outside the market. According to a pure market logic, they might be expected to sell up and move out, thus permitting a smaller rural population and a more rational pattern of mechanized farming. But the opening of transnational labor markets enables households to avoid this step and thereby to hold on to a measure of continuity with the self-sufficient peasant economy of old.

A similar dualism seems to be developing in at least some regions of Hungary. However, due to the rationalization which took place in the collectivized decades and the way in which decollectivization was implemented, the lingering "peasant" sector is nowadays smaller in

---

[7] As in the past, migrants distort the census figures. It is likely that a part or even the entirety of the increase in the rural population would disappear with a closer focus on actual residence. Even if they register for some purposes in their migration settings, many do not deregister in their natal villages.

I have not returned to Wisłok Wielki since a brief visit in 2005, when the main change I noticed was the establishment of a new Roman Catholic parish with a resident priest. I was told that production and the agrarian structure had not changed significantly in recent years, and that embryonic touristic development had not compensated for the loss of jobs at the socialist sawmill in Rzepedź.

Hungary. Traditional peasant ideals of self-sufficiency at the level of the household were undermined by the symbiosis with socialist cooperatives, which resulted in an extraordinary increase in the proportion of final agricultural output that was formally attributed to small-scale producers (households). Since the demise of that socialist synthesis, many Hungarian villagers have simply given up small-scale agriculture altogether. The long-term decline in the size of the rural population was reversed in the 1990s, as in Poland, but in contrast to Poland the decline has resumed in the last decade. The present figure is just over 30%. Village residents are demoralized but, as in Poland, given the investments they made in their homes in the socialist era, they have no incentive to move to towns. Many own non-viable smallholdings, which if they are lucky they can rent out to a new private farmer. Some even cease subsistence production on their remaining garden plots. As Bea Vidacs has shown (2015), many villagers have given up the traditional ritual of pig-sticking, because it is cheaper to buy meat at the local branch of a German-owned supermarket (*Lidl* or *Penny Markt*). One might say that Hungarian villagers have entered a new stage of modernity, compared to the decades of late socialism, because they expend less energy on dirty, demanding, labor-intensive tasks and have more free time to watch television, or to participate in an expanding range of activities at the Culture House. However, many feel nostalgia for the socialist decades, in which they worked incredibly hard, but enjoyed the fruits of this labor (in terms of consumer goods, above all housing) in ways not open to them today.

On the basis of these brief illustrations we can see that the Central European countryside is certainly not immune to the wider forces of globalization and neoliberalism: supermarket penetration as well as new migration options and EU subsidies to farmers have all had an impact, in Poland as well as in Hungary. The details continue to vary as a consequence of different histories. I argue that the history of the socialist decades was decisive in shaping present patterns in both countries. The reactionary political currents that are particularly virulent in rural Hungary today are surely related to the sudden decline of the rural-agricultural sector after 1990 (see Chapter Eleven). In this respect, as in many others, the Polish rural sector shows greater continuity. Both relative and absolute poverty indicators for the rural sector remain roughly twice as high as urban levels.[8] This country remains a *locus classicus* for the study of that vast group classified by Teodor Shanin as the "awkward class," because its peasants have never been easy to accommodate in the standard classifications of modern social theory. It might be argued that the Polish peasantry has lost much of its historical distinctiveness, and that other social classes have become equally "awkward" as they improvise pluralist strategies of survival in postsocialist variants of neoliberalism, irrespective of whether they live in towns or in the countryside. But the possibilities to accomplish social reproduction via "self-sufficiency" remain very different in the countryside (see Gudeman and Hann 2015b).

Whereas in Hungary the era of neoliberalism has brought a sharp decline in the position of farmers and the standard of living of the rural population vis-à-vis urbanites, in Poland it can be argued that neoliberalism has helped the rural sector as a whole to overcome at least some of the consequences of the backwardness and isolation that persisted under socialism. This is evident in improved pension provisions for farmers, and in the narrowing of the gap between rural and urban fertility rates. At the same time, the present transnational constellations continue to facilitate the persistence of large numbers of households, especially in "Poland B," i.e. the less developed eastern provinces, which operate according to the rhythms of the peasant economy of old rather than the agribusinesses of the twenty-first century. Compared to most Western states, the rural population is large in both Poland and Hungary—much larger than warranted, a hypothetical agrarian economist might say, for an efficient agricultural sector. One conspicuous result of the socialist era, when households in both countries found it easier to invest in consumption than in productive machines, is a large stock of improved housing in the countryside, often scattered outside village centers. This provides millions, including transnational migrants, with an anchor or refuge from the constraints of neoliberal capitalism. The Polish post-peasants who remain, as Maria Halamska puts it, "outside the market" in their villages

[8] See Halamska (2011, 51). I have not been able to trace a comparable figure for Hungary, but I suspect it would be similar.

do not form a cohesive class, but they are a major long-term hindrance to the emergence of a more efficient agrarian structure, as they were under socialism.[9]

Social Class, Work, and Workfare in Tázlár

Stratification patterns in Tázlár were touched upon in Chapters Two and Three. Prior to the socialist era, land was the prime determinant of social class. The transfer of labor was a means to reproduce this hierarchy. Prosperous households in need of labor to farm their larger acreages hired day laborers (*napszámos*) at peak periods. The institution of farm servants (*cseléd*) was at least equally important. Poorer households formed links with the wealthy via their children, who were typically allowed to visit their native families every second Sunday and remunerated in kind rather than in cash. These arrangements often persisted over generations. Poverty was endemic but it was especially severe during the Great Depression. In 1932 the local government provided aid to 331 village residents who would otherwise have faced starvation. The able-bodied were obliged to perform public work (*közmunka*) in return for the wheat they received (Szabadi 1997, 109).

Such public works programs were superfluous in the socialist decades. The institution of the *cseléd* disappeared in the course of the 1950s. The practice of day-laboring faded even earlier as the last major landowners were expropriated in the post-war land reform. Most left the village; wealthy farmers who remained were pilloried as *kulák*, the class enemy, in the repressive climate of the 1950s. Power holders targeted everyone who met the criteria laid down nationally. One well-known case in Tázlár was that of Pali, born in 1929 into a family of poor peasants but adopted at the age of seventeen by an unrelated, more prosperous family which lived on a neighboring farm and lacked a male heir. Pali's rural-proletarian background did not prevent his being classified as "*kulák*

[9] In retrospect, it seems to me that villagers in Wisłok Wielki were quite right to be cynical about the Solidarity movement in 1980–81. Although articulate working class and intelligentsia leaders claimed to be speaking for the entire nation, rural constituencies lost out; this is reflected in the recent success of populist parties [see Malewska-Szałgin 2017].

progeny" in 1950 and sent off to the army for 27 months of forced labor. Back in the village, he again ran into trouble with the authorities in 1956 for allegedly damaging a statue of Lenin. He was imprisoned for four weeks before the charges were dropped for lack of evidence. Eventually he was allowed to resume work on a family farm now reduced in size to ten acres (Pavlovits 1990, 41–42). Following collectivization in 1961, to his surprise, Pali was proposed as chairman of one of the three new cooperative groups. He served until 1971 in this capacity, and even after the cooperatives fused in 1974 to form the Peace Agricultural Cooperative, he was a prominent member of the leadership committee. His responsibilities had a deleterious effect on his own farming activities, for his wife and two sons struggled to compensate for his frequent absences.

From the middle of the century onwards, poor peasants flocked to industrial workplaces. As noted in Chapter Three, many commuted to their new jobs while continuing to reside in the countryside and engage in farming on a part-time basis. The old ideal of the family labor farm was rapidly supplanted by a system in which at least one member of the household engaged in wage labor. Even these workers contributed significantly to production based on the "household plot." The cooperatives were charged with facilitating small-scale production, regardless of household composition. Not everyone approved of the new institution, especially its collective sector. In the words of the village chronicler, "There was never any concrete link between the results of the cooperative and the incomes of individual members. . . . Members remained convinced that the performance of the socialist sector was bureaucratic and ineffective. The leadership could not make working for the cooperative attractive to its members" (Szabadi 1997, 140–41). Many, including Pali, the chairman, continued to plough small plots with a horse in the traditional way. Despite their suspicion of socialist institutionalized cooperation, villagers continued to cooperate according to their own norms, free of bureaucratic interference. Work groups were common at harvesting. New forms of working together developed to facilitate the labor process, e.g. when Pali joined forces with an unrelated household in the village center to share the costs of maintaining the single horse that sufficed to meet their farming needs. Voluntary cooperation was most conspicuous in house-building, which peaked during the 1960s–1970s. These were primarily joyous occasions blending productive labor with eating and drinking. Wedding celebrations also required extensive cooperation. The sums raised in this way constituted a communal endowment for the new couple. These weddings were a graphic demonstration of material prosperity and of the value attached to the post-peasant way of life (Hann 2014a; Sárkány 1983).

Wage-workers made redundant for poor performance, or even for the theft of socialist property, generally had little trouble in finding another job which would bring more or less the same remuneration, either in the factories of nearby towns or within the village. Lax labor discipline was related to what economist János Kornai (1980, 1992) called the "soft budget constraint" that lay at the heart of the inefficiency of socialism. White-collar positions proliferated for both men and women in the Peace cooperative's headquarters. Manual jobs as tractor-drivers or laborers were generally a male domain. Men and women worked in the brigades of the Kiskőrös State Farm, which built up large vineyards on the outskirts of the village. Women had other wage-labor jobs available to them for the first time, notably in ancillary units of urban factories and later in small-scale units operated by the cooperative itself. These jobs required little or no skill and seemed on the surface to be extremely monotonous. Yet they were appreciated not only for the income they brought and the pension rights which accrued, but also for their sociality. They were possible because, in line with the general socialist policy, a kindergarten was opened in the village in 1962. All children had their midday meal provided at the daycare center. Patriarchal traditions undoubtedly persisted and women continued to shoulder the greater burden of domestic tasks, including the raising of animals in the yard and tasks in the vegetable garden. Nonetheless, the socialist shift to wage-labor that emancipated male villagers from the dependencies of *cseléd* status was experienced as progress by women as well as men.

Within the cooperative a distinction emerged between members, generally those who took significant items of equipment and land into the collective sector when they joined, and the expanding workforce, most of whom were not members (*tag*) but employees (*alkalmazott*). The labor force of the State Farm was more unambiguously proletarian. These employees were more likely to stem from poorer families (the better-off encouraged their children to obtain qualifications and move away from the village). The distinction between the member and the employee had implications for social security entitlements but neither group could be considered "precarious" labor. Members were entitled to an "allowance" (*járadék*) if they handed over their plots to the cooperative when they became too old to work them. But it was also still possible to transfer property to one's children in the traditional way. There was also continuity in terms of values: the traditional emphasis on physical work in a labor process under one's own control continued to dominate (Fél and Hofer 1969; Lampland 1995).

The efflorescence of household economy that I witnessed during my first fieldwork in 1976–67 should not be idealized. Many villagers had punishing routines, e.g. getting up at dawn to commute to a factory job, returning in the early afternoon, and then working till late in the evening in their fields or around the farm. The work they carried out "for themselves" was not necessarily less alienating than that undertaken in the factory. I argued that a higher form of socialism was desirable in order to curtail the opportunities for such self-exploitation (Hann 1980a). My diagnosis was influenced by the fact that new social inequalities were emerging within this socialist symbiosis of public and private. Male and female villagers were again being recruited as day laborers to meet the needs of prosperous families, especially those who, encouraged and subsidized by the late-socialist state, had invested in vineyards and needed labor at peak periods. Payment was in cash, usually supplemented by generous hospitality throughout the day (food and also drink, including alcohol). This payment was not taxed or officially monitored in any way. Until late in the socialist era it was not legally possible for family farmers to employ workers, either permanently or temporarily. But the "market socialist" state turned a blind eye to these developments. In short, economic prosperity in this nominally collectivized community was increasingly characterized by stratification patterns and commodification of labor similar to trends in the capitalist West.

The main changes of the 1980s and 1990s have been outlined above (see Chapter Three). There was a rapid decline in employment opportunities in the village. The workshop which produced shoe uppers lasted until the end of the century before liquidation. The only ancillary unit which has continued to flourish in the new century is an enterprise which produces plastic bags. It was bought out by its managers and, after cutting back on staff, stayed in business by paying wages commonly reported to be significantly below the national minimum. In the absence of any alternatives, even these jobs are coveted. The local government has not been successful in attracting investment to the village. Men tend to be more mobile than women, e.g. as lorry drivers. One woman returned to the village after a spell in domestic employment in New York and was able to find work at the cooperative's shoe workshop while it was still operating. But she found this work dissatisfying and chose to return to the US after a short period, eventually marrying her much older employer and staying on permanently. Some villagers are critical and report that she is much missed by her four children, now young adults scattered around the country and abroad.

The motivations to migrate are clear. If wage-labor jobs can be found locally at all, the wages they pay are meagre. Unlike in the socialist era, when wages were similarly low, the labor discipline is now harsher. Owners (such as the proprietors of the plastics workshop) stress that their budgets cannot afford the flexibility of the socialist era, that no jobs are secure in this climate, and so there can be no opportunities for relaxed socializing at the workplace as in socialist days. In the socialist era, the factory jobs (the same logic applied to many white-collar workers) were complemented by the persistence of the family-labor farm, i.e. the production of agricultural goods both for auto-consumption and for sale. Here one could exercise more control over one's labor process and, while the work was sometimes grueling and smelly, the material rewards were considerable. This option is hardly available in the new century. Most households still make some use of their vegetable gardens (primarily women's work, as it always has been) but almost everyone agrees that, since the end of the socialist subsidies, the labor-intensive raising of animals no longer pays. Most families no longer bother to slaughter a pig. The housebuilding boom came to an end in the 1980s. According to some local estimates, up to one quarter of village houses nowadays stand empty and potentially available for purchase—but there are no buyers. In short, the workaholic village I knew in the 1970s has morphed into a village in which remaining residents of all age-groups spend a lot of their time sitting in front of the television. The range of goods potentially available in the monetized economy is greater than ever before, but village lifestyles are constrained by lack of cash. They get by through transfer payments from the state combined with some minimal gardening for subsistence.

Very few villagers have the resources to build up capitalized family farms. Those who have succeeded with vineyards or poultry have need of non-familial labor. If they employ others, full time or part-time, they are legally obliged to register this labor. In some cases (in Tázlár there are very few) long-term relationships have been established, apparently congenial to both employer and employed. A wealthy employer is able to provide a range of supplementary benefits, including housing. Long-term trusting relationships may make it easier to circumvent the rules of the state. For example, it used to happen quite often in the richer villages of the region that a worker was made redundant and replaced by a neighbor. The first man then drew unemployment benefit, before returning to his old employer when his neighbor replaced him at the job center. The deception lay in the fact that, in practice, both were expected to be at the beck and call of the employer, especially at peak periods (see Hann 2006; these rules were tightened after 2010).

Due to the demand for seasonal labor, the institution of the *napszámos* has persisted. In the 1990s and 2000s, this need was met mainly through a seasonal influx from Transylvania. Ethnic Hungarians, but also Romanians and Roma, could earn enough during the summer season in Hungary to keep them going in their native communities for the rest of the year. This was only feasible to the extent that the state continued to turn a blind eye to this illegal employment, as it had in the last decades of socialism. This only began to change under Viktor Orbán in the third decade of postsocialism. Under pressure from the EU, the Hungarian state is now obliged to control who is working where, and to sanction those farmers who hire labor illegally in order to avoid having to pay their social insurance contributions. This creates dilemmas, of course. The farmer with the largest vineyard acreage is working with his son and daughter to expand the estate and to develop new bottling and marketing capacities. He employs one full-time worker, skilled in operating all the sophisticated machinery, and pays the prescribed employer's contributions. But in spite of the machines, he still depends significantly upon seasonal labor to harvest his grapes (because not all vines are equally suited to mechanical harvesting). If he were to declare every last *napszámos* employed, his margins would be significantly cut. Those who work for him understand this and accept that the money they receive would have to be reduced if their employer were to pay the prescribed contributions. As foreign citizens, they do not consider it likely that they would draw any long-term benefit from completing all the paperwork which the state bureaucracy formally requires them to complete. The daily rate in 2014–15 was less than twenty euros for a ten hour day. The generous provisioning of food and drink which characterized such work parties in the past has been eliminated.

In addition to immigrants from Romania, some local families, too, are dependent on the *napszám* work as a source of income—as was the case before socialism, and again in the last socialist decades. Some of these families have long histories of alcohol abuse (cf. Cash 2015). Other villagers comment that extending the reach of the state to ensure that every day of labor is recorded, in order to comply with social insurance and pension regulations, does not serve the interests of this vulnerable section of the community. Rather than risk expanding their vineyards and increasing their dependency on such labor, it is said that entrepreneurs will not invest at all; or they will invest only in machine-harvestable vines; or they will hire only foreigners, who are unlikely to object if social insurance contributions are not paid.

As in the 1930s, the local government now organizes "workfare" (*közmunka*) in order to help local families in need. After tentative beginnings under the previous socialist government, these schemes were expanded nationwide after 2010 under the national-conservative government led by Viktor Orbán (Szőke 2012). During this period, swingeing cuts have been imposed on social expenditure, including unemployment benefits (Szikra 2014). However, far from imposing neoliberal principles, the government has explicitly celebrated its illiberal paths in every domain. It has intervened in the economy in drastic ways. Political leaders, notably the prime minister himself, have evoked traditional peasant values and laid heavy emphasis on the moral value of work. Whereas socialist ideology had emphasized the importance of productive labor in conditions of full employment, the message today is that workfare schemes can lead the unemployed back to employment on the regular labor market. Even while receiving *less* than national the minimal wage, participants receive *more* than basic welfare allowances. They are supposed to internalize the discipline of labor, setting a good example in their households, and contributing to a national revival. Critics allege that long-established public sector jobs are being axed and substituted by *közmunkások*; they point out that such schemes seldom in fact help individuals to find regular long-term jobs. By including such workers in the statistics of those gainfully employed, the government is accused of concealing its poor record in addressing the root causes of unemployment. On the other hand, researchers into rural workfare have documented a high degree of acceptance and even popularity at the local level, especially in small communities where state funding has dried up (Váradi 2016).

Although workfare schemes have been introduced in urban contexts as well, including the capital city, they have been particularly salient in the countryside.[10] The detailed implementation guidelines have changed frequently and there is considerable regional variation. Schemes typically run for a few months at a time. Activities are scaled back during the winter months, because most of the tasks are outdoor and seasonal. Many are directly connected with the land, including the maintenance of parks and sports fields. The numbers involved also vary. Villages with a large Roma population commonly have high numbers of participants (Szőke 2012). Although the scheme is nominally administered by the employment office of the district to which the village belongs, in practice the local mayor has the most important voice in determining who should be invited to participate, according to his own assessment of who is "deserving." Though it might be far-fetched to make comparisons with the "clans" found in other postsocialist countries such as those discussed above, these workfare schemes have undoubtedly placed significant resources in the hands of local leaders.

I spoke with the long-serving mayor and with the twelve participants in the Tázlár workfare program in 2013 and 2014. Men and women were equally represented. Their ages ranged from early 20s to late 50s, and they were certainly not subject to any blanket stigma in the community. The mayor stressed that he considered each individual case carefully on the basis of what he knew about the person and his or her household needs. If the worker did not turn up punctually and work in a disciplined manner, dismissal could follow; or, more likely, no new contract would follow when the present contract expired. All contracts are short-term. The men had a small stock of machines and were most visible in the central park and in maintaining pavements and verges throughout the village. The women spent a lot of their time in

[10] Jakab (2014) provides an account of how an intellectual unable to find employment appropriate to his qualifications was obliged to join a poorly organized workfare scheme in Budapest in order to qualify for basic social benefits.

vegetable production on the twelve hectares of community-owned plots just outside the village. The mayor relied heavily on a male "brigade leader" to ensure that tasks were carried out as agreed; he was dissatisfied with the performance of the female participants, who he thought spent too much time being convivial. In four years he was not aware of anyone who, on the basis of workfare experience in the village, had proceeded to regular employment.

In 2015 I was surprised to find that, within the framework of the "Start program," workfare in Tázlár had been significantly expanded from 12 to 34 participants. Two workfare beneficiaries were carrying out clerical work in the municipal office. As throughout the country, however, the main emphasis of the Start projects was on productive activities on community-owned plots. In Tázlár they had decided to specialize in the labor-intensive branch of courgette (*cukkini*) production. Roughly one third of their output is used by the daycare center, thus saving the costs of purchase. A further third is sold on the open market, thus generating a small but significant source of additional income for the community. Finally, one third (of inferior quality or at any rate appearance) is distributed among the workforce and consumed by their families or fed to their animals.

The new mayor (elected in 2014) lives quite close to the community plots. He and his wife, who is an elected councilor, supervise the labor themselves on a regular basis. Like his predecessor, the mayor stresses the need to maintain discipline. But he is also flexible enough to allow a good worker to take holiday time when he is needed for some other, more urgent task as a day laborer in the private sector (e.g. harvesting elderberries or grapes). It is possible to combine both jobs in the same day. In no sense can the program be considered punitive. As Monika Váradi (2016) argues, workfare has been embedded in the fabric of the community. It exemplifies the "human face" of government policy. At one point in the summer of 2015, when the courgettes needed to be harvested every day, the Tázlár mayor requested his workforce to put in an extra shift on Saturday or Sunday. Only 7 out of 34 turned up, despite the assurance that they would be generously compensated with days off in lieu once the peak period was over. The mayor was not pleased, but he was in no position to enforce sanctions. So far only one worker has ever been dismissed ("she only managed to peel five carrots in an entire morning—a hopeless case"). One par-

Figure 8. Berci at home on his farm with his favorite horse (photo by Chris Hann, 2104)

ticipant had recently left the program for a job in the private sector but was made redundant again shortly afterwards.

These villagers work to produce courgettes but they are not themselves substitutable "cucumbers," as Karl Polanyi once caricatured the capitalist labor market.[11] Each individual has his/her own history. Let me introduce Berci, the elder son of Pali, the cooperative chairman, whose biography I sketched above. Berci was born in 1961 and I have known him since he was a schoolboy in the 1970s. At this time his father still lived on his farm about a mile outside the center. Berci has lived there alone since 1999. A marriage in the 1980s was short-lived. He took over responsibility for the family farm when Pali became infirm and moved into the center with his wife; but unlike his father and younger brother, Berci was not content to become a full-time farmer. His trade as a tiler offered few opportunities locally and he changed jobs frequently before the end of the socialist era, alternating factory work in a nearby town with stints working for the cooperative as a shepherd and as an unskilled worker at the shoe workshop. His longest period of employment was with the local oil enterprise. Made

[11] In notes titled "Community and Society" formulated in 1937, Polanyi described the "treatment of human labor as a commodity, to be bought and sold, like cucumbers" as a "grotesque perversion of common sense." Cited in Dale (2016a, 168, note 77).

redundant when this firm imposed massive cuts in 2004, Berci has not had a regular job since. Workfare suits him because he generally enjoys the tasks set by the mayor. He is praised by his employer for carrying them out well and setting a good example to the others. Berci's contracts have always been renewed, but he knows that the job is insecure. During the summer months he could earn more in ten days as a *napszámos* than he does from working an entire month as a *közmunkás* (just over 50,000 forints or roughly 160 euros in 2014). But he would not consider such an alternative—the discipline of day-laboring is harsh, and besides, such work is only available for relatively short periods of the year. Berci's outgoings are limited, partly because he lunches most days with his widowed mother, who lives alone in the village center. She cultivates a plot here, while he keeps a few chickens, pigs and sheep at the old family farmstead. He is especially proud of his horses, a love he has inherited from his father, though nowadays these animals serve no economic purpose.

Villagers not taken on for the *közmunka* scheme and lacking other sources of income may be forced to meet cash needs by working as *napszámos*, legally or illegally. As noted, expenditure can be kept low through subsistence gardening. The concept of *precariat* has been developed with reference to urban, industrial work (Standing 2011). But it might be extended to rural contexts such as postsocialist Tázlár, where work opportunities have greatly diminished since the socialist era. As a result, migration becomes a common strategy, especially for younger people. Few villagers are so vulnerable that their subsistence is threatened, but even the most uncertain, precarious jobs abroad are preferred to a rural rhythm which involves some two or three months of intensive labor for new elites and nine or ten months of vegetating.

In this context, virtually all villagers welcomed the expansion of the workfare programs. I heard criticism from a successful vineyard owner who deplored the fact that taxpayers were funding a "social cooperative" (*szociális szövetkezet*) for the workshy.[12] Yet even this individual conceded that working for the community in this way was a healthy

[12] [Criticism became more common a year later following a significant extension of the scheme through the construction of a new community pig sty: not even under socialism, it was pointed out, had hogs been raised collectively.]

form of self-discipline for those concerned, and preferable to previous arrangements whereby able-bodied villagers had been able to draw state benefits while working illegally in the private sector. No one in Tázlár supposes that those employed growing courgettes are more likely to find "real" jobs as a result of this experience. A new government might eliminate the schemes with a stroke of the pen. But for the time being, although no one ever phrased it to me in quite this way in Tázlár, this public opportunity to work is a popular response to the polarizing impact of market society over the two preceding decades. The jobs may be temporary and precarious, with little if any prospect of leading to long-term employment on the regular labor market; but communal work in one's native village is an attractive alternative to the uncertainties of migration or the more strenuous fluctuating rhythms of day-laboring.

Conclusions

Anthropologists have been generally cautious in applying class analysis in their investigations of the postsocialist countryside. The vocabulary of class is politically loaded due to its deployment in socialist ideology, but the deeper problem arises from the conditions of rural life and its evolved social relations. Rather than stress inequalities in land ownership and income, anthropologists have attended to the less visible mechanisms which lie behind the statistics, such as access to social capital and personal networks. In the Weberian terms employed by Christian Giordano, when the state cannot create the conditions for bureaucratic and legal legitimacy, successful private farmers need first and foremost to be "political entrepreneurs"; clans (in the extended sense) seem more significant than class.

Ethnographic methods cast light on informal activities and intangibles that are hard to illuminate statistically but crucial to outcomes. Alexander Nikulin (2011) has noted that, when contemporary Russian sociologists conduct village surveys, the answers they receive to questions about the family economy are systematically distorted (a century ago, in the original *zemstvo* studies, the more serious distortions concerned questions about family composition). New forms of patronage often entail complicity in pilfering and other forms of informal-ity, which no one likes but everyone must learn to live with. What we label "corruption" may be increasingly recognized as such by the local actors. Embryonic class formation is nurtured by persistent ideas about a common moral economy. Such links have a stronger significance in rural than in urban settings because of the "face to face" nature of these communities. Thus Tommaso Trevisani, who exposed the naivety of Roy's view that the resilience of collective institutions could be viewed in terms of a neo-tribal solidarity group, nonetheless identified a lingering moral dimension in Uzbekistan, where older ideas of responsibility are available for manipulation by power holders. However, even if there has been considerable long-term continuity of elites, the bases of power today are different. All complex bureaucratically regulated economies have their "informal" or "grey" zones. But today's private farmers in Uzbekistan and many other parts of the postsocialist world differ both from their Soviet-era precursors and from contemporary Western farmers, scheming to achieve the best deal they can from the regulators of the EU's agricultural policies. They differ also from most urban communities in that perceptions of class conflict are less likely to develop where people live alongside each other and work for each other, and where the continued availability of the subsistence plot means that the laborers have not yet been fully reduced to the status of dispossessed proletariat. Whether the persistence of ideas of harmony at the level of the community and occasional symbolic acts of generous redistribution have a significant impact in modifying perceptions of polarization and equalizing life chances is an open question requiring further empirical research.

Contemporary rural communities in Poland and Hungary, like those in post-Soviet Central Asia, are shaped by their histories. The failure to push through mass collectivization in Poland did not inhibit limited modernization in the spheres of consumption and housing, but it had far-reaching consequences for production and the entire political economy. While in Hungary the end of the socialist system increased rural-urban disparities, in Poland the gulf was always more considerable. This is reflected in the large number of farms that produce little if any economic value, but which retain sentimental value for owners who earn their living as migrant laborers. A new class of capitalized family farmers is emerging in the era of neoliberalism, supported by EU policies, but smallholder resilience and the migration options make it impossible to recognize a proletariat in any orthodox sense.

Finally, zooming in again on the village of Tázlár, where older forms of class inequality have reappeared in new forms since 1990, I emphasized continuities in the peasant valuation of manual labor as a fundamental moral dimension of the economy. Workfare is commonly viewed as a repressive instrument of neoliberalism but, at least in the countryside, these programs have been almost universally welcomed, both by the participants and by other villagers. The workfare measures implemented in Tázlár in the 1930s and again today are very different from the Speenhamland system of poor relief analyzed by Karl Polanyi (1944). The men and women who receive a job from the mayor are registered in a national scheme. They perform a full working week for the community, thereby accumulating long-term entitlements as well as their daily bread. Even if most of those hired descend from the poorer strata of this community, this employment is socially inclusive and is not perceived as degrading by the participants or by other villagers. From the point of view of economists such as János Kornai, these programs are inherently flawed. They are a regrettable legacy of the decades of market socialism, when Hungary established a welfare state for its citizens "prematurely," before the economy warranted such generosity (Kornai 2007). But it is possible to view the workfare programs of the 2010s as a benign element of what Polanyi termed the "double movement," as a humane defensive response on the part of society to the polarization induced by the postsocialist variety of neoliberal "market fundamentalism" [cf. Block and Somers 2014].

CHAPTER SIX

Civil Society at the Grassroots: A Reactionary View

(1992, 2004)

Introduction[1]

In this chapter I am concerned with the adequacy of concepts such as democratization and civil society for understanding contemporary social transformations in Eastern Europe. I argue that more attention should be paid to the needs and anxieties of citizens as they themselves express them, in the context of their experiences under socialism. From this angle, the discourse of civil society, particularly when linked to an extreme model of market economy, is an ideological product alien to most citizens. Many villagers regret the passing of an age when dogma and ideology were less obtrusive in their community and posed less of a threat to their welfare.

The rhetoric of civil society was widely used by Eastern European intellectuals in the 1980s, aided and abetted by influential commentators in Western countries (Arató 1981; Garton Ash 1989; Michnik 1985; Hankiss 1990). Whereas English essayist Timothy Garton Ash offers portentous insights into the heroic struggles of entire peoples, Budapest sociologist Elemér Hankiss operationalizes the concept of civil society by counting voluntary associations, particularly interest group associations. Their declining number is evidence for him of the "demobilization" and "atomization" which occurred in the socialist

---

[1] *This chapter is based on Hann 1992b. It was written in response to an invitation from political scientist Paul G. Lewis, who was keen to include a micro-level contribution from a social anthropologist in a multi-disciplinary collection on civil society. The concluding section is adapted from Hann 2004.*

period. Hankiss interprets the ebullient "second economy" of János Kádár's Hungary as contributing to exaggerated individualism, the alienation of citizens and their withdrawal from public life. He also thinks, however, that this sector might contain seeds of more humane ways to resolve basic problems of social values and cohesion. His premise is that a healthy society is spun out of the multiple webs of spontaneous but formally constituted associations, whereas the imposition of a single monolithic web under socialism made a decent society impossible.

My perspective as a foreign anthropologist is inevitably very different from that of Hankiss. Like him, I am concerned in this chapter primarily with Hungary (some of the arguments have a degree of validity elsewhere in Eastern Europe—for example in Poland and Yugoslavia—but conditions in Ceauşescu's Romania were entirely different). During most of the Kádár period Hungarian socialism was not driven by ideological dogma, but rather by pragmatic policies which gave citizens considerable scope to pursue their ambitions as consumers. Hungarian society was transformed by these policies, for which it is difficult to find a simple label. The term *polgárosodás* is one which many Hungarians themselves are only now becoming acquainted with. It is usually translated as embourgeoisement, *polgár* corresponding both to "bourgeois" and "citizen." But clearly socialist transformation differed from the bourgeois course on which Hungary had barely embarked in the pre-socialist period. Perhaps a better English equivalent would be "modernization." I remain impressed by the fact that, under socialism, millions of rural citizens were dynamic producers of agricultural commodities, acquired new homes with electricity and bathrooms, and gained unprecedented access to state-provided education and health care. This sort of material progress may constitute the essence of *polgárosodás* for many citizens, even when it is accompanied by a severe diminution of the free, autonomous associations found before 1948. Kádárist pragmatism might have been unattractive to Western observers in ethical terms, but it enabled the majority of citizens to improve their living standards dramatically, among them many of the poorest and least integrated sections of the rural population in settlements such as Tázlár, to which I now turn.

Civil Society and Local Politics in Tázlár

Few inhabitants of Budapest (population around two million) have heard of Tázlár (population around two thousand), a settlement on the flat sandy soils of the Danube-Tisza interfluve, only a short drive from the Yugoslav border. The larger neighboring village of Soltvadkert is better known nationally, thanks to the diligence and ingenuity of the Lutheran German settlers who form its most salient ethnic group, especially in the wine sector. Tázlár was repopulated later and its ecology is generally poorer (Hann 1979, 1980a). Although both settlements were allowed to develop "specialist cooperatives" following collectivization, those in Soltvadkert were much more dynamic. At the time of my fieldwork in the 1970s, political institutions were held in low esteem in Tázlár. The council chairman was of poor peasant origin and widely reputed to be corrupt: for example, he would not authorize the electrification of a farmhouse outside the village center until the appropriate bribe had been paid. He was also thought to be ineffectual in securing public funds for local development. Since the building of a large Culture House in the early 1960s, associational life in the village had stagnated. With religious denominations strictly excluded from secular domains and no other autonomous organizations of significance active in the public space, it might be supposed that the dynamic energies of the community in this period were chanelled overwhelmingly towards private accumulation. This diagnosis would be fully consistent with the arguments of Hankiss, noted in the introduction to this chapter.

In all the instant mythologising which followed the revolutionary upheavals of 1989, it is often forgotten just how far Hungary had already travelled down the road of reform before this date. In Tázlár the appointment of a non-socialist chairman of the specialist cooperative in 1982 was a landmark. The appointment of an agronomist of Soltvadkert origin put an end to an era of leadership instability characterized by repeated interventions by the external authorities. The rest of the decade witnessed significant economic consolidation in the cooperative. Farming operations were streamlined and initiatives taken to create new jobs in non-agricultural activities (small factories employing mainly female labor in manufacturing shoe uppers and plastic bags). Most of the cooperative's machine park was privatized to employees, who then entered into contractual agreements with the cooperative and competed for farmers' business with other private tractor owners. The outstanding new investment was in a vast vineyard, following a pattern pioneered in other specialist cooperatives of the interfluve and supported with state subsidies. Unlike traditional peasant vineyards, certain operations were now mechanized. However, family labor remained indispensable at peak periods. "Ownership" rights were sold to individuals, who shared the costs and the profits with the specialist cooperative. Studies have shown that the yield in such private member joint farms (*tagi közös*) can reach double that of an equivalent area of collective vineyard without such devolution of ownership and cultivation rights (Simó 1987, 85). This was a good example of Kádárist pragmatism towards the rural population and it helped to win the specialist cooperative respect in the community.

Outside the cooperative, however, there was little to match this dynamism. On the political front the former council chairman was a broken man after 1983, when he received a suspended jail sentence for corruption. He was replaced by the headmaster of the village primary school, who resigned from the (always minuscule) local cell of the Communist Party in 1989, when it had become clear that the days of socialism were numbered. By 1990, he was letting it be known that he favored the restoration of religious instruction in state schools, as the only way to ensure adequate moral training for youth.[2] In addition to school and council, the same individual was responsible for directing the village Culture House—a thankless task, as he readily admitted, especially given the difficulties in attracting younger villagers.[3] Offi-

[2] However, the churches were by no means well supported in Tázlár in the 1980s. The Roman Catholics who comprised the largest congregation were bitterly divided following a personal rift between the parish priest and the community's long-serving female cantor. After an unsuccessful appeal to the bishop for a new priest, the absence of the apathetic majority was augmented by a boycott on the part of several members of the devout minority.

[3] In an article about the Tázlár Culture House written for a new newspaper published in neighboring Soltvadkert, the Director wrote "In recent years people have lost the habit of patronizing the Culture House because of more difficult material circumstances and their second jobs, and even third jobs. Our existing groups (zither, drama, puppets, women's club etc.) are working well enough, but the situation of young people cannot be resolved. It is no consolation to know that it's the same everywhere. How can we make plans without their participation?" *Vadkerti Újság* 2, no. 5 (1990): 14.

Figure 9. Discarded plaques of the socialist village (photo by Chris Hann, 2016)

cially sponsored organizations such as the Women's Club attracted only small numbers to their perfunctory meetings. Perhaps the most active formal association in Tázlár in the 1980s was the Hunting Association. Cooperative officials and Party members were prominent in the membership, as elsewhere in Hungary (Pünkösti 1986; Szász 1985). But, by 1990, this too had disintegrated owing to a failure to agree on new officers and the Tázlár association was swallowed up by the larger association in Soltvadkert.

There was thus a dearth of active local associations or corporations when Tázlár residents went to the polls in 1990, first in the spring to elect a new parliament, and then in the autumn to elect a new mayor and local council. The revived Smallholders' Party had a strong base in this region. One of its leading activists was a Tázlár resident who looked set at one stage to become the party's parliamentary candidate. In the end he stepped down in favor of a better-known and respected veterinary surgeon, who was comfortably elected. During the summer of 1990, when I visited the village, the Smallholders' Party was maintaining its high profile. No other party was well established, although several had a small core of activists: the Hungarian Socialist Party (successor to the Communist Party), the Christian Democratic People's Party, and the Agrarian Alliance. Neither the Hungarian Democratic Forum nor the Free Democrats, the largest political forces in the country, were able to establish a formal presence in Tázlár. The Smallholders scored a symbolic victory when they took over the space in the village council offices previously reserved for the Communist Party and put their emblem prominently on display in the window.

It is perhaps not surprising that there was strong support for the Smallholders' Party in a region in which family farming had retained its vitality thanks to the specialist cooperatives. But there were also paradoxes here, which came more into the open by the time of the local elections in September 1990. At one level there were plenty of voters ready to respond to certain elements of the Smallholders' message, and in particular the promise to create fully independent family farmers on the basis of the land owned by the family in 1947. To implement this principle literally implied the dismemberment of the specialist cooperative. The activists certainly saw matters in these terms. Some of them belonged to the families which stood to gain most from the policies of "1947 restoration" (see Chapter Three). However, many of those who voted for a Smallholder in the parliamentary election of May 1990 were reluctant to elect a Smallholder as village mayor five months later. The local campaign was exciting. In conversation in August 1990, the initiator of the Smallholders' local organization spoke honestly about personal rivalries among the activists, and also about deep-seated reservations concerning the Smallholders' program throughout the community. He complained that, although he always found massive support for his radical program when he canvassed farmers individually, when he spoke out against the cooperative leadership at a public meeting his support melted away. He attributed this to a "duality" (*kettősség*) in the nature of his fellow-villagers, rooted in the diverse traditions of their community, which made it very hard for them to accept a leader from within, from among themselves.[4]

Other contenders for the new post of mayor experienced similar problems: if X had the right educational background, the problem was

[4] Indeed there was a fair amount of gossip and slander about this would-be leader. His descent from a family which had been active in local administration before the socialist period carried no particular weight. Criticism focused on his lack of education, and on the fact that he did not farm himself and had virtually given up his occupation as a private motor mechanic in order to devote himself to researching the early history of the community. His family life (his wife, a former accountant at the cooperative, had died of cancer only a year earlier) was also placed under the microscope and found wanting by local opinion.

that he could not understand the needs of ordinary farmer; if Y fulfilled the latter criterion, this had to be set against a worrying drink problem; and so on. There was general surprise that the out-going council chairman chose not to run for mayor (he explained that he had enough to do looking after the school and the Culture House, but was easily elected as an ordinary councillor). In the end six candidates were nominated. The most extraordinary campaign was run by a local entrepreneur, standing as an Independent. Possessing neither inherited wealth nor a prestigious name nor any impressive paper qualifications, this man had nonetheless managed to build up a dynamic restaurant business in the 1980s. He had business interests which spread into neighboring communities. However there were many adverse comments about some aspects of his career. For example, rumors circulated following a fatal drug incident at one of his restaurants. This candidate's manifesto emphasized his local origins and his determination, if elected, to promote community development in vigorous and radical new ways. He would commission a new village emblem and publish a local history monograph. He would build new roads and negotiate with foreign capital to open a petrol station in the village. He would open up new marketing avenues for local farmers in Budapest and even in Austria. He would organize "market research" to determine the priorities for commercial development within the community; he even floated a scheme for an independent local bank. There was no mention whatsoever in this candidate's manifesto of the future of the specialist cooperative. Instead he summed up the message of numerous sociological studies of contemporary Hungary when he stated proudly in his manifesto that hitherto he had preferred not to get involved in local politics on the grounds that "I know just two important things, family and business, and I've devoted all my time to these two areas."

Victory went by a large margin to another Independent, the socialist council's retiring executive secretary, a woman who had married into the community, had worked for the socialist administration since the 1950s, and who was thought to favor strengthening the specialist cooperative rather than dissolving it. The entrepreneur did not accept the result. He took his objections through several stages of increasingly acrimonious appeal and gained national publicity, but all to no avail. (According to my informants, if anyone was guilty of electoral malpractice it was he, for his services to voters were by no means confined to offers of transport to the polling booths.) The election left a legacy of bitterness (the village was "like a wasp's nest" for months afterwards, according to one friend). I tell the story in this detail in order to show how difficult it is in a place like Tázlár to create a democratic, party-based political culture at the local level. Independents, many of them ex-Party members, did well in the local elections in most parts of Hungary. This led some observers, particularly intellectuals in the capital city, to condemn old apparatchiks for clinging to power and to rehearse once again their arguments about an atomised civil society.

However, it is possible to take a different view of this local society and of the elites who would diagnose atomisation. The leading voices in almost every major party in Hungary in 1990 were agreed that the country needed to proceed rapidly towards a genuine "market economy" (*piacgazdaság*) and that state interventions and subsidies needed to be curtailed. The Smallholders' Party was progressively isolated in its insistence on a return to the 1947 version of private property landholding, but this nonetheless remained the dominant ideological flavor right across the political spectrum. No wonder that farmers who had experienced the more subtle property relations of the specialist cooperatives were skeptical. They had very good reason to be suspicious of pure market triumphalism, if that implied a withdrawal of state support for small farmers, not to mention the specific subsidies which Tázlár enjoyed because of its unfavorable endowment. Many farmers I talked to believed that it was vital for the security of the community to preserve the specialist cooperative in its established form, farming its own collective sector as well as continuing to service the farms of its members. The cooperative chairman (who did not join any political party) emphasized the need to give priority to production and to pull together to defend collective achievements. Far from being rejected as a hangover from socialist ideology, this stance won widespread support and admiration.

In other words, the recent transition in Tázlár might be characterized as a vote of confidence in a number of individuals identified with the *ancien régime*, and, at least implicitly, in the specialist cooperative. The latter is associated not only with existential security for all and substantial prosperity for many, but also with a positively valued public identity and social cohesion. By contrast, the forces associated with the new political parties, particularly the Smallholders, seemed to stand for the

Figure 10. The current symbol of the village government of Tázlár (photo by Chris Hann, 2016)

atomisation of society, for a world of pure market agents in which all farmers would suffer as the state withdrew its supports.

To return now to the arguments of Hankiss, I propose that a focus upon the presence or absence of organized interest groups and autonomous associations is inadequate for a diagnosis of the condition of society.[5] In Tázlár not even football provides a very satisfactory basis for public sociability or an enduring local patriotism. The small group of men who gather regularly for scratch matches on the pitch maintained by the cooperative include the village doctor, the former council chairman discussed above, and a number of small businessmen. They are not a very representative group. Most men in these age groups are too busy with other activities: tending their vineyards, seeking out and transporting materials, or getting on with the next phase of their self-help housing. But it would be absurd to present these accumulation strategies as anti-social. Men and women combine in groups with kin and neighbors for most of these activities (Sik 1988). The specialist cooperative has both enabled the persistence of older forms of inter-household cooperation and stimulated new ones (e.g. in the large-scale vineyards). In short, far from atrophying in the socialist period, Tázlár continued to develop its own style of social cohesion alongside its remarkable economic transformation, and both were underpinned by the specialist cooperative.

The Richer Neighbor

I do not claim that Tázlár is a representative community. It was probably unusually low in cohesion in the pre-socialist period, and it has experienced an unusual variant of collectivization. It might also be

[5] [The counting of such associations was a favorite preoccupation of civil society researchers in the 1990s. In Hungary the number of "non-profit organizations" rose from below 9,000 in 1989 to 43,000 by 1995. See Jenkins 1999.]

objected that "social cohesion" can hardly be adequately explored in a single small community, and that scale factors should be taken carefully into consideration. In this context it is instructive to look briefly at some developments in Soltvadkert, which has some five times as many inhabitants and is economically much more advanced than Tázlár, for which it serves as a market center (and, increasingly, as a leisure center). The residents of Soltvadkert seem to spend less of their energy nowadays on accumulation. They have their comfortable houses and their cars, and many have second homes at a nearby lake resort which is also beginning to attract a few of the new rich in Tázlár. They have lively cinema programs (including "drive-in" movies in the summer season) and a flourishing Sports Association, with teams participating in national leagues. But many Soltvadkert citizens spend their leisure time at home, in private ways familiar to most westerners (cable television has enjoyed considerable success in recent years). By 1990, Soltvadkert could also boast a range of clubs and associations far greater than these of Tázlár, from stamp-collectors to pigeon-fanciers. In future it is likely that these will attract members from the smaller villages of the district.

One interesting example of an interest group in Soltvadkert was the local branch of the Small Tradesmen's Alliance. There was considerable anger in spring 1990 when the Hungarian Democratic Forum (about to become Hungary's main governing party) called a public meeting to re-establish this body under its pre-socialist name "Craftsmen's Association" (*Ipartestület*) at precisely the same time as the officials of the existing organization summoned their members to a meeting intended to reach the same goal via a negotiated name change. For the Forum activists, such an admission of organic continuity with the socialist period was unacceptable. They envisaged the Association as a successor not to the socialist organization but to the Association dissolved in the late 1940s. However, many members did not wish to repudiate the socialist organization, and they certainly did not wish to risk losing the assets which it had built up. I quote at length from an account which appeared in the local newspaper:

> The Soltvadkert Craftsmen's Association can look back on a distinguished past, and it can claim proudly that it has maintained its identity, even when certain factors dictated that it was not called the Craftsmen's Association, but instead the Small Tradesmen's

> Alliance. In the past it was precisely this organization which tried even in the difficult years to draw its members together, to represent their interests as well as conditions permitted, and to offer them protection against attacks from a variety of political currents.
>
> . . . Now, when there is talk of "renewing the country, unity and democracy," and these are the aims of the governing party, the need for drawing together and unity is greater than ever. That is why we find the initiative of the Hungarian Democratic Forum concerning the establishment of a new Craftsmen's Association incomprehensible.
>
> We ask: shouldn't this question be entrusted to the craftsmen, businessmen and traders themselves to decide? We think they are well able to decide their own fate and future independently, in the interests of their own common goals.
>
> The attendance of members at the two simultaneously convened meetings proved unambiguously which of the two had a quorum. The Forum meeting was attended by at most ten persons, whilst the meeting arranged by the craftsmen themselves to renew their Association attracted about seventy, a clear majority of those eligible. We were able to hear a serious debate about all the details of the report presented by the representative of the Small Tradesmen's Alliance concerning its proposed evolution into a Craftsmen's Association . . . [6]

This episode seems to me to exemplify the arrogance of some of those who came along at the end of the socialist period in Hungary to proclaim that everything done in that period was tarnished, and that the only way forward was to start again, or to restore some golden age associated with 1947 (or even earlier). That is not at all how many ordinary citizens perceived matters. Tázlár and Soltvadkert are in many ways untypical, but I suggest that the pragmatic style of market socialism which gave rise to the specialist cooperatives made itself felt in less spectacular ways throughout Kádár's Hungary. The election of a large number of independent and ex-communist candidates across the country, and perhaps also the very high abstention rates, indicate

6 *Vadkerti Újság* 2, no. 7 (1990): 7–8.

a failure on the part of the new elites to understand the value attached by many ordinary people to achievements of this particular socialist regime. It is possible to interpret the 1990 electoral results (as Hankiss presumably would) as evidence for the destruction of an earlier civil society and the difficulty in building a new one. But it is worth remembering that a village like Tázlár hardly had even an embryonic civil society before socialism. It became well integrated into the national society and experienced unparalleled material prosperity as a result of reformist socialist policies. Those who believe that the path to a more democratic political future lies in the rejection of gradualist pragmatism (in favor of "shock therapy" and rush to capitalism in the Polish manner) are pinning their faith in a naive representation of the Western historical record and an equally naive model of the role of "the market" in a mature industrial economy. The evidence from Tázlár suggests that the preconceptions of the new elites are not widely shared by their citizens.[7]

Ernest Gellner and the Church of Civil Society

The most common response of liberal intellectuals to analyses such as that laid out in the previous section is to bemoan economistic bias, crude consumerism and the political immaturity of the masses, for

[7] Evidence from the grass-roots of a number of other ex-socialist societies reveals a similar picture: see Skalník 1993, Dragadze 1991. [I continued to monitor civil and local-political developments in Tázlár (and Hungary in general) after this article was written in 1992—see Hann 2003a, 2004, 2006. Events at the beginning of the new century were instructive. Viktor Orbán did not take kindly to his defeat at the polls in May 2002, when he argued that the return of a socialist government spelled the end of democracy. His Fidesz party triumphed in Tázlár, as it has consistently ever since, replacing the Independent Smallholders' Party as the "natural" representative of the countryside, in opposition to socialists and liberals with their bases in the cities. The defeated party organized rallies and a nationwide network of "civil circles" (*polgári körök*). In Tázlár in the summer of 2002 most villagers were unsure if their settlement had one of these circles or a regular branch of the Fidesz party. In any case the activist group proved to be short-lived. Only in 2014 did Fidesz again organize actively in the locality, this time in order to topple a long-serving mayor—see Hann and Kürti 2015].

which the socialists alone are to blame. But it remains instructive to look more closely at the concept of civil society. It is one of those terms where it seems especially important to distinguish *Begriffsgeschichte* from the concrete development of the phenomenon at issue. The concept was not in use for most of the nineteenth and twentieth centuries, though it is safe to assume that its object of reference underwent certain changes in this long period. As noted above, civil society was rediscovered in the last years of the Cold War as a result of a curious coalition of Eastern European "dissidents" and left-leaning intellectuals in the West (see Hann 2000b). In its revived post-Cold War career it is again helpful to distinguish between words and things, between the rhetoric of civil society and the actual course of social change. Ernest Gellner was one of the enthusiasts for the reinvention of the concept of civil society, regardless of its "muddled" history, because it seemed to him the best term to encapsulate the most attractive features of the open, liberal and individualist society of which he approved (Gellner 1994).[8] It is worth recalling that Gellner began his career with an attack on Oxford linguistic philosophy (1959). He was more interested in understanding the concrete development of "things." Nevertheless, linguistic idealism and "speech act theory" exerted pervasive influences on his adopted discipline of social anthropology. Gellner was obliged to recognize that even Bronisław Malinowski, the founder of the modern British empirical, fieldwork-based tradition, verged on a suspect idealist epistemology when exploring the magical power of certain Trobriand words (Gellner 1998). Words, including social science concepts, do indeed have material effects in society.

The phrase civil society, whether in a local translation or left in English (where it may secrete an extra hint of mystery), has been taken up in a magical sense in many parts of postsocialist Eurasia. At first *społeczęstwo obywatelskie* (Polish) or *polgári társadalom* (Hungarian) appeared in the obscure, semi-clandestine publications of tiny groups of intellectuals. With the collapse of socialist regimes, the concept of

8 [It is curious to note that Gellner did not attach much importance to formal organizations; associations do not figure at all in his 1994 book, his major work on civil society. I recall from conversation his scorn at the notion that you could quantify the strength of civil society by counting up the organizations. See also Hall 2010, 356–60.]

civil society entered into the programs of new political parties and into the mass media. It signified utopian conditions of democratic participation and tolerance, the antithesis of "totalitarianism"; more precise definitions were seldom forthcoming. It suited new power holders to have a term of the "motherhood and apple pie" ilk, from which no one could possibly dissent. A decade on, in countries such as Poland and Hungary where more or less stable political institutions have emerged, the term has already faded from the public sphere. However, in Russia I am told that the concept of *grazhdanskoe obchystwa* still seems to have a certain magical aura.

These performances have impacted on society in various ways. New groups of enthusiasts have emerged, primarily as a consequence of the adoption of one specific notion of civil society by governments and foreign Foundations and aid organizations. Partly because the latter needed a quantitative measure for their own bureaucratic reasons, the health of a civil society came to mean (especially in the Anglo-Saxon world) the number of associations it had, more specifically the number of non-governmental organizations (NGOs). There are distinguished precedents in Western intellectual history for a focus on associations, notably in the work of Tocqueville. However, the emphasis on NGOs and the "third sector" (Russian: *tretiy sektor*) that was supposed to be an autonomous force beyond the spheres of state and market was both a simplification and a distortion of the two principal classical strands of civil society theorizing—that which refuses a state versus society dichotomy (e.g. Ferguson) and that which identifies civil society with the atomistic world of the market (e.g. Marx). In the dislocation of post-socialist transformation, the establishment of free associations became a priority of public policy. The channeling of public money through these new organizations led to many distortions. At its most harmless, this could lead to sports clubs that had previously functioned under the control of the state or a trade union continuing for most practical purposes unchanged, but now classified as embodiments of civil society. At the other end of the spectrum, the unregulated proliferation of clubs and associations led in some circumstances to some very "uncivil" consequences and even interethnic violence (see Chapter Nine).

The routing of a high proportion of aid funds through these NGO channels can make already weak states even weaker. Governmental programs to dispense aid and technical assistance inevitably become caught up in local political rivalries (Wedel 1998). The foreigners who appeared on the scene, not only as businessmen but as the purveyors of democracy and civil society, can afford to pay higher salaries than local organizations, and so the receiving country's best university teachers and civil servants are easily persuaded to change sectors. These new elites commonly end up changing countries as well, for following extended contracts and regular training periods abroad, they often became unemployable in their home countries (Mandel 2002; Sampson 2002). This has resulted in envy towards those who succeed in the new foreign-funded NGO sector. The logic of the current situation leads the most talented to put all their energies into learning English, management studies and of course the jargon of civil society project management, rather than obtain other qualifications and enter established professions. The emphasis on free associations and organizations obliges donors and even governments to set about creating the missing "non-governmental" bodies (known as DONGOs and GONGOs respectively, see Mandel 2002) that are essential if the flow of "aid" is to continue.

"Civil society" has therefore brought changes in the living conditions of specific social groups, but the impact on the wider society has been modest. Many postsocialist citizens have experienced a decline in state provision, e.g. in the value of pensions, or in education and health, without experiencing any compensating material benefits from an NGO. Some of the consequences have been unintended, and even the opposite of what was intended, notably the brain drain abroad. Of course not all projects have failed, and some NGOs, both foreign and domestic, have creditable records. But however laudable the intentions, I argue that the general thrust of civil society intervention has been misconceived. Few would object to the decentralized principles stressed by the British Foreign Office's "Know-How Fund." But even schemes like this one were experienced as experiments in social engineering. The main difference to socialism was that the new interventions had a foreign slogan, foreign managers and foreign criteria of success regarding what makes a decent society. Current programs of "civil society export" amount to the imposition of a specifically Anglo-Saxon notion of social cohesion. Yet most people (perhaps even many among the new Westernized elites) would prefer to adapt their own ideals, typically based on kinship or religious or ethnic loyalties rather than on formal associations and individual agents. Civil society export can lead to the abortion of local processes of change, embryonic or already well advanced, a very undesirable outcome from the point of view of the anthropologist.

The obvious anthropological alternative is to expand the definition of civil society beyond the Enlightenment heritage of liberal individualism (Hann 1996a). This would allow us to recognize other ways of achieving accountability, participatory politics, tolerance of group differences, and other desiderata associated with a concept that has become inescapably normative. Ernest Gellner rejects this approach. In this context he is perhaps untypical of contemporary anthropologists, e.g. when he characterizes tribal society as a "tyranny of cousins" and rules out the possibility of an Islamic civil society (1994). It is true that some critical intellectuals in Muslim countries agree with this stance and prefer to emphasize the modern, Western associations of civil society, for instance in the field of gender rights, when they challenge the traditions of their own societies (Eickelman and Anderson 1999). But others have argued that the ethnocentric bias of scholars such as Gellner leads them to deny the real presence of civil society in Islamic societies, even when the classical Western criteria are applied (See Kamali 2001, who follows a model specified by Shmuel Eisenstadt). The more satisfying anthropological approach is one which pays close attention to local patterns of sociality and investigates how issues of political and moral accountability can be resolved in civil ways that may differ from modern Western solutions. To date, the pioneers of such enquiries into cross-cultural ethical systems seem to be political theorists and philosophers (Chambers and Kymlicka 2002).

Instead of entering into these debates, too many anthropologists have responded to the civil society vogue by accepting the Anglo-Saxon, neoliberal definition and restricting the focus of their fieldwork to the NGOs. Though sometimes able to offer valuable insights into the impact of new associational forms, such studies too often ignore local patterns of sociality outside the organizations. Yet many of these patterns either persist unaffected by the NGOs, or develop in new ways as a consequence of external interventions. It is disappointing—though often readily explicable in terms of funding conditions and logistics—when anthropologists, the only members of the academy equipped, through the methods of participant observation, to penetrate the complexities of local societies, end up spending much of their fieldwork speaking English to other foreigners engaged in civil society development projects.

For Gellner, socialist societies could never provide an attractive alternative to the standard liberal model. The difference, compared to Islamic societies, is that socialism, at least in Eastern Europe and Russia, emerged on the immediate periphery of the industrializing West, so that in principle the problems of "translating" civil society should be greatly reduced. It is nonetheless depressing to have to note that a distinguished tradition of civil society theorizing in Germany has been swamped by the Anglo-Saxon vogue. The German concept of *bürgerliche Gesellschaft* has been largely replaced by the Anglicism *Zivilgesellschaft* (similarly in Hungary, where *polgári társadalom* has been supplanted in recent years by *civil társadalom*). At any rate, in the postsocialist countries, perhaps unlike other parts of the world, I detect no intellectual ferment around the concept of civil society. Many people have become cynical. A decade after the collapse of socialism, I found that no academics in Moscow took the notion of civil society very seriously. It was simply a buzzword to be inserted into any foreign grant application, just as a phrase about Russia's cultural or spiritual renaissance was obligatory in grant applications within the country. Things have gotten to the point where civil society seems to be a symptom of the diseases of non-democratic governance and intolerance, rather than a cure to these problems (Hann 2003a). As in other parts of the world, in Russia the crudities and abuses of the foreign NGO sector lead people to react by reaffirming older loyalties. This seems to be one factor behind the resurgence of ethno-national sentiment, and also of continued nostalgia for socialism and the popularity of political platforms which exploit that heritage all over Eurasia. The discomforting implication of this anthropological relativizing of the concept of civil society is that many postsocialist citizens (perhaps in many countries a majority) feel that they enjoyed a more civil society under the old regime than they do today: not, of course, in the sense that they had more free associations and more participatory forms of governance, but in the sense that their personal and social lives were more secure and their communities more firmly anchored in a moral framework, one which emphasized values of mutual support and civility.

Let me give a concluding example from Eastern Europe. There is a wide measure of agreement that Roma groups have experienced new and intensified forms of social exclusion following the transformation of socialist economic planning and social security services. The new democratic conditions require that even such marginalized groups have adequate political representation, but ensuring effective Roma participation has proved highly problematic. Some attempts to improve matters have focused on strengthening Roma civil society, in the sense of funding new organizations and projects to promote Roma goals. Daniela Tarnovschi is a sociologist who specializes in Roma civil society in Romania.[9] This civil society came into existence in 1926 with the establishment of the first formal organization to represent Roma interests. There was no Roma civil society in the socialist period, but it re-emerged promptly in 1990 and the number of Roma associations expanded impressively after facilitating legislation was passed in 1996. It may be too soon to judge the impact of the large number of organizations and projects on the general conditions of Romania's Roma population, numbering some 5% of the total population. My point is simply that an anthropological approach cannot limit itself to these new organizations, but would also need to explore through fieldwork what other Roma think of the new elites who control these civil society interventions. To understand the problems of the Roma today it will certainly be necessary to analyze their situation under socialism, but perhaps also to consider alternative models of how to organize social and political participation. It is possible that older structures based on the office of the "Gypsy King" can be incorporated into the new structures of formal associations, but it is also possible that many Roma will resist such incorporation. Thus, even if one insists on retaining the narrow definition of civil society, focusing on formal organizations, it will be necessary to undertake research outside these limits in order to understand the circumstances in which this new model of civil society spreads or fails to spread.

Despite mounting evidence that the promotion of an impoverished notion of civil society is not working, the magic of the concept still seems strong for large swathes of Anglo-Saxon academia. How

---

9 See Tarnovschi 2003; for more information about Roma organizations and projects see the website of the Ethnocultural Diversity Resource Centre: www.edrc.ro

do we explain this enchantment? I do not think it can be attributed solely to cynical instrumentalism, and in any case this begs the question of why the term civil society retains its mysterious power for so many donors and governments. Another of Gellner's favorite metaphors is useful here. Echoing Karl Popper, he liked to refer to the partisans of "closed" systems of thought, such as Marxism and psychoanalysis, as "churches" (e.g. Gellner 1964). I suggest that the partisans of civil society, a concept which, in his estimation, exemplified the open, liberal vision of society, are in danger of becoming another intellectual church. It is ironic, too, that one of the major temples should be the London School of Economics, home not only to Gellner but to Malinowski and Popper before him.[10]

This new church of civil society can be compared to the secular religion it has replaced across much of Eurasia, the Marxist-Leninist variety of socialism. Both are varieties of non-spiritual religion. Their visions of the good life are somewhat different, as are the techniques they employ, but both suffer from a common deficiency. By proclaiming that salvation is to be found here on this earth, through improvements in human institutional arrangements, neither is able to connect with the transcendental, with that sense of the sacred which so many human beings appear to need. Ernest Gellner used to argue in the case of socialism that its promise of a better future in this world must have contributed to its delegitimation, once it became clear to everyone in the stagnation and corruption of the Brezhnev years that there was no longer any prospect of improvement. My sense is that the salvation promises of civil society will have an even shorter life span. Many enthusiasts of the 1980s and early 1990s have already lost faith. Outside academia the church is struggling, at least in the postsocialist world. The combination of a continuing flood of rhetoric but dwindling material transfers and mounting moral revulsion may be enough to send civil society back to the conceptual graveyard from which it was so recently exhumed.

---

[10] [I refer here to the LSE's "Centre for Civil Society," which began publishing an annual report *Global Civil Society* in 2001.]

CHAPTER SEVEN

Socialism and King Stephen's Right Hand

(1990)

Introduction[1]

This chapter proceeds from the assumption that politics everywhere and at all times can be illuminated by an anthropological exploration of the "symbolic" dimension (Cohen 1974; Geertz 1980; Kertzer 1988). It is argued that political anthropologists can offer distinctive insight into processes of legitimation in contemporary socialist societies. Even before the era of *glasnost'* the states of Eastern Europe, including the USSR, had long moved out of the "heroic" phase of Leninism-Stalinism. Populations were no longer mobilized *en masse* through socialist rhetoric and the great majority of citizens were no longer terrorized by "security forces." However, the ruling powers have experienced increasing difficulties in grounding their legitimacy in rapid economic modernization. With only a few exceptions, historic patterns of underdevelopment vis-à-vis the west have reasserted themselves strongly since the mid-seventies. In these circumstances, the symbolic dimension becomes of central importance to the state in its efforts to ensure political stability. We might expect this dimension to gain in importance as the economic situation deteriorates. Yet, even before economic decline became so serious, scholars examining the Soviet ritual system had pointed to significant changes in the symbolic sphere, including a shift towards powerful "traditional" symbols such

[1] *This chapter derives from Hann 1990d. It was the unplanned product of two short sojourns in Hungary in the summer of 1988, during which I discussed the subject of King/Saint Stephen with both rural and urban dwellers in all age groups, including non-believers as well as practising Catholics.*

as those of national identity (Lane 1981; Binns 1979–80). Such adaptations by the authorities may not succeed. Some anthropologists argue that Marxist socialism, unlike other ideologies, contains within itself subversive strands which frustrate conservative legitimation strategies (Kideckel 1983). Symbols and rituals may have dynamics of their own which cannot be manipulated at will by new elites. Some symbols may be contested by rival social groups. In the context of modern states, opposition movements are just as beholden to the symbolic dimensions as the regimes which they reject (Kertzer 1988).

The present study investigates how different groups interpreted and exploited King Stephen, who has long been a potent, multivalent symbol for Hungarians, in the summer of 1988. Such symbols are the ones most likely to gain in prominence at times when power holders have no ready answers to pressing political and economic problems. I shall trace how Stephen was caught up in a crisis management program on the part of the state, but also in a projected revival on the part of the Catholic Church, and a great deal more besides.

Anniversaries

King Stephen is known internationally and to Hungarians as the ruler who converted his previously nomadic people to Christianity and established their state, superseding the old "tribal" structures, in more or less its present territory in the Carpathian Basin of Central Europe. He was canonized by the Roman Catholic Church within half a century of his death in 1038, and his feast day is celebrated on August 20, the day of his burial. Secular markers have been laid down for this same day by the socialist state. It has become "New Bread Day," and since 1949 has been a public holiday as "Constitution Day." In the village of Tázlár the council chairman organized a ceremony at his offices on August 20, 1988, at which all three celebrations were given equal prominence. He explained to me that prior to this year only the secular symbols had been recognized on state premises, with Stephen confined to the church. In the inter-war period, however, the highest state leaders (including Admiral Miklós Horthy, a Protestant) took part in a commemorative procession of which Stephen was the main focus; these central rituals were echoed all over Hungary with festivities that typically included the wearing of folk costumes and fireworks.[2]

Stephen has a vital association with the most important symbols of Hungarian statehood, notably his own Holy Crown. This was taken to Fort Knox at the end of the Second World War, on the occupation of Hungary by Soviet troops. Its return by President Jimmy Carter in 1978 generated enormous publicity in Hungary. Secretary of State Cyrus Vance was drawn into elaborate ceremonies, which were widely perceived as an important mark of foreign recognition for János Kádár's reform-minded regime (Beeson 1982, 256). Since then the crown has been kept in a specially constructed chamber of the National Museum, forming the closest Hungary has to a national shrine. Succeeding years have witnessed more and more discussion in academic and public life, in all media, of the complicated history of Hungarian identity. This has to be understood in the context of economic crisis, but also of a much more relaxed political climate which has encouraged a radical reappraisal of the earlier socialist decades. The mass media have been able to discuss figures who were "non-persons" for a generation, socialist accretions to Hungarian heraldic emblems and flags have been discarded in favor of "purer" traditional versions, and in early 1989 even the Revolution of 1956 was completely reassessed. Another vital contextual element was the long-simmering conflict with Nicolae Ceauşescu's Romania over treatment of the Magyar ethnic minority in Transylvania. It was against this background that the Hungarian state decided in 1988 to commemorate the 950th anniversary of the death of King Stephen, the founder of a state which had included the Transylvanian territories that are the focus of present concern.[3]

[2] Since the drafting of this paper in Autumn 1988, the pace of political change in Hungary has accelerated dramatically. In 1989 the Roman Catholic Church was allowed to organize a public procession in Budapest on August 20 without hindrance. For the tone of public comment see the articles in *Reform,* August 18, 1989, 6–7. The symbol of Stephen was prominent in the publicity of the newly established opposition party, the Hungarian Democratic Forum.

[3] A typical slogan for public consumption (this one was offered in various languages to accompany a set of colored slides issued for the occasion) read literally: "950 years ago died King Saint Stephen [sic], founder of the Hungarian State." Indicative of the climate of opinion in state circles was the fol-

The state saw the anniversary as an occasion to rehabilitate a national hero who had largely disappeared from view under Stalinism. It was happy to promote pageantry and special exhibitions to encourage tourism. The actions of the secular authorities may also be understood as a response to demands from below: the state was following public opinion rather than dictating to it. But in addition to the state, the Roman Catholic Church in Hungary also perceived an opportunity in 1988 that was too good to miss. For the Church, Stephen was Saint Stephen (the Hungarian designation is *Szent István király* literally "Saint Stephen king").[4] His state was a bulwark of western (Latin) Christianity. However, unlike the Catholic Church in that other great stronghold of the West in Eastern Europe, Poland, the Catholic Church in Hungary has in recent decades experienced an accelerating decline in its position in the life of the nation. This can be documented in obvious ways, including levels of church attendance, but it needs also to be understood less tangibly, in terms of the image presented by the Church and its leaders in society, including the intelligentsia. The explanations are complex, but include historical factors (such as the presence, unlike in Poland, of significant Protestant minorities—who also happen to be strongly associated with the Transylvanian regions) as well as characteristics of the socialist period, among which the "consumerist" orientation which dominated economic policies in Hungary from the 1960s onwards is the most

lowing editorial statement by a distinguished and well-connected journalist: "This year the entire country has been commemorating the 950th anniversary of Stephen's death. Although this is no centenary, the political leadership, the Catholic Church and, indeed, the general public, all felt that we should not wait another 12 years to celebrate him on the millennial of his coronation. At a time of refinding their national identity, Hungarians should reach back to their oldest roots . . ." (Boldizsár 1988, 5).

[Further developments cannot be chronicled here. Twelve years after these lines were written, under the first government of Viktor Orbán, to mark the millennial the Holy Crown was transferred from the National Museum to a politically more potent location in Parliament.]

4 Precise names were of some importance in 1988. In at least one major settlement, the southern city of Pécs, there was a debate about whether to restore the word "Saint" in the designation of "Stephen's Square," the religious title having been officially dropped by the state in the Stalinist period. After strong representations by local citizens it was duly restored.

important. But by 1988 the church had cause to feel that a revival was overdue. It had a new leader, László Paskai, who was raised to the status of Cardinal as the anniversary celebrations reached their height in 1988.[5] There was a widespread feeling among non-Catholics as well as Catholics that, as the long consumer boom seemed to be over, the Church had both an opportunity and a duty to preach a renewal of spiritual values. The anniversary of Stephen's death was therefore a convenient one, all the more so as it could be linked with a year of Marian devotion, in a manner I shall explain below.

In the background to the Church's treatment of the Stephen anniversary was another anniversary relating to an event that many contemporary Hungarians can actually remember. This was the 50th anniversary of an International Eucharistic Congress organized by the Catholic Church in Budapest in 1938. That congress was planned to mark the 900th anniversary of Stephen's death. By all accounts, it provided a focus for a range of national/secular and religious/spiritual energies similar to those unleashed in 1988. But, whereas the conservative government of that era could depend upon the Catholic Church as a natural ally of the state, the Church-state relationship was more problematic for a socialist government, especially following the highly antagonistic relations of the early decades of socialism (Beeson 1982, 257–87). Nevertheless, in 1988 both state publishing houses and the various Church organs gave substantial publicity to the events commemorating 1938.[6]

---

[5] Paskai had become primate of the Hungarian Catholic Church in 1987 after the death of Cardinal László Lékai in 1986. The latter, though popular and respected, was felt by many to have been too accommodating to the secular authorities. His successor was not well known, and had little in the way of charisma, but most ordinary Catholics were ready to give him a chance. For a well-informed discussion see Eibner 1988.

[6] See Gergely 1988, Seredi 1988. The latter is an abridged one-volume reissue of a massive three volume comparative study of Stephen and his age, first published in Budapest in 1938. There was apparently some reluctance among leading historians in 1988 when they were invited at short notice to organize an academic meeting devoted to Stephen. They were afraid, not unreasonably, that the published proceedings of a hastily convened Workshop would be compared unfavorably with the scholarship of their predecessors. See Glatz 1988, 239–52.

The Image of Stephen Through the Ages

To understand different attitudes to Stephen in 1988 it is insufficient to restrict the enquiry to what different groups in society are doing with Stephen in the contemporary context. The accumulated layers of mythology begin long before 1938. Although the sources available are inadequate, especially for the earlier centuries, it seems that he emerged very early as the crucial figure in the legitimation of statehood and territory, complementing the older *mythomoteur* of the Hungarians that was rooted in nomadism (Armstrong 1982, 47–51).[7] This image was first dramatically formulated in Stephen's canonization in 1083 (when King Ladislas, not a direct descendant of Stephen, instigated the proclamation of the first Hungarian saints in order to consolidate his own position on the throne) and by the convenient identification and location of a suitable relic, Stephen's right arm, in the following year.

According to a recent study of the text known as *Saint Stephen's Exhortations*, in which the monarch provides some political and ethical tips to his son Prince Imre, Stephen is shown to be an exemplary Christian monarch of the period:

> . . . the *Exhortations'* political theory ideologically separated the rulers' power from society's older, pagan, barbarian sector on the one hand, and placed it under the control of society's new, Christian, feudal sector on the other. King Stephen established the relationship between the Hungarian state and contemporary Europe and underpinned the sovereignty of the ruler in terms of

[7] The Hungarian sources I have consulted include various popularizing works disseminated in 1988 by both secular and religious publishing houses, a more scholarly collection of commentaries and documents (Györffy 1973), and the monograph of the leading contemporary authority on the period (Györffy 1977). See also Berend (1988). Hungarian historians have been claiming since the beginning of the twentieth century that they are now at last in a position to dispel the myths and give their readers the truth about Stephen (see Karácsonyi 1904). However, there remain significant differences of interpretation between scholars of opposing world views, and even some discrepancies as to "facts," some of which have been highlighted by the Catholic historian Thomas von Bogyay (1979).

> theology. In terms of ethics he regulated the relationship between royal power and society. On the theoretical level this early feudal, Christian monarch exists in a twofold functional relationship; between royal dignity and universal Christianity, and between king and politically active members of his society. Herein lies the basis for that dynamic development of the medieval state that neither barbarian nor despotic systems ever knew. (Szűcs 1988, 97)

Jenő Szűcs is concerned here to link Hungarian political developments to the Christian west rather than with the authoritarian regimes of the east, a topos which is dear to many intellectuals in Hungary today. This distinguished historian insists that Stephen had no ambition to be an absolutist ruler, and even recognized "an early precursor of what constitutional history calls the right of resistance" (*ibid*). But an anthropological history will be more wary of supposing a sudden rupture with the "tribal" past. Violent conflicts erupted after Stephen's death. These remained close to the surface long after the political stabilization achieved under Ladislas. This may help to explain the relatively low profile of Stephen in Hungarian popular culture in succeeding centuries. In folk tales and folk beliefs he is overshadowed by Ladislas himself, who also became a saint, and by another ruler who, though not achieving sainthood, approximated better the ideal type of the "Good King": Mathias Corvinus. Stephen's low profile in the eyes of his folk is unsurprising when one reflects on the social tensions of those early centuries. Hungarians did not all give up their pagan beliefs immediately, and not all did so willingly. Absolutist or not, the power of the new state was surely experienced by many as something novel and unwelcome.[8] Stephen's image was that of a distant potentate. It was cultivated in later centuries by several chronicles and by highly stereotyped representations, showing Stephen clad in royal robes and crown, holding the same ceremonial regalia (lance, cross, sword etc.). The circulation of these texts and portraits was limited. Although Stephen's sarcophagus

[8] I am indebted to Mihály Sárkány for drawing my attention to the fact that Stephen's representations are largely restricted to the sphere of state political domination. Gábor Klaniczay (1988) argues that the failure of the legends concerning Stephen to connect with pagan or folk mythologies was consistent with a wider European pattern. For comparative discussion see Wilson 1983.

was placed in the Byzantine style in the cathedral of Székesfehérvár, and although relics were displayed in other religious centers, no major cults developed around the founder of the state.

This was to change in later centuries. Following the retreat of the Ottoman Turks and the consolidation of a strong Habsburg state, a common theme of Jesuit activities during the Counterreformation was adapted to the Hungarian context. This involved the idea of Stephen offering up his country to the protection of the Blessed Virgin Mary. The virgin, now officially deemed to be "the Queen of Hungary," came to function as a sort of partner for Stephen.[9] Only in the age of modern nationalism, when political society expanded to include the mass of the peasant population, did Stephen make the transition from remote potentate to prime national hero. His role was highlighted by the periods of Ottoman occupation and Habsburg absolutist domination: Stephen was needed precisely to remind all Hungarians that they could lay claim to a long history of independent statehood. This process was in full swing in the latter half of the nineteenth century, when Hungarian national identity was very strongly emphasized, both in relation to Austria and toward the subject peoples of the Habsburg monarchy. Monuments to Stephen were erected all over the country, including the famous equestrian statue next to the Mathias Church in Budapest (unveiled in 1906). Stephen remained primarily a political symbol, yet the Roman Catholic Church played the major role in popularizing him. The largest ecclesiastical building in the new capital was called after him; and there was now systematic propagation of his embalmed "Holy Right" (Hand) (the Hungarian omits the word hand—*Szent Jobb*). The 1938 Congress in Budapest was the culmination of Stephen's celebration in Hungarian nationalist ideology, in the context of the deep-seated discontent which pervaded the country after the territorial losses

[9] This was not altogether an invention, since historical sources dating from the German Bishop Hartvik's legend, compiled in the early twelfth century, facilitated the consolidation of a link with Mary (Klaniczay 1986, 76). Stephen's church at Székesfehérvár was dedicated to Mary and, most conveniently, Stephen had died on a major Marian feast day, that of the Assumption (August 15). It is tempting to suggest that the ruling class which forcibly imposed a Christian feudal state on a recalcitrant tribal society went out of its way to encourage devotion to Mary to compensate for the female deities which Hungarians were being asked to abandon.

Figure 11. Statue of King Stephen on the Fishermens' Bastion, Budapest (photo by Chris Hann, 2013)

of the Trianon Peace Treaty in 1920. Artists produced countless monumental representations of the Saint King in these years.[10]

While the modern Hungarian nation can in some ways be seen as the product of a "revival" of the nineteenth century, essential icons of this national movement were by no means new and artificial. Rather, they were built upon cultural foundations developed over many centuries among elite groups and already partially diffused into popular culture. The Stephen tradition was consistently prominent from the moment of Ladislas's restoration. In this sense, Stephen can indeed be seen as the omnipresent builder of the nation.

[10] A typical example was a giant tapestry by Noémi Ferenczy, on which "The holy king is seated in front of a church, palace or royal mansion under construction as he receives the homage and gifts from his people. By showing a wall still in the process of being built the artist wished to refer to Saint Stephen's work as a nation builder." See Gizella Cennerné Willhelm, *The Image of Saint Stephen in Hungarian History*, a brochure accompanying the exhibition at the Hungarian National Museum August-October 1988 (Budapest, 1988).

This link has not been seriously weakened in the socialist period. Not much was heard about Stephen in the first decades of socialist rule, the messianic phase-of a new "secular theology" which had no room for kings or saints and little for national symbols of any kind. However, with the maturing and later the souring of the "Kádár settlement," the last decade has witnessed a strong resurgence of historical thinking among Hungarians, including government spokesmen, churchmen, and large numbers of artists and intellectuals. The theme of Stephen became prominent in popular discourse long before the 1988 anniversary, thanks in particular to a rock opera based on Stephen's life, performed with spectacular success by some of the country's most gifted popular musicians in 1983. I began to realize how the Stephen symbols were continuing to function as a result of discussing the impact of this work with friends in Budapest.[11]

The most important aspect for the majority of Hungarians was undoubtedly a general patriotic one. The rock opera was a celebration of the life and work of Stephen as a national hero. He was shown, amidst great spectacle, to be the founder of the state and the vanquisher of all challengers. Anachronistic from the point of view of contemporary verisimilitude, but in keeping with the nationalist spirit of the work, some of the costumes could be identified with the Transylvanian regions contested over the centuries with Romania. Stephen's crown, lance, insignia etc. were all prominently displayed, not only at the public performances (initially in the open-air, in front of vast crowds, before transferring to a downtown theatre for a successful run) but also on the covers of books, magazines, records, film posters and so forth.[12]

Yet, Stephen's opponents are also Hungarians, wild men who boast loudly of their patriotism, and denigrate Stephen for (among other faults) bringing in foreign troops to the country and acknowledging "a God who cannot speak Hungarian." These pagans look to their leader Koppány to preserve their old tribal society. Some of their pre-

---

[11] For a wider range of opinions and information about this rock opera see Koltay 1984. For criticism of the enterprise from an academic authority, see Klaniczay 1984. For more radical (*samizdat*) analysis of the political motives of the work (and of the authorities in allowing it to be staged) see Emericus 1984–85.

[12] The film version scored a *succès d'estime* at the 1984 Cannes Festival, under the title *Étienne le Roi*.

Christian motifs also figure prominently in the content and publicity of the opera, and this strand, too, is dealt with respectfully by the artists. This bears out John Armstrong's theory (1982) that the Hungarians have continued to make use of a double legitimating myth: alongside Stephen they have also needed to stress the distinctiveness of their origins, as nomads, when compared with their neighbors who all became settled agriculturalists much earlier in history. At the same time, these signs of difference served to emphasize the antiquity of the Hungarian people. One design could be readily associated with the unorthodox but strongly patriotic theories of a popularizing archaeologist concerning the Hungarian settlement of the Carpathian Basin.[13] This rock opera emphasized Stephen's political significance and was presumably seen in these terms by the authorities who permitted performances. It was entitled King Stephen, rather than Saint Stephen. However the work in no way belittles his religious significance. Christians in the audiences were not made to feel that their saint was being distorted to fit a socialist mold. Much of the music has a hymn-like quality, and some of the lyrics convey a powerful religiosity.[14]

The ability of this musical extravaganza to offer different messages to different people did not stop there. Among intellectuals, there were those who quickly tired of the publicity given to the opera. Some were inclined to see it as an attempt by the authorities to stimulate an anodyne patriotism to divert citizens' attention away from the serious problems facing the country at home and abroad. Others, knowing that some of the artists involved were themselves thoughtful commentators who had in the past smuggled political messages into their pop songs, looked for layers of profundity in the lyrics of King Stephen. When Stephen faced his most awkward dilemma—was he prepared to use highly unpleasant methods to preserve the unity of the nation and the

---

[13] Gyula László is the archaeologist and the image in question derives from a celebrated find in Transylvania. See László and Rácz 1977.

[14] For example several Latin texts are set to music to good effect. The hero sings verses such as the following: "Speak my God/ Make manifest to me/ Your infinite power/ Show me the meaning of my life/ Speak my God/ Give me a sign now/ Give me strength to fight/ Let my life be worthy of you/ Beautiful and good/ Grant then/ That in Accordance with your wish/This should become Your country/ And I shall entrust my life to You."

structure of the state?—audiences could detect parallels with Hungary's modern situation, compromising in order to survive. More specifically, some saw a subtle commentary on the post-1956 settlement: like Stephen's firm handling of his own internal counter-revolution, it could be seen as painful but essential. Of course the commentary was not exact, some interlocutors told me (by this point setting the text aside and relying on their subjective interpretations); for whereas in Stephen's time the threat to the Hungarians came from powerful states to the West, everyone in Hungary knew from which direction their statehood was threatened in the second half of the twentieth century.

The "Holy Right"

The music from the King Stephen rock opera was still being frequently played (even in church services) at the time of the 1988 anniversaries. The constellation of messages was broadly as identified above. The authorities placed greater emphasis upon Stephen's role as a modernizer, a leader who wished to incorporate his people into Europe, just as the new and technocratic communist leadership of Károly Grósz attempted to present itself as tackling a serious economic crisis by improving its relations with western partners. These policies included new elements of political pluralism as well as attempts to improve the economy.[15]

The Stephen symbol was more dramatically taken up in 1988 by the Roman Catholic Church. Policies of tough resistance to the atheistic socialist government were epitomized in the 1940s and 1950s by the hard-line stance of Cardinal József Mindszenty. When dogmatism faded on the government side after the Kádár settlement, the Church took some time to adapt and find a new direction. The 1970s saw the development of a much warmer relationship with the secular authorities, which did little to reassure believers. Some began to complain that their own leaders were going too far in fruitless dialogues with socialists committed to consumerist reforms, whilst neglecting the moral and

[15] Grósz replaced János Kádár as party secretary in May 1988, before losing the political struggle to "reform communists'" (most prominent among them Imre Pozsgay) in 1989. See Lendvai (1988, chapter 10).

spiritual foundations of their faithful.[16] Criticisms of the stance taken by the hierarchy in Hungary were often emphasized by comparisons with the strength of Catholicism in Poland, especially after the election in 1978 of a Polish cardinal as Pope. During the 1980s there was an emerging consensus among Hungarian Catholics that some major initiative was needed to regain lost ground; the Stephen anniversary provided an ideal opportunity.

The most conspicuous example of the Church's harnessing of the anniversary was the decision to launch the country's most holy relic, Stephen's Right Hand, on a nationwide tour to all diocesan centers and certain other places of religious significance, culminating in extensive (and televised) ritual exposure on August 20, Saint Stephen's Day. The history of this relic is complex.[17] The leading contemporary scholar regards its authenticity as highly probable. It seems clear that it was first invested with great symbolic significance in the period of feudal consolidation which took place under King Ladislas, half a century after Stephen's death. It was venerated in the medieval period, but it did not become an object of popular devotion throughout the country. This point seems to be confirmed by a divergence of views among scholars as to when the relic left Hungary: it was probably either in the course of the Tatar invasion of 1241, or in 1541, when much of the country was under Ottoman occupation. Nor is there agreement among the experts

[16] Concerning the controversies generated by Father György Bulányi and his "basis community" groups, see the condemnatory letter of Cardinal Joseph Ratzinger (1987).

[17] Although the 1988 nationwide tour of the "Holy Right" regularly included a talk by a senior churchman about the history of the relic, I was unable to locate a full scholarly analysis. Conflicting published accounts, including that of Györffy 1977, are probed by Ruffy 1988; see also Szántó 1988. From a comparative anthropological perspective it is significant that it was the right hand which came to outweigh various other Stephen relics in circulation (cf. Hertz [1909] 1960). The power of the right arm (later reduced to knuckles and fist when the relic was divided) is evidently linked to the domination established by Stephen in his new state. In Hungarian *jobb* means "right" (opposite of left), but it also means "better" (comparative form of *jó*, "good"). In the early medieval period it was apparently interchangeable with *jog* which later became the standard Hungarian term for "law," as well as "right" in the sense of "title" or "claim." This semantic field is not dissimilar to that found elsewhere in Europe, both east and west of Hungary.

as to when and in how many stages a complete right arm was shortened into the stump of the hand which has been displayed to pilgrims over the last few hundred years. It turned up in Dubrovnik in 1590, where it became an object of mass devotion. Its return to Hungary was organized in 1771 by Maria Theresia, the reigning Habsburg monarch, upon advice received from a Jesuit, György Pray. Pray was a key figure in the intellectual revival which was just getting under way in Hungary, and which can be seen as laying the groundwork for the era of mass nationalism.[18] Between 1777 and 1882 the Holy Right was preserved in a chapel of the Royal Palace in Buda, where it was in the custody of a German order, the Knights of the Star Cross. After 1882 its guardians were regular Hungarian clergy, but its location was still not conducive to mass pilgrimages. The major new departure, greatly increasing the exposure of the Holy Right Hand, came in the inter-war period when it was given pride of place annually in the August 20 procession in Budapest. In 1938 it was circulated all over the country as part of the 900th anniversary celebrations and the International Congress held in Hungary that year. Photographs of the "golden train" used to take the relic around the country in 1938 were reproduced in the Catholic press in 1988. After 1950 the Holy Right was prominently displayed in Saint Stephen's Basilica in Budapest, but procession outside was prohibited.

Of course the rituals of 1988 differed from those of 1938 in numerous ways. Black cars replaced the golden train, and ceremonies were confined to the spaces inside and immediately adjacent to the major religious centers visited by the Holy Right. Newspapers, both secular and ecclesiastical, reported the speeches made on these occasions by the two sets of authorities, religious and secular. The reporting styles were remarkably similar, with the Catholic press concentrating on formal lists of religious dignitaries present in order of seniority, exactly as the socialist media listed the secular apparatchiks. (This mimesis was a good illustration of why some Hungarian Catholics had come over the years to perceive their own leadership as little different from the hierarchies of secular power.) Typically, the secular representatives would empha-

[18] Pray purported to discover authenticating texts in medieval Latin accompanying the relic. These disappeared mysteriously in the mid-nineteenth century. They were apparently found again in 1940 and even photographed, but both the pictures and the original disappeared at the end of the war.

size Stephen as the founder of the nation-state and as a modernizer who "chose Europe," whilst the religious authorities stressed his activities on behalf of the Church; but sometimes the latter, too, placed greater emphasis upon his nation-building activities. The state spokesmen were gracious in recognizing the role of the Church in Hungarian history, whilst the Church spokesmen gave full recognition to Stephen's activities outside the specific sphere of religion. Beneath the compliments and mutual congratulation of the formal speeches, Church and state were out to claim Stephen for rather different legitimating purposes, with the emphasis on the national importance common to both camps.[19]

The rituals were apparently much the same throughout the summer's touring, though local themes were highlighted wherever possible. The village of Tázlár falls in the diocese of Kalocsa. When the Holy Right visited for a weekend in mid-June there was great play on the fact that this was the diocese of Anastasias (Asztrik), the bishop who brought Stephen his sacred crown from the Pope at the turn of the millennium. Later in the summer, just before the saint's feast day, a newly commissioned statue of Stephen was unveiled on the square in front of the cathedral, and a new permanent exhibition of ecclesiastical treasures was opened with formal speeches from representatives of both church and state, who had combined to organize it.[20]

---

19 In the media, church spokesmen regularly digressed into secular topics, above all concerning Hungarian identity and the values of a "small nation." For example, the Archbishop of Kalocsa declared that "The future of the small nation can be summed up in three words: to be different. This is Saint Stephen's program. This is the guarantee of progress and victory." (reported in *Új Ember*, July 3, 1988). Secular speakers frequently invoked "our national relic" and sometimes noted ideals more commonly associated with religious teachings, including family values and the need to improve moral standards. For another example of the "dialogue" between church and state spokesmen on these ritual occasions, see reports on speeches delivered at Vác in early August in the newspaper *Katolikus Szó*, August 28, 1988.

20 Newspaper reports (*Új Ember*, September 11, 1988) introduced the sculptor as Károly Kirchmayer, adding the recognition he had received as a "Trades Union Congress Prize winner." This article went on to quote the bishop's clear awareness that, in consigning many of the cathedral's most treasured objects to the exhibition room, he was launching them into new contexts which would include cultural education within Hungary, the edification of tourists and the circulation of the objects via the national network of museums.

Inevitably, most publicity focused on the major celebrations in the capital, outside Saint Stephen's Basilica, on August 20 itself. There was prolonged applause from the massive congregation thronging the square and adjacent streets when it was announced that the secular authorities were extending an official invitation to Pope John-Paul II to visit Hungary. In a long letter, read out on this occasion, the Pope gave a careful appreciation of Stephen's role in Hungarian history. Relations with Romania over the Transylvanian issue were exceptionally strained at this time; standing guard ceremonially on the public podium beside the Holy Right was a female writer dressed in the folk costume of one of the best-known districts of Transylvania.[21]

Another exceptionally interesting weekend in the tour was that which the Holy Right spent in Székesfehérvár, center of the state and church in Stephen's own time, and the site of his grave, from which various relics had disappeared so mysteriously. The cathedral already housed a relic that was supposedly part of István's head, with a history almost as confused as that of the Holy Right, but not so infused with either patriotic or religious significance (at least not in recent times). When the Holy Right arrived at the cathedral entrance it was greeted by the Head Relic (*Fejereklye*) and both were placed together in the sanctuary. The local bishop made a speech in which he suggested that, with these two relics together again, Stephen could be perceived almost as a "living figure." More secular messages were conveyed by the county secretary of the Patriotic People's Front, an organization under the control of the socialist authorities. He suggested parallels, by now familiar to audiences, between Stephen's state formation at the beginning of the millennium, and the current need at the end of the millennium to "catch up with the European leaders, by modernizing economic and social life."[22]

I observed proceedings in the southern city of Szeged, close to the Yugoslav border, on Sunday September 25. Crowds were large and very well ordered, marshalled by hundreds of stewards. Mass was celebrated by the local bishop and temporary stands were erected to enable a total congregation of several thousands to participate (including many

21 A full account of the celebrations of August 20, including the complete text of the papal letter, can be found in *Katolikus Szó*, August 28, 1988.

22 *Ibid.*

outside the cathedral). Most of us joined a queue to file past the Holy Right, positioned in front of the main altar. We were allowed only a few seconds to view the object itself, and not a great deal longer to inspect a small accompanying exhibition of photographs and texts. Outside, however, there was ample opportunity to buy souvenirs of the occasion, which ranged from expensive reprints of the 1938 commemorative albums to cheap lapel badges. Several private entrepreneurs were vying for position alongside the stalls of the major ecclesiastical publishers, and the hot dogs were cheaper than some of the prayer cards on offer. I have no doubt that for some pilgrims to Szeged on that September Sunday the occasion provided a satisfying religious experience, simply because of the throng and the sense that, after so many years, the Catholic Church was able once again demonstrate its vitality on the city streets.[23] At the same time, for many Catholics (I suspect the large majority), it remained a rather superficial occasion. Families were out for the day (some had travelled from nearby Vojvodina especially for the occasion), and although grandmother might be close to tears as the memories of a 1938 visit to Budapest came flooding back, her children looked more keen to visit the Sunday market (which was open for business as usual), and her grandchildren were frankly bored by both. In short, I doubt whether the Stephen celebrations evoked intense "private" religiosity. I do not think the Church even tried to exploit Stephen in this way. By and large clergymen themselves were content to praise Stephen for his national role, and for building up the institutional framework of the church in Hungary. For more profoundly evocative areas of consciousness they could draw on other resources. Herein lies the secret of their great advantage over the secular authorities.[24]

---

[23] The effervescence reminded me of what I observed when the city of Kraków was transformed during John Paul II's first return to Poland in June 1979.

[24] In addition to emphasizing Stephen's political contribution, some interpreters sought also to direct attention to another level, the familial. This was attempted most clearly by the Pope himself in his letter (*Katolikus Szó,* August 28, 1988): "his family life was similarly exemplary. He was a caring husband to Blessed Gizella of Bavaria, sister of the Emperor Henry. Inspired by deep faith he established a monastery next to his palace in order to be able constantly to pray for his family and his people. He sought to provide for his succession like a good father worrying about the fate of his people." Even here the family element is subordinated to the political.

The Marian Complement

The modern representations of Stephen, certainly those of the last hundred years or so, show a very male figure, often astride a horse which is also of exceptionally powerful appearance. This seems to fit well with the main role that Stephen is called upon to play, as national hero for a Hungarian people that has had to fight to maintain its territory in a hotly contested area of Europe. He is able to play this role equally well for Protestants, as well as for the small population of Eastern-rite Catholics (Uniates or Greek Catholics, see Chapter Ten), and indeed for all Hungarians.[25] The significance of this role was highlighted in 1988 by the poor relations between Hungary and Romania. Church leaders regularly highlighted the plight of the Hungarian minority in Transylvania, even though these Hungarians are mostly Calvinists who, for doctrinal reasons, take a dim view of rituals such as those which have evolved around the Holy Right. The point here is that Stephen remains important for the legitimation of a state identity which would have included the Transylvanian territories. The Roman Catholic Church can thus commend itself to all those Hungarians who still have not accepted the borders established at the Trianon Treaty (1920), which the present secular authorities, in contrast to the pre-socialist regimes, are prevented from openly contesting. The Church is thus able to insinuate more through the Stephen symbol than is possible for the socialist authorities, even in purely secular contexts.

But the Church can also penetrate further zones of identity which socialists neglect or ignore. I suggest that the figure of Mary plays a very different and complementary role to that of Stephen in Hungarian

[25] The position of the Orthodox and Eastern-rite (Uniate) Catholics in Hungary is interesting, as they have historically viewed Stephen as a convert to the Byzantine rite rather than to that of the Roman Church. Uniates, or Greek Catholics as they are commonly known, see him as the forerunner of the combination which they practice today, viz. political recognition of the papacy and membership of the international Catholic community, combined with loyalty to the rites and customs of the East. The itinerary of the "Holy Right" included a weekend at Máriapócs, which is not only a major center for Hungary's 200,000 Uniates, but also a center of Marian devotion for all Hungarian Catholics.

Catholicism, and that this role was seen especially clearly in 1988. Formally, as stated above, Mary is the Queen of Hungary, just as she is the Queen of Poland. In practice, despite the political origins of the modern Marian cults in the Counter-Reformation period, her role has not spilled over to the "political" sphere as it has in Poland. The contrast may well predate the appearance of lasting and significant Protestant minorities in Hungary, for there was never a single dominant cult center such as Polish Catholics had at Częstochowa (Szajkowski 1983). Although Mary has her cult centers in Hungary, they have been largely devoid of political significance in the life of the nation.

In recent years the Polish Pope has done much to stimulate Mariology in many parts of the world. He has promoted a combination of established (though far from ancient) elements of the folk tradition in Christianity—contact with the deity through the mediation of Jesus's mother—with a more modern emphasis upon spiritual meditation that posits Mary as the source of enduring Christian values, including those most threatened in contemporary materialist civilization. The Catholic Church's declaration of a Marian Year in 1987–88 therefore offered Hungarians the chance to link their national celebrations with an active strand in international Catholicism. Stephen was reputed to have offered up his kingdom to Mary. Many of the sermons and church publications connected with Stephen in 1988 make a great play on this relationship. In some contexts they appear as equivalents: for example, both Mary and Stephen could be asked to intercede on behalf of ethnic brothers in Romania.[26] However, at other times it is apparent that they are by no means interchangeable, and that the renewal of Christian commitment which the Catholic Church in Hungary called upon its followers to make in 1988 had a spiritual dimension that focused solely upon Mary. The future of the people/nation was dependent upon Mary's motherly love and concern, qualities not strongly associated with Stephen.[27]

The implication, it seems to me, is that the virile, male symbol of national identity is inadequate in itself. It needs to be subordinated to some "higher" symbol. As Stephen offered up his country to Mary,

---

26 See Cardinal Paskai's speech, reported in *Új Ember*, July 31, 1988.

27 See later sections of the same speech by Cardinal Paskai, *ibid.*

so today Catholics are encouraged to renew his offering by dedicating themselves to her. Thus, in the modern setting, the Virgin Mary is for Hungarian Catholics both a symbol of their international Catholic identity, and at the same time a focus for moral anxieties and spiritual needs for which neither Stephen nor the deity himself are available. Village grandmothers are not the only Catholics who pray devoutly to Mary, but I doubt that many Hungarian Catholics address Stephen with such intensity.

These suggestions are inspired by recent anthropological approaches to the sexual division of labor in religion and ritual, and to the question of gender in religious symbolism. Whereas John Davis (1984) sets out to explain sharp imbalances in the degree of religiosity shown by men and women in both Catholic and Islamic areas of the Mediterranean, Cornelia Sorabji (1989) has shown in her work on Bosnian Muslim identity that in Sarajevo certain ritual activities of men relate primarily to an international context of identity (as Muslims), whilst those of women connect to the national level (as Bosnians). The roles are complementary and equally respected. Caroline Walker Bynum and others (1986) have set themselves the still more ambitious task of explaining *why* the central symbols of religious systems should be gendered as they are.

I suggest that the Stephen-Mary polarity works to express different aspects of identity in contemporary Hungary. Two levels need to be distinguished analytically. Firstly, this symbolic pairing is reflected in the "sexual division of religious labor" among Hungarian Catholics. Men view Stephen more enthusiastically than do women, while the latter are more prominent as devotees of Mary, in associations such as Rosary Societies, which were ubiquitous in Catholic parishes in the pre-socialist period. Secondly, and more significantly, I argue that for both men and women Mary is a figure of richer and deeper potential than Stephen, able to meet more fundamental identity needs. If this generalization is correct (there is certainly huge variation according to generation as well as education, place of residence and many other factors), the pattern which emerges is the reverse of Sorabji's Bosnian model, since in Hungary it is the male side which emphasizes a national identity and the female side that is associated with an "external" and international religious identity. However, it is also the female side which seems to bear greater "internal" religious weight, i.e. Mary serves as the major focus for spirituality, "private" religiosity, as Davis would predict (1984, 18).

The state's problem is that not only does it have to compete hard with the Roman Catholic Church to uphold its own claim on Stephen as a national figure, but it really can put up no fight at all when the ground shifts away from specifically national symbolism. In theory the equivalent complementary elements, both the "international" and the "internal," are supplied by socialist ideology. Perhaps Marxism-Leninism functioned to meet these needs, for some of its faithful, for a short period of history. But socialism in Hungary, as a result of the course it has followed under the Kádár settlement (though the picture does not seem much different under other kinds of socialist regime), has long ceased to be able to operate in these dimensions. Whilst the Catholic Church can claim Stephen as a saint and national hero, and invoke Mary to satisfy other identity needs, the secular authorities can orchestrate rival claims about Stephen—but that is all they can do. There is nothing in contemporary socialism that equips it symbolically and emotionally to undertake this distinctive "female" role.

Conclusion

This chapter has touched briefly upon five phases in Hungarian history, a pre-Christian (tribal) phase, a feudal monarchy phase, an absolutist monarchy phase (foreign—i.e. Habsburg-dominated), and finally the phases of bourgeois nationalism and socialist nationalism. The original Stephen was the instrument of the transition from phase one to phase two, a very radical transition by any standards. His symbolic importance in the life of the nation has been great, at least since the consolidation achieved under King Ladislas, when Stephen was elevated to the company of the royal saints. However, he did not fit the image of other "popular" saints, and his importance remained primarily political: the strong right hand which destroyed the old society earned him respect but did not endear him to the people. The Stephen symbol acquired a new role when Hungary fell under foreign rule, and again when political society was widened to include all members of the nation. This process began at the end of phase three, and seems to be culminating in phase five, when we can observe both the socialist state and the Catholic Church making extensive use of Stephen for their different legitimating purposes. I have suggested that the symbol was modified through the different phases of Hungarian history, and that it was always a question of reworking older materials rather than starting afresh. In the contemporary situation it is not unusual to find images of Stephen surrounded by a kaleidoscope ranging from pre-Christian insignia to nineteenth century folk costumes. All this facilitates the simultaneous communication of rather different messages.

My argument is that the Stephen symbol, when complemented by that of Mary, provides Hungarian Catholics with a totalizing ideological system that operates at individual and international levels as well as the national. The socialist state, though to some extent successful in appropriating Stephen as a national hero, has not succeeded in adding suitable symbolic foci for other human identity needs. For the state, then, participating in a competition to appropriate this symbol, rather than fostering legitimation, may in the end highlight serious deficiencies of socialist systems. The present state has had increasing recourse to powerful symbols of the national past because it has, in effect, given up the very elements in its own ideology which might have provided alternative sources of symbolic support. The more utopian elements of the socialist program were jettisoned in the name of Kádárist "pragmatism" after the disasters of the Stalinist era. So long as economic performance was satisfactory, legitimation problems were not urgent. But as soon as the economy began to weaken, compensating efforts in the symbolic dimension were called for. Hence the authorization of rock operas on the theme of King Stephen, and the state's initiative in organizing joint church-state celebrations of Stephen's 950th anniversary. But, given that no secular authorities can ever entirely succeed in appropriating Stephen from the Catholics, and given that in the symbolic world of Hungarian Catholicism Stephen has powerful allies beyond the reach of secular manipulation, first and foremost the Blessed Virgin Mary, it would seem more logical for the state to concentrate upon improving its performance in more prosaic dimensions—sponsoring fewer historical extravaganzas and turning instead to radical economic and political reforms.

Appendix[28]

I stumbled on the Stephen celebrations in the summer of 1988 by accident, during visits that were not intended to be field trips at all. Twenty-five years later I went back to take note of changes. In 2013 there were no surprises to compare with the spectacular revival of the cult of the Holy Right and the sense that an entire socio-political order might be coming to a close. There were no posters to celebrate Constitution Day, only a ubiquitous government poster carrying the slogan "united for the country." The crowds along the banks of the Danube included large numbers of visitors from Transylvania, many wearing folk costume and displaying large loaves of "new bread." I found that, in the capital as in Tázlár, Stephen and Mary were continuing their ritual collaboration. Now, however, they were working together to legitimate the postsocialist political order, rather than to offer an alternative order to that of the socialists. Some of the festivities had a strong religious coloring, but the day had retained its ludic character, epitomized in the fireworks which brought it to a close. No statesmen made speeches on the main holiday (though they did so in the days before—indeed a cabinet meeting was held on August 18 in Székesfehérvár, the city which houses Stephen's sarcophagus). A galaxy of dignitaries, including Prime Minister Viktor Orbán, attended Holy Mass on August 20 at St Stephen's basilica. However, they left the oratory to Cardinal Péter Erdő, who dutifully invoked Mary alongside Stephen in his sermon while pointing out that the country still needed the guiding hands of both. Overall, the events corresponded to Zdzisław Mach's characterization of state rituals: "at times of relative social peace they become routinized, and then people's participation in them gives legitimation to the political authorities without people being aware of the ideological significance of their behavior" (Mach 1993, 157). Participation on August 20, nowadays as under socialism, is voluntary and seemingly devoid of party-political content. Yet, as Mach shows, such events have profound implications for the legitimation of a political order.

---

28 *This appendix draws on an essay written for a Festschrift for a good friend in Kraków, Zdzisław Mach, which contains a fuller description of the rituals of St Stephen's Day as I witnessed them in 2013 (Hann 2014c).*

Figure 12. Procession of the "Holy Right" of King/Saint Stephen in downtown Pest (photo by Chris Hann, 2014)

If the 1980s were characterized by competition for the custody of the nation's most sacred symbols, in the 2010s it is hard to detect any means to oppose the present power holders in the symbolic dimension. But is this in fact an era of "relative social peace" in Hungary? In comparison with the late 1980s, my sense is rather the opposite: both among intellectuals in the capital and among villagers in Tázlár, I have the impression that multi-party democracy has brought not only contestation but rancor and intensifying social divisions. On August 20, these divisions are ostensibly transcended. With the implementation of his "National Cooperation Program" since 2010, Prime Minister Orbán has merged the cause of his party with that of the nation to form a seamless unity which the socialists could never match. Although he began his career as an outspoken critic of Soviet power and a fervent advocate of "rejoining Europe," the Prime Minister has in recent years frequently placed Brussels in the structural position previously occupied by Moscow. Without the financial benefits of EU membership, Hungary's economy would collapse, yet the political rhetoric of the ruling party emphasizes only the constraints.[29]

[29] In terms of political economy, the constellation is curiously similar to that of the socialist era. Hungary benefited during those decades from substantial Soviet subsidies, but these did not prevent the great majority of Hungarians

Like some Polish populist politicians, their equivalents in Hungary claim to be more faithful to Christian values than their neighbors and allies in the West, emasculated by the anodyne discourses of human rights and multiculturalism.

Two years later, on the eve of the national holiday, I attended an open-air revival of the rock opera discussed above in central Budapest. I noted (as did reviewers) that applause for the pagan Koppány and his allies was more vigorous than ever. This had to do less with the merits of particular songs and performers than it did with the widespread perception in the audience that this small nation is nowadays exposed to new forms of colonization—from Europe and the capitalist West. In the more formal speeches and ceremonies during the following day, migration and "security" issues were prominent. Significant numbers of refugees had been visible for months in Budapest's public sphere, notably in the "transit zone" at the recently refurbished plaza in front of the monumental Keleti train station. The government had intensified its efforts to prevent "illegal migration," notably through the construction of a barbed wire fence along the southern border with Serbia, the transit route for most of these unwelcome strangers. Hungarians are well aware of the opprobrium which this fence has brought them in other European countries, but Viktor Orbán and his government have defended their actions. Large posters all over the country proclaim: "We do not want illegal migrants." The ugly fence, the authorities insisted, is necessary in order to ensure that migrants cross the border where they are supposed to. In short, they claimed to be acting as good Europeans, the heirs to Stephen's Christian legacy, oblivious to the fact that Stephen himself had ruled over a population of great ethnic diversity.

In the speechmaking on August 20, 2015, the coarsening of the nationalist tone was unmistakable. The Prime Minister's principal representative spoke of an increasingly insupportable burden for the nation, while at the morning military ceremonies the Minister of Defense declared that "This is our homeland, not some sort of house with a passageway through it." In the main religious rituals late in the

from viewing the Soviet Union as a radically alien other. Otherness is more problematic when it takes the form of "Europe" (i.e. the EU), but as Armstrong (1982) pointed out, the Hungarian experience of a dual *mythomoteur* goes back a long way.

afternoon, when the sacred relic of Stephen's right hand processes through the streets around the Basilica which is named after him, Cardinal Péter Erdő invoked Stephen's teachings to call for a more tolerant approach to solving the problems posed by the unprecedented deluge of immigrants. Pope Francis later echoed these sentiments. But I found that, outside the liberal intelligentsia, these sentiments were not in line with public opinion. Villagers in Tázlár pointed out that their children had been unable to find work at home and compelled to move to Britain: how, then, could Hungary be expected to welcome newcomers from outside Europe? As the "migrant crisis" escalated in the following weeks, even senior figures in the Hungarian Roman Catholic Church expressed their support for the intolerant stance of their government.[30]

[30] See Hann 2016a.

CHAPTER EIGHT

Ethnicity in the New Civil Society: Lemko-Ukrainians in Poland

(1997)

> *I remember twenty years ago a Karen remarking to me, "I hope the British will stay in Burma for two hundred years." "Why?" "Because we do not wish to be ruled by Burmese." Even at the time it struck me that sooner or later this would become a problem. The fact is that the question of minorities is literally insoluble so long as nationalism remains a real force. The desire of some of the peoples of Burma for autonomy is genuine, but it cannot be satisfied in any secure way unless the sovereignty of Burma as a whole is interfered with. . . . Whenever A is oppressing B, it is clear to people of goodwill that B ought to be independent, but then it always turns out that there is another group, C, which is anxious to be independent of B. The question is always how large must a minority be before it deserves autonomy. At best, each case can only be treated on its merits in a rough and ready way: in practice, no one is consistent in his thinking on this subject, and the minorities which win the most sympathy are those that have the best means of publicity.*
>
> (Orwell 1970 [1947], 323–47)

Introduction[1]

The concepts of ethnicity and of civil society were not yet common currency when George Orwell wrote the above lines in 1947, but they have become pervasive in the sociological, anthropological, and political

[1] *Earlier drafts of this chapter were presented at conferences in Cambridge in March 1990 (Poland: Cultural, economic and political perspectives for the 1990s—orga-*

science literature of recent decades. They have certainly been widely used in commentaries on Eastern Europe in the immediate postsocialist period, where ethnicity and nationalism are commonly presented as the major threats to the extension of democracy and citizenship rights, for which civil society has come to serve as a shorthand. This latter term is often invoked to imply an autonomy from the state that in the conditions of modern industrial societies can only be mythical. Much of the rhetoric of civil society postulates an undifferentiated "people" opposed to the established forms of socialist statehood, but it seems to me that this is hardly any improvement on the rhetoric of totalitarianism, to which it stands as a sequel (Hann 1990b, 1995b). We need to be much more sensitive to the diversity of social and political relations of different East European countries under socialism, a diversity which remains evident in the 1990s. No general model of "civil society" can illuminate cases as divergent as the Czech and the Romanian, or the Polish and the Macedonian.

As for ethnicity, the intellectual terrain is still more confusing and contested. Despite much criticism of "primordialism," many still think of ethnicity in terms of fixed and clearly bounded groups possessed of a unique culture: in other words, in the ideological terms of modern nationalism. Political borders do sometimes coincide with more or less salient cultural boundaries, such as those marked by linguistic or religious differences, but until fairly recently this has been, in most parts of the world, the exception rather than the rule (Gellner 1983). Modern nationalist movements have struggled to create an unprecedented congruence between the political unit (the state) and the cultural unit (the nation). In areas as culturally heterogeneous as East and Central Europe, they face formidable obstacles. It is true that the proportion of the population constituted by national minorities has declined sharply in the course of the twentieth century. But, as Orwell noted

nized by Frances Pine and Chris Hann) and at Miskolc in July 1993 (Hungarian Sociological Association meeting: panel organized by László Kürti on Minority Issues and Inter-Ethnic Conflict in Eastern Europe). I am grateful to participants on both occasions, and also to Paul Robert Magocsi for a critical reading. Thanks also to a longstanding friend in Zyndranowa, Teodor (Fedor) Gocz. The paper was updated in the light of a field trip in summer 1994 (when Jacek Nowak kindly met me at Żdynia) and eventually published as Hann 1997.

for Southeast Asia, the emergence of each new sovereign state always seems to uncover another oppressed ethnic group, which then campaigns to establish its own separate unit. The new units have promoted their identities through the same basic repertoires as those pioneered by the national movements of the nineteenth century. Their members are expected, now as then, to take for granted that they can have but one ethno-national affiliation, which necessarily constitutes their "basic, most general identity" (Barth 1969, 15). The recent collapse of the socialist bloc has seemingly strengthened such forces in Central Europe. For example, no sooner have Slovakia and the Czech Republic separated to form their own states than we start to become aware of Hungarians who aspire to secede from the former, and even of Moravians who would like some form of autonomy within the latter.

Yet at the same time as we witness an apparent resurgence of ethnonationalism in East and Central Europe, elsewhere in Europe there is no shortage of voices proclaiming that the hegemony of the sovereign nation-state is already over. Eric Hobsbawm does not believe that ethno-nationalism in East and Central Europe can significantly obstruct the economic and political forces that are inexorably undermining nation-states everywhere (Hobsbawm 1992). Though it may be premature to claim that the development of a common European culture has progressed as rapidly as political and economic integration in the so-called European Union, it is clear that some of the distinctive features of "national traditions" have already been undermined by transnational trends. A whole academic industry has recently grown up around "globalization" and "McDonaldization." Some of the contributors to this literature have recognized, however, that increasing homogeneity in consumption styles may proceed in tandem with new ways of asserting local and personal identities. In the emerging "world civil society," local cultural transformations take place alongside and in a dialectical relationship with large scale transformations of political and economic structures. If the term ethnicity is applicable at all in such contexts, it can no longer be in its familiar sense to indicate a bounded cultural group with aspirations to nationhood (Robertson 1992; Friedman 1994).

Poland is in many ways an ideal country in which to explore these issues. Its modern history and cartography exemplify the rise of nation-state ideologies. The Polish state partitioned by its neighbors in the late eighteenth century was a political unit of great ethnic diversity, exhibiting the cultural pluralism that Ernest Gellner believed to be typical of agrarian states everywhere. The national movement of the nineteenth century won substantial cultural and political autonomy for Poles in the province of Galicia, then under Austrian administration, and prepared the ground for the re-emergence of the Polish state after the First World War. The most important marker of national identity for most Poles was the Roman Catholic religion. However, approximately one third of the population of interwar Poland was not of Polish ethnicity (in this period a similar proportion of the population of Czechoslovakia was neither Czech nor Slovak), and national consciousness was far from developed among many of the remaining two thirds. Nationalism was very strong in the interwar decades, but it was only following the establishment of new borders and massive population transfers after the Second World War that the size of Poland's national minorities dropped sharply. By the early 1990s the population was estimated to be almost 97 percent Polish in terms of ethno-linguistic composition (Hołuszko 1993, 6) and President Wałęsa could even declare that his country did not have any minorities.

Although the culmination of this long-term trend toward ethnic homogenization took place under socialist rulers, and although (in Poland as elsewhere) some socialist politicians were not averse to playing the national card, legitimation proved elusive. In the case of Poland, moral consolidation was impeded by singularly unsuccessful management of the economy. The decade of struggle which began with the launching of Solidarity in August 1980 (there were of course earlier protests) can be taken to exemplify the political path toward a resolution of the contradictions of socialism.[2] But who were the people who

[2] In Hungary, where the scale of demographic dislocation in the years immediately preceding socialism was much smaller, solutions were sought via gradual economic reforms and the expansion of informal economic opportunities for the population. This approach might seem closer to the classical Western prototype for the emergence of a free civil society. For an elaboration of the contrast, see Szelenyi 1989. The stirrings of "civil society" in Hungary were strongly associated with increased national sentiment, much of it focused on the fate of Hungarians in Transylvania (see Joó 1994). The Hungarian Democratic Forum successfully mobilized this sentiment in 1990. In Poland the end of communism was associated with calls for more recognition of minorities. Although nationalists have not exercised much influence

waged this struggle, and what kind of society has replaced the socialist society? Solidarity was never in reality the homogenous unified movement that it was sometimes taken to be in the West. It would be naive to suppose that only a few bureaucrats and enterprise managers had any vested interests in the preservation of the established practices of the People's Republic. In the heady days of 1981 it was abundantly clear within the rural population, where I was working at the time, that the country's farmers had several incompatible objectives. This diversity was reflected in the divided wings of the Rural Solidarity organization. By 1989 there were conspicuous tensions between the Solidarity leadership as it entered power and those (for example, members of the "official" unions) who still took their primary job to be the defense of workers' interests, even when some of their industries used the most antiquated technology and would according to rational economic criteria inevitably have to be liquidated. Such tensions contributed to the fragmentation of the movement once the socialist enemy had been replaced by a primitive capitalism based on the market and liberal individualism.

How could Solidarity or any other postsocialist government hope to transcend particularist conflicts? One obvious strategy was to ground legitimacy in ideals and symbols that would overcome sectarian strife and unite the population. Some Solidarity leaders looked for such powerful ideals in Western democratic traditions, and some of them invoked "civil society" as a cover term to indicate respect for individual liberties and rule of law, in contrast to the abuse of state power under socialist collectivism. But another impressive strand in much of the intellectualist literature associated with Solidarity asserted the rights of groups to collective self-expression. This pluralist standpoint was explicitly extended to cover ethnic minorities as well as trade unions. The Ukrainian minority, for example, was the object of a spate of media publicity and scholarly publications in the paradoxical liberalization that took place in Poland in the later 1980s.[3]

---

at the governmental level, right-wing groupings have become prominent in many localities with multiethnic traditions, including the historic diocesan center of the Lemko-Ukrainians, Przemyśl. (See Chapter Nine.)

[3] Zięba 1988; see also the resolution passed by Solidarity's Congress in 1981, translated in Information Centre for Polish Affairs (UK) 16 (Nov. 4, 1981); also various contributions to *Studium Papers* 12, no. 2 (1988).

However, other strands were also strong. The legitimacy of Solidarity as a popular movement and of later postsocialist governments came to depend to a very significant degree on a common national identity and a common Roman Catholic religion, from which some Polish citizens were excluded by definition. How is it possible that at least some members of one minority group could feel more comfortable under a repressive socialist empire than they felt in the apparently free and democratic society which replaced that empire? Is the group in question now reconstructing a primordial identity that was lost, suspended, or otherwise tampered with in previous generations? Or have these people all along been the object of manipulation by external elites and their ideologists? How do these questions about group identity connect with the "shock therapy" economics of Jeffrey Sachs? In this chapter I explore these questions in relation to people I call provisionally the Lemko-Ukrainians, among whom I first carried out fieldwork in the period 1979–1981 (Hann 1985, 1988).

Who Are the Lemko-Ukrainians?

The case of the Lemko-Ukrainians illustrates a number of problems commonly found in border regions, and among ethnic collectivities more generally, as well as difficulties with the social science concepts for addressing these problems. As usual in such cases, conscious processes of ethnogenesis in recent generations cannot be grasped without knowledge of the dynamics of settlement and culture in earlier centuries.[4]

The political border most relevant to this chapter was stable for many centuries, though the people living to the north of it have been subject to long-term manipulation from outside forces that culminated in violent intervention and mass deportations in the 1940s. The Carpathian ridge that now separates southeast Poland from northeast Slovakia was, from the middle of the fourteenth century, the political frontier between Poland and Hungary. During the period of the Habsburg Dual Monarchy, there was still a political frontier between Austrian-

[4] No comprehensive account can be attempted here. For two significantly different introductions in English, see Best 1990 and Magocsi 1987. [These works have now been superseded by Magocsi 2015.]

administered Galicia and the Hungarian territories to the south. But what was the significance of this frontier for the human populations that settled in this border country in the later medieval period? The mountains were inhabited by people who shared not just a natural environment but a range of cultural practices that distinguished them from neighboring populations to the north and to the south (though these boundaries were not sharply defined in all sub-regions, and they did undergo some adjustments through time). The political frontier, like the group boundaries in the foothills of the mountains, was always permeable, even when attempts were made by customs officers and other state representatives to control such movement. The inhabitants of this section of the Carpathians are the products of a continuous cultural stream that was not rudely interrupted until the twentieth century, when the pressures to make political and cultural boundaries coincide led to disaster.

It is important not to begin by reifying "the Lemkos." This is the term most commonly used in scholarly literature of the last half century to designate the Eastern Slav inhabitants of that section of the Carpathians that falls within the boundaries of the present Polish state. I maintain that this ethnonym is the imposition of outsiders, and see the Lemkos as a classic instance of an "invented" identity. The scholarly literature has created the false impression of a bounded unit, a distinct people, or society, or culture, ethnic group, nationality, or even nation, to be slotted in alongside other such units in taxonomies of bounded groups that both anthropologists and politicians can work with. But I also acknowledge that this label has been accepted as a self-designation by some of the people to whom it has been applied. It must therefore be taken seriously in the renewed debates about identity that have opened up with the demise of socialism.

The inhabitants of the wider Carpathian region came under the influence of a number of nationalist movements, among them the Hungarian, the Slovak, and the Romanian. Some were also attracted to more diffuse pan-Slavic and Russophile orientations. However, the fate of those now designated Lemkos was determined most decisively by two modern national movements, the Polish and the Ukrainian (Mach 1993). Ukrainian nationalists insisted that, according to basic linguistic and religious criteria, this population always formed the westernmost part of the Ukrainian nation. The principal agents of this nationalism over a long period were the clergy of the Greek Catholic church.[5] The Polish position was more complex: it did not rest on a simple ethno-national claim, nor was it based on some putative "civic" alternative claim. The Lemko territory historically formed part of the Polish state, yet it was self-evident that its people differed from the Polish peasants of the plains. Their Christianity was that of the eastern liturgical tradition, and their language could not (unlike that of the distinctive Górale highlanders of the Zakopane region) plausibly be classified as a dialect of Polish. Polish gentlemen scholars were the first to use the term Lemko in the middle of the nineteenth century, deriving it from a feature of the local dialect that struck them as distinctive and apparently amusing. It was not used to designate any form of group by local people, let alone a supra-local ethnic community.

With the growth of the Ukrainian national movement in the late nineteenth and early twentieth centuries, seeking greater autonomy from the dominant Polish group in Galicia, just as the Poles had begun somewhat earlier to seek their autonomy from Vienna, scholarship became more politicized. Polish authors pointed to the unique features of the folk culture of these mountain dwellers, emphasized also the role of Vlach pastoral migrants from the Balkans in the formation of this culture, and argued that, in some regions at least, the residents were in fact Poles who had only acquired their apparent eastern characteristics after settlement in the mountain regions. They claimed that the resulting melange had no stronger intrinsic links with Ukraine than with Poland: it could therefore find an appropriate home within the Polish state, with which it had ancient historical links (Bujak 1929; Pieradzka 1939).

Among the factors which complicated the propaganda struggle was the development of pan-Slavist currents in the later Habsburg period, which contributed to terrible retribution on the part of the Austrian authorities when "Russophiles" were accused of treachery during the

5 The very existence of this Church can, however, be seen as an expression of Polish imperialism in the age of the Counter Reformation. It was set up following the Union of Brest (1596) to wean millions of East Slavs away from their original Orthodox faith. (See Chapters Nine and Ten.) For a recent overview of the links between religious and secular identities in this region see Magocsi 1988.

Figure 13. The seventeenth century church of Saint Paraskeva, Kwiatoń, central Lemko zone (photo Chris Hann, 1994)

First World War. Even before this war and the demise of the Habsburgs, large scale migrations out of this region, particularly to North America, led to questions of identity being posed in new contexts. It can plausibly be argued that Lemko identity was more clearly articulated in communities in Pennsylvania (such as those immortalized much later in Michael Cimino's film, *The Deerhunter*) than in the homeland (Magocsi 1993b). Religious divisions were also accentuated by developments in the diaspora, where Greek Catholic emigrants from the Lemko districts came into contact with other Eastern Slavs who had never left the Orthodox Church, and then proceeded to re-implant Orthodoxy in the homeland. In the interwar period the new Polish authorities worked hard to undermine the position of the Greek Catholic Church. Because of its strongly nationalist character they sought to drive a wedge between the Lemko districts and the much larger numbers of Ukrainians further east. The severe economic difficulties of the depression years rendered many villagers and entire parishes prone to convert to Orthodoxy (and also to experiment with other religions and sects).

Despite these intense political and religious debates, which also influenced the establishment of a short-lived Lemko Republic in the immediate aftermath of the First World War, it is doubtful that any clear notion of Lemko identity was generally disseminated at this time. Polish scholars and officials popularized the designation in the inter-war decades, but its widespread adoption in the diaspora communities was not matched by any comparable level of acceptance in the homeland. Remarkable though it may seem, in the 1930s many villagers were still lacking a modern ethno-national identity. In answer to the questions of the ethnographer Roman Reinfuss, they would declare themselves to belong to a local cluster of communities, and they would say they were *Rusnak*.[6] Reinfuss was the most thorough of a number of Polish ethnographers who underwrote the academic legitimacy of the category Lemko, contributing, among other works, rigorous papers that attempted to resolve the problematic eastern border of Lemko territory.[7]

Socialism

The question of which identity to adopt was transformed in the aftermath of the Second World War, when the Lemkos were forced to leave their homelands in an early application of what half a century later we have come to term "ethnic cleansing" (Hann 1996b). Many were transported to the Soviet Union in 1945, when the establishment of Poland's new frontiers was accompanied by a large-scale, non-voluntary exchange of populations. In 1947, in the course of a brisk military campaign called Operation Vistula (*Akcja Wisła*), most of the remainder were dispersed across the territories which Poland gained from the defeated Reich. No more than three related families were allowed to settle in the same location. For many years they were unable to return even for brief visits to the Carpathians, though from the late 1950s small numbers managed in more or less clandestine ways to move back permanently. Most of the Lemkos I have known have fallen into this latter category and belong to the older generation. There are no official statistics indicating their number in the Carpathian home-

6 *Rusnak* here does not mean Russian in the modern sense, but harks back to the age of Kievan Rus' before the divisions of the East Slav national groups. It is often translated as Ruthenian.

7 To the north and west the boundary with Poles was clear; to the south lay the state border and beyond it Hungarians and Slovaks; but to the east the Lemkos' neighbors were East Slavs with cultural traits that varied only slightly and inconsistently from their own, hence the inordinate problems in determining a precise line on the map. See Reinfuss 1948–49. [See also Hann 2012.]

lands, but it is probably fewer than ten thousand. Poles have come to constitute a large majority. Large areas were not repopulated at all but were allocated to the state for farming or forestry, or allowed to degenerate into natural wilderness. Following these traumatic experiences, the minority was classified by the Polish authorities as simply "Ukrainian," in contrast to the pre-socialist period when every effort was made to emphasize their distinctiveness from other Ukrainians. However there was more continuity with pre-war policy in attitudes to the Greek Catholic Church, which following the Soviet precedent was proscribed in 1946. Some of its property was reallocated either to the Orthodox Church or to the Roman Catholic Church, but a very substantial part was destroyed.

Formally, the authorities of the Polish People's Republic could claim that they respected the rights of the minority group: educational and cultural rights were exercised through a handful of secondary schools and higher education facilities, a government-controlled Socio-Cultural Association and its newspapers, and a sponsored choir. In reality, citizens of Lemko-Ukrainian background experienced continuous discrimination in every walk of life, just as many of them had under the previous regime. Their old churches and cultural treasures were desecrated, and even the names of their villages were altered for more Polish-sounding names. The focus for much of the anti-Ukrainian sentiment was the period of armed struggle between 1944 and 1947. Films and popular novels, as well as more scholarly works, sought to justify the deportations by alleging that Ukrainian terrorists had perpetrated countless atrocities on Polish civilians in the Carpathian region. In fact, the great majority of the Lemko population played no part in these events, of which they too were frequently the victims.

Many of the resettled Lemkos have sought to assimilate into Polish society, whenever this was possible. These trends have been well documented by Polish social scientists (Kwilecki 1974; Nowicka 1980; Pudło 1987). By contrast, this traumatic history may have induced some inhabitants and former inhabitants of the Lemko lands to identify themselves definitively as of Ukrainian nationality, but the picture remained anything but simple. The term Lemko was proffered by some as a kind of lower-level, "ethnic" designation to complement a Ukrainian "national" identity. But at least some activists considered it to be a national identity in its own right, perceiving the imposition of a Ukrainian identity to be a consequence of repressive socialist rule. It was virtually impossible for most Lemko-Ukrainians to build any close links with the Ukrainian Republic, or even to visit their own relatives there. Links with the communities in North America, where the debates about identity persisted with little basic change over decades, remained significantly stronger.[8] Comparable debates proceeded in adjacent sections of the Carpathians also populated by East Slavs. The districts most remote geographically from the urban centers of the Ukrainian nationalist movement were more likely to generate alternative collective identities, sometimes favoring pan-Slavic or Russian levels, sometimes an "independentist" orientation, and sometimes content to emphasize a "regional" level within a larger national identity. Within the Lemko territory the more western parts had subscribed to the "Old Ruthenian" orientation in Austro-Hungarian days and been the slowest to accept the blandishments of Ukrainian nationalism, whereas in the eastern districts where I worked it seems that a Ukrainian national identity was strongly implanted even before the military operations of the 1940s. These regional differences persisted as the deportees trickled back to their homeland from the late 1950s.

The legacy of the past was felt particularly strongly in the field of religion. All members of the Ukrainian minority were theoretically assured access to Orthodox churches. This organization played a major part in the persistence of minority identity, both in the diaspora and in the homeland. Despite the lack of official recognition and the confiscation of its property, the Greek Catholic Church maintained a covert existence in a few localities. For example, in Komańcza some Lemko-Ukrainians were able to avoid deportation because of the need for labor created by the old Habsburg-constructed railway line that passes through the mountains at nearby Łupków. Here and in a few other villages Greek Catholic services were held under the protection and on the premises of the Roman Catholic Church. However, as in other villages where the old *cerkiew* was not physically destroyed, in Komańcza, too, custody of the old buildings passed to the Orthodox Church, the only eastern rite Church that enjoyed state recognition. About one quarter of the local Lemko-Ukrainian population attended this church.

---

[8] See various issues of *Carpatho-Rusyn American*, vols.10–11, 1987–1988.

In other cases the *cerkiew* underwent a facelift in order to make it more suitable for Roman Catholic services: the old iconostasis was often removed and replaced by Latin sacred art, often accompanied by Polish patriotic images and texts.[9] The state did little to protect ecclesiastical property from vandalism by immigrant farm workers and forestry personnel. A few outstanding buildings were removed to a skansen in the town of Sanok for conservation, but when a Lemko-Ukrainian sought to establish a museum in his native village of Zyndranowa, on the basis of the fine farm buildings he had inherited, his efforts were repeatedly obstructed by the communist authorities. That Teodor (Fedor) Gocz eventually succeeded in establishing his own private museum probably owed much to his sideline displays of souvenirs from the military battles fought in the Dukla pass area, close to his village. The authorities found it difficult to condemn these activities, particularly once they had attracted the attention and support of the fraternal state on the other side of the pass; and so the museum in Zyndranowa was tolerated, though no public support was extended to consolidate its archives and library holdings.

The climate of increasing tolerance in the last years of socialist power brought some significant changes in the Lemko homelands. Some new churches were constructed, both Greek Catholic (Komańcza) and Orthodox (Zyndranowa). The ingredients in each case were strong local initiatives, an influx of North American dollars, and the conviction that only their Church was the true embodiment of ethno-national traditions. Whereas previously it had been logical for the Greek Catholics to blame the Polish state for suppressing their churches and inciting the spread of Orthodoxy, in the new climate they again came into conflict with those of their "co-ethnics" who believed firmly that they belonged with Orthodoxy, and not with any version of Catholicism. Less controversially, there was general pleasure in the establishment of an annual Lemko cultural festival in the mountain homelands. The first *Watra* was held on a small scale in 1983. Within

[9] For example, the *cerkiew* at Zęgiestów retains its distinctive eastern architecture externally, but the interior has been redecorated with Polish Marian images, the national colors are draped around a signed message from the late Cardinal Wyszyński, and a huge painting on the ceiling proclaims *Polonia semper fidelis*.

a few years it was attracting large numbers of Lemkos and other Ukrainians, from all parts of Poland and from abroad.

Lemko-Ukrainians were frequently of two minds concerning the forces that threatened and eventually conquered the socialist state. On the one hand they were appreciative of the promises to respect and improve minority rights. Solidarity campaigners in the region in 1981 gave prominence to the need to put an end to the cultural destruction taking place in the former Lemko villages, and new ethno-national associations were formed. However, some Lemkos had doubts about the new social movement and very few were active in Solidarity. They were concerned about what they perceived to be its nationalist and clerical character. At the village level, I found in 1980–81 that Lemkos were quicker than their Polish neighbors to blame the new movement for the worsening economic situation. In the religious sphere they were extremely critical of Roman Catholic bishops who, they said, were so intent on Latinization that they obstructed Greek Catholic initiatives as well as the Orthodox. I collected evidence to support these points from the highest ranks of the Greek Catholic Church in Poland.[10]

A New Civil Society?

The position of the Lemko-Ukrainians after 1989 provides an interesting test case for those who would see that year as a watershed, as a point of sharp change between a repressive totalitarian regime and a free and democratic civil society. Superficially there have been plenty of positive changes. The new civil society has provided the Lemko-Ukrainians with the opportunity to organize their own political parties, independent of the old state-controlled Socio-Cultural Association. Several groupings have emerged, but the activists in the homeland region do not always see eye to eye with each other, let alone with those who seek to mobilize the members of the diaspora communities in other parts of Poland. The most effective organization appears to be that based in south-western Poland in Legnica, which favors an "autonomist" orientation. In contrast, most of those who have returned to the

[10] Interview with Father Stefan Dziubina, Przemyśl, October 1982.

mountains would prefer either a Ukrainian or a "hyphenated" version of identity, insisting on Lemko distinctiveness within the Ukrainian nation.

These disagreements have spilled over into the cultural sphere. Thus, the *Watra* festival that developed in the late socialist period to celebrate Lemko traditions has itself, after socialism, become a contested event. A much smaller festival is now organized separately in Legnica in August by those who feel that the homeland *Watra* in late July has been hijacked by outside forces. I attended the homeland *Watra* in 1994 at the remote permanent site where it has been consolidated in recent years in Żdynia, in the central Lemko zone, close to the border with Slovakia. Estimates of the numbers attending were in the order of ten thousand. The number of cars and buses with Ukrainian plates indicated that a very large number of these were from the neighboring state. I arrived by car and gave a lift to an old lady along the last section of the dusty track. She had lived in Ukraine since 1945. The only disappointment of her trip so far had been her inability to arrange transportation to visit her native village, just a few miles away across the mountains.

Outside the festival grounds, many visitors were selling the merchandise that Ukrainians and others have been retailing on local markets throughout Poland since the collapse of the Soviet Union. Some of these people never entered the festival proper, for that required payment of a modest entry fee. For them, the festival was really just an excuse to join an organized party for a relatively cheap trip to a country that possessed a convertible currency and a range of goods not readily available at home. During their short stay in Poland these visitors spent their limited resources very carefully; they lived in their buses or in their own tents, and had brought all their own provisions with them.

Inside the festival gate the first enclosure was given over to refreshments. The most popular item of consumption on a sweltering weekend was chilled Żywiec, brand leader among Polish beers. Books and other products of the recent proliferation of publishing activities were sold at small stalls, mostly by individuals, both Polish and Ukrainian, rather than publishing firms. (I was able to purchase a copy of Oleg Iwanusiw's powerful photographic compilation *Church in Ruins*[11]

[11] Ontario: St. Catherine's, 1987.

Figure 14. Lemko folklore on stage at the Watra Festival (photo by Chris Hann, Żdynia, 1994)

from a Ukrainian for a fraction of its price in the West.) Beyond this zone of commerce was the main entertainment arena, where spectators could sit on a sloping field as the Polish and Ukrainian national flags fluttered at either side of a specially constructed stage. The greater part of the weekend's entertainment was provided by well-rehearsed troupes from all over Ukraine, who completely overshadowed the Lemko participants. I had been told that one of the highlights would be a performance by a local folk group, *Lemkovyna*. However this group turned out to be an excellent choir, based in L'viv. Some of the comperes spoke and told jokes in the Lemko vernacular, but others used standard literary Ukrainian. The public proceedings of the festival had no overt religious element, though I was told that the Greek Catholics were campaigning to be allowed to hold services on the closing Sunday.

In these conditions it is unsurprising that some Lemko-Ukrainians have ceased to attend the festival, and no longer regard it as an authentic expression of *their* culture. At the end, I was introduced to a retired teacher in a nearby village who offers part-time instruction in the Lemko vernacular to a few dozen local children. She refuses to recognize this tongue as simply a dialect of Ukrainian, and is currently working on pedagogical materials, including a dictionary and a grammar book, that will enable such education to become more widely available for Lemko communities in Poland. She had not attended the *Watra*, in spite of its physical proximity, and was particularly angry over the way in which Greek Catholic clergy originating outside the region were attempting to eradicate the specific features of Lemko identity in her own village (for example, by preaching in standard literary Ukrainian).

In the following days I spoke with other activists who had attended the festival and were dismissive of this philologist's efforts to build up a separate Lemko cultural identity. Yet they too had ambivalent feelings about the expansion of the festival. On the one hand, they were proud that so many people had assembled to celebrate a culture that, according to some Polish social scientists, had seemed just a few decades earlier to be on the verge of extinction. Nonetheless these activists realized that local people had little control over the gathering and they advised me not to be taken in by appearances. In reality, they said, the Polish authorities in this new era of so-called democracy were still sowing the seeds of conflict within the Lemko-Ukrainian community, just as earlier Polish governments had done. One leader emphasized the postsocialist governments' evasion of the legitimate economic demands of the autochthonous group, notably the refusal to return, or to provide adequate compensation for, the forests that were nationalized after the deportations of the 1940s (he had collected signatures at the festival for a petition protesting against this injustice). Another, Fedor Gocz, the founder of the private museum in Zyndranowa, preferred to emphasize the dimension of religion and claimed that nothing had really changed in Poland, except that a red ("communist") theocracy had been replaced by a "black party," that is, the Roman Catholic Church. Gocz had taken the lead in establishing a new Orthodox church in Zyndranowa in the 1980s. In 1993 a young Greek-Catholic priest moved into the village and recruited most of the local Lemkos to the eastern rite services he held in the old church, now under Roman Catholic control. The activist Gocz saw this development as a provocation from the higher levels of the Roman Catholic hierarchy, sanctioned by the state, intended to weaken and divide local people. The Orthodox Church now suffers from the suspicion that, simply because it was allowed to operate in the decades of socialism, it must be somehow tainted; its positive role in conserving Lemko-Ukrainian identity is easily overlooked.

For the founder of the private museum in Zyndranowa, the official enthronement after nearly half a century of a new Greek Catholic bishop in Przemyśl is a sign of a new conspiracy among the different Catholic churches, rather than recognition of or concession to the Lemko-Ukrainian people. At the same time, both activists and lay people are well aware that in other parts of the Lemko region Roman Catholics exercise their power to frustrate the aspirations of the Greek Catholics. Events in Przemyśl at the time of the Pope's fourth pilgrimage to Poland in 1992 made it obvious to all that the dominant church remains unwilling to concede parity to a non-Western liturgical tradition (see Chapter Nine). The Roman Catholic bishops of Tarnów and Przemyśl have continued to obstruct the restitution of property to the Greek Catholic church, effectively continuing the policy of divide and rule that has characterized ecclesiastical as well as secular politics throughout the century.

After 1989 Fedor Gocz was promised state support without strings attached for his private museum in Zyndranowa. Some funds were released through the nearby municipal museum at Dukla. By 1993, however, the local government agency to which responsibility had been devolved was pleading lack of funding, and the future of Gocz's museum was again plunged into uncertainty. For the time being the museum persists essentially as a private institution with occasional inputs from voluntary groups of sympathizers, which is more or less how it functioned during the last two decades of socialism. Its founder is therefore understandably skeptical of claims that 1989 has brought any substantial changes in the status of the Lemko-Ukrainians and the prospects for the survival of their culture.

It can be seen that Lemko-Ukrainians remain divided in all fields, political, cultural and religious. They are extremely vulnerable to outside manipulation. Should they be recognized as a group separate from the Ukrainians? If so, are they genuinely autonomous or might they form a component of some other group, perhaps a group embracing all the East Slavs of the Carpathians? This case of contemporary identity formation shows the essential arbitrariness of attempts to impose order on continuous cultural variation through the drawing of sharp boundaries. The people classified as Lemko have many complex and cross-cutting identities. They have a lot in common with other Ukrainian groups in Poland, and also with the inhabitants of the Prešov region of Slovakia, and somewhat less with the more distant inhabitants of the Transcarpathian oblast of Ukraine. All of these groups have been classified over the last half century as ethnic Ukrainians: the term Lemko has never had any currency outside southeast Poland, and it would seem that the term Rusnak/Rusyn has been steadily losing its symbolic power in these adjacent regions for most of this century. Many Lemko-Ukrainians probably feel, on the basis of their biographies in Poland, stronger links to ethnic Poles than to the main mass of Ukrainians, and the economic predicament of those who now visit from the Ukraine serves to accentuate this sense of difference. Many Lemko-Ukrainians have new senses of place following their complex migrations, where many have acquired religious, professional and recreational identities quite different from those of earlier generations. Nowadays they have ever increasing opportunities to participate in diverse forms of global culture. Their links with the Americas have been strong for a century, and the end of socialism has precipitated a more general transformation of culture in and around their central European homelands. The nearest branch of McDonald's is now not very far away, in a Kraków that is being rapidly incorporated into the European heritage circuits and attracting huge numbers of international tourists. This is also the city where much of the academic work to consolidate a separate Lemko culture is now proceeding, at the Jagiellonian University.[12]

This complexity tends to be flattened when academics as well as laypersons imagine that they can capture the fundamental qualities of identity in something they term "ethnicity." Thus when a foreign observer of Carpathian East Slavs in Poland in the late 1980s talks of "a movement that is providing them with a concrete Lemko identity" (Magocsi 1990, 208), this is no more innocent than the past imposition upon the same people of Russian, Polish and Ukrainian identities.[13] The same observer is right to point to some evidence that "since the Revolution of 1989 there has been a revival promoting the idea of a distinct national identity" among the people he terms Carpatho-Rusyns

---

[12] Some Lemko-Ukrainians are suspicious of the attention being paid to them by Poles in a spate of publications, many of them touristic in character rather than strictly academic. They point out that past Polish publications devoted to the Lemkos, while presenting them as a separate group, sometimes tried to assimilate them to Polish society (as noted above for the 1930s); see Duć-Fajfer 1993.

[13] Magocsi's use of the adjective "concrete" is doubly unfortunate here. Apart from conveying exactly the essentializing approach to identity that I argue against, the Polish term *beton* had some very specific associations with right-wing nationalist orientations in the very period in which Magocsi locates the flowering of Lemko identity.

(Magocsi 1993a, 97). There is some irony in the fact that such views seem to be more popular in the diaspora (both home and abroad) than in the Carpathian homeland, but in any case scholars ought to make it clear that these stirrings are a replication of earlier attempts to invent and impose a nation, rather than a revival of any spontaneous or primordially given identity at either the Lemko or the Carpatho-Rusyn level. In spite of all claims to scholarly neutrality, intellectuals are once again the chief catalysts of the cultural production of identity that is now proceeding according to classic nineteenth century schemas: for example, through struggles to control the folk festivals, to present Lemko history and to standardize the "language."

Although it is too early to reach any definitive conclusions, my own impression is that these efforts to construct an "imagined community" (Anderson 1983) of Lemkos have had relatively little impact on the majority of those so designated, for whom such questions remain academic.[14] The persons to whom the labels are applied do not see themselves as a nation, or as an ethnic group, or even as a "people." Most of them are more concerned with a range of pragmatic issues, above all their economic conditions, for the new market economics has done no favors for those who struggle to make a living off the land, particularly in relatively unproductive mountain environments. The identity issues do not seem so urgent to those born after the deportations (all of the activists mentioned above belong to the older generation). The uncertainties that some of these people have experienced in their collective identities are a consequence of their geographical isolation and the particular historical conditions in which they have experienced the rise of nation-states all around them. An optimistic interpretation might see them as exemplars of postmodern fragmentation and the shift away from the nation-state as the primary level of identification for its citizens: from this vantage point, these latecomers to the age of modernity are well placed to reject the seductions of nationalism and show their neighbors how to rediscover multicultural pluralism in postindustrial forms.

---

[14] Apart from my own short visits to the Lemko region in the 1990s, I base this paragraph on the current work of Jacek Nowak. See Nowak 1993. [See also Nowak 2000; on the nature of religious diversity in the heart of the Lemko homeland in the new century, see Pasieka 2015.]

To Critique or Not to Critique?

The fate of these geographically peripheral people who have fallen between the stools of strong rival nationalisms over the last century should alert us to the essentialism of all nationalist discourse. Magocsi is right to criticize the *obiter dicta* of those contributors to his recent edited volume who simply assert that the Carpathian East Slavs are a component of the Ukrainian nation (1993c). It is not clear, however, that Magocsi's alternative, seeking to repeat nineteenth century nation-building programs on a reduced scale, is a viable one in the current remaking of Lemko identity. It is surely high time to solve Orwell's problem by recognizing the futility of reifying such identities, regardless of whether we call them nations or ethnic groups, and in this case regardless of whether we pitch them at Lemko or at Carpatho-Rusyn level. We must look beyond borders rather than aim to create new ones. Recent initiatives to establish a "Carpathian Euroregion" intended to increase contacts between all the people of the mountains are an indication that such hopes may not be entirely utopian.

But when it comes to drawing conclusions from this analysis, in terms of political strategies in the contemporary Polish state, we encounter a paradox. Exposing the constructed or invented character of the categories Lemko and Ukrainian might be taken to imply that no such category warrants any special recognition in the new, postsocialist society. Taken to an extreme, approaches that emphasize pluralist cosmopolitanism and the "mongrel" or "hybrid" nature of all identities would leave no room whatsoever for the study of ethnic or national cultures. At best, the social scientist writing from this perspective will have to devote a little space to explaining why some people erroneously hold on to these reifications. Is this a sensible or realistic strategy to apply in postsocialist Eastern Europe? Most citizens of modern Poland are deeply conscious that the Poles constitute a "historic nation." In contrast to their eastern and western borders, their southern border is viewed as stable. They are conscious that most of their territory consists of lowland plain, but they are proud too of what they perceive to be their mountains—particularly of the Tatra region around Zakopane, but also of the less dramatic Carpathian zones adjacent to it (including the ranges known as Beskidy and Bieszczady).

For historical reasons that cannot be further explored here, many Poles tend towards an extremely exclusivist view of their national state, which they strongly associate with the dominance of the Latin variant of the universal Catholic Church. Neal Ascherson (1990) has recently explored the case of the White Russian minority of the Białystok region, some of whom also felt a certain ambivalence towards Solidarity. I think he is right to label the Dmowski heritage "almost totalitarian," but I am less sanguine than he is concerning the prospects of overcoming that heritage. In short, the civil society which now exists in this part of the world is Polish civil society, not world civil society, and within this context it is still important to retain a concept of national minority, despite the danger of reification. Some kinds of collective rights must be granted to people such as the Lemko-Ukrainians, not because such reifications exist primordially, nor because the constructions of some minority activists have acquired a degree of recognition, but because of the strength and character of modem Polish nationalism—itself of course a reification, from which the East Slav elements that have contributed much to Polish culture over centuries have been systematically expunged. Whatever the confusions in Lemko-Ukrainian self-identifications, they know (and are continuously reminded) that they are different from ethnic Poles, and like other minorities they have reason to fear the "totalitarian" elements in Polish nationalism and clericalism.[15]

The new elites which have governed Poland since 1989 can claim some credit for extending limited initiatives of the late-socialist period. There has been improved recognition of Lemko-Ukrainian culture and its survival seems more secure now than at any time since the deportations of the 1940s. New publishing houses and museums have sprung up. There has been a cultural efflorescence in areas remote from the original homelands, where it is clear that earlier reports of assimilation were somewhat exaggerated. The authorities must proceed very cautiously, because improved recognition of the Lemkos, (for example through allowing their dialect to enter the school curriculum) can easily be interpreted as a revival of the Polish state's earlier policies to separate

[15] For a perceptive discussion of how other kinds of cultural minority may become more vulnerable in the course of postsocialist democratization see Mucha 1992.

them off from the main body of Ukrainians. In practice the new political climate has made it easier for new organizations to institutionalize longstanding divisions within the Lemko-Ukrainians, but the authorities have so far resisted demands from Lemko "independentists" that they be awarded formal recognition as a separate national minority.[16]

The future is uncertain. At the time of writing, the postsocialist authorities have yet to own up to the fundamental injustice of Operation Vistula in 1947. But even if they did and even if more financial resources were available, it will be very hard for Polish governments to act upon what has become in the twentieth century a long tradition of prejudice, which has resulted in the Ukrainian being stereotyped almost as negatively as the Gypsy or Jew (Chlewiński 1980). The population movements of the 1940s made the situation of the Lemko-Ukrainians particularly vulnerable. They were not merely deprived of their homeland, but forced to live among Poles who had themselves been deported from more eastern regions, and whose anti-Ukrainian sentiments were particularly strong. It is the very fragmentation of the Lemko-Ukrainians after 1947, when their traditional local identities were abruptly terminated, that makes it imperative for activists to attain some kind of supra-local identity today.[17]

It may seem odd that the socialist state which, through its media and its education system, disseminated such negative images of Ukrainians, might still be preferred by at least some Lemko-Ukrainians to the re-emergence of a genuinely independent, sovereign Poland. But

---

[16] [This policy later changed. In the new century, when a question concerning ethno-national identity was included in the census, it became necessary to choose between Ukrainian, a recognized national minority, and Lemko, a recognized ethnic group. Nationwide, in 2002 only 5850 respondents declared a Lemko identity, a much smaller number than expected. Of these, 1642 resided in the homeland (where an additional 789 citizens declared themselves Ukrainian). See Hann 2012.]

[17] The resilience of malignant ethno-nationalism among people who have been uprooted from their homelands should not be surprising. This can help us understand the unevenness of Polish nationalism, which seems to take more virulent forms among those displaced from cities in the borderlands (e.g. Lwów, Wilno—today L'viv, Vilnius) following their incorporation into the Soviet Union. These groups differ from the Lemko-Ukrainians in that their national consciousness was already highly developed in the period preceding resettlement.

there is really no paradox here. This minority, though it counts few intellectuals in its membership even today, is well informed about the inter-war period. Ukrainians may have been second-class citizens under socialism, but under earlier regimes they were third-class or worse. A free civil society can have only one status of citizen and must respect the rights of its ethnic minorities with more than fine words alone. Yet President Wałęsa prefers to ignore their existence, and the worry must be that, in courting votes for future elections, nationalist elements already active in Polish political culture will gain stronger emphasis at the national level. Add the continuing pressures towards clerical uniformity and it is not difficult to understand the reasons for apprehension among the people whose inability to control their own destiny in the modem age of sovereign nation-states is summed up in the continued application to them (but not for the most part by them) of the problematic term Lemko.

Conclusion

I have argued in this chapter that the end of one-party rule in Poland has not necessarily benefited minority groups in Polish society and for some people it has been prejudicial. Improvements in the position of the Lemko-Ukrainians began in the later decades of socialism. The continuation of this trend since the late 1980s, when leading intellectual voices called for greater attention to be paid to minority rights, has been undermined in the case of the Lemko-Ukrainians by their internal divisions. Some of their leaders believe that, behind the rhetoric of freedom and democracy, the new state authorities are systematically reproducing these old divisions, in both secular and ecclesiastical domains. They fear that the threat to their identity from Polish nationalism and Roman Catholic clericalism is actually greater in the new conditions of civil society than it ever was under communism. At the same time it is evident, particularly among the younger generation, that the distinctive bases of group identity are being eroded by the rapid growth of a "market economy" and further incorporation into increasingly global patterns of consumption.

Ethnic and national identities are the constructions of intellectuals, and such inventions must always be subjected to rigorous critique. But those who expose the fallacies of primordialism and insist on the critical exposure of apparently spurious collectivities risk being pushed into a position where they claim that no two individuals share the same culture. Such "postmodernists" risk assimilation, as far as their political stance is concerned, into the camp of those intellectual descendants of the Enlightenment who have been running economic programs in postsocialist Eastern Europe. Just as the "shock therapy" devised and implemented in Poland was hardly a recipe for a civil society, in that it was not a morally defensible way to organize economic and political life in a complex industrial society, so the postmodern deconstruction of minority identities is politically naive, given the elemental power of the majority culture that defines this society within its present frontiers as the *Polish* nation-state. The Lemko-Ukrainian minority in Poland is a latecomer to such globalized social conditions, and the legacy of past manipulation makes the task of even well-intentioned state authorities extremely difficult. But if an attractive civil society, pluralist and democratic, is to flourish in these territories, it is certain to require decisive state action to counter the double hegemony of the free market and Polish nationalism.

CHAPTER NINE

Postsocialist Nationalism: Rediscovering the Past in Southeast Poland

(1998)

Introduction[1]

Since the collapse of socialist regimes in 1989 few subjects in Eastern Europe have attracted as much attention as nationalism. Academic studies have been carried out from many disciplinary perspectives, by scholars native to the region as well as many outside it, and nongovernmental organizations have undertaken numerous policy-oriented initia-

---

[1] *This chapter derives from Hann 1998e, an article based on research financed by a grant from the Economic and Social Research Council (No. R000236071, "The Politics of Religious Identity: the Greek Catholics of Central Europe"). I am greatly indebted to my main partner in this research Stanisław Stępień, Director of the Southeast Scientific Institute in Przemyśl, who in addition to local data collection and extensive interviewing among the Ukrainian minority in the city in 1996–97 has in countless ways helped to inform and educate a puzzled outsider. He is not responsible for any errors of fact or interpretation in this text, which is based primarily on short annual field trips (no longer than one week) every year between 1994 and 1998. The language I used during these visits was Polish (also in interviews with members of the Ukrainian minority). The same disclaimer applies to others who have provided useful comments on earlier drafts: Klaus Bachmann, Janusz Mucha, George Schöpflin, and Kai Struve. I am also grateful for the comments of participants at two conferences in November 1997: "Poland: Social and Cultural Paradigms," in Berlin, organized by Michał Buchowski and Édouard Conte, and "Structuring of Identities in Twentieth Century Europe," in Warsaw, organized by Marian Kempny. In 1998, seminar participants at the Free University of Berlin, at the Wissenschaftskolleg zu Berlin, and at Viadrina University Frankfurt (Oder), as well as the anonymous referees for* Slavic Review, *all provided useful comments.*

tives.[2] Eastern European developments have figured prominently in discussions of "ethnicity" and "identity politics" globally (Ignatieff 1994; Brubaker 1996). It might be an exaggeration to claim major conceptual advances in the recent scholarship, but at any rate few would now argue that national loyalties re-emerged in some "natural" form after a generation in the socialist "deep freeze" (metaphors widely employed in the early 1990s; see Offe and Gaines 1996).

Anthropologists have made significant contributions to this field, sometimes with highly specific case studies, sometimes tackling larger regions and complex historical processes (Bringa 1995; Karakasidou 1997). In addition to the short-run factors that can precipitate malignant forms of nationalism in the postsocialist conjuncture, Katherine Verdery has shown the importance of recognizing how an idea of the nation was used and abused by socialist powerholders, and of the roles played by intellectuals in the formation of national symbols in even earlier periods (Verdery 1991a, 1996). When history is embraced in this way, it becomes more difficult to formulate elegant general theories to encompass very different national experiences. In a recent survey, Peter Niedermüller has complained of "a certain theoretical and methodological stagnation" in this research field (1997, 246). His own preferred remedy is to distinguish a number of "discourse strategies" that together provide contemporary Eastern Europeans with a convincing and satisfying "cultural logic" by which to organize their daily lives. I find Niedermüller's work stimulating but I shall argue that his anthropological concern with "cultural ordering" needs to be complemented with more concrete investigations of changing institutions and, above all, of the new political contexts.

Coverage of the region in the recent literature has been uneven, since scholars, publishers, and philanthropists tend to invest more resources where the problems have been most conspicuous. Hence there is a large literature on former Yugoslavia, and especially on

[2] See Augustinos 1996, Holmes 1997; see also the journal *Nationalities Papers*. Among the many initiatives of recent years have been the establishment at the Central European University of a Centre for the Study of Nationalism, financed by George Soros and directed in Prague by Ernest Gellner until his death in 1995, and the *Project on Ethnic Relations*, based in Princeton, New Jersey and funded primarily by the Carnegie Corporation.

Bosnia. By contrast, the literature dealing with the peaceful breakup of Czechoslovakia is still scant. So too, especially in view of the size of their populations, is the literature on contemporary nationalisms in Ukraine and Poland. My focus in this article is limited to Poland and to one part of that country's Ukrainian minority, whose collective awareness is heavily dependent on its minority status. I do not address the more complex phenomenon of nationalism in Ukraine itself; I do, however, wish to broach some aspects of contemporary Polish nationalism.

The Polish case can be instructive precisely because it is not commonly perceived to pose problems. Poland has been almost entirely free of the ethnic violence that has occurred elsewhere. Even anti-Roma prejudice has not been a significant problem (of course, the Roma population is relatively small). Postsocialist constitutions have guaranteed the rights of all "national and ethnic minorities."[3] These documents have been followed up by an active Parliamentary Commission. Nonetheless I suggest that the potential for nationalism is deeply rooted in contemporary Polish society. Far from withering (or "freezing") under socialism, it continued to grow. While the overt promotion of political nationalism of the sort known in the interwar period was precluded, state control of education and culture helped to ensure that the nation, rather than any sub-national or supra-national entity, became the dominant focus of loyalty and identity. Above all, it suited the Roman Catholic Church to promote the nation as the basic principle of cultural ordering.

I approach the Polish case in terms of the model put forward by Ernest Gellner (1983). This model, much more abstract and long-term than is usual in social and cultural anthropology, contrasts the cultural diversity of the polity of the Agrarian Age with the homoge-

---

3 In Poland, as elsewhere, the terminology is problematic. Polish social scientists generally classify an ethnic group is a "national" group if it possesses its own state. In practice, however groups such as Roma and Lemkos have often been classified, like Ukrainians, as a national minority. The vocabulary is also confusing because the term nationality is often popularly used to describe another form of belonging, that of legal citizenship. The nationalism that I am concerned with in this article is of the sort commonly labelled "ethnic," but this term can also be misleading. The terms ethnic and ethnicity can be employed in more complex ways: for example, some citizens of contemporary Poland declare themselves to be of Lemko ethnicity (*etniczność*) and Ukrainian nationality (*narodowość*) (see Chapter Eight).

neity of the succeeding Industrial Age. The territory of what is today southeast Poland and western Ukraine was culturally diverse in Gellner's sense for many centuries. Leaving aside smaller groups and specific local identities, three main groups lived alongside each other in roughly equal numbers: Roman Catholics, Greek Catholics, and Jews. The generalized identity that had most salience was religious, for until late in the nineteenth century, in both towns and rural areas, national identity in the modern sense was weakly developed.[4] In the cities and hinterlands of Przemyśl and L'viv, most Roman Catholics spoke a west Slav dialect, while most Greek Catholics spoke an east Slav dialect. But other combinations were not unknown: there were Greek Catholic Poles and "Ruthenians" who followed the Latin rite. All-embracing secular designations in the modern sense of ethnicity either did not exist at all or were only weakly internalized and of limited significance in social interaction. People's identities were basically "polytactic" (Elwert 1989). The more or less lumpy features that we nowadays refer to as "ethnic groups" or "cultures" existed, but not as sharply bounded units asserting exclusive rights over territory. Rather, identities cross-cut each other, and different ties and allegiances were activated in different contexts. Alongside anthropologists such as Gellner and Elwert, historians capable of escaping the mind-set of nationalism have also considered this sort of cultural pluralism to be the more common condition of humanity (McNeill 1986).

Gellner liked to illustrate his theories from the Habsburg Empire, which provided more fertile soil for the growth of a Polish national movement than the other imperial powers that divided the Polish state between them in the late eighteenth century (Brock 1969). The Poland that was reinvented as a political entity after the First World War was still culturally diverse, but it promptly embarked upon the assimilating and excluding strategies of a "nationalizing state" (Brubaker 1996). About one-sixth of the population was Ukrainian, and Ukrainians

[4] Cf. Tomaszewski (1993, 246), who cites the case of a peasant in the middle of the nineteenth century who declared his identity and his language to be "Mazovian." For the Lemko-Ukrainian region of the Carpathians, see Reinfuss 1948–49. Another identity term that received census recognition in the eastern borders of pre-socialist Poland was *tutejszy* (of this place). For classic ethnographic documentation see Obrębski, 1976 [1936].

outnumbered Poles in many parts of the southeast; another sixth was made up of Jews and other minorities (Tomaszewski 1985, 52). Religious distinctions corresponded ever more closely to ethnic boundaries, but increasingly it was the secular, ethnic identity that was "sacralized." The condition that Gellner associates with industrial modernity was eventually achieved more through political contingencies and violence than through the spread of capitalist enterprise. Following wartime genocide, border changes and large-scale population movements, voluntary and involuntary, and a final burst of ethnic cleansing in 1947, socialist Poland emerged as one of Europe's more homogeneous states (Hann 1996b). By the 1970s it was reported that only 1.3 per cent of the population was not ethnically Polish (Wiatr 1977, 137). Within this country, the continuing role of the Roman Catholic Church in defining the mainstream of Polish cultural identity has been widely recognized, obscuring the degree to which the principal focus of sacralization became the ethnic community itself, that is, the Polish nation.

Even before the demise of socialism, however, signs were emerging that the cultural homogeneity of modern Poland was less complete than it seemed to be.[5] Since the collapse of socialism, ethnic diversity (especially in Poland's borderlands with Germany, Belarus, and Ukraine) has been more openly acknowledged (Babiński, Mucha, and Sadowski 1997). Does this mean that the new democracy is allowing citizens to rediscover their polytactic identities? While this may be happening for some groups, including Silesian Germans, as far as the Ukrainian minority in Przemyśl is concerned the strength of Polish nationalism continues to inhibit polytacticity, just as it did throughout the decades of socialism. Ernest Gellner's model of the modern polity, envisaged as perfectly congruent with just one cultural group, is an ideal type and undoubtedly an oversimplification of the empirical reality in contemporary Poland, but I shall argue that the nationalist goal of creating and sustaining this congruence continues to structure Polish society and to preclude plurality and polytacticity.

[5] For example, there has been a surge of interest in Polish-Jewish relations past and present, led by academics at the Research Center for Jewish History and Culture in Poland at Jagiellonian University in Kraków. See Krajewski 2002. On the Lemko-Ukrainian minority, see Chapter Eight; see also Michna 1995, Nowak 1996.

The Past in the Present: Greek Catholic Ukrainians in Przemyśl

Anthropologists are usually more interested in the politics of the past in the present, in how people represent their history, than in history *wie es eigentlich gewesen*. In both oral and literate cultures, the past has a social function in the present. It is not only the recent past that functions in this way. Many Poles and Ukrainians in this region nowadays have a conviction that, once upon a time, the city of Przemyśl and the surrounding territory belonged exclusively to them. Strong claims of primordial propriety are embedded in today's ethnic cultures. But the fuel for the mythologizing of origins and a distant past is obtained from events relatively close to the present. Today Przemyśl is a city which lies in southeast Poland on both sides of the River San, about 10 kilometers from the border with Ukraine. Out of a total of just under 70,000 inhabitants, the number of people identifying themselves as Ukrainians is almost certainly fewer than 2,000.[6]

Apart from a recently established Orthodox parish with about 100 members, the Ukrainians are Greek Catholic. The Greek Catholic Church, sometimes known as the Uniate Church, and in Poland today officially as the Ukrainian Catholic Church of the Byzantine Rite, combines the theology of the western, Roman Catholic Church with the practical religious life of the eastern, Orthodox tradition.[7] It was formed in the era of the Counter-Reformation when the secular and religious authori-

[6] There are no official statistics for contemporary Poland's ethnic minorities. The total number of Ukrainians, including Lemkos, is thought to be between 250,000 and 280,000 (Hołuszko 1993). The minority associations, however, claim higher figures, perhaps approaching 400,000. Ukrainians in Przemyśl quote 2,000 as the upper limit for their community there. The active membership of the Ukrainian Socio-Cultural Association and the Greek Catholic parish is nearer to 1,000. Some people give a figure of "400 families." They often point out that the city has many more inhabitants of Ukrainian descent who no longer acknowledge this fact.

[7] I use the name Greek Catholic, which dates from the Habsburg period, because this is still the designation preferred by the people themselves, as well as being the name most commonly used to describe them by the Polish Roman Catholic majority. For further discussion see Halecki 1958, Hann 1993d, Keleher 1993.

ties of the predominantly Roman Catholic Commonwealth of Poland and Lithuania wanted to incorporate their many Orthodox subjects into the Catholic Church (following the principle of *cuius regio, eius religio*). They did not aspire to change the actual practices of these subjects: such a transformation would have been uncharacteristic of a generally tolerant Commonwealth and unacceptable to the Orthodox bishops. It was sufficient that the bishops should agree formally to recognize the Pope and to amend a few points of theology that have remained to this day obscure and irrelevant to the mass of the faithful. Even so, union proved controversial and in some regions it generated violent resistance. The Union of Brest (1596) was not finally ratified in the diocese of Przemyśl until 1692. From its inception until the Second World War, this Greek Catholic Church operated in political and cultural frameworks dominated by western powers. During these centuries the practical religion of the Greek Catholics moved closer in some details to that of the Roman Catholic Church, for example, in styles of singing and iconography. Despite this seeping Latinization, however, the calendar and the central rituals and liturgy of the Greek Catholics remained virtually identical to those of Orthodoxy and unlike those of the Roman Catholic Church. Religious differences were therefore available as the principal "raw material" in this region for the later emergence of national communities.

In summarizing the complex history of Przemyśl and its hinterland we can make a crude division between the more distant past that is available primarily through history books, museum exhibitions, and so on, and the history of recent generations in which, alongside more abundant textual materials, popular memory assumes a greater significance. The first important date for the first sort of history is 981, when a monk in Kiev provided the record of a settlement called Przemyśl, without clearly establishing its nature or the composition of its population.[8] In the early centuries of the next millennium, various groups of eastern and western Slavs intermingled here, the bearers of Orthodox and Latin Christianity, respectively. In the town and hinterland of Przemyśl, the former seem to have been more numerous in the earliest

[8] For the history of the city see Fenczak and Stępień 1993; see also the early monographs of Hauser 1991 and Lewicki 1994, and the successive volumes of *Polska-Ukraina, 1000 lat sąsiedztwa*, published in Przemyśl since 1990 by the Południowo-Wschodni Instytut Naukowy.

phases of permanent settlement, but the latter were more successful in consolidating institutions of secular and religious power. In 1340 Casimir the Great succeeded to the title of duke of Galicia (Halicz, Halychyna), and the definitive incorporation of this territory into the Polish state was completed in 1387 by Queen Jadwiga. This state and its successors deservedly enjoyed a reputation for pluralism and tolerance, but the cultural diversity of the Agrarian Age was structured hierarchically. The Greek Catholic Church experienced Latinization, and upwardly mobile East Slavs tended to adopt the language and secular culture of the higher status group. "Ruthenians" could become Poles for social purposes ("Polonization"). Some became Roman Catholics and in time identified fully with a Polish culture that was not yet a national culture in the modern sense of being open to the masses as well as to elites. Others, however, did not change their religion or forget their East Slav origins. Modern Ukrainian history texts present the position of the East Slavs in this Polish state as essentially one of colonial dependency (cf. Verdery 1983). This relationship did not preclude assimilation in the other direction at lower levels of the hierarchy: when Roman Catholic peasants migrated into areas where East Slav dialects and eastern Christianity predominated, they were likely to experience "Ruthenization"; or they might change their religion but hold on to their West Slav language, thereby expanding the possibilities for polytacticity. Very few present inhabitants have any conception of the complexity of these interactions, which included high rates of intermarriage (in this respect the Jewish group always remained an exception).

In 1772 in the course of the "first partitions" Galicia became part of the Austrian empire (from 1867 the Austro-Hungarian empire). National identities emerged throughout Central and Eastern Europe in more or less their modern form in the Habsburg era. Romantic poems, novels, and nationalist historiography all contributed to the dissemination of myths, such as those of Cossack heroes (or villains, depending on your point of view) and of Poland as the "Christ of Nations."[9] Churches also played a key role in these processes. Habsburg rulers

[9] The novels of Henryk Sienkiewicz are sometimes singled out by Ukrainians in Przemyśl as promoting images of their nation as a land of "butchers and bandits." See Sosnowska 1997, 20–22. For further discussion of the creation of Polish national imagery, see Skurnowicz 1981. For wide-ranging comparative discussion, see Hosking and Schöpflin 1997.

were generally well disposed toward the Greek Catholic Church, which in a critical period from the middle of the nineteenth century became the leading agent of Ukrainian nationalism (Himka 1984). It suited the Austrians to allow Ukrainian consciousness to grow in eastern Galicia as a counterweight to increasing Polish nationalism. By the end of the Habsburg period even the peasant inhabitants of remote mountain regions were being called upon to profess a national identity, something they had not had to do previously. The tangle of secular and religious identities was also much influenced by developments outside the region, notably the rapidly expanding diaspora communities in North America (Magocsi 1993b). The main options at this time were either Greek Catholic Ukrainian or Roman Catholic Pole, but East Slavs could also choose a "Ruthenian" (Rusyn or Rusnak) option and the Orthodox Church began to gain ground among Greek Catholic peasants not attracted to the Ukrainian affiliation. They paid a high price when Austria went to war with Russia in 1914.

With the First World War, we move into the period where social memory assumes greater importance: even if no actual participants remain alive, grandparents can recall the tales told to them. Przemyśl was an Austrian military fortress until it fell to the tsar in 1915. Within three years both empires had disappeared. Supporters of a newly proclaimed republic in western Ukraine attempted to include Przemyśl, but they were defeated by Polish forces in 1918–19. This period is kept vividly alive in the memories of Poles and Ukrainians. The fighting that took place in Przemyśl in the autumn of 1918 was not large scale or in any way glorious, but it did provide the new Polish nation with young heroes: among the dead were a number of schoolboys who gave their lives for the national cause. Designated "Eaglets" in emulation of the heroic "Eagles" who defended L'viv against the Ukrainians, their heroism was celebrated in a special exhibition mounted in Przemyśl's city library in 1997.[10] On the Ukrainian side, the memory of that heroic defeat continued to provoke violence in the interwar decades. During this period the proportion of Polish, Roman Catholic inhabitants in the city increased, while peasants in the surrounding countryside became increasingly aware of possessing a Ukrainian national identity.

[10] The city library was formerly a synagogue and remains recognizable as such, but the city's Jewish history is otherwise almost invisible today.

The state was concerned about the threat posed by Ukrainian nationalism and deeply mistrustful of the Greek Catholic Church. Many in the Roman Catholic Church shared these negative views. The entire interwar period was one of economic hardships and of rising ethnic antagonisms, between Poles and Ukrainians and between each of these groups and Jews (Tomaszewski 1993; cf. Korzec 1991). The erection in 1937 in Przemyśl of a monument to the Eaglets of 1918 was one indication of nationalist sentiment.

These factors were exploited during the Second World War by the Nazis, who recruited Ukrainians to assist them in the administration of the Polish territories they occupied. When Adolf Hitler and Joseph Stalin carved up Poland they made the River San part of their frontier, thus dividing the city of Przemyśl in two (most of the old town lies to the east, that is, in the area occupied by the Soviets in 1939). The monument to the Eaglets was demolished in 1940 by Ukrainians acting on German orders. The following years generated more scores to be settled after the Nazi defeat. Alongside the struggle between the Nazis and the Red Army there were conflicts between Polish and Ukrainian "partisans." These were particularly fierce in Wolhynia, to the northwest of the Przemyśl region and now part of Ukraine. These years yielded a further storehouse of submerged memories that were brought to the surface, especially among Poles, after the collapse of socialism (they were "submerged" only in the sense that it was not possible to discuss them openly in the public sphere; they could of course be discussed and transmitted privately).

The new borders imposed by Stalin saw Ukraine expand dramatically westwards, though not quite as far as the San. Centuries of cultural pluralism came to an abrupt end as large numbers of ethnic Poles moved from towns and villages incorporated into Ukraine to occupy the former German lands that now passed to Poland, while Ukrainians moved in large numbers in the opposite direction. In 1945 it was still possible to pretend that these were voluntary movements. No one could claim this of the further violence that occurred in 1947, which has vividly survived in Ukrainian memories. Ostensibly as a consequence of continued guerilla activities by the Ukrainian Insurgent Army (*Ukrayins'ka Povstans'ka Armiya,* UPA), the leading Ukrainian partisan organization, most remaining Ukrainian and Lemko-Ukrainian communities within Poland's new borders were evacuated by the Polish army in Operation Vistula (*Akcja Wisła*). Their inhabitants were resettled in lands to the west and north that had formerly belonged to Germany, where they typically found themselves outnumbered by recently arrived and hostile Poles. In Ukrainian memories Operation Vistula nowadays figures as the brutal climax of a longstanding Polish program of ethnic cleansing (Hann 1996b). Many who experienced deportation, like the few who managed to avoid this fate, concealed their national identity in the new conditions (Babiński 1997). In Przemyśl, as elsewhere, many children in families where one or even both parents were Ukrainian learned only the Polish language and lost all contact with Ukrainian culture. Repression of Ukrainians was relaxed in 1956, however, when they became an officially designated minority, entitled to maintain their culture under the auspices of a national Socio-Cultural Association. Branches of the association, including the one established in Przemyśl, organized cultural activities at the local level. With basic civil rights restored, it became possible for Ukrainians to return to their native region. Many could not return to their former homes and farms, for these had been allocated to Poles, and for them Przemyśl became a popular alternative, a place where Ukrainians of diverse origins could start to build a new community. Many who made this move recall the risks and dangers. Some speak of a "blockade" by ethnic Poles, determined to prevent them from finding work and accommodation in the city.

The Polish socialist authorities, anxious to present themselves as the legitimate representatives of the Polish nation, could not play a nationalist card against Russia directly, but they could and did do so against Ukraine, especially by emphasizing "terrorist" atrocities by UPA on the territory of the new Polish state up to 1947 (Potichnyj 1980). The "cultural ordering" of socialist Poland was nationalist rather than socialist, even though official historiography was restrained in comparison with some other cases (cf. Verdery 1991a). Diaspora groups helped to sustain this ordering, which was underpinned by the Roman Catholic Church and enormously boosted by the election of Karol Wojtyła to the papacy in 1978 and his regular "pilgrimages" to his native land thereafter. In the last decade of socialism, the symbols and rituals developed by the Solidarity movement confirmed that the vast majority of Polish citizens considered their *pays réel*, the source of their most powerful sources of identity, to be not the People's Republic but the Polish nation (see Mach 1993; Kubik 1994)

Meanwhile the revival of a Greek Catholic parish in Przemyśl (under the protection of the Roman Catholics) in the thaw of 1956 was one of the main attractions to returning Ukrainians. This Church continued to serve as a vehicle for the expression of national identity. Its fate exemplified the differences between Polish and Soviet models of socialism. In Ukraine, Stalin had liquidated the Greek Catholics in 1946. History was rewritten and the Union of Brest was reclassified as an act of Western imperialist aggression against the Orthodox Church. Greek Catholics were merged into Orthodox congregations, though some persisted in the so-called catacomb churches (Keleher 1993; see also Bociurkiw 1996). In Poland most clergy were deported to the USSR in 1946, though a few continued to work "underground" after being dispersed with their parishes in the course of Operation Vistula. The Greek Catholic bishops of Przemyśl both died in Soviet camps. However, although Greek Catholics were denied official recognition in the People's Republic of Poland, they were not explicitly proscribed or actively persecuted. Their history was not so much rewritten as simply ignored. Some of the Church's property, including their cathedral in Przemyśl, passed to the Roman Catholic Church (though it was re-appropriated between 1952 and 1956, and the adjoining monastic buildings were used for a variety of secular purposes). Other Greek Catholic properties were transferred to the Orthodox Church, which continued the expansion it had begun in this region in the first half of the century. From 1956, most Ukrainians in Przemyśl attended Greek Catholic services in a Roman Catholic building, the centrally located former Jesuit church, nowadays known as the Garrison church. Others joined an Orthodox parish when this was formed in 1984 and given use of another former Greek Catholic building on the city boundary.[11] Both eastern Churches maintained a low profile; until the very end of the

[11] The socialist state consistently supported an institution that was expected to encourage defections from the dominant Roman Catholic Church. For some, this made the Orthodox Church highly suspect; they were also repelled by its often marked Russian features. Yet for many Greek Catholics, conversion to Orthodoxy was preferable to attending regular Roman Catholic services, because the form and content of the Orthodox rituals were so much closer to their own.

socialist period, only the Orthodox could organize their Jordan rituals publicly at the bank of the River San.[12]

It was not only in Przemyśl and not only in the sphere of religion that the Ukrainian minority was constrained to maintain a low profile in the People's Republic: in political and social life they were almost invisible. Apart from the anti-Ukrainian stream that was allowed in popular culture, which focused on UPA terrorism, their past was ignored. In 1988 the Roman Catholic Church joined in the general celebrations of the millennium of the establishment of Christianity in Rus' by Prince Volodymyr. This was an important event in strengthening a sense of national identity for many Ukrainians, but for others it served only as a reminder of divisions within the contemporary eastern Churches between Orthodox and Greek Catholics. Neither political nor religious unity prevailed in the minority community. The research of Polish social scientists indicated that the socialist state was a more successful "nationalizing state" than its predecessor; assimilation into the dominant Polish Roman Catholic society was the order of the day (Kwilecki 1974; Nowicka 1980).

Postsocialist Conflicts: The "Defense of the Carmelite Church"

Since 1989 a struggle over one particular building has taken precedence over all other struggles concerning the politics of the past in Przemyśl. I shall focus on this case in order to show how the analysis of nationalist discourse needs to be complemented by an investigation of concrete institutional factors.[13]

In Poland the political events of 1989 were significantly less dramatic than in several neighboring countries. As a result of the "round-

[12] Jordan rituals on January 19 correspond to the Latin Epiphany, but are celebrated more prominently in the eastern Church. See Hann 1998c.

[13] The section that follows is based on later oral accounts and a considerable volume of local and national journalism. The most detailed narrative of events is that published by Stanislaw Zółkiewicz, one of the leading protagonists, between October 22 and December 10, 1991, in the regional newspaper *Pogranicze*.

table talks" and compromises that were years in the making, Poland had a non-communist government in office well before the collapse of walls and iron curtains elsewhere in the region. Like most Polish towns, Przemyśl had a very active Citizens' Committee, pro-Solidarity and anti-communist, which triumphed in the local government elections of 1990.[14] This quickly secured the replacement of a number of socialist and ex-socialist public officials, for example the county conservation officer, who was replaced on the grounds that he held no appropriate professional qualifications. In addition to Citizens' Committees and political parties, new possibilities for participation in the public sphere were offered by special-purpose associations. Prominent among these were nationalist groupings and veterans' associations, which took advantage of virtually unrestricted media freedom to publicize all those issues it had not been possible to discuss publicly under socialism, notably the history of problematic relationships with eastern neighbors. Much was now published for the first time about atrocities committed by UPA and by Ukrainian sections of the Wehrmacht against Polish civilians in wartime Wolhynia. Particularly popular were the books of Wiktor Poliszczuk, whose accounts of Ukrainian nationalist violence were considered all the more authentic as they came from the pen of a Ukrainian author.[15] The nationalism of the new Polish discourses fits well into the model of successive temporal cultural orders outlined by Peter Niedermüller (1997): the interwar period was presented as a period of positive development in the life of the nation, rudely interrupted by the war and then by socialism, following which the "purity" of the nation had to be newly asserted in all areas of social life.

---

[14] The Citizens' Committee list included a Ukrainian, a widely respected doctor. National identity issues seem to have played no role in the 1990 elections. However, this Ukrainian counsellor was not re-elected when he sought a second term in 1994, and since that time there has been no Ukrainian member. Right-wing parties (mainly *Porozumienie Centrum* and *Konfederacja Polski Niepodległej*) have been the strongest forces in both local and national elections in Przemyśl since 1993.

[15] See Poliszczuk 1993. This and other books by Poliszczuk and by Polish authors holding similar views were widely available in Przemyśl bookshops, which do not stock any materials in Ukrainian. Poliszczuk himself apparently lives in Canada, although he publishes principally in Polish.

But expectations concerning the redress of old grievances were also raised among the Ukrainian minority. They focused on the injustices of Operation Vistula in 1947, which could at last be openly discussed, and on religious freedoms. The latter problem complex was dominated by intractable property issues. The few remaining Greek Catholic clergy were able to step out from the shadow of the Roman Catholic Church to voice their demands for autonomy and restitution. The Polish Pope had consistently upheld the right of the Greek Catholics to full equality with the Church of the Latin rite. Early in 1991 he appointed Iwan Martyniak to be the new Greek Catholic bishop of the ancient see of Przemyśl. From this point on, the aspirations of the Greek Catholic community centered on regaining possession of their former cathedral, which had been transferred to the Roman Catholic Carmelites by the Communist Party in 1946. Restitution had already been formally requested by the Greek Catholic cardinal in Rome.

As soon as Greek Catholic demands were articulated, however, a group of lay Roman Catholics formed an Association for the Defense of the Carmelite Church, which opposed any transfer of ownership to the Greek Catholics.[16] This group did not deny that the building had been used by the Greek Catholics before the communists intervened in 1946, but it argued that, in this case, the simple course of erasing the evils of communism could not be followed. Their reason was that this church had formed part of a Roman Catholic Carmelite foundation between its foundation in 1630 and its suppression by Emperor Joseph II at the beginning of the Habsburg period. It was allocated to the Greek Catholics only in 1784, after they had refused the offer of the city's Jesuit church, located on a less imposing site lower down the same central hill. Members of the Defense Association argued that this act of violent appropriation was contrary to natural justice, and to specific laws enacted by the Polish Republic in 1928. They insisted that it had never received any legal sanction. Thus the Carmelites had been fully entitled to regain their former property in 1946—all the more so as this religious order had itself been the victim of illegal appropriation by the Soviet authorities in L'viv. The association even traced descen-

[16] The association had a total of thirty-three members, including four city counsellors and six Solidarity activists. Fourteen members held a degree, most in the fields of engineering and economics.

dants of the founder's family, who issued public statements asserting that it would be disrespectful to them if the Carmelite church in Przemyśl were to pass again into foreign hands.

The Greek Catholics offered a quite different interpretation of the past, emphasizing the elements that suited their case. The building was said to incorporate materials from an even older Orthodox church. They claimed that they had only abandoned construction of a new cathedral on another site because of a clear understanding, shared with Roman Catholics in the late eighteenth century, that the transfer of the former Carmelite church was irrevocable. Some Greek Catholics asserted that the building had been legitimately purchased from the Austrians. They persuaded certain members of the founder's family to endorse their view that it should now belong to the eastern rite church. They also claimed that their ownership had been confirmed in a 1925 Vatican Concordat and was consistent with many other cases all over the world where a church founded by one rite of the Catholic Church had passed into the hands of another. Finally, in perhaps their most telling point, Greek Catholic Ukrainians emphasized that Roman Catholic Poles had not disputed this church's ownership when they had ample opportunity to do so, in the generation preceding its confiscation in 1946. Therefore, despite all protestations to the contrary, the Defense Association was in effect seeking to profit from the morally indefensible socialist appropriation.

Each side was able to make a case in the realms of historical discourse, offering a blend of fact and interpretation. Practical outcomes, however, are determined elsewhere. At first it seemed that a compromise would prevail. The Papal Nuncio in Warsaw Józef Kowalczyk, Polish Primate Józef Glemp, and Archbishop of Przemyśl Ignacy Tokarczuk agreed at a meeting with the newly appointed Greek Catholic bishop that the building should be returned to the Greek Catholics for a five-year period only; within this period the Greek Catholics were to set about building a new cathedral church, with Roman Catholic support. As soon as this compromise was made public, the group of lay activists began to organize protest campaigns in the local media, which they later took to the streets. An elderly lady went on a hunger strike. Senior Roman Catholic clergy were accused of being KGB intelligence agents, others were condemned for refusing to hear the confessions of members of the Defense Association. Some junior clergy sympathized with the activists and helped to frustrate attempts to mediate in the dispute.

The protesters argued in the same "us" versus "them" terms that Solidarity had deployed successfully over the years against the socialist authorities, the difference being that "us" no longer referred to an all-inclusive "people" but to members of the Polish ethnic community. They argued not only that Poles had a legally clear-cut right to retain the Carmelite church, but that the city's Polish heritage was coming under a more general threat from Ukrainians. This issue of church property was central in fomenting a climate of mistrust in Przemyśl at the very time when the Pope himself was due to visit the city in June 1991. Eventually John-Paul II had little choice but to back down when the activist group refused to end their occupation of the building. He left the former Greek Catholic cathedral in the hands of the Carmelites, but during his visit gave the minority the Garrison church which they had been using unofficially for many years, the former Jesuit church which they had rejected in 1781, in favor of the Carmelite church.

In these early postsocialist years in Przemyśl numerous other historical events over which a veil had been drawn in the socialist decades were manipulated and contested. The Polish nationalists operated mainly through the instrument of their newly formed associations which, they claimed, represented the long-suppressed voices of civil society. They had heavily overlapping memberships, were often far from civil in their operation, and drew their *raison d'*être from the violence of the past. Claims to be representative of local society were rendered dubious by the fact that prominent leaders of these associations were not natives of Przemyśl but *repatrianci*, Poles "repatriated" from lands incorporated into Ukraine in 1945.[17] The violence most commonly evoked as evidence of Ukrainian brutality was that which took place in Wolhynia, not violence in Przemyśl or any other region of contemporary Poland. The most aggressive of the new associations, however, was that formed to re-erect the local monument to the Przemyśl Eaglets of 1918. Its president, Stanisław Zółkiewicz, was perhaps the most influential individual in Przemyśl in the early 1990s, though he

[17] It is commonly alleged that many of these activists were members of the Communist Party before 1990, but I was not able to verify this.

never held any elected office. Too young to have participated in the events of the 1940s, his motivation apparently derived from childhood memories of Ukrainian terrorism, and from being a witness in 1950 in L'viv to Ukrainian desecration of the graves of the Poles who had defended the city in 1918–19.[18]

The Ukrainian minority was never in a position to compete in the local media or with the barricades and candlelit vigils organized by the defenders of the Carmelite church. Having lost that battle, however, they too looked continuously to the past and pursued claims for other items of property appropriated by socialists. They enjoyed some successes, though their principal claim (for the former bishop's palace, converted in the 1960s to function as a state museum) has so far made no progress in the courts.[19] They also sought to commemorate martyrs who had fallen in the struggle for an independent Ukraine, including those killed on Polish soil in the first years of socialism. Attempts to erect public monuments led to several conflicts with the authorities and, in one case, to the imposition of a heavy fine on a Greek Catholic priest. These initiatives were viewed as treasonable by the Polish activists, who opposed Ukrainian moves to have their deceased heroes reburied in consecrated ground; in some cases bodies were exhumed secretly in the dead of night.

After the church controversy in 1991, the heady enthusiasms that had followed the end of socialism gave way to a climate of mistrust and intolerance. The city government came increasingly under the influence of Polish extremists, who were determined to oppose initiatives from the capital to improve relations with Ukraine. The clearest example of friction between capital and periphery was the initiative taken by Warsaw

[18] The expression of national memory in this cemetery has remained a source of concern on both sides; Ukrainians have recently reacted strongly to a Polish attempt to commemorate the Polish heroes who gave their lives "in defense of the Fatherland." See the interview with Zółkiewicz in the city newspaper *Życie Przemyskie*, May 1, 1996.

[19] Some Poles argue that a Church known as the Ukrainian Catholic Church can have no legal claim to a building constructed a century earlier by a Church with a quite different name when the region was under Austrian rule. The Association for the Defense of Polish Property specializes in property issues and is opposed to any form of foreign ownership. Its deputy head is a lawyer who also serves as a vice-president of the city.

in 1995 to move the biennial Ukrainian Cultural Festival to Przemyśl from its usual location at Sopot on the Baltic coast. As with the decision of the religious hierarchy in the case of the Carmelite church, the officials failed to reckon with the strength of Polish nationalist opinion in the city. After a campaign that featured the defacing of posters advertising the festival and an arson attack on the Ukrainian Socio-Cultural Association, the festival eventually went ahead in an atmosphere of considerable tension, with a high security presence. The activists objected to public money being spent on such festivals. They tried to prevent its organization in Przemyśl again in 1997, but were again overruled by Warsaw. They also obstructed the organization of a Polish Cultural festival in L'viv in 1996, recognizing that such an event in the city which is often paired in the imagination with Przemyśl would strengthen the claims of the Ukrainian minority in their own city.[20]

At the height of the festival controversy in 1995, the historian Stanisław Stępień, an ethnic Pole who has served since 1990 as director of the South East Scientific Institute, an independent research institution in the city that works to promote better interethnic relations, was stung by nationalist criticism to publish the following diagnosis of the local political climate under the title "We Should Not Stay Silent Any Longer":

> Since the time of the infamous "Defense of the Carmelite Church" against Catholics of the Eastern rite, when . . . before the visit of the Holy Father in 1991 Przemyśl walls were daubed with slogans like "Kowalczyk, Glemp, and Tokarczuk have sold Poland to the Ukrainians," no one apart from Archbishop Tokarczuk has publicly condemned those who carried out and inspired those events. They therefore felt that they had avoided all sanction, indeed the present city authorities even began to reward them for their endeavors, while most people unfortunately acquiesced through their silence. Especially politicians in various

[20] Another issue on which central and local governments have clashed concerns the Carpathian Euroregion. Although membership was strongly encouraged by the authorities in Warsaw, the city council in Przemyśl decided in 1995 that it was not in their interests to seek closer cultural or economic links with neighboring states. See Hann 1998d.

> offices were afraid of that small but noisy group, of being accused by them of a lack of patriotism, of not being *real Poles* [*prawdziwymi Polakami*], or, heaven forbid, of having some Ukrainian ancestors. This wrong, which went publicly uncorrected, has led to a situation in which that group, which styles itself "patriotic," has effectively terrorized a city of 70,000 people. Usurping for itself the right to speak in the name of the whole of society, it has imposed its own representatives on various public bodies. It denigrates parliamentarians, state officials, clergy, and scholars. It accuses scientific research institutes of "falsifying the history of Poland."[21]

Contestation of the past was carried out in a rapidly changing present, in which mundane changes in the economic sphere were of great importance. For the first time in half a century Ukrainians became visible and audible in Przemyśl as a result of the liberalization of cross-border travel and, in particular, of regulations governing petty trade. People travelled from all over Ukraine and even further afield to sell and buy at a bazaar said at its peak in the early 1990s to be second in size only to that of the capital. Small-scale commerce fitted in well with the new precepts of freedom and market economy. It certainly offered a badly needed economic lifeline to a city in which many socialist enterprises were being closed. For this reason the petty commerce was condoned as a somewhat disagreeable necessity, even by the more nationalist Poles who did not like to see so many foreigners in their city. The authorities in Warsaw and their Western advisers expected new trading partnerships to produce positive social benefits. No doubt some benefits have accrued, but petty trade of the sort unleashed throughout the regions bordering on the former Soviet Union also carries dangers. The conditions of the markets and the traders often left much to be desired (few could afford to stay in hotels, and in any case Przemyśl at this time had no hotels to offer them), as did the quality of the goods they sold. The influx of Ukrainian traders and wild rumors about "mafias" tended to confirm the

---

[21] Stanisław Stępień, „Dłużej milczeć nie wolno," *Życie Przemyskie*, June 17, 1995 (emphasis in original).

negative images long harbored by many Poles. Since the numbers of Poles who took advantage of opportunities to travel eastward was much smaller, it is doubtful whether the new economic circumstances did much to improve intercultural understanding. On the other hand, the new phenomenon of mass unemployment created a reservoir of discontented people, especially among the young, who were susceptible to the rhetoric of extremists (see Chapter Two).[22]

Although controversy has also surrounded some other buildings, the Carmelite church has remained the principal symbolic focus for the minority issue. Having won the main battle in 1991, the nationalists made various alterations to the interior to highlight its Polish affiliation. One wall was covered with a large map of Poland with its pre-1939 boundaries and a plaque that features the Polish national eagle with a swastika in one claw and Ukraine's national symbol in the other. The text underneath reads: "To the innocent Polish population barbarously murdered by UPA bands in the southeast borderlands of the Republic in the years 1942–48," followed by the signature of Stanisław Zółkiewicz. In 1992 the Carmelite clergy, supported by the nationalists, launched an attempt to transform the exterior of the church by removing the tower and dome that were added in the nineteenth century by the Greek Catholics. At first the county conservation officer gave his permission and demolition commenced. He then changed his mind, only to be accused of pro-Ukrainian bias and in effect hounded out of office after the 1993 elections by a coalition of nationalists and ex-socialists. The issue simmered while a successor was appointed. Eventually the job went to the previous, ex-socialist incumbent, who to no one's great surprise acceded to nationalist demands. Permission was denied by the Ministry in Warsaw, however, and for several years the remnants of the great dome provided a conspicuous reminder on the skyline of the tradition that the Polish activists wished to obliterate, a symbol of Ukrainian culture in the city, even if the building would never again be theirs.

[22] Przemyśl Ukrainians believe that anti-Ukrainian graffiti writing and the more serious outbursts of violence in recent years, such as arson attacks at their Ukrainian Socio-Cultural Association and at the Southeast Scientific Institute, are the work of "hooligan youth," but that these eruptions are encouraged and even financed by their elders.

Figure 15. Destruction of the tower of the former Greek Catholic cathedral (photo by Stanisław Stępień, 1996)

The dome was finally demolished in 1996, the 400th anniversary of the creation of the Greek Catholic Church in this region, in circumstances that again highlighted the tension between the city government and the authorities in the capital. To the earlier historical justifications a new one was added in public discourse on the Polish side: the claim that the canon law of the Carmelites prevented any building belonging to them from being adorned with any form of tower or dome. Hence the dome would have to come down, irrespective of what the secular authorities might have to say. Against this, the national conservation officer insisted that state conservation law had priority over any such canon law. Various Polish "experts" declared that the dome was structurally unsound (no one took this argument very seriously—even if true, such problems could have been remedied) and that it did not harmonize architecturally with the rest of the building. No one asked the Ukrainians for their opinion.

As with the earlier conflicts in 1991, these various strands of discourse were rendered brusquely irrelevant by direct action.[23] In scenes that read in media accounts like high farce, the county conservation officer, after ordering that demolition proceed, hid himself away from

[23] This account of the most recent transformation of the Carmelite church is based on the article by Jagieńka Wilczak, "Spór w rozbiorce," *Polityka*, December 7, 1996, 30–32.

Figure 16. The Carmelite church with its new "western" spire (photo by Stanisław Stępień, 1997)

his office so as not to be able to take the countermanding call that he knew would follow from the Ministry in Warsaw. The Carmelite clergy and demolition workers sealed themselves off from the world, as had the occupiers of the church in 1991, in order to be able to ignore last-minute instructions to desist. A year later, apparently in disregard of their own canon law, the Carmelites erected an elegant new tower in place of the demolished dome. Thwarted, the national conservation officer in Warsaw had to content himself with the observation that the dome, far from being Eastern Orthodox in character, had in fact been modelled on St. Peter's in Rome. To a foreigner the new tower might even be thought to have a more distinctive oriental character than the dome it has replaced. But that is not how these matters are perceived by either the Polish or the Ukrainian community in Przemyśl.

Some Ukrainians wept when the dome was dismantled, but they felt powerless to influence the course of events at any stage. Questioned about responsibility, some of them conceded that only a tiny minority of the Polish population were responsible. Others gave more thoughtful answers, arguing that this active minority was giving expression to prejudices that were deep and widespread throughout the Polish population. Although their bishop has decided not to question the Pope's gift establishing the former Jesuit church as their cathedral on a permanent basis, and although major redecoration of this building was completed in 1997, some Greek Catholics still do not feel at home in this church.

Confrontation is continuing in 1998 over plans to erect a new bell tower and to remove the Jesuit symbol and Latin inscription from the facade of the building.[24]

Conclusions: Prospects for Polytacticity

Peter Niedermüller (1997) refers several times to Poland in his review of the role of history in postsocialist discourse strategies. The strategies that he labels "renovation" and "reconstruction" imply that the postsocialist national community can resume an earlier trajectory by rebuilding on basically unproblematic pre-socialist foundations. However, Niedermüller pays little attention to the concrete institutional contexts which become crucial when one moral principle—the provision of restitution or compensation to all those who suffered or justly at the hands of socialist powerholders—comes into conflict with an even stronger principle, that which attaches the highest moral worth to the Polish nation and the Roman Catholic Church. This has been the

[24] Although the church was given to the Ukrainians by the Pope himself, they know that many Poles still consider it a Polish church (*kościół*). Some therefore favor a return to the plan of erecting a new cathedral, a *cerkiew* with an explicitly eastern design and acoustics better adapted to eastern hymns, which would be undeniably "ours." For details, see the somewhat one-sided presentation by Niemiec 1998. The journalist cites three Polish "experts" who all agree that Ukrainian proposals to alter the exterior of the former Jesuit church are contrary to conservation codes. One adds that such alteration would be contrary to ecumenical aspirations. Whereas some Poles justify the demolition at the Carmelite church on the grounds that the addition of the dome in the nineteenth century was an alteration of the original building, Greek Catholics point out that the Latin inscription they now wish to remove from the Jesuit church was added at the time of major renovation in 1900. The Polish reply to this, as reported by Niemiec, is that this inscription is not merely a name on the church but a religious invocation to God that bears witness both to the Roman Catholic origin of the building and to the sacrifices made by the people of Przemyśl in renovating it at the turn of the century. She adds an unsupported assertion: "Among the inhabitants of Przemyśl the memory of that social action is still living" (69). [For more detailed material on Ukrainian attitudes, based on interviews with members of the minority in Przemyśl, see Hann and Stępień 2000; for the general picture, see also Mokry 1997; for details of improved interethnic relations in the early years of the new century, see Buzalka 2007.]

case since 1989 in Przemyśl. The usual strategy of "renovation" was trumped in this case by the evocation of an earlier wrong perpetrated against the Polish side. The motivation for evoking an unjustifiable appropriation in 1784 lay in memories and media evocations of acts of violence committed this century between Poles and Ukrainians.

Many Poles in Przemyśl readily concede that the Ukrainian, Greek Catholic minority also suffered wrongs under socialism. According to their rationalization, however, compensating this group materially is not warranted, because this would involve returning more real estate than the present minority population could possibly use (similar arguments are sometimes advanced in the Jewish case). To provide full compensation would now threaten the "Polish character of the city" and make it an attractive place for Ukrainian migration. Such opinions compete with other views, such as the pluralist multiculturalist view according to which, although the city now lies unambiguously within the Polish state and has a predominantly Roman Catholic Polish population, the rights of linguistic and religious minorities should be respected and actively cultivated. Almost all Poles agree, at least publicly, that the Ukrainian minority that exists in the city has a right to be there and to cultivate its traditions. But at the same time there are many Polish inhabitants who doggedly insist that this minority is very small and that "it should have no right to dictate to the majority."[25]

There is a strong conviction among members of the Ukrainian minority that historically, primordially, all territory east of the San River and large districts west of it belonged to them. Following the deportations of the 1940s, most of the Ukrainians who were indigenous to

[25] For an example of this viewpoint, see the interview with Andrzej Matusiewicz, president of the city, in *Życie Przemyskie*, November 18, 1992. He spoke as follows: "We must answer the question: is Przemyśl to be a town of both nations, that means of the Poles and the Ukrainians who live here, or is Przemyśl to be a Polish town that observes minority rights. . . . I am an advocate of the Polish character of this town—of course not in a nationalistic sense. There is in Przemyśl a Ukrainian minority, it was here in the past, and it has a right to be here. Above all else, however, it must respect the law of the state in which it is living. It cannot be privileged just because it is a minority." Matusiewicz is a lawyer who acted on behalf of the Carmelites in the church controversy described above. He explains in this interview that his professional involvement in this case has no bearing on his position as president of the city.

what is now southeast Poland have been more or less integrated into other regions of Poland and Ukraine. The latter have no right of return and there is no evidence that the former will ever move back in large numbers to the Przemyśl region, irrespective of compensation policies currently under discussion.[26] Nonetheless, the Polish nationalists in the city profess concern. Both their discourses and their practices illustrate in extreme forms how the past can become a focus for controversy in the conditions of postsocialist democracy.

I have tried in this chapter to situate this Polish nationalism in multiple time frames, including the long-term and the postsocialist conjuncture. Long-term issues include the status of Ukraine as a sovereign nation and of the Greek Catholics as a hybrid of east and west. The basic story is a simple one: after many centuries of cultural pluralism, the dominant trend of the twentieth century in this part of central Europe was to create culturally homogenous "nation-states." The most drastic steps to this end were taken in the 1940s. In the wider context, the political culmination of this trend was the breakup of the Soviet Union, Czechoslovakia, and Yugoslavia in the 1990s. But no matter how drastic the measures taken and how painful these separations, the goal of perfect congruence between political and cultural boundaries is always illusory. All over the region, and especially in "borderland" territories, there are minorities in analogous situations to the Greek Catholic Ukrainians of Przemyśl. Many have managed to retain more complex identities than are nowadays regarded as the norm in this region, where, as we have seen, pressures to make national identity coincide with religious affiliation long ago modified an earlier polytacticity. The very existence of such minorities serves as a reminder that national identity is a contingent phenomenon, and a relatively recent development in this part of the world.

There are grounds for supposing that polytacticity may be making a comeback in some parts of Eastern Europe, including Poland. The creation of a Euroregion and the relaxation of some customs controls are intended to contribute to greater movement across borders. More enlightened minority legislation, especially when supplemented by the financial resources necessary for educational and other cultural pro-

[26] This is confirmed by the Przemyśl Ukrainians themselves, almost all of whom have relatives settled in other places, including some who now speak only Polish and have been assimilated into the mainstream of Polish society.

vision, may prove conducive to the reassertion of regional and local identities. The case of the Lemko-Ukrainians, at least some of whom seem able to reconcile the two strands of this identity, is but one of many illustrations of how this phenomenon is unfolding in Poland (see Chapter Eight). On the other hand, policies enunciated by the new liberal elites in Warsaw may not be constructively implemented in the peripheral areas where most citizens of non-Polish ethnicity live; legislation alone does nothing to bring about greater tolerance toward minorities by the dominant group.

Janusz Mucha, one of the leading scholarly investigators of majority-minority relations in contemporary Poland, has recently sought to expand the terms of the discussion (1997a, 1997b). By questioning the value of a distinction between ethnic or national minorities and other kinds of cultural minorities—the disabled, atheists, youth subcultures, even women—he in effect introduces a new, broader approach to polytacticity. It is an attractive approach with much to recommend it: for example, in terms of their impact on local public opinion, youth groups known as Skins and Punks have probably been as conspicuous in Przemyśl in the 1990s as any public activities undertaken by the Ukrainian minority. To adopt the social science vocabulary of pressure groups and subcultures assumes that Polish society can be approached sociologically in basically the same way as, say, Britain or the United States. Moreover, there is little doubt that in some situations the Ukrainians of Przemyśl will not identify themselves with the Ukrainian traders conspicuous in their marketplaces, but will feel instead that they have more in common with their Polish neighbors and workmates. In short, everyone, even the most committed members of ethnic and national groups, is to some extent polytactic in everyday life. Have I not exaggerated the importance of one strand in contemporary identities, implying that this is the only strand which matters and neglecting a host of other factors pertinent to identifications?

There is the further issue of what general conclusions to draw from this case study.[27] The Przemyśl region is poorly understood in the rest

[27] When I presented an earlier version of this article at a conference in Poland, some participants were politely dismissive. In the context of the present Polish state, they asserted, the problems affecting Greek Catholic Ukrainians in Przemyśl were quite exceptional, a marginal phenomenon in the wider society.

of Poland, and this is at least partly due to the fact that its problems are remote from most Poles' daily experience. I do not pretend that the city is representative. It is worth repeating that postsocialist power holders in Warsaw have made numerous positive gestures toward ethnic minorities, and that in Przemyśl itself the great majority of citizens have played no active part in fomenting ethnic hatred. We might adopt a different perspective and suggest that, in comparison with the Yugoslav situation, Polish-Ukrainian relations have evolved very positively. Considering that, here as in the Balkans, direct and indirect memories of ethnic violence remain so widespread, one might marvel at the relative tranquility of the area. To take an optimistic view, the controversies that have arisen in the 1990s may be seen as the last efforts of an older generation to stir up trouble in changed political circumstances. As Poland's democracy is further stabilized, these problems can be expected to recede and the prospects for better relations with Ukrainians should improve.

Yes, maybe, but as the first postsocialist decade draws to a close Greek Catholic Ukrainians in Przemyśl still have good reasons to conclude that Polish nationalism is a dominant structuring force, not only in their city but more generally in Polish society, and that Ukrainians serve as this nationalism's most significant enemy or "other."[28] Why else would hundreds, probably thousands of "mixed" families in Przemyśl continue to foreclose some of their polytactic options by denying that they have any Ukrainian ancestry? The dominance of a national identification among members of the minority community is shown in the fact that, though differentiated in terms of place of origin, occupation, and even religion, they all agree on the importance of marriage within the group, in order to be able to pass on what they see as their Ukrainian heritage. Since most of these people have previously lived and worked in other parts of Poland, their many negative experiences with Poles, cannot be attributed entirely to the unique local environment in Przemyśl (though the recent conflicts here have undoubtedly strengthened their Ukrainian

[28] Formerly this role was played more conspicuously by Jews. Although, as has often been noted, it is perfectly possible for anti-Semitism to linger and even to flourish without any significant presence of Jews, the virtually complete disappearance of Jews from cities such as Przemyśl has perhaps been a further factor in the canalization of hatred toward Ukrainians.

self-identification). In short, the events in Przemyśl have been unique, but they cannot be dismissed as the peculiarities of one city. They confirm patterns long evident in nationwide sociological surveys, which have not changed very much in the new political climate of the 1990s. Secure in the possession of their own national culture, Poles are almost entirely ignorant of the equivalent Ukrainian culture, and the popular images remain overwhelmingly unsympathetic.[29] The cognitive map of most Poles has not accommodated Ukraine which, if it does not fall apart altogether, is expected to remain at best a backward eastern neighbor long after Poland has assumed her rightful place in the European Union. Poles are used to conceptualizing themselves as sandwiched between two powerful neighbors, and they have varying mixtures of hatred and respect for both Germans and Russians. For complex historical reasons, Ukraine simply does not fit. The problem facing Poland is not just how to deal with a minority numbering a few hundred thousand, but how to classify the 52 million citizens of a newly sovereign country, much of which they, Poles, once dominated.[30] Until Poles come to terms with this history, a major constraint on postsocialist polytacticity in Przemyśl will remain in place.

---

29 See Jasińska-Kania 1992. In recent years immigration from the Balkans has apparently caused Romanians and Gypsies to be viewed even more negatively than Ukrainians, while attitudes toward Jews/Israelis have softened somewhat. See "Stosunek naszego społeczenstwa do innych nacji: Kommunikat z badań," *Centrum Badania Opinii Społecznej* (November 1997). Many Poles tend to excuse negative views toward Ukrainians with the claim that Ukrainians categorize Poles in precisely the same way. With the exception of a small group of extreme nationalists in western Ukraine, this is not the case: see Klaus Bachmann, "Na czym polega problem polsko-ukraiński," *Rzeczpospolita*, September 27–28, 1997, and further correspondence in the issue of November 8–9. One positive way to address the negative images held by Poles would be to follow the model set by the Polish-German Schoolbook Commission, which has, since the 1970s, helped both sides come to terms with a history of mutual mistrust and prejudice. See various contributions to Becher 1993. The recent "Komunikat historyków polskich i ukraińskich" issued jointly by Polish and Ukrainian historians could be a useful beginning.

30 The history of Poland's domination of western Ukraine is too intricate to enter into here (for a recent balanced assessment, see Magocsi 1996). In very general terms, I see this as a problem of postcolonial recognition analogous to the problems faced by France in Algeria or by England in Ireland.

CHAPTER TEN

Polish Civil Society, the Greek Catholic Minority, and Fortress Europe

(2000, 2002)

> The Polish situation is specific. Poland is a one-nation country within the borders designated by Stalin; a country whose euphoria experienced after the defeat of communism is clouded by the deep crisis of its economic structure. In Poland one can see most clearly what the "Black Hundreds" is about—it is not, after all, about struggling with ethnic minorities, which are not threatening anybody with anything. It is about the shape of Poland itself, the nation and its culture, the state and its guiding principles. It is a dispute neither between the right and the left, nor between Christian democracy and social democracy. None of these designations makes much sense today. It is a dispute between two ideas of nation and state: between the idea of a civil society and an open nation on the one hand and, on the other, the idea of a "Catholic State of the Polish Nation" and intolerance toward those who are different. The former uses the language of democratic debate; the latter, the language of insinuation and hatred. For the former, the nation is a community of culture; for the latter, a community of blood.
>
> Adam Michnik (excerpted in Augustinos 1996, 138)[1]

[1] As Gerasimos Augustinos notes (1996, 138), "Black Hundreds was an anti-revolutionary and anti-semitic organization founded in Russia at the time of the 1905 revolution that was opposed to change."

Introduction[2]

A Catholic minority in Poland? Surely there is some mistake here. Everybody knows that the Catholic Church has long played a leading role in Polish national life. Since the redrawing of frontiers and the migrations, mostly forced, of many millions of people in the 1940s, well over ninety percent of the population has belonged to the Roman Catholic Church. This gave the Church its unique strength in the struggle against communism, when it seemed to represent the whole of Polish society against an illegitimate state.

I write "seemed" because my fieldwork during and immediately prior to the Solidarity period demonstrated that things were not in fact quite so simple. Certainly the ability of the dominant Church to project itself as a force for both national unity and democratization has weakened in the postsocialist years. Rather than lead the struggle for a new, open "civil society," the Church is frequently in tension with such an agenda. The new tensions between society and its dominant Church expose more fundamental ambiguities in the concept of civil society. After considering how to define and use this term, I shall turn to ethnographic and historical materials to show why it has proved difficult to establish a more civil society in the area of southeast Poland where I have carried out field research. The Greek Catholics have been the main victims of a continuing lack of *civility* there. However, this is not merely a local or a regional problem, nor is it just a religious problem. I argue that it is symptomatic of a more general anti-Ukrainian prejudice that is widespread throughout Polish society. While it is relatively easy to formulate general theories of civil society which guarantee individual rights, including basic religious rights, this does not help very much in situations where one religion is dominant, where religious identities are strongly identified with secular ethno-national identities, and where other sources of collective well-being have been seriously, perhaps irrevocably, weakened. In these circumstances more specific

---

2 *The opening sections of this chapter are adapted from Hann 2002, while the penultimate section and final concluding paragraph originate in Hann 2000a. My thanks are due to the editors of these volumes, based on conferences which they convened in Kraków and Frankfurt (Oder) respectively.*

safeguards are necessary if a multifaith, multicultural civil society is to flourish. At the end of the chapter I briefly consider some of the steps that might be taken to achieve such a goal.

Civil Society and Religion

First it is necessary to define civil society. I tend to agree with Ernest Gellner's view that, when one considers the intellectual history, this term is an incoherent "muddle" (1994, 60). Yet despite this conclusion, Gellner joined many other social scientists in finding the term useful in the positive and normative analysis of contemporary societies, preferable to still vaguer terms such as "democratization" (see Chapter Six). Jürgen Kocka has recently characterized civil society as a coherent utopian project of Enlightenment Europe. He outlines its main features as follows:

> [A] modern, secularized society of free and self-reliant individuals who would manage their relations with one another in a peaceful and reasonable way, through individual competition as well as through voluntary cooperation and association, without too much social inequality and without the tutelage of an authoritarian state. For that purpose certain institutional arrangements were needed: the guarantee of individual rights, the protection of the family, markets, an arena for public debate, the nation state, due process of law, constitutional government and parliamentary representation. These demands were intrinsically linked to a new conception of social relations: work, achievement and success—not birth and privilege—should determine the distribution of wealth, status and power. Education should be of the utmost importance. The public use of reason should replace legitimation by tradition. Private and public life should be clearly distinguished. (Kocka 1997, 499)

The renewed vitality of the concept of civil society owes much to its deployment in the later years of socialist rule in Eastern Europe, where it was contrasted sharply with the presence of an authoritarian state. While Kocka refrains from specifying the form of state power that will be necessary to guarantee the "institutional arrangements" of civil society, some popular usages have pitted civil society *against* the state in any form. This was readily understandable in socialist conditions (Hann 1990a, 1990b, 1996a). Some formulations restrict civil society to the realm of associations, to nongovernmental organizations, or to the voluntary or "third" sector. In the absence of any general agreement on how to operationalize civil society in empirical analyses, I favor retaining the breadth of Kocka's ideal type. Indeed I am inclined to broaden it further by suggesting that a civil society must be one in which the free individual citizens can also express their collective identities in conditions of tolerance and civility.

Where does religion fit in to such an approach? Jürgen Kocka starts out by specifying a "secularized society of free and self-reliant individuals." However, other historical accounts have pointed out that the foundations of the modern individual are intimately connected with new religious currents (Seligman 1992). Many authors resolve the issue by applying the distinction introduced by Kocka at the end of the above quotation. Religion is considered a facet of the individual's private identity. As such it enjoys state protection, in much the same way as the family is protected. The general civil rights of an individual who belongs to a small religious minority should not be any different from the rights of those who belong to a dominant religious tradition.

European countries vary enormously in the ways in which they implement these ideals. France endeavors to maintain a sharp line between the public and private, so that Muslim women who wish to wear a headscarf in the public domain encounter the same criticism that they encounter in Turkey, where Islam is the dominant tradition, but the Kemalist state is resolutely secular and seeks to maintain a sharp public/private distinction. Britain and Germany offer "softer" models. The former has an "established" Church, but Anglicanism has a long history of accommodation to other traditions. In Germany, Muslims may feel they have fewer rights in the eyes of the state than the mainstream Protestant and Catholic Churches, but their status is secure and quite different from that of the Church of Scientology.

Religion, in the form of the Roman Catholic Church, continues to play a more prominent role in politics as well as in social life Poland than in any of these Western countries. The Polish People's Republic did its best to undermine the power of the Church, but it failed. It did not try to eliminate religion altogether. Instead (rather like the Kemalist regime in Turkey) it tried to confine it to the private sphere. One of the side effects of attempts to weaken the Roman Catholic Church was a willingness on the part of socialists to cooperate with smaller churches that posed little threat. The Orthodox Church was able to expand in the socialist period—hence the apprehension I noticed among some members of this minority during the Solidarity period and later (Hann 1985, 197; see Chapter Eight). They were worried that a Poland governed by a strong movement claiming to represent all the Polish people and closely attached to the Roman Catholic Church would provide a less hospitable environment for ethnic and religious minorities.

By and large these fears have not been born out in the aftermath of socialism. Successive Polish governments have paid more attention to the protection of minorities, which clearly is specified in Article 35 of the new Constitution as adopted by the National Assembly on April 2, 1997. However, from the point of view of broad definitions of civil society it is not self-evident that the postsocialist state is a major improvement on its predecessor. Certainly the state has become more constitutional and some representative institutions work more effectively. However, under the influence of the dominant church it has adopted new policies in areas previously regarded as matters of private sphere, notably in the curtailing of abortion. In the villages and small towns of Poland, which is where most people live, it is difficult today, just as it was in the communist period, to live as an atheist. To point this out is not to deny that in certain respects Polish society has become highly secularized. Some aspects of secularization have accelerated in the postsocialist years with greater exposure to Western media and consumer goods. Yet Poland, having thrown off the unwanted collectivity of socialism, continues to exhibit two extremely powerful and congruent forms of collective identification, with the Roman Catholic Church and with the Polish nation, which rather fly in the face of Jürgen Kocka's "modern, secularized society of free and self-reliant individuals." In the following sections I shall explain why this situation poses special problems for people who, though committed Catholics, constitute a religious minority that is highly correlated with a non-Polish ethno-national group.[3]

3 [For a recent ethnographic study of the limitations of pluralism in a multi-religious district of the Carpathians, see Pasieka 2015.]

The Decline of Polytacticity

The region that is now the southeast corner of Poland has a tangled history which is not untypical of Eastern Europe as a whole (see Chapter Nine). It is a polytactic history in which linguistic boundaries showed a high degree of congruence with religious boundaries. Three main traditions dominated the medieval and early modern periods. The Roman Catholics mostly spoke Western Slavic dialects, the Orthodox spoke Eastern Slavic dialects, while Jews had their own, much less permeable boundaries. Politically this region was under Eastern Slavic control until its incorporation into the Polish state by Casimir the Great in 1341. In the following centuries Poland (in the guise of the Polish-Lithuanian Commonwealth) remained a state of many languages and religions. They did not all enjoy equal status. On the contrary, polytactic agrarian polities were typically hierarchical. In this case, Western Slavic cultural elements were more highly valued, such that an upwardly mobile Eastern Slavic would tend to assume the languages of the West (Latin and French, as well as Polish) and the Roman Catholic religion. Poles were often more numerous in the towns, while "Ruthenians" tended to be the more numerous element in the countryside. In some areas, to be a Pole meant to be a nobleman and a landlord, while the peasants were entirely Ruthenian.[4] But there were also many Roman Catholic peasants, speaking dialects of Polish. Following complex migration processes, some persons and groups changed their language and/or religion, giving rise to new combinations of Western Slavic speakers who practiced the Eastern strand of Christianity and vice versa. Meanwhile Jews maintained their distinctive economic niches, both in towns and in villages, and were subject to different laws and administration.

This polytactic agrarian state was far removed from the Enlightenment ideal of a civil society. It nonetheless provided a political framework for peaceful coexistence and extensive cultural as well as economic exchange, particularly between the two major Christian

[4] I use the old term Ruthenian to describe this Eastern Slavic population because it is anachronistic to speak of Ukrainians before the emergence of this national identity in the nineteenth century.

traditions. This was exemplified by the case of the Greek Catholic Church, which came into existence through the Union of Brest in 1596 and allowed Orthodox Christians to become Catholic without having to give up their Eastern rite, or what I have elsewhere termed their "practical religion" (Hann 1988, 1993d).

Polytacticity remained the norm until the middle of the twentieth century, but the process of dissolution began under the region's last imperial rulers, the Austrian Habsburgs, to whom Galicia was allocated following the first partition of Poland in 1772. The nineteenth century was the great age of national movements in Europe, each struggling to control a quite new form of state. In the spirit proclaimed by Johann Gottfried Herder, intellectuals formulated a concept of collective secular belonging, based on a common language, which was increasingly standardized and purified of foreign elements. It took some time to persuade peasant Western Slavic dialect speakers that they shared a common identity with their Polish landlords. In 1846 these peasants still showed more sympathy with the Austrian Emperor than with elites fighting for Polish national liberation, who were perceived as the class enemy. Gradually, however, the abolition of feudal ties, constitutional and political reforms, increasing literacy, communications revolutions, and greater social and geographical mobility (including international migration) facilitated the dissemination of national consciousness.

Among Eastern Slavs, the same process unfolded more slowly, due primarily to weaker traditions of statehood and economic backwardness. In eastern Galicia there were tensions between those who struggled for the relatively novel ideal of a Ukrainian national identity and those who felt more attached to the term *Rusyn* (Ruthenian) and its cognates, and sympathized with the Russian Czar on pan-Slavic grounds. The new secular identities were very closely bound up with religions. Much of the most powerful imagery of the new Polish nation was Christian, especially because the Roman Catholic Church was able to put itself forward as the embodiment of the national identity in the absence of a Polish state. The Greek Catholic clergy played a vital role in the early expansion of the Ukrainian national movement, and this Church remained strongly identified with the Ukrainian cause throughout the twentieth century.

Wilsonian principles of national self-determination at the end of the First World War led to the creation of a new Polish state. However, approximately one-third of its citizens were not Polish in the ethnic sense. We can speak of the continuation of polytacticity in the interwar decades. We may speak, too, of further gains for civil society, since the state proclaimed itself to be a republic and elections were held to new representative institutions. However, this civil society did not function well, particularly from the point of view of minorities. Polish farmers were resettled in eastern zones where Ukrainians were denied equal rights to acquire land. The promise to establish a Ukrainian-language university was broken. Perceptions of the role of the Greek Catholic Church in strengthening Ukrainian nationalism led to more defections to Orthodoxy and hence to the creation of a separate Apostolic Administration for those parts of the Carpathian region where the Ukrainian cause was not yet well entrenched, by agreement between Warsaw and the Vatican (see Best 2000). Economic depression and rising nationalist sentiment both contributed to increasing anti-Semitism in the 1930s. The decisive rupture with polytacticity came during and after the Second World War. In the decades following Operation Vistula, in 1947, when almost all remaining Eastern Slavs were evacuated from what was now the southeast corner of the state, high rates of geographical and social mobility and socialist educational programs contributed to a homogenization of culture and high rates of assimilation among most minority groups. Unlike all previous Polish states, socialist Poland approximated to monoethnicity.[5] The authorities trumpeted this in their own way, since playing the national card was one of the few ways in which they could attempt to bolster legitimacy.

The Changing Status of the Greek Catholics

Given the links between ethnicity and religion, this transition to monoethnicity entailed for the Roman Catholic Church a more dominant position in the society than ever before. Even before Operation Vistula, following the forcible elimination of the Greek Catholic Church in the Ukraine in 1946, this Church had its property confiscated. Its bishops were deported to the USSR, where they died in camps. Some of the

[5] Jerzy Wiatr gives a total figure for all minorities of only 1.3%. (1977, 137).

spoils were divided between Roman Catholics and Orthodox, though many fine buildings were destroyed or left to disintegrate. As an institution, the Greek Catholic Church seemed to be defunct. However it refused to die. In Poland as in the Soviet Ukraine a few clergy managed to maintain the Greek Catholic tradition by holding services "underground," in the diaspora created by Operation Vistula. Ecclesiastical responsibility for the Greek Catholic Church was vested by the Pope in the Roman Catholic Primate. With Roman Catholic support, after the political thaw of 1956 Greek Catholics were able to expand their pastoral activity over much of the country, holding their services in Roman Catholic churches and administering sacraments and life cycle rituals in the prescribed ways.

From the point of view of civil society it is worth looking a little more carefully at the exact status of the Greek Catholic Church in these years. Few would consider Operation Vistula and the various decrees that authorized massive property confiscation to be legitimate actions of a law-governed state. Yet the socialist authorities after 1956 treated these decrees as having full legal force and steadfastly refused to recognize the Greek Catholic Church as an "ecclesiastical legal person" in the way that other religious communities were officially recognized by the state (Czech 1992). On the other hand, the authorities did not ban the Church and persecute its members in the way Greek Catholics were persecuted in Ukraine. Polish Greek Catholics had a lot of freedom, but only through the protection received from the dominant Church. This was a relationship that could work well, but it also gave rise to tensions and suspicions. Sometimes the Greek Catholics felt that their efforts to re-establish their own tradition met with obstruction from Roman Catholic priests and bishops who preferred to promote the religious variant of cultural assimilation, i.e. conversion of all Catholics to the Western, "Latin" rite.[6] In 1971 and again in 1980 Greek Catholics signed mass petitions in which they pleaded for the independent recognition of their Church. The matter was referred to a commission, set up in 1980 to regulate relations between the state and the

[6] Such opinions were expressed by no less a figure than Stefan Dziubina, Vicar-General of the Greek Catholics in Poland between 1977 and 1981. See his autobiography, Dziubina 1995.

Catholic Church, which finally reported to parliament in May 1989, shortly before Poland became the first Soviet bloc country to allow the holding of partially competitive free elections.

The statute that followed was a disappointment to Greek Catholics as it still made no explicit mention of their Church. While specific units of the Church could now obtain recognition as "legal persons," the Greek Catholic Church was still subsumed in the encompassing identity of "the Catholic Church." Another mass appeal (with 5,500 signatures) was submitted to the (postsocialist) parliament in December 1990, asserting that the omission of any reference to Greek Catholics was tantamount to a continuation of their uncertain existence hitherto, outside of the law. By this time the matter of separate recognition was more urgent because, as socialist power throughout the region collapsed, the prospects for regaining confiscated property suddenly improved. Much of this property had passed to the Roman Catholic Church, which was no longer in the convenient position of being able to say to Greek Catholics that it would really like to be able to do more to help them, but that it could not countermand the dictates of the socialist state.

The postsocialist state plainly preferred to leave these issues to the Catholic Church to negotiate internally, but this was where Greek Catholics felt vulnerable. A modification to the new Statute, approved in October 1991, declared that the "Catholic Church in Poland existed in all of its rites," but this too fell short of the explicit institutional recognition sought by Greek Catholics. They had to endure further disappointment in 1992, this time at the hands of the Vatican, when a papal Bull attached the revived Greek Catholic diocese of Przemyśl to the Metropolitan of Warsaw, i.e. to the Roman Catholic Primate. Once again the Greek Catholics protested at treatment which seemed to them to subordinate the Eastern Catholic Church to the country's dominant Roman Catholic tradition. These protests may have had some impact, for in 1993 the Pope elevated the Bishop of Przemyśl to the status of Metropolitan, giving him formally the same rights and status as the head of the country's Roman Catholics. But since the latter community is at least three hundred times larger, and since the two Greek Catholic bishops are of course heavily outnumbered by their Roman Catholic colleagues on the Polish Episcopate, the main executive body of the Catholic Church in Poland,

Greek Catholic perceptions of inferiority and powerlessness have not gone away.[7]

Postsocialist Civil Society, Civility and Culture in Przemyśl

The end of socialist rule brought more dramatic changes in many fields, including the opportunities open to ethnic minorities. It soon became clear that many groups were much more numerous than had been admitted under socialism. Like others, Ukrainians transformed the state-controlled Socio-Cultural Association they had had since 1956, and a host of new secular organizations came into existence at national and local levels.[8] Many of these had branches in the south-east, for in addition to those who had managed by one means or another to avoid deportation in 1947, from 1956 onward there was a steady trickle of return migration. But of course the culturally dominant community also enjoyed new freedoms. It was possible to organize political parties to articulate nationalist viewpoints that had been banned from the public sphere under socialism. In addition, it became possible at the local level to organize new associations for a great variety of purposes, some of them previously taboo. Such tendencies look at first glance like an unambiguous step forward for the cause of civil society. Doubts arise when one starts to look more closely. Let me turn first to the close-up view preferred by the anthropologist.

The importance of religion for ethno-national identity is stressed by majority and minority alike in Przemyśl, the small city introduced in the preceding chapter, which is located close to the Ukrainian bor-

[7] Some Greek Catholics in Poland would prefer an arrangement which placed them within the jurisdiction of the Greek Catholic Cardinal in L'viv, Ukraine. This is precluded by the Vatican's preference in recent times for linking its own hierarchy to that of sovereign nation states. [For further comparative analysis of the fate of the Greek Catholic Churches in the postsocialist years, see Mahieu and Naumescu, 2008.]

[8] A full listing of secular and religious Ukrainian organizations (including some which prefer the "regional" designation Lemko to the national classification Ukrainian) can be found in Czech 1993, 290–304.

Figure 17. Epiphany rituals beside the River San, Przemyśl (photo by Stanisław Stępień, 1998)

der.[9] The Greek Catholic parish is at least as important a focus for the minority community as the secular *Dom Narodowy* ("National House"). Through participating in weekly services (held entirely in Ukrainian), observing religious holidays, and ensuring the transmission of religion within the home, they maintain their Ukrainian culture. Greek Catholics emphasized that they had deliberately chosen to marry within their group; when pressed to specify the drawbacks of marrying outside, they typically drew attention to clashing religious holidays. Following this logic, they agreed that there was no real problem in marrying a Ukrainian who was Orthodox and shared the same ritual calendar, though some were critical of the Orthodox Church's close links with Russia and Russian national traditions. What repelled most members of the minority from the Roman Catholic Church was its strong identification with Polishness.[10]

[9] No official figures are available but it is estimated that 1000–2000 attend Greek Catholic services at major holidays; some speak of "400 families." Identity concealment has continued in the postsocialist years. An Orthodox parish was established in 1984, but this is attended mainly by recent migrants who were brought up in that faith; the great majority of Przemyśl Ukrainians and of the recent return migrants have remained faithful to the Greek Catholic Church, which resumed functioning here in 1956.

[10] Stanisław Stępień and I probed into the emotional preferences of members of the Ukrainian minority, which led them to rank participation in Orthodox rituals ahead of Roman Catholic services. See Hann and Stępień 2000.

The minority has made significant gains in both religious and secular spheres since the collapse of socialism. For example, Epiphany (Jordan) rituals on January 19 can now be celebrated in public once again. Perhaps the most significant secular gain has been the establishment of a new Ukrainian-language primary school in the city in 1991, extended to serve high school pupils in 1995. The initiative for this was taken locally, but its success owed much to support from the Ministry of Education in Warsaw, which overruled the many objections raised by the local authorities. Religious instruction is given inside the school by Greek Catholic clergy. Indeed, many of the activities of ostensibly secular associations are strongly influenced by the Church. This applies also to property compensation claims, where the most intractable issues have concerned ecclesiastical property (though ownership of the building which houses the secular *Dom Narodowy* is also contested). The minority has enjoyed only limited success in pursuing these claims. A seminary has been returned to the Greek Catholic Church, as has a church to the Basilian order (it served as the state archive for most of the communist period). But the Greek Catholic bishop's palace has served for many years as the County Museum, and all requests for its return have been refused by the City and county level authorities.[11] For the Greek Catholic minority one building had greater material and spiritual significance than any other. As soon as their new bishop was appointed in January 1991 they made formal representations for the return of the distinctive hilltop building which had served as their cathedral until its confiscation in 1946 and later allocation to the Roman Catholic Carmelite order. This opened a chapter of major conflict in the city which, even at the turn of the new century, had still not completely subsided (see Chapter Nine).

Polish nationalists have used their dominance of the postsocialist public sphere to foment anti-Ukrainian sentiment in numerous contexts. These groups are only weakly represented on the city council in Przemyśl, yet they have exercised a baleful influence throughout the 1990s. As noted in Chapter Nine, they have opposed the city's participation in the Carpathian Euroregion, an initiative which has attracted

[11] [The palace was eventually returned to the Greek Catholic Church in 2001, though it continued to function as a museum until 2008, when the collections were transferred to a new building.]

support from Warsaw and from international sponsors, but which is unwelcome to the nationalists because it is perceived as a dilution of national sovereignty. City councilors opposed proposals from Warsaw that Przemyśl should host the country's Festival of Ukrainian Culture in 1995 and 1997. Young men plastered the city with anti-Ukrainian posters and there was a serious arson attack on the Ukrainian club. This is why I speak of a decline in civility in the postsocialist years.

Greek Catholic Hybridity and the Boundary of Europe

At this point I switch from the micro-level analysis of the ethnographer to the more macro analyses preferred in other social sciences. The construction of a European identity on pragmatic political and economic foundations has in recent years been found wanting. Political actors, notably the Commission in Brussels, and other analysts have increasingly sought to define Europe in terms of a common culture (Shore 1993; cf. Goddard, Llobera, and Shore 1994). However, if we take the Ural Mountains as the standard geographical specification of Europe's eastern boundary, the territory legitimated from Brussels continues to exclude the greater part of the continent. Restrictive definitions of Europe have been encouraged in the decade following the collapse of socialism in eastern Europe (it should be remembered that the rhetoric of "rejoining Europe" began in some places well before this collapse). The emphasis is on a shared history and traditions and there is commonly an emotional and evaluative tone: we hear a lot, for example, about the "values of European civilization," particularly when people in peripheral parts of Europe are considered to fall short of those standards. The evaluation is not simply the arrogant declaration of those in the west who feel themselves closer to the sources of all that is good about the continent; the same opinions are heard from many people in the east who feel themselves, or at least a part of their societies, to be far removed from "Europe" in this laudatory sense. But moralizing judgments of this kind does not help us to define the boundaries of this highly valued European culture or civilization.

Such views are deeply entrenched in the literature on nationalism, which is often seen as taking more destructive "ethnic" forms in the east, compared to benign "civic" forms in the west (Ignatieff 1994; cf. Gellner 1997). Recently, in an epilogue to a scholarly collection on problems of nationhood and ethnicity Erhard Busek argued that, just as a nation must be grounded in a common culture, so "the real definition of Europe comes from culture" (1996, 170). Busek is a well-meaning pluralist who is not out to defend a homogeneous, unitary culture. Yet his long list of products of European culture contains nothing from anywhere east of Germany. Russia is discussed quite separately, on a par with North America. In short, Busek's vision of "village Europe" is very strongly biased to the west.

Another scholar who seems to draw the eastern boundary of Europe a long way west of the Urals is Samuel Huntington, for whom "Europe ends where Western Christianity ends and Islam and Orthodoxy begin" (1996, 158). His recommendation is to allow in to the European Union only those countries which would make the Union "coextensive with Western civilization as it has historically existed in Europe" (1996, 161). Civilization is defined by Huntington as "culture writ large" (41). It is based on "values, beliefs, institutions and social structures" and as a result it forms "the most enduring of human associations" (43). So the political boundary should, in the view of this scholar, be underwritten by cultural factors. Unfortunately, as Huntington acknowledges, these boundaries are not always clear-cut. For him there is no civilizational divide between Germany and Poland, for both belong to one and the same Western tradition. In his view the civilizational divide lies at the other end of Poland. More precisely, it follows an internal frontier within Christianity, that which marks the eastern, Orthodox tradition off from the western, Catholic or Protestant heritage.

Huntington's position is clearer than that of Busek and his claims can be subjected to empirical scrutiny. The Greek Catholics are now, at the end of the twentieth century, the dominant Church in the western districts of Ukraine and they have a significant minority presence in Poland as well as Slovakia, Hungary, and Romania. Greek Catholic priests and bishops belong to the global organization of the Catholic Church with its center in the Vatican. Yet their rite is not the Latin rite or a modern vernacular version of that rite. It derives from Byzantium not Rome, and is practically identical to that of Orthodox Christians. The papacy, and not least the present Polish pontiff John Paul II, has consistently held that no single rite has priority within the universal Catholic church. In theory, Greek Catholics have every right to hold on to their traditional religious culture. In reality, things have never been this simple.

Recent conflicts in Przemyśl are perceived on all sides to be conflicts about national identity, for which religious orientation is the most salient cultural marker. The Greek Catholics assert their right to exist and develop their culture in a city that, they point out correctly, has historically been multicultural. The Roman Catholics (not all of them, but the most articulate political activists among them) assert that the city has become a Polish city, and that any remaining citizens who are not ethnic Poles should respect the primacy of the dominant culture. Polish nationalism finds an echo on the Ukrainian side of the border, where the Greek Catholic Church is once again in the vanguard of the national movement. The same social force, nationalism, is strong on both sides of the Polish-Ukrainian border and it expresses itself in quite similar ways. It seems difficult to judge one side to be more "European" than the other. From the perspective of Samuel Huntington no such judgment is necessary, since Greek Catholic heritage allows him to define western Ukraine as an integral part of European civilization. Where local people in Przemyśl, both Roman Catholics and Greek Catholics, today see sharply opposed national cultures, he sees civilizational unity. Greek Catholics in Ukraine also fail to endorse the civilizational boundary postulated by the American political scientist. Their prime focus of allegiance is the Ukrainian nation, with its boundaries extending far into the east.

On the ground, in Przemyśl as in L'viv, just a short distance away across the border, people tend to speak of "Polish culture" and "Ukrainian culture" as having ancient separate existences. They do not see them as the contingent products of a social order that used to be multicultural—and, of course, multireligious. Whereas today there is a strong preference for marriage within the national and religious community, half a century ago this was not yet the case. Even in the interwar years, when tensions between Poles and Ukrainians were rising, half of all Christian marriages in Przemyśl were inter-denominational, i.e. they took place between a Pole and a Ukrainian.

Borrowings and mutual interaction were also important within the sphere of religious culture more narrowly construed. Two extreme positions can be identified. The first would be the claim that the Greek Catholics continued to develop the Byzantine artistic traditions that had been integrated into their faith before the Union of Brest in 1596, entirely unaffected by the new social and political context in which they found themselves. This intuitively implausible claim does not survive close scrutiny in any field of artistic production. For example, prior to the emergence of the Greek Catholics iconic styles in this region were influenced by Russian schools as well as Balkan and Byzantine models.[12] From the seventeenth century onwards it is very clear, especially in the more western districts, that the sacred art of the Greek Catholics came under the influence of western Christian, models. This is evident in many stylistic details and in the production of icons in "folk" style, entirely lacking the austerity and mystery of earlier representations. By the nineteenth century the Virgin Mary was being realistically portrayed as a human figure in an iconography that owed more to Rome than to Byzantium (see Figure 18).

But was the sacred art of the Greek Catholics so transformed by closer contacts with Western traditions that it entirely lost its eastern character? This is the accusation commonly levelled against Greek Catholics by the Orthodox. They allege that, in reality, the imposition of "Latinization" contradicted the official position of the Catholic Church, which proclaimed that the eastern rite enjoyed parity with the western. Such allegations are confirmed in numerous everyday details, for instance in the gradually increasing unwillingness of the Greek Catholic Church to allow the clergy to have beards and wives, as was normal in the eastern tradition. If the entire religious culture of the Greek Catholics was assimilated to that of the dominant Roman Catholics, this could be construed as support for Huntington's assignment of the Greek Catholics to the culture and civilization of the west, i.e. to Europe.

---

[12] The leading academic authorities on the icons of this region disagree in their interpretations. Klosińska (1966, 1989) speaks of a distinct "Carpathian School" and thereby, in line with the approaches of many other Polish scholars, emphasizes discontinuity with eastern traditions. However, Biskupski (1991a, 1991b), while carefully acknowledging the influences from the west, locates this art unambiguously within Ukrainian traditions.

Figure 18. Images of the Immaculate Heart of Mary and St Nicholas hang side by side in the (ex-Greek Catholic) Orthodox church of the Dormition of the Virgin Mary in Przemyśl (photo by Chris Hann, 1998)

But neither extreme position is tenable. Certainly the formation of the Greek Catholic Church facilitated contact with the west and many practices were affected by influences that came not only from Poland but also from Germany, Italy, and elsewhere. Changes took place not only as a result of the west exercising its greater power, but also because there was interest and demand at the grass roots for elements of Western culture. This is evident, for example, in the mass production of icons in folk style in the eighteenth century (Molnár 1995). But this acceleration in cultural changes following western models did not mean the destruction of eastern traditions altogether. Even if images of the Virgin Mary came increasingly to follow Italian styles, they still followed eastern themes and often formed part of an eastern iconostasis that had no equivalent in the west. The basic forms and language of religious services, the script and the ritual calendar remained eastern. Their church architecture in some districts underwent westernizing changes but in others, especially in Carpathian villages, the design of wooden churches followed a distinctively eastern evolution, with subtle regional variations (see Buxton 1981). There have been periodic attempts to defend, revive, and purify this Church by ridding it of its western accretions. This is happening again today in Przemyśl as the Greek Catholics appropriate the former Jesuit building and insert a large iconostasis. Not only to their Roman Catholic neighbors but also in their self-representations, it seems that the Greek Catholics have all along remained an eastern Church.

The concepts of syncretism and hybridity offer a better way to capture the complexity of the Greek Catholic position.[13] Some members of this Church may indeed have seen themselves as a synthesis of eastern and western elements. The danger with this term is that it implies that these western and eastern cultural streams were radically separate, integrated wholes until the Greek Catholics began to disaggregate them and form their new combination. But this again would be an oversimplification of a more complex reality, for there were many borrowings between east and west in the centuries before the Greek Catholics came into existence. The Virgin Mary of Częstochowa is a national icon of the modern Polish nation, but who can deny the affinity this representation bears to eastern iconographic traditions?

Samuel Huntington sees cultures as bounded units which maintain their essential integrity and identity over the long term. This approach is congenial to the nationalist, who believes each nation to have its unique culture. It is then easy to extrapolate to higher levels, as Huntington does when he talks about civilizations, and as many other scholars and politicians are now doing when they talk about a European cultural identity. The exercise is futile, not only because it neglects internal cultural differentiation but because the search to specify an external boundary is inherently misconceived. The Greek Catholic case is therefore instructive: the hybridity of their art and architecture shows the flaws inherent in Huntington's approach. For most of the last four centuries the main institutional and political links of the Greek Catholics have pointed westwards. Their iconic art has undergone western influence over an even longer period. Yet it also shows continuity with an eastern tradition. The east-west contrast is useful for some purposes, but closer analysis shows that neither is monolithic and that there has always been a great deal of interpenetration. This region defies simplistic classification. In some respects

13 [I have explored the theme of hybridity further in Hann 2003b, 2005a, 2014b. The Greek Catholic Churches of Central Europe were investigated comparatively in an important volume arising out of teamwork at the Max Planck Institute for Social Anthropology in the years 2003–2008; see Mahieu and Naumescu 2008.]

ties to the west were more significant, in other respects ties to the east mattered more. Neither Huntington's line, which includes Greek Catholics in the west, nor an alternative sharp line that would leave them with the Orthodox in the east, is an adequate reflection of the encounters that have taken place in this region of Central Europe within a common Christian civilization. The boundary between Byzantine and western traditions of Christianity is very old, but it is not primordial. It has been flexibly and creatively adapted and crossed by many actors, religious and secular. This is tacitly acknowledged by Huntington himself when he classifies Ukraine's nationalist western regions with the West.[14]

Conclusions

As Adam Michnik noted in the article from which I quoted at the beginning of this chapter, many citizens had utopian hopes for what might follow socialism. These were bound to be disappointed. Initially Greek Catholic Ukrainians had hopes that they too would receive compensation and justice, along with all the other victims of socialism. In retrospect this was naive. The evidence that I uncovered in Przemyśl suggests that the fundamental problem of reconciling national identities with civic institutions has not been solved at all (cf. Holmes 1997; Khazanov 1995; Latawski 1995). Many members of the minority that I have been discussing would critique Michnik's formulation that Poland is a country of one nation. This liberal is on the side of those who wish to see an open civil society, but his use of the word culture in the singular is problematic. Members of the Ukrainian minority would argue that, even within the Catholic Church in Poland, two quite separate cultures persist alongside each other.

[14] It is ironic that it is the more Russified, eastern regions of Ukraine which in recent years have upheld more "civic" definitions of the nation, held by some scholars to be the monopoly of the West, while the Greek Catholics in western Ukraine rank among the more fervent "ethnic" nationalists, emphasizing the uniqueness of their Ukrainian culture. [See Hrytsak 2006 for analysis of how national identity came to triumph in the former Galician districts, long before Ukraine's descent into violent conflict in 2014.]

Too many commentators and advisers to Eastern European governments were prone to wishful thinking in assuming that passing better laws in Warsaw, promoting voluntary associations and strengthening local democracy at the expense of the discredited communist state, would be conducive to the birth of a healthy civil society. Even the old communist constitution had been unexceptionable in its declarations concerning minority rights.[15] The difficulty lay in ensuring that such principles would be implemented. Poland's postsocialist constitution makes only brief reference to the protection of national, ethnic, and religious minorities (compared, for example, to the new Slovak and Czech Constitutions), though the establishment of a parliamentary Commission for Minority Affairs has led to constructive initiatives in various parts of the country. However, this has not been enough to resolve tensions in places like Przemyśl, where a similarly titled commission established at municipal level failed to have any impact. Certainly many voluntary associations flourished outside political structures, but most have been organized by a relatively small group of embittered anti-Ukrainians. They have taken advantage of new media freedoms to disseminate their highly emotive version of the past, which focuses on Ukrainian nationalists' terrorist actions of the 1940s.

The awkward fact is that, from some points of view, members of the minority were better off under the socialist regime, which did not grant them much by way of legal recognition but at the same time did not tolerate the nationalist excesses that have caused a general decline in civility in recent years. That was also a regime which guaranteed its citizens security of employment. It is usual to identify civil society with individualism and market competition, but high unemployment and endemic economic insecurity can contribute to a decline in civility.

---

[15] Art. 81 read as follows: "1. Citizens of the People's Republic of Poland irrespective of their nationality, race or creed have equal rights in all areas of the life of the state, of political and economic life as well as in social and cultural life. Contravention of this principle by any discrimination, direct or indirect, or restriction of rights according to national, racial or religious criteria, will be liable to punishment. 2. The spreading of hatred or contempt, the provocation of discord or the humiliation of a human being on the basis of differences in nationality, race or creed, is forbidden."

This can affect young people most strongly: there is evidence that anti-Ukrainian sentiment is by no means restricted to those old enough to remember the suffering of the 1940s, but is strong among the young people of Przemyśl (Jestal 1994).

Since nobody argues for a return to socialism, the question arises as to how the minority can best be protected in the current postsocialist conditions. This can be addressed institutionally at several levels, of which I shall mention just a few. The first is the level of local political institutions. A respected Ukrainian doctor who had been a very active member of Solidarity was a member of the Przemyśl Citizens' Committee in 1989 and then of the first postsocialist council in the city, but he was not re-elected in 1994. Since then the Ukrainian minority has had no representation. It is dispersed in all wards across the city, and it seems that no one expects Polish voters ever to elect another Ukrainian to the council. Given these conditions, legislation to promote a system of minority self-governments along the lines pioneered recently in Hungary would seem desirable.

At the national level of politics, state-periphery relations have been thoroughly destabilized in postsocialist conditions. The present Polish state does not have the resources to ensure that its writ is effective in matters where, for the sake of maintaining a civil society, it *needs* to be effective. The history of the former Greek Catholic cathedral in Przemyśl (Chapter Nine) suggests that central state institutions need *strengthening* if minorities are to be protected. Local transgressions need to be met with firm sanctions.

Poland's dramatic rupture with socialist economic practice in 1990 ("shock therapy") probably contributed further to social dislocation and the tendency to embrace extremism in the name of the national community. It follows that a clear commitment to rebuilding the social democratic role of the state, not the old centrally planned and state-owned economy but the welfare and social security responsibilities that people valued highly from the socialist period, is also desirable. A clear lead from the state in educational policy is similarly called for. History teaching would benefit from approaches that were not focused so exclusively on the Polish nation, which would convey to pupils at least some basic data about the culture and history of Poland's immediate neighbors as well as minority groups within state boundaries.

The new postsocialist Constitution deals with religious minorities in the same article that it treats national and ethnic minorities.[16] Since the great majority of Greek Catholics in contemporary Poland are ethnic Ukrainians, the national identity that has persistently evoked some of the most negative stereotypes among Poles, the conflation of religious and ethno-national identities seems particularly justified in this case.[17] Many Poles still have difficulty in accepting Ukraine as a sovereign nation, with cultural traditions on a par with their own or with those of Russia. It is paradoxical that the secular identity which poses such problems of recognition should in southeast Poland be tied to a religious identity uniquely close to that of the majority—a sister Catholic Church. This is the precarious condition of the Greek Catholics, whose fate I have traced from premodern polytacticity through their active role in the age of nationalism and their survival strategies under socialism, down to contested re-emergence in the 1990s. There is a danger that the pressures on the minority could increase further when Poland joins the European Union, if this is accompanied by renewed modernist attempts to make political and cultural units congruent, but then at a level higher than the nation state, i.e., to present the cultural boundaries of Europe as those of Latin Christianity. The alternative is to see in Greek Catholic traditions a source of creativity and cultural hybridity of the sort that Eastern Europe urgently needs if it is to construct a more civil society out of the wreckage of socialism and the legacies of malignant ethnic nationalism.

We need better understandings of the political and economic factors which give rise to assertions of cultural boundedness, even in contexts of intensive interaction. In the particular case I have considered in this chapter, differences in religious tradition have persisted over time, but the history of the Greek Catholics points to flexibility and the con-

[16] An ethnic minority is one that does not possess a corresponding state—thus the Lemkos (see Chapter Eight) constitute an ethnic minority, while Ukrainians are a national minority. Some sociologists apply a more general concept of "cultural minority" to refer to any group or category outside the "dominant culture." See Mucha 1989, 1992, 1997a, 1997b.

[17] By no means all Ukrainians in Poland are Greek Catholic: large numbers are Orthodox. On negative stereotypes of Ukraine see Klaus Bachmann, "Na czym polega problem polsko-ukraiński," *Rzeczpospolita*, September 27–28, 1997 (see also Chapters Two and Nine of this volume).

tinual potential for hybridity rather than a "fault line" that must forever divide a continent. As we enter a new millennium, it is time to recognize the long-term unity of Eurasia and to abandon the search for tidy sub-divisions in its western zone, Europe. There can be no justification in history or in anthropology for turning Christianity's internal frontier into the external frontier of a new "Fortress Europe."[18]

18 [For later analysis of Poland's eastern border when this metaphor had become a reality, see Follis 2012]

CHAPTER ELEVEN

The Visegrád Condition (Freedom and Slavery in the Neoliberal World)[1]

Introduction: The V4

In February 1991 at Visegrád in Hungary, overlooking the bend in the Danube north of Budapest, leaders of the first postsocialist governments of Czechoslovakia, Hungary, and Poland signed agreements of regional cooperation based on their countries' long-term civilizational commonalities. With the "velvet divorce" in Czechoslovakia, in 1993 the three members became four. Institutionalized forms of cooperation have been consolidated at many levels since accession to the European Union in 2004. The presidency of the Visegrád Group (also referred to as the V4) rotates annually between the four capitals.[2]

This institutionalization over more than a quarter of a century helps to justify addressing these four countries together as a unit. The nomenclature seems preferable to invocations of a fuzzy "Central and Eastern Europe." Within the V4 there is, of course, great diversity. Economic policies have not been fully harmonized; the most striking contemporary difference is the fact that Slovakia alone has joined the Eurozone (in 2009). Historically, too, Slovakia is exceptional because

---

1 *This chapter was written in Autumn 2017 and draws on preliminary field research in 2016 and 2017 in Kiskunhalas. The content also reflects the agendas of the "Visegrád Anthropologists' Network," established in October 2017 at the Max Planck Institute for Social Anthropology: http://www.eth.mpg.de/4638135/Visegrad_Network*

2 For an outline of the consolidation of the Visegrád cooperation before and after EU accession from a "relational power" perspective, see Végh 2018. (This assessment does not take account of the tensions associated with the "migrant crisis" since 2015.)

unlike the other members it cannot look back on centuries of medieval statehood. In terms of the strength of contemporary religiosity, the big exception is Poland. From the religious point of view, Slovenia and the three Baltic states, which joined the EU at the same time as the V4, share the same Western (Latin) Christian civilizational tradition as V4 members. Croatia did not accede to the EU until 2013, but its Catholic nationalist traditions constitute a similarly strong affinity to Poland. If one were to prioritize the economic variables, including the ways in which Western capital, including financial capital, has transformed economy and society in recent decades, then Romania and Bulgaria, and perhaps also other countries with Eastern Christian civilizational traditions, would have to be drawn into the comparisons. We might even wish to consider the former German Democratic Republic as an honorary member of the V4; the *neue Bundesländer* have benefited from massive transfers from the West, but economic and socio-cultural dislocation are still widespread a generation after reunification.

In short, postsocialist Eastern Europe can be sub-divided in a variety of ways, depending upon the criteria one chooses to privilege. Several countries outside the V4 display close affinities to it, whether of a long-term historical nature, or in terms of contemporary political economy, or both. For some purposes it makes more sense to work with larger sets, such as "the postsocialist world" or "structurally peripheral European states" (a set that could extend from Moldova and Kosovo to Greece and Portugal). For other purposes it will be appropriate to consider smaller units. Regional variation within countries is considerable: disadvantaged districts of eastern Poland may have more in common with deprived eastern districts of Hungary than with wealthy districts in western Poland, where most investments have been concentrated in the postsocialist decades. Capital cities and other touristic locations have prospered throughout the postsocialist world. It is fortunate that many anthropologists still work in less privileged places, seldom visited by foreign tourists, or journalists, or even other social scientists.

The following assessment of the Visegrád condition does not aspire to be comprehensive. But for the purposes of this chapter the substantive commonalities between the contiguous states making up the V4 are greater than those to be found in alternative classifications. These characteristics are poorly understood. The "migration crisis" that erupted in Europe in the summer of 2015 has increased the salience of this grouping, both for citizens of its member-states and in the perceptions of other states. There is a widespread view (especially in countries of the "old EU") that in their reluctance to admit non-European refugees, in particular in their rejection of "quota allocations" by the European Commission in Brussels, the V4 are reneging on principles of EU solidarity from which they are massive net beneficiaries. I shall return to this controversial theme at the end of the chapter. First I provide a short macro-level outline of postsocialist developments in these countries, referencing pertinent anthropological studies as well as some from other disciplines. I then turn to my own observations in a county of Hungary that illustrates some of the larger trends rather well, and which due to its location at the border with Serbia has proved to be an instructive location to explore both ethical and economic dimensions of recent population movements.

Privatization and Personhood

Even within socio-cultural anthropology, the literature on postsocialist transformations is now vast. Some of the most fruitful contributions, empirical as well as theoretical, engage with countries outside the V4, but their main conclusions are no less valid within it (e.g. Creed 2011; Verdery 2003). Whereas most investigations of Eastern Europe in the socialist period concentrated on transformations taking place in the countryside, urban settings have become more common since 1990. Thematically, the range has expanded. Topics have reflected what is happening "on the ground" in postsocialist states, notably the attention paid to national sentiment and social exclusion. Theories have generally been adapted from those in vogue elsewhere in the world. Changing styles and standards of knowledge production in socio-cultural anthropology have undoubtedly impacted on research in this region, but this chapter will not probe into epistemological issues.[3]

[3] According to Mihály Sárkány, more knowledgeable of the history of socio-cultural anthropology than most of his contemporaries in western countries, the end of socialism came "at an unfortunate moment." The discipline was not able to contribute as effectively as it might have to understanding the

One original perspective on the dramatic changes of the 1990s in Hungary was provided by a study of a former model socialist steel city (Sztálinváros, later re-named Dunaújváros) that focused on the creative ways in which residents appropriated apartments built in the socialist era, of which they had now become owners (Fehérváry 2013). Differentiation through taste and culture are shown to be more significant than relationship to the means of production. Fehérváry documents the extent to which, well before 1990, the authorities promoted aesthetic options that allowed Hungarians to make discriminating "bourgeois" choices. Compared to other socialist countries, in terms of output statistics at least, Hungarian market socialism was rather successful: Fehérváry notes the inadequacy of the "shortage" paradigm of János Kornai; many goods were readily available, but poorly packaged local brands could never satisfy those who aspired to the "normal" condition of Western middle classes. The arrival of market capitalism after 1990 did little to alter the basic consciousness of lagging behind. Nevertheless a few of Fehérváry's key informants succeeded in achieving "transcendence" by constructing new family houses, complete with gardens, "American kitchens," and luxurious bathrooms as their inner sanctum. Although the production of steel has continued in Dunaújváros, the persons we encounter in Fehérváry's monograph show no traces of socialist class identities rooted in production.

Whereas Fehérváry focused on consumption and the home, other anthropologists of Eastern Europe in the 1990s investigated changes in personhood through factory studies. Works by Michel Foucault were becoming increasingly popular throughout the social sciences and notions of "self-regulation" seemed ideally suited to making sense of the postsocialist context, in which central planning and democratic centralism yielded to new forms of management and adminis-

---

transformations of the 1990s due to the unsettling impact of postmodern critique, which "hindered the choice of a firm paradigm" (2002, 563).

Tensions between foreign researchers and native scholars who also self-identify as anthropologists, and between both of these and counterparts working in the traditions of "national ethnography" or folklore, cannot be explored here (see Kürti and Skalník 2009; for my own position see Hann 2013a). Works by all types of researcher will be cited in this brief review, the selection criteria being largely pragmatic (accessibility in English).

tration and the old class rhetoric appeared to lose all traction. Many large enterprises were privatized to transnational corporations (TNCs). Exemplary research in a baby-food factory in the Polish provincial city of Rzeszów demonstrated how new managers sought to impose their rhythms and norms (Dunn 2004). The post-Fordist factory institutionalized new techniques of discipline to promote nothing less than privatized personhood (it was not just the factory that was privatized). The responses of the workforce could hardly be classified as resistance: for this there was no precedent, and job insecurity was a good reason not to cause trouble. But Dunn describes how local notions of value continued to reflect a mixture of Catholic social teaching and socialist ideology. At the level of discourse, everyone wanted to leave socialism behind, but the informal networks of *znajomości* which lubricated the old system persisted in new forms alongside the scientific management of neoliberal capitalism; older forms of sociality rooted in kinship and community could not be easily eradicated. Similar tensions were found among factory workers in East Berlin, where the strength of brigade ties seems to have exceeded anything recorded by anthropologists for the V4 proper (Müller 2007).

The dislocation of the 1990s was an irruption of Karl Polanyi's "market society" in a dramatic form that made the "disembedding" accomplished by nineteenth century liberalism seem mild and gradualist in comparison. The disintegration of both national central planning and the international coordination of COMECON led to mass unemployment and increased inequality throughout Eastern Europe (Swain and Swain 2018). The convulsions in Eastern Europe were less turbulent than those experienced in the Russian Federation, where the contraction of the state was accelerated by the collapse of the Rubel in 1997 (see Humphrey 2002a). Nevertheless, "surviving post-socialism" was a challenge everywhere (Bridger and Pine 1998). Women who had been drawn into the labor market under socialism now found themselves disproportionately vulnerable to redundancy (Pine 1998). Male "losers" of the transformation processes in Poland demonstrated their creativity and resilient agency through gathering herbs in forests, scavenging for scrap metal, digging up "bootleg" coal, and other activities that might be illegal but were morally legitimate for the "degraded" themselves (Rakowski 2016). Urban postsocialist "culture of homelessness" was a new form of poverty, yet one that showed significant continuities with the "hidden poverty" of the socialist era (Nagy 2009). The flow of investment from the West did little to assuage existential uncertainties. Foreign direct investment was concentrated in regions with good communications westwards. While the triangle between Vienna, Bratislava, and Budapest recorded dynamic growth, the closure of socialist-era industry and mining in north-east Hungary and eastern Slovakia accentuated regional inequalities. Workers at the new Audi plant in Győr were found to be more discontented with their foreign bosses than workers exposed to similarly radical restructuring in the former Eastern Germany (Bartha 2013).

New class structures emerged through somewhat different processes in rural areas. Government policies ostensibly supported capitalized family farming, but the size of the rural population and the collapse of the old COMECON markets hindered any such transition. When cooperative farms were dismantled, control (not necessarily legal ownership of land) often passed to the former senior officials: "green barons" replaced the "red barons" (Swain 2013). For large sections of the rural population this meant the (re-)emergence of a capitalist rural proletariat. These processes were also visible in Poland, which had managed to avoid mass collectivization, but which faced the same challenge of establishing viable new structures. The consequences were especially transparent where former State Farms were privatized (Buchowski 2004).

EU Admission, Financial Crisis and Deepening Marginalization

Following years of negotiation and gradual preparation (including the necessary budgetary adjustments), all four members of the V4 (along with other postsocialist states of Eastern Europe) were admitted to the European Union in 2004. Politicians of almost every hue hailed this achievement (and sought a share of the credit), but there was little euphoria on the ground. Regional development transfers continued, but they did little to create sustainable employment. Access to agricultural subsidies turned out to be a formidable bureaucratic challenge for most farmers. The major change was the expansion of migrant labor to the "old EU." This had become significant in various sectors in the 1990s. It now became legal, though some countries (notably Germany) sought to protect their high-wage labor markets from a sudden influx. The British government had no compunction in opening its labor market with immediate effect (on the basis of predictions that greatly underestimated the actual flows which ensued). A decade later the consequences of this decision were manifest in the Brexit referendum.

This labor mobility, along with the greater mobility of capital, had far-reaching implications for the V4, dramatizing vast differences in wage levels in every segment of the labor market. The rhetoric of politicians replicated textbook economic theories: with the help of judicious transfers via the EU social fund, within a relatively short period of time, the new members would be effectively integrated and wages and prices harmonized. Nothing of the sort has come about. Instead, new chains of east-west exploitation have emerged. While Poles have flocked to work in Britain, their neighbors from outside "Fortress Europe" have found myriad ways to enter Poland, where they fill some of the gaps left behind by the migrants, inside and outside households (Follis 2012; cf. Uherek 2009 on Ukrainians in the Czech Republic).

The global financial crisis that began in 2007–8 had a severe impact (though less severe in Poland than elsewhere in the V4), obliging governments to cut back further on the legacies of the socialist welfare state. The steady advance of neoliberalism, marked by the Maastricht Treaty (1992) and by the introduction of the Euro in 1999, undermined earlier assumptions that the central institutions of the EU would be able to act as a countervailing force to the power of capitalist markets. The argument now was that, to maintain global competitiveness, there was no alternative to austerity. Given the "democratic deficit" of the EU, thinly camouflaged German domination functioned increasingly to exaggerate the market outcomes rather than to correct them, leading to a potentially fatal "trap" (Offe 2016).[4]

[4] As far as the Eurozone is concerned, economists are fully aware that the gains of a currency union (lower "transaction costs") have to be weighed against the political risks involved. Since economic performance varies greatly across a macro-region as the diverse as the EU, monetary union can only function effectively if the countries in surplus are willing to invest in those that "underperform" (Salais 2013). Politically, however, it is as difficult to persuade the "winners" of this economic unification (above all Germany) to implement this elementary Keynesian principle as it is to persuade "losers" (such as Greece) of the necessity to impose austerity (see also Bohle 2016).

The situation in which the EU finds itself as a result of the neoliberal turn and the creation of "Euroland" (Streeck 2017) has long been clear to academic observers. Yet while the politics of the north-south divide are heatedly debated, awareness of the new peripheralization of Eastern Europe remains limited. Statistics for unemployment, outmigration, and poverty indicate that the countries that are both eastern and southern have suffered the most. In comparison with Bulgaria and Moldova, the V4 is closer to the powerful economies of the north. Communications by road and rail have improved considerably, making them attractive to TNCs. The greatly enhanced role of these corporations renders the old binary of "state versus market" increasingly redundant (Crouch 2011). As with many other phenomena, this global trend was particularly salient in the tabula rasa opened up with the collapse of socialism. For example, automotive TNCs are among the largest employers in all four of the Visegrád states. TNCs also dominate in retail and service sectors. The supermarket products available to consumers are as diverse as those available in the same supermarkets in the old EU. The prices may be a little lower, but the differential is nowhere near as great as the differential in wage rates. From time to time there is public outcry when it becomes known that a product sold in the new EU with exactly the same branding as in the old EU turns out to contain quite different, inferior ingredients.

Anthropologists of the V4 have explored multiple facets of this evolving market society. Some have continued to take inspiration from the Foucauldian approach followed by Dunn (2004), since the rhetoric of flexible persons taking responsibility for the self has remained ubiquitous. Self-identifications have been influenced by intensifying European integration and global mobilities (Galbraith 2014). A representative collection (Makovicky 2014b) includes studies of Poles who struggle for orientation in a Euroregion in which old stereotypes of egalitarian resourceful highland pastoralists mingle uneasily with top-down notions of "enterprising citizenship," and of confident Slovak au pairs who seem perfectly aware of the constraints on their ability to fashion new selves during their temporary employment in London.

A generation after the systemic changes, some anthropologists are asking whether it is time to move beyond culturalist notions of personhood, with the implication that this is in some sense common to all members of a national-state, and instead re-embrace the concept of class in order to achieve a deeper understanding of the consolidation of capitalist hegemony. Working class consciousness has diminished as a result of the general discrediting of socialism, in combination with the opportunities that allow a few to move upwards into the middle classes, and many more to migrate abroad. Class consciousness is also weakened by the barrage of media images that emphasize the nation as the ultimate object of identification (Kalb 2009; Kalb and Halmai 2011). The deepening of neoliberal structural peripheralization has intensified rent seeking, thinly disguised by invocations of the need to create a national capitalist class. Most conspicuously in Hungary, in sectors ranging from agriculture to finance, the state blatantly subverts "free market" competition, hitherto touted as the natural condition of both a healthy economy and a healthy society, in order to reward its clientele, and above all the entourage of the Prime Minister (Magyar 2016).

Interventions have been especially visible in the case of labor—a "fictitious commodity" in the language of Karl Polanyi (1944). The cutting back of social entitlements, including unemployment benefit, has been accompanied by the large-scale introduction of workfare schemes, notably in Hungary (Szőke 2012; Hann 2016b, 2018) but also in Slovakia (Makovicky 2013) and elsewhere. Large sections of the population can nowadays choose, at least theoretically, between workfare, migration, and local labor for a minimal wage that is perhaps one quarter of that found in the old EU (see Chapter Five).

Unemployment has indeed declined in recent years, but dissatisfaction has not gone away. It is reflected in support for anti-establishment, "populist" parties such as PiS in Poland and Jobbik in Hungary (which has become the most credible rival to the Fidesz party of Viktor Orbán). This populism has a history that plays out in different ways even within the same country (Hann and Kürti 2015). Even the "political culture" of the Czech Republic, where on the whole populism has assumed less malignant forms, is marked by a lack of trust in democratic institutions and civil society (Skalník 2009). Similar conclusions have been reached for villagers in Carpathian Poland, whose imaginaries of their state and nation are not so much postsocialist as "post-peasant," while continuing to bear the imprint of the world view of the peasantry of past centuries as described by William Thomas and Florian Znaniecki (1918–19). The state was to some degree "tamed" under socialism, but with the closure and downsizing of socialist enterprises and few alternatives to international migration, Polish highlanders consider the distant authorities in Warsaw to be neglecting their basic responsibilities. Common stereotypes of liberal politicians, parliamentary institutions, and democracy itself do not bode well for the consolidation of a tolerant, inclusive society (Malewska-Szałgin 2017). Labor migration and foreign tourism have little impact on these deep-seated populist worldviews. The challenge facing researchers is how to explain new coalitions between the "dispossessed," in both urban and rural settings, and educated elites who mobilize them for illiberal causes.[5] Postsocialist populations are far more mobile internationally, but the "moral dispossession" (Hann 2011, 2015c) experienced by very large sections of society (including apparent "winners" of capitalist transformation) leads not to a new cosmopolitanism but to a neo-nationalist shrinking of identifications.

To grasp these often paradoxical developments it is again helpful to recall Polanyi's concept of the "double movement" (Polanyi 1944). The enthusiasm for the free market in the wake of socialism, in the context of global trends, led inexorably to a situation in which the forces of "social protection" gained ground. This reaction to the market could take many forms. In the V4, the forces attempting to salvage the social rights built up in the later years of socialism were politically weak, reflecting their more general weakness in the EU. As a result, the way was open for unscrupulous politicians to foment antagonisms by blaming ethnic minorities and strangers (Feischmidt 2016). Internally, the primary "other" and scapegoat for all ills is often the Roma minority (Stewart 2012). Externally, resentment has often been channeled to "Brussels" and a bureaucracy represented as too large and too liberal in its failure to uphold the primacy of Christian national identities. The financier and philanthropist George Soros is perceived to epitomize the global forces threatening the integrity of the Hungarian nation.[6]

[5] In western Europe since the 1950s the expansion of higher education has been associated with electoral support for left-of-center parties, but the recent constellation in the postsocialist countries appears to be very different (Thomas Piketty, research in progress).

[6] On the surface, Orbán and his Fidesz party are careful to show respect for Jewish traditions (and for the Israeli state). In the official rhetoric, a common

Numerous anthropologists have illuminated this ongoing double movement by focusing on cultural phenomena, from religious revival to the politics of memory, nostalgia, heritagization and new forms of public ritual. In some parts of the postsocialist world the opening of the religious marketplace provided new opportunities for Christian missionaries, but in the V4 countries the revival of established denominations repressed under socialism was the more conspicuous trend (Hann and the "Civil Religion" Group 2006, Hann 2010c). The Roman Catholic Church in Poland consolidated its dominance, even in exceptional areas of ethno-religious diversity (see Chapter Eight; Pasieka 2015). Religious resurgence did not always mean a reversal of secularization trends, e.g. in the frequency of religious observances. But the churches aspired everywhere to assume a more prominent role in collective representations. Since 1990, every country has witnessed a more or less continuous ratcheting up of a specifically national cultural canon. In Hungary this process became more extreme after 2010. Here too, however, efforts to displace the alleged hegemonic status of leftist-liberal thought with rightist-conservative alternatives often lacked ideological coherence. Rather, policies in the sphere of culture served above all to shore up the power of elites beholden to the Fidesz-led government (for example, with regard to theatres see Kristóf 2017).

All power holders look to myth and ritual to legitimize, even to sacralize, their domination. Again, Hungary has led the way in efforts to evoke loyalty through traditionalism. As noted in Chapter Six, the country can draw on two major sources. In addition to celebrating its European, Christian past, invoking the defeat of the Ottomans as a precedent for repelling the new Muslim invaders of today, Hungarians indulge in fantastical imaginations of their tribal origins in Asia, where they roamed with their animals before becoming tied to the soil as cultivators, and where their spirituality was expressed through shamans rather than the institutions of a multi-national Church. Neopaganism flourishes in contemporary Hungary (Kürti 2015). This is

Judeo-Christian civilization is threatened by Islam. However, long traditions of anti-Semitism are manipulated in more or less subtle ways by influential public figures; the demonization of Soros, a native of Hungary but also a Jew, corresponds to this pattern.

a domain in which regional and national minority groups, such as the Ukrainian minority in southeast Poland, can assert their difference to provide entertainment for the majority (Buzalka 2007). Festivalization and heritagization have boomed (Kürti 2011; Pusztai and Martin 2007). Folk dancing, which in Hungary played a mildly subversive role in the late socialist decades, has remained a highly politicized form of cultural expression in the postsocialist era (Taylor 2008). In an era of accelerating globalization, the distinctiveness of a regional identity such as that of the Górale of upland Poland can be readily enlisted in support of national identity politics (Schneider 2006). Meanwhile softer forms of identity celebrations are increasingly entrenched at the level of villages and neighborhoods (Hann 2017, 2018). The elevation of products such as paprika and *pálinka* to the status of Hungaricum lends them an additional aura that feeds into national sentiment and a more general nostalgia for an era of purity that preceded globalization and the mass importing of inferior foreign produce (Gille 2016).

In the case of the *neue Bundesländer*, it was demonstrated in the 1990s that "nostalgia" for the socialist past, e.g. its distinctive material culture, was shaped to a considerable degree by the new forms of Western domination (Berdahl 1999; cf. Bach 2015). Similar arguments can be made for the V4 countries (not taken over in the same way and less developed in the presocialist era) and for the postsocialist world as a whole (Todorova and Gille 2012). The strength of national sentiment in the V4 is linked to a temporality that privileges a pure peasant folk culture and a collective memory that has great difficulty accommodating the socialist decades. With the demise of the futurist visions of socialism, there is a pervasive sense that "time is out of joint." Elites compete to provide a useable past and to transmit it through symbols, rituals and schoolbooks (Pine, Kaneff, and Haukanes 2004). Many V4 citizens acknowledge in private that their lives were transformed for the better in the last decades of socialism. In the public sphere, however, even in the third decade of postsocialism, such sentiments cannot be articulated. Instead, in the new ritual calendar, in churches and in schools (many now again in ecclesiastical hands), and in new institutions such as Budapest's Museum of Terror, the socialist era has to be vilified while capitalist democracy is celebrated (Hann 2015c).

Contemporary Bács-Kiskun

I turn now to explore the contemporary Visegád condition more concretely in the Hungarian county that I have studied since the 1970s. In 2010 Daimler-Benz opened a large new factory in Kecskemét, southeast of the capital on the Great Plain, where the transport network was good and labor was plentiful due to transformations on the land and the decline of the agro-industries of the socialist era. The deal to build Mercedes cars in the largest town of Bács-Kiskun county (pop-

Figure 19. The main entrance of the new Mercedes factory in Kecskemét (photo by Chris Hann, 2017)

ulation a little over 100,000) was not, of course, the product of self-regulating market mechanisms. It was brokered initially by a socialist-led government in 2008. Within a few years the massive buildings and tall chimney of this enterprise (adorned with the city's coat of arms) dominated the flat landscape west of the city. Seismic political shifts in Budapest and in the county have not impeded the enterprise's steady expansion. By 2017 over 4000 people were employed in this factory. Thousands more have jobs in smaller, Hungarian-owned firms in the vicinity which supply parts. The enterprise has been highly profitable. My tour group was told, at the end of a guided visit to the enterprise in August 2017, that work would begin soon on "Kecskemét 2," a new plant next door to the first that would create a further 3000 jobs.[7]

In the socialist decades, Bács-Kiskun was known above all for its dynamic agricultural sector, notably in wine and fruit production. The county experienced unusually flexible forms of collectivization (see Chapters Two and Three). Much industrial investment was channeled into food-processing branches, such as the canning factory dating back to the pre-socialist era that was the largest employer in the county town. But socialist planners also invested in smaller market towns of the county that had previously been entirely lacking industrial jobs. For example, the town of Kiskunhalas was transformed by the 1970s. Because of its location close to Hungary's sensitive border with Yugoslavia, Halas (the full name is commonly abbreviated) became a garrison town for both Soviet soldiers and the Hungarian army. Some of the latter (including officers) stayed on in the town after their retirement. Some conscripts also ended up as permanent residents, working alongside local rural-urban migrants in the factories of the new industrial parks that mushroomed to the east of the Budapest-Belgrade railway line in the 1960s and 1970s. Not that the town lost its agricultural character completely: most residents of the new urban blocks had access to gardens, where they produced a range of items for household consumption, and often for sale as well. To the end of the socialist era the State Farm remained the largest employer. Unemployment was almost unknown in those decades, even among the Roma minority.

The history of Halas's socialist enterprises has yet to be written. Contrary to some stereotypes, production profiles were far from stagnant. Several large enterprises experienced radical restructuring. One was taken over in 1988 by Levi-Strauss (at this point, the county town of Kecskemét had no comparable experience with a TNC). But none of the other large enterprises were able to continue production at the same level with the same labor force following the "system change."

[7] This is not my normal method of field research but my request to the company's headquarters in Stuttgart for research access was turned down. My tour group in August 2017 consisted mainly of pensioners resident in Kiskunhalas. It was organized by the state railway enterprise. After brief sightseeing in the city-center, a tour of the factory was the highlight of the day's program.

The privatizations of the 1990s followed the usual pattern. Unskilled workers, notably Roma, were the first victims. Some of these successor enterprises have persisted to the present day, mostly in Hungarian ownership. Few new businesses have been established and there was a sense of crisis in 2009 when Levi-Strauss, by far the largest firm with almost 500 employees, decided to relocate to Romania. This was at the very same time that Mercedes-Benz was about to open its doors in Kecskemét. But to commute to the car factory would mean an hour in each direction and this is difficult. For a start, the costs of fuel would make a significant dent in the assembly-line worker's income of approximately 500 Euros. Since the commencement of the project, the costs of accommodation in the county capital have risen steeply. Successive mayors of Halas have tried to attract new investment, including Mercedes suppliers, but road communications are poor. It is said that rail transport will boom when plans to upgrade the Budapest-Belgrade line with the help of Chinese finance are finally implemented, but there is no guarantee that this will happen or that the decline in the town's population can be reversed.[8]

Travelers who leave the state highway that runs 5 kilometers through the town to inspect its historic center are likely to form positive first impressions: numerous public buildings and the main square have been renovated with the help of central government funds (said to originate in Brussels). The Museum has been substantially expanded thanks to a major gift from a Transylvanian-Hungarian émigré in Germany. To the west, the "garden city" that took shape in the socialist era contains attractive detached homes for the middle classes. Similar developments are under way in the vicinity of a scenic lake immediately

[8] The population of Kiskunhalas began to decline in the last socialist decade; it was stable between 1995 and 2005, but decline has accelerated since. The official figure of 27,000 for 2017 is dubious for a number of reasons, notably for including large numbers of people who live and work elsewhere (in particular Britain and Ireland). The present mayor (elected 2014) is a member of Fidesz. Halas was late in conforming to the dominant trend in provincial Hungary. In 1990 the Free Democrats were the strongest party in the town but, after the 1990s brought only massive disillusionment, voters elected a socialist (and former State Farm director) as their mayor until 2010, when the socialist vote collapsed.

to the north. But south of the center, Roma are the principal inhabitants of a neighborhood where overcrowding and squalor are visible. It is said that ethnic Hungarians are being forced out of these districts, since their property and persons are increasingly vulnerable. Roma and poor Hungarians work alongside each other in the workfare program, typically sweeping the pavements and streets and maintaining parks and flower-beds (Hann 2016b). But there is general agreement among the town's Hungarians that little has changed as far as Roma work discipline is concerned. Even when agricultural bottlenecks are acute and day laborers are essential (e.g. in harvesting paprika), ethnic Hungarians are reluctant to hire members of the minority. The same goes for the new TNC employers in town (Tesco, Aldi and Lidl). Only the Roma deputy mayor of the town seems to find it profitable for his waste disposal and recycling enterprises to hire large numbers of his co-ethnics.

East of the highway, where no tourists venture, the socialist industrial estates create a desolate impression. One factory cuts its maintenance costs by allowing sheep to graze freely in its extensive gardens. Its owner László, now in his 70s, does not disguise his nostalgia for the heyday of the old firms. His neighbor Pál, also well over 70 but still exercising day to day control in one of the largest successor enterprises (with almost 100 employees), offers an angrier political analysis of the 1990s. He says that the country's economy was effectively "castrated" to serve the interests of foreign capital. Pál graduated from the Technical University in Budapest and recalls with pride the factory's high production standards before 1990. This was attributable not just to the ingenuity of the engineers, but also to the skilled workers below them, some of whom he was able to offer jobs when it became apparent that the enterprise would have to be broken up. Pál does not understand why the government did not do more in those years to protect national interests against sharks from abroad. Like others in his generation, he points out that many of the products nowadays imported from the west or produced by TNCs in Hungary have a shorter life and are less reliable than the products of the now defunct socialist enterprises. László agrees. To survive, they have been forced into international niche markets where their main advantage is the low cost of labor. Both are in the process of handing over the company to younger family members, but they are anxious about what the future holds. They enjoy participating in social events with co-workers from the socialist era. Like other entrepreneurs, they organize a family day in the summer and/or a Christmas party. They probably invest more in this respect than firms of similar size in most western countries, yet the bonds of the workplace are obviously weaker today than under socialism.

Ignác is about 20 years younger than Pál and László, but he too received his training under the *ancien régime*. His metalwork atelier was founded in the mid-1980s in the backyard of his house and now occupies one small block of a forlorn estate. Unlike the factories of Pál and László, no name is visible on the outside wall. There is no indication that Ignác has built up a business that employs almost 40 workers and operates in international markets (mainly supplying high-value products to Germany). Ignác asserts that for the last two decades he has reinvested all profits in capital equipment, and that no ministry or local mayor has offered significant help. Fortunately his only son, socialized into this workplace from his earliest years, has acquired the necessary skills (manual as well as managerial) and seems certain to take over in due course. Ignác's main complaint is the shortage of skilled workers. He is scathing in his assessment of how standards in vocational training have declined in Hungary. In his eyes, the Mercedes plant in Kecskemét has contributed to a general process of deskilling. Wages might be higher than elsewhere in Hungary, but for Ignác the assembly line is just a modern form of slavery (*rabszolgaság*). He deplores the fact that many young people are moving abroad to work, motivated solely by money, though the jobs they take in the west are mostly devoid of skill and job-satisfaction. By contrast, his employees have more meaningful tasks, and the time they spend in the factory is organized "in the Hungarian way" rather than "in the German way" (i.e. with the discipline and monotony of the assembly line). Recently Ignác has hired locksmiths from across the border in Serbia, providing them with free accommodation in Kiskunhalas during the working week. These employees, he says, might otherwise have sought work in Germany, where they would certainly earn a great deal more money than he is able to pay them. But because the cost of accommodation and subsistence is so much higher in Germany, and because a job in Halas allows these workers (members of the Hungarian minority in Vojvodina) to return every weekend to their families, Ignác hopes he will be able to hold on to them. He was an activist in the Free Democrats in the early

1990s but (as he says retrospectively) he quickly concluded that this party, dominated by intellectuals in the capital, was never interested in addressing the problems of small towns such as Halas. In recent years Ignác has supported Jobbik. He also supports local charities and cultural events to cultivate distinctive national(ist) traditions of popular song (*magyar nóták*), in which he enjoys participating.

Work "in the Hungarian way" is also remunerated in the Hungarian way. It is an open secret that employers declare most of their workers at the state-prescribed minimum rate, in order to reduce their tax liabilities. Of course, this impacts negatively on the workers' pension entitlements. In practice, many employers find creative ways to supplement the earnings of those individuals who perform well. The ensuing murkiness has a divisive impact on the workforce, quite apart from its consequences for the grey or shadow economy that reaches back to the "second economy" of the socialist era (Hann 1990a, 1990b). Recent measures to lower the rate of taxation and introduce more severe fines are intended to change these patterns, but in Kiskunhalas no one is expecting any significant improvement. On the contrary, there is sympathy for the predicament of the entrepreneur who (according to the widespread perception) would surely go out of business if he (seldom she) was completely honest in his dealings with the taxation office. The idea that Hungarian employers should pay wages at Western European levels is simply laughable. The popular posters of the Jobbik party which call for "equal pay for equal work" evoke a double response. First, employers like Ignác point out that the work is not the same, i.e. that the productivity of his workers interacting with their machines "in the Hungarian way" will never compete with the likes of Mercedes. Second, if it is argued that at least the TNCs, together with those Hungarian-owned enterprises that are successful in global markets, should pay much higher wages, the objection that many Halas residents have internalized is simple: why, then, would those jobs stay in Hungary? It is generally accepted that the country can only be competitive through low labor costs.

This is the context in which increasing numbers of Hungarians, mostly young, some with tertiary qualifications, have been taking up jobs in other EU states, especially in Britain, where the labor market was opened to them with the accession of the V4 in 2004. There is a hardly a family in Halas that is not affected in one way or another.

Figure 20. Ignác and his son outside their metalwork atelier in Kiskunhalas (photo by Chris Hann, 2017)

The decision to leave is to some extent a matter of choice, usually heavily dependent on the advice and support of relatives or friends in one's neighborhood or one's school. Sometimes the risk element is minimal and the migration is planned as a very short-term phase in the life-cycle, framed in the neoliberal language of entrepreneurial "self-fashioning" (cf. Sekeráková Búriková 2014 concerning young Slovaks in Britain). But temporary migration is often prolonged and, when the most talented and hardworking gravitate abroad, the impact on the sending communities is detrimental in moral as well as economic terms. This is why, in the opinion of the older generation, small towns throughout provincial Hungary have been unable to sustain the growth paths launched by socialist industrialization policies (cf. Makovicky 2014a on the Polish-Czech border country).

This is also the context in which to understand the negative reaction of the great majority of Hungarians, including residents of the villages and small towns of counties such as Bács-Kiskun, to the influx of non-European migrants that became dramatic in the Summer of 2015 (Hann 2016c; see also Chapter Six, above). Concern about this dramatic configuration of human mobility has been manipulated assiduously by Viktor Orbán's government. In 2015–17, some refugees were accommodated temporarily in a disused barracks on the outskirts of Halas. I heard rumors of violence in the "reception center" and later of incidents in the

Figure 21. Billboard of the Jobbik party in Kiskunhalas calling for equal wages for the same work. The top line reads "We live in the center of Europe, but our wages are a quarter [of the European level]. (photo by Chris Hann, 2017)

town, including thefts from the nearby Tesco store. It turned out that the stories had no foundation and in any case this reception center was soon closed. But the climate has remained poisonous as a result of the government's continuous efforts to mobilize public opinion: ultimately against Islam as a threat to Christian civilization, and at the same time against liberal cosmopolitans in Brussels and Budapest who are alleged to be complicit in undermining national identities. As noted above, George Soros is the ogre whose alleged "plan" to open up European borders is portrayed as the culmination of his lifelong capitalist dedication to the free movement of both capital and persons. This propaganda resonates in places like Kiskunhalas and Bács-Kiskun more generally. Even in expanding Kecskemét, many sympathize with this populist view of the world. The market society that was implemented in the first postsocialist decades in Hungary (not least by the socialist party) caused convulsions in communities accustomed to the securities and steady accumulation of socialism. One of the saddest consequence is the gulf that has opened up once again between town and countryside, and between Budapest (where left-liberal elites are concentrated) and the rest of the country. To place these trends in a broader world historical picture, there can be no better guide than Karl Polanyi.

Freedom, Responsibility and Slavery

In the early 1990s all members of the V4 experienced the elixir of freedom and socialists were everywhere defeated in the first democratic elections. The fact that successor parties to the Communists triumphed in later elections can be interpreted as evidence of the strength of the new democratic institutions. In addition to bringing individuals basic freedoms that were denied during the socialist decades, including the freedom to travel, postsocialist transformations seem to have entrenched a democratic political culture. Yet these freedoms remain fragile. Many parties have proved unstable; the institutions remain susceptible to authoritarian abuses and corruption at every level. Government interference in the judiciary in Poland and Hungary has been a matter of concern to the Brussels Commission and the European Parliament. In Hungary, the exemplary "illiberal democracy,"[9] Fidesz (the party in power since 2010) exercises its power over the media to distort and suppress oppositional voices. So much for freedom in the public, political sphere.

As for the economic sphere, liberals take it for granted that the privatization of state property and the extension of markets add up to a massive increase in the freedom quotient. Many foreign companies have undoubtedly profited from the new freedoms to invest and make money in the V4, as have significant numbers of local entrepreneurs. But large numbers of citizens have paid a high price for these freedoms, as I have indicated in the previous section of this chapter, and elsewhere in this book. How can we compare the freedom of young men and women in Kiskunhalas today to choose between migrant labor in London and local workfare with the range of choices made by their parents and grandparents (whether or not to move into the town, and which factory to work for)?

---

[9] This phrase was used by Viktor Orbán in a speech to ethnic Hungarians at Băile Tuşnad, Romania, in 2014. George Schöpflin, a Fidesz member of the European Parliament, argues that Orbán's intention was to emphasize his opposition to economic (neo)liberalism rather than to question liberal values as the basis of a free and democratic society (Schöpflin 2016).

Similar points were made by Dunn (2004, 167) following her fieldwork in Poland in the mid-1990s. Four decades of exposure to socialist ideology have helped to ensure that Marxist critique has considerable traction among older citizens of the V4 countries. But simultaneously there is an enduring suspicion of the tradition of scientific socialism, based on notions of class antagonism, which brought so much brutality and suffering. Many of those who suffered were in a later phase among the prime beneficiaries of socialist rule. This quagmire of ironies is sufficient reason to consider alternatives to the historical materialism of Marx and Lenin.

Questions of freedom were of central importance to Polanyi at various points in his career. It has been argued recently that they underpin virtually everything he wrote (Brie and Thomasberger 2018). Before the First World War, as a student in Budapest, he gravitated towards a left-liberal "freethinker" position. The war brought illness, followed by exile to Vienna, where he engaged with Marx (and behind him, Hegel). Polanyi participated in debates about value and the viability of an economy that was not integrated by markets and the price mechanism. He rejected what he perceived to be the economic determinism of later Marxists. Instead, drawing on ideas common at the time among members of the "Christian left," with whom he interacted intensively in Britain during his second exile, Polanyi stressed individual responsibility as the cornerstone of freedom and of human society itself. By the time he drafted "Freedom in a complex society," the concluding chapter to *The Great Transformation* (1944), he was ready to draw conclusions.

What is Polanyi's mature position? Claus Thomasberger (2018) argues convincingly that, even before the horrors of Auschwitz and the gulag became known, Polanyi had witnessed enough to reject the hubris of the European Enlightenment. It was a mistake to imagine that man could emancipate himself and his world through any simple act of transformation based on human will. Liberalism, with its emphasis on the market and a notion of freedom that pitted the individual against society, was the ultimate cause of the economic and political catastrophes of the early twentieth century. Against this, Polanyi argues (drawing on the theologian Reinhold Niebuhr) for recognition of, and resignation to, "the reality of society." The word "resignation" is perhaps misleading, for Polanyi never countenanced *acceptance* of the market society that had emerged as a reaction to liberalism. Scholarly critique of liberal and libertarian philosophy was a vital component of the political struggle against Fascism.[10] As a scholar, he continued this work in North America, scene of his third exile, where he formulated the program of a substantivist economic anthropology grounded in a holistic view of the embeddedness of economic institutions in society.

Ambivalences and confusion have crept in concerning Polanyi's precise political loyalties, in part due to the simple fact that Polanyi was hardly free, in the United States of the 1950s, to write entirely freely about socialism. He rejected the rigid evolutionism of historical materialism and recognized that to substitute omniscient planners for the self-regulating market could also become a dystopia if put into practice in a non-democratic way. The answer was therefore to democratize socialism, in the workplace and in society more generally. There is no doubt where Polanyi's sympathies lay in the first decades of the Cold War. He saw more grounds for hope in the USSR and its allies, even under Stalin, even after suppression of the 1956 revolution in his native Hungary, than he could identify in the market societies of the West, even after the New Deal and the extension of the welfare state after 1945 in Western Europe. The course of events in the V4 since 1990 would confirm him in this preference. The positive reminiscences that one hears in places like Kiskunhalas today would suggest to him that the dialectic is not over. He would be concerned that nationalist reactions to the failure of the latest attempt to impose a market utopia could again lead to some form of Fascism.

It may not be altogether fanciful to compare Polanyi's ruminations on freedom in what he frequently referred to as the "machine age" with those of an earlier European philosopher with similar humanist instincts. Johann Gottfried Herder lived in a society that was still fundamentally preindustrial. Just as Polanyi deplored Fascism, Herder detested slavery (still endemic in the Atlantic economies of his time). Herder seems to have thought that a human being could only find his *Glück* in the culture and environment in which he was born (see Gossiaux 2016).[11] Would he condemn the pressures that lead many young

[10] See Brie and Thomasberger 2018, especially the chapters by Thomasberger and Fred Block.

[11] A sentiment that is, of course, congenial to the anthropologist, whose *métier* has traditionally depended on being able to assign unique socio-cultural groupings to particular places.

residents of Kishunhalas to migrate to London as free wage-workers in the same terms that he would condemn the warmongers whose activities generate more clear-cut cases of forced migration? Would he agree with Ignác, the locksmith introduced in the previous section, for whom work on a car assembly line, even if undertaken in the *Heimat*, can be characterized as a form of slavery?

The vocabularies of Herder and Polanyi could hardly be more different. Whereas the latter urges recognition of "the reality of society," the former celebrates the *Genie* of peoples, their distinctive *Nationalcharakter*, the originality and value of each and every *Kultur* or *Nation*. This is why Herder is commonly viewed as a founding father of anthropology, whereas Polanyi is the cosmopolitan polymath, whose seminal contribution to the sub-discipline of economic anthropology was a fortuitous accident. Yet Polanyi too had a strong sense of belonging to a nation—Hungary. The two thinkers resemble each other in their suspicion of mobilities.[12] The end of socialism in the V4 has undoubtedly brought great increases in the mobility of both capital and labor, but has this served the common good? Would these two Central European moralists profess some sympathy with the slogan of the Jobbik party that "everyone should be able to prosper [flourish/thrive] in his/her native land"? They would surely agree that some of the choices facing individuals today are unfortunate. The invention of the Euro and the institutionalization of market models which can never be adequately compensated by redistributive regional policies would push both Herder and Polanyi to take the side of those urging resistance to present, neoliberal forms of Europeanization and globalization.[13]

The tragedy is that this resistance is currently being championed, almost monopolized, by virulent populists. The V4 is regularly

---

[12] In comparison with Kant, Hegel, and most other contemporaries, Herder's career was marked by great mobility, not all of it entirely voluntary. Polanyi's successive migrations were noted in Chapter One.

[13] Polanyi was deeply attached to Hungary, but he was not an economic nationalist and would have no time for the corruption and repression of liberties practiced by the current regime in Budapest as a form of reaction to the failure of the market utopia. Rather than a universal currency akin to the gold standard, he envisaged a world of large trading blocks and the persistence of national currencies to regulate unequal relations within such blocks. Experience in Euroland confirms the wisdom of this view.

pilloried by powerful voices in the West, who identify the refusal to accept quotas of migrants allocated by Brussels as a lack of civilizational *Salonfähigkeit*. It is commonly suggested that the transfers made by the old EU to the new EU in the name of regional policy should be reduced or suspended until the latter have learned to practice "European values."[14] Of course, the V4 leaders insist that it is they who best represent the values of Christian Europe. Domestic critics in Budapest and other capitals deplore the stance of their own governments and endorse universalist precepts based on human rights. The multiple blaming games surrounding the "migrant crisis" are perhaps best seen as a distraction that affords scope to nationalist politicians in the V4 to become ever more strident. While there are indeed grounds for concern at the national level, above all pertaining to political and jural freedoms, opposition politicians and liberal intellectuals should not exaggerate the danger of Fascism in villages such as Tázlár or small towns such as Kiskunhalas. There may even be some truth in the claims of V4 leaders that their critique of Brussels *diktat* is a beacon of light for democracy, because it reflects existentially-grounded opinions that are widespread throughout Europe, but not reflected in elite policymaking. One conclusion is certain: both the nationalism currently espoused by the V4 (especially Hungary and Poland) and the (neo)liberal elite consensus represented by the EU Commission are incompatible with the notions of freedom and responsibility espoused by the socialist Karl Polanyi.

[14] The value of these transfers to the V4 is significant but Thomas Piketty (2018) has argued that it adds up to less than the value of the profits repatriated by TNCs, to which a large proportion of regional development funds flow. At one level the Kecskemét factory discussed above would seem to exemplify the exploitation of Hungarian labor by German capital. But, as noted, jobs at the new factory in Kecskemét are attractive because they pay far better than local employers. Since few of the up-market cars manufactured here are sold in Hungary, the nature of the value chain and the exploitation is moot (all the more so as Chinese investors up their stake in Daimler-Benz).

CHAPTER TWELVE

Conclusion: Building Social Eurasia

At the beginning of this book I posed two general questions: first, what light can socio-cultural anthropology throw on the rise and fall of Marxist-Leninist-Maoist socialism, and by extension on other moments of rupture in human history? And second, what impact has work on these recent transformations in Eurasia had upon the discipline? The latter question is the easier to answer. The total number of foreign anthropologists specialized in the former Soviet world has not grown much (if at all) since the Cold War. Work on postsocialism has fed into diffuse anthropological concerns with temporality and memory, as well as material transformations of markets, property relations and political processes. But it would be difficult to claim that the contributions from socialist and postsocialist Eurasia have been a catalyst for original trends in the discipline at large. The most ambitious and original attempt to theorize socialism remains that of Katherine Verdery (1996), but this has not been taken further by other researchers and there is no equivalent model for the study of postsocialism. On the contrary, it is implicitly assumed that no such model is needed, since the elimination of imposed, unnatural socialist institutions allows countries and cultures to resume their historically diverse trajectories.

The first question is more important and more complex, since it involves moving beyond the details of ethnographic case-studies to grasp long-term changes in human economy and the embeddedness of production, distribution and consumption in other social institutions. I shall answer the question here in three steps, each with some help from Karl Polanyi, each signifying a more expansive temporality.

Beyond his seminal contributions to economic anthropology in the 1950s, a fresh look at the oeuvre of Polanyi can help us to theorize both socialism and its denouement in the era of neoliberal globalization. Polanyi can still inspire—but it behooves us to apply his framework creatively and critically (cf. Fraser 2014).

Short Run: After Brexit

My delay in completing this book allows me to speculate on how Karl Polanyi might perceive the state of the world in 2017, following a British referendum in June 2016 in which a majority of voters opted to leave the European Union ("Brexit"). Parochial though this event may seem in the light of Britain's declining global significance, it is a major reversal of the trend to unify the states of the European macro-region, a trend which began not long after Karl Polanyi left Europe for North America in the wake of the Second World War. Polanyi would surely speculate on wider conclusions (just as, in *The Great Transformation*, he offered much more than an interpretation of British economic history). He might structure his interpretation by drawing once again on his conceptualization of the three fictitious commodities.

Of the three fictitious commodities, the neoliberal commodification of labor in a European Union that since 2004 has included the four Visegrád countries was undoubtedly a prime cause of the referendum outcome in Britain (Goodwin and Milazzo 2017). Migration poses challenging questions to left-leaning intellectuals. Karl Polanyi was himself a migrant several times over. Nowadays, however, regardless of social stratum, citizens are not leaving Eastern Europe because of violence and persecution. Most take advantage of EU labor mobility to occupy low-skilled jobs in Britain, where they have at least basic language skills, because these jobs offer them opportunities preferable to anything available to them at home. The conditions in which they live and work are demanding. Young people delay marriage (if they marry at all) and have fewer children, while their parents and grandparents in Eastern Europe bemoan the absence of their loved ones.

It is sometimes claimed that these patterns of labor migration are not essentially different from those of earlier generations. Thanks to cheap air flights, the situation of migrant workers in Britain is quite unlike that of the millions who took steamships to North America before the First World War. Nowadays it is possible to fly home for a brief Christmas sojourn, or even at short notice for a weekend to attend an important family ritual. This is more like the situation of hundreds of thousands of villagers who, in the late Habsburg era, migrated to cities such as Budapest from distant provinces such as sub-Carpathian Ruthenia. Many of them entered domestic service for the new bourgeoisie, but they were not obliged to work through every weekend and could catch a train home when they needed to. If this analogy is accepted, the present commoditization of labor is not radically new. The major difference is the nature of the labor market in the receiving country. As a result of the decline of its old industrial regions, Britain exhibits stark regional differences. It is easy to manipulate populist, xenophobic sentiments in such regions: should the unemployed in ex-mining communities of Wales or Northumberland be expected to migrate to Southeast England to compete with Poles and Hungarians to wash dishes or pick strawberries? Analyses of the Brexit vote suggest that economically disadvantaged regions tended to vote more strongly for leaving the EU. Of course, they may soon rue this choice in material terms, since they stand to lose the redistributive funding made available by the EU they have come to abhor.

Karl Polanyi introduced the concept of the double movement to help us grasp such reactions to the intensification of market society. The deeper cause of Brexit is not migration from the Visegrád countries but the institutions of a global neoliberal order. A great deal of the responsibility lies in Brussels, where the ideals of those who sought in the last century to promote European unity on the basis of shared values and social protection have been largely buried. But some of the responsibility lies at the level of the nation-states. Social tensions are inevitably accentuated by the scaling down of public expenditure, especially for social security, in both receiving and sending countries. In the Visegrád states, the payment of higher wages (reflecting actual productivity) and the preservation of levels of public spending attained in the socialist era would diminish the incentives to migrate. In this sense, as Zoltán Pogátsa (2016) has argued, "A sustainable solution to Brexit therefore lies in the east." Ultimately it is a question of taking "social Europe" seriously, so that the decision to seek work elsewhere becomes a genuine choice, an expression of freedom rather than a practical necessity.

The second of Polanyi's fictitious commodities is land. I have devoted considerable space in this book to agricultural land in Tázlár, a community that was launched by the commodification of the *puszta* in the late nineteenth century. Due to its poor soils, much of this land now has little value as a productive resource. Elsewhere in Hungary, however, and around the globe, landgrabbing is a central problem, because the ownership of "real property" is the most attractive option when capital is available in abundance and all other assets are uncertain. A much broader conceptualization of the environment is needed, for the deleterious impact of contemporary market capitalism's reliance on "cheap nature" (Moore 2015) far exceeds anything Karl Polanyi could have imagined.

Polanyi would perhaps be even more astonished by the evolution of monetary institutions in the last half century. Money, too, is for him a fictitious commodity. Present arrangements in Europe, notably the structural imbalances within the Eurozone, have contributed to deepening inequalities both between north and south, and between regions within each member state. The intensification of financialization in order to maximize profits has led seasoned observers to conclude that this might truly be the endgame for the capitalist mode of production (Streeck 2016). Streeck's analysis leans heavily on that of Polanyi. He too argues passionately for another "great transformation," one that will prove more durable than Keynesian social democracy.

It is instructive to compare the insights of Karl Polanyi with the social vision of a great Central European thinker of a later generation. I have referred to Ernest Gellner many times in this book (and outlined a more careful contrast to Polanyi in Hann 2015b). He published *Conditions of Liberty: Civil Society and Its Rivals* in 1994, barely a year before his death. The subtitle is an allusion to Karl Popper's *The Open Society and Its Enemies*. After surveying the intellectual history of "civil society" and finding it to be messy and unsatisfactory, Gellner nonetheless argues (by means of comparisons with the "ideocracies" of socialism and tribal Islam) that this slogan encapsulates the essence of a healthy pluralist society, one in which "we" should want to live. He wrote this book in the early 1990s, when he had already left Cambridge and was teaching for the Central European University in Prague, the city in which he spent his childhood. We met on several occasions in those years. I recall that Ernest was far from sympathetic to local developments, whether in politics (the "velvet divorce") or in the economy (where Václav Klaus was doing his best to emulate Margaret Thatcher). But though he pushed "civil society" as a sociological concept, Gellner in this late work refrains from any concrete engagement with postsocialist societies. He contents himself with a virtuoso *tour d'horizon*, insisting on the need for markets ("economic decentralisation") and overlooking the deleterious consequences for social order that were already vividly apparent in the course of the region's rapid incorporation into capitalism's global political economy.

Two decades later it is time to conclude that the liberal agenda of civil society failed to provide that healthy open society to which the liberal Popperian in Gellner aspired. In Hungary and Poland, the main subjects of this volume, too many persons have found their opportunities and freedoms constrained in recent years. Almost everywhere, from university departments of history and the social sciences in the capital cities to one-party monopoly in the countryside, the tide has turned against pluralism in favor of populist nationalism. This is exactly the double movement that Karl Polanyi would have anticipated. It is of a piece with Brexit, and with other variants of populism throughout western Eurasia. There is little sign anywhere in the world that evolving reactions to neoliberal marketization will be anything but malignant.

Long Run: After Speenhamland

Most preindustrial rural societies were characterized by class exploitation and alienation. In the socialist era, following the quite different forms of oppression that characterized the Stalinist period, a new combination emerged which allowed villagers in places such as Tázlár to combine new forms of wage-labor with Chayanovian family farming. Thanks to new technologies, drudgery levels were significantly reduced. Self-exploitation became more voluntary, since alternatives to farming were readily available. The postsocialist era has seen the intensification of class differences and new forms of precarity—typical symptoms of neoliberalism. Workfare, the most controversial policy of the present Hungarian government for dealing with the adverse consequences for employment of the country's weak structural position in contemporary capitalism, is hardly neoliberal in the sense of an economic philosophy based on free markets. Yet to characterize it as a Foucauldian disciplining of the labor force seems just as inadequate. At least in villages such as Tázlár, the *közmunka* programs have been generally welcomed, both by the participants and by other villagers.

Such programs need to be assessed in historical perspective. One salient thread of Polanyi's *The Great Transformation* is the discussion of the Speenhamland system of poor relief in early industrial England (see Block and Somers 2014, 114–49). In this system (named after a village in Berkshire where the arrangements were first introduced in 1795), the community topped up the low incomes of those inhabitants whose families would otherwise have faced hunger. Polanyi was scornful of a practice which was thoroughly degrading of the worker and held wages down. Others, notably Thomas Malthus, disapproved for different reasons. They held that any public interference in the emerging capitalist labor market was mistaken because it reduced incentives (in this case the incentive to move away from Speenhamland, where the dispossessed could no longer afford to buy bread, and instead to move to a town such as Birmingham or Manchester, where English industry was booming). The Speenhamland measures persisted until 1834, when this system of poor relief was definitively abolished. Traditions of community solidarity which reached back to the Middle Ages gave way to a "free market" for labor; human beings were reduced to the status of a commodity, "like cucumbers," as Polanyi himself put it (see Chapter Five, above).

The workfare measures practiced in Tázlár in the 1930s and again today are very different from Speenhamland. Today the men and women who receive a job from the mayor are registered in a national scheme, they work a full week for the community rather than for private entrepreneurs, and they accumulate entitlements to health care and pensions as well as their daily bread. This employment is not perceived as degrading by those allocated such work, or by other villagers. But how long will this modification of the pure logic of the market last in postsocialist Hungary and what are its deeper implications for the morale of society?

Rather than compare the Speenhamland system with today's workfare schemes, from a *longue durée* perspective I find it more fruitful to compare Speenhamland with the Hungarian variety of Marxist-

Leninist-Maoist socialism. Each lasted for four decades. Each marked the era of maximum disruption to the rural economy, as the historically evolved peasantry was transformed by industrialization. Speenhamland provided poor villagers with basic security against the unprecedented uncertainties of the new market economy. Socialism did the same, initially in very destructive fashion, but then rather more creatively and effectively from the 1960s onwards. Some villagers migrated to occupy new positions in the urban industrial division of labor, but many of these migrants maintained both material and emotional ties to their villages. With the exception of Poland, farming in the Visegrád states was primarily the responsibility of large socialist institutions, which guaranteed employment to all. Accumulation was possible via the household plot. The counterparts of the English rural poor, who after Speenhamland were left with no option but to join the urban proletariat and sever their rural connections, were able in market socialist Hungary to build modern houses, buy cars, and in numerous respects achieve higher living standards than urban workers. The peasant-workers were incorporated into the national society where they were granted all the entitlements of social citizenship.

The gradualist model of socialist industrialization is the context in which to grasp the revival of workfare schemes in the Hungarian countryside in the last decade. Karl Polanyi would surely have saluted the convergence of rural and urban living standards in the socialist era as a relatively humane implementation of the great transformation, promoting the re-embedding of economy in society. Other economists have taken a different view, as I noted in Chapter One. Rather than welcome the extension of universalist social citizenship, János Kornai condemned "premature welfarization" (see Kornai 2007). From the (neo)liberal economist's point of view, the *közmunka* programs are inherently flawed, a legacy of the misguided generosity of the decades of market socialism. From this point of view, Hungary has yet to reach the turning point of 1834. But for the villagers who vote for Viktor Orbán, these schemes are a humane intervention as well as a welcome opportunity for the genuinely needy. The jobs may be tedious and precarious, but communal work in one's native village is widely perceived to be an attractive alternative to the uncertainties of migration or the more strenuous demands of day-laboring.

Very Long Run: After the Bronze Age

To compare and contrast a particular socialist path of industrialization (I am not claiming that Hungary is representative) with the path of a capitalist pioneer two centuries before is already an unusual level of analysis for a social anthropologist. But it is possible to be much more ambitious and reach back further into the historical origins of the tensions which have played out in modern history as a dialectic of state and market or, to phrase this dialectic in Polanyian terms, of redistribution and exchange as the dominant forms of integration.

As Jack Goody showed in many publications (e.g. 2006, 2010), it is a Eurocentric error to attribute a "breakthrough to modernity" to a fortuitous constellation of circumstances in the North Atlantic from the sixteenth century onwards. Instead, Goody draws attention to "alternating leadership" between Western and Eastern Eurasia during millennia of intensive connectivity. Since the urban revolution of the Bronze Age, based on the rural surplus that was enabled by plough agriculture, "merchant cultures" evolved new patterns of property transmission and status differentiation in the realm of consumption. They also developed new political institutions. The roots of what Western Enlightenment thinkers termed "civil society" are to be found not just in Greece but in cities right across Eurasia, whose contributions to democratic government and "civilisation" have been systematically overlooked and distorted by Eurocentric scholars (Goody 1998, 261–78).

Goody emphasizes the crucial role of exchange (trade and markets) in the transmission of goods, technologies, and ideas across Eurasia. He says little about the necessity to mitigate the potentially disruptive consequences of what Polanyi termed "price-forming markets" for human flourishing in the Aristotelian sense. This mitigation and amelioration took place in two basic ways. First, humans invented new forms of religion or cosmology bearing in unprecedented ways on ethical standards, which ushered in new forms of communal responsibility. Second (often closely linked to the new moral universalism), while social inequality grew and this was reflected in consumption patterns, the principle of redistribution was consolidated in the context of new forms of centralized polity and what we nowadays term inclusive social citizenship. These agrarian civilizations were threatened to their foundations by the developments that began in North-West Europe in the late eighteenth century, but the basic dialectic has persisted. The response to the rise of commercial society, *laissez-faire* or market society in Polanyi's descriptions of nineteenth century Britain, could only be a reassertion of the ethics of redistribution, a rejection of the preposterous proposition that *eudaimonia* could be attained through the selfish pursuit of individual advantage.

Seen from such a perspective, Marxist-Leninist-Maoist socialism is a particularly dramatic instance of a dialectical double movement that dates all the way back to the emergence of complex economies and differentiated societies in Prehistory. Simply to conclude that this socialism failed is short-sighted. As Goody pointed out, "electoral socialism" has had a profound impact on many parts of the world that never experienced Marxist-Leninist-Maoist dictatorship (Goody 2003). The aspiration to enjoy happiness in a decent and secure community is universal to our species. It certainly remains strong in the Visegrád states, at the interface between advanced West and backward East. In Tázlár, even diehard opponents of the socialist ideology they experienced in the 1950s and 1960s appreciated the improvements that they had experienced in their lives by 1990. Neither the militant post-socialist liberals nor today's populist power holders in Hungary and Poland can dismiss the accomplishments of their Marxist-Leninist predecessors. The search is still on for the elusive balance that would fulfill Karl Polanyi's call for "freedom in a complex society." If *Vorwärts immer* was a utopia, so too was the promise of market society after 1990. In the continuing evolutionary ratchet, the short-run crisis for Hungary, the V4, and the rest of the EU is a consequence of the abandonment of "social Europe." The long-term solution for the disorder of the European macro-region (and arguably of the planet) is the abandonment of neoliberal economic dogmas and a resumption of the dialectic of "social Eurasia."

References

Abrahams, Ray, ed. 1996. *After Socialism: Land Reform and Social Change in Eastern Europe*. Oxford: Berghahn.

Alexander, Catherine. 2004. "Value, Relations, and Changing Bodies: Privatization and Property Rights in Kazakhstan." In *Property in Question: Value Transformation in the Global Economy*, edited by Katherine Verdery and Caroline Humphrey, 251–73. Oxford: Berg.

Anderson, Perry. 1979 [1974]. *Lineages of the Absolutist State*. London: Verso.

Anderson, Benedict. 1983. *Imagined Communities: Reflections on the Origins and Spread of Nationalism*. London: Verso.

Andrews, Geoff, ed. 1991. *Citizenship*. London: Lawrence and Wishart.

Appadurai, Arjun, ed. 1986. *The Social Life of Things: Commodities in Cultural Perspective*. Cambridge: Cambridge University Press.

Arato, Andrew. 1981. "Civil Society Against the State: Poland 1980–81." *Telos* 47: 23–47.

Armstrong, John A. 1982. *Nations Before Nationalism*. Chapel Hill: University of North Carolina Press.

Ascherson, Neal. 1990. "The Borderlands." *Granta: New Europe!* 30: 41–64.

Augustinos, Gerasimos, ed. 1996. *The National Idea in Eastern Europe: The Politics of Ethnic and Civic Community*. Lexington, MA: D. C. Heath.

Babiński, Grzegorz. 1997. *Pogranicze polsko-ukraińskie: Etniczność, zróznicowanie religijne, tożsamość*. Kraków: Nomos.

Babiński, Gregorz, Janusz Mucha, and Andrzej Sadowski, eds. 1997. *Polskie badania nad mniejszościami kulturowymi*. Białystok: Wybrane zagadnienie.

Bach, Jonathan. 2015. *What Remains: Everyday Encounters with the Socialist Past in Germany*. New York: Columbia University Press.

Barth, Fredrik. 1969. "Introduction." In *Ethnic Groups and Boundaries: The Social Organization of Cultural Difference*, edited by Fredrik Barth, 9–38. Oslo: Scandinavian University Press.

Bartha, Eszter. 2013. *Alienating Labour: Workers on the Road from Socialism to Capitalism in East Germany and Hungary*. New York: Berghahn Books.

Becher, Ursula A. J., ed. 1993. *Zwanzig Jahre gemeinsame Deutsch-Polnische Schulbuchkommission: Reden aus Anlaß der Festveranstaltung in Braunschweig am 10. Juni 1992.* Braunschweig: Georg-Eckert-Institut.

Beckert, Jens. 2009. "The Great Transformation of Embeddedness: Karl Polanyi and the New Economic Sociology." In *Market and Society: The Great Transformation Revisited*, edited by Chris Hann, and Keith Hart, 38–55. Cambridge: Cambridge University Press.

Beeson, Trevor. 1982. *Discretion and Valour: Religious Conditions in Russia and Eastern Europe.* London: Harper Collins Publishers.

Bell, Peter D. 1984. *Peasants in Socialist Transition: Life in a Collectivized Hungarian Village.* Berkeley: University of California Press.

von Benda-Beckmann, Franz. 1979. *Property in Social Continuity: Continuity and Change in the Maintenance of Property Relationships through Time in Minangkabau, West Sumatra.* The Hague: Nijhoff.

von Benda-Beckmann, Franz, and Keebet von Benda-Beckmann. 1999. "A Functional Analysis of Property Rights, with Special Reference to Indonesia." In *Property Rights and Economic Development: Land and Natural Resources in Southeast Asia and Oceania*, edited by Toon van Meijl, and Franz von Benda-Beckmann, 1–14. London: Kegan Paul International.

———. 2006. "How Communal is Communal and Whose Communal Is It? Lessons from Minangkabau." In *Changing Properties of Property*, edited by Franz von Benda Beckmann, Keebet von Benda-Beckmann, and Melanie Wiber, 194–217. Oxford: Berghahn.

von Benda-Beckmann, Franz, Keebet von Benda-Beckmann, and Melanie Wiber. 2006a. "The Properties of Property." In *Changing Properties of Property*, edited by Franz von Benda-Beckmann, Keebet von Benda-Beckmann, and Melanie Wiber, 1–40. Oxford: Berghahn.

———, eds. 2006b. *Changing Properties of Property.* Oxford: Berghahn.

Berdahl, Daphne. 1999. "'(N)Ostalgie' for the present: Memory, longing, and East German things." *Ethnos* 64 (2): 192–211.

Berend, T. Iván. 1988. "Szent István a magyar történet századaiban." In *István és Kora: A 950 éves hagyaték mai leltára*, edited by Ferenc Glatz, and József Kardos, 9–17. Budapest: MTA Történettudományi Intézet.

———. 1990. *The Hungarian Economic Reforms 1953–1988.* Cambridge: Cambridge University Press.

Best, Paul J. 1990. "The Lemkos as an Ethnic Group." *The Polish Review* 35 (3): 255–60.

———. 2000. "The Apostolic Administration of the Lemko Region 1934–1944." In *The Lemkos of Poland: Articles and Essays*, edited by Paul Best and Jaroslaw Moklak, 219–34. Cracow and New Haven: Carpatho-Slavic Studies Group and Historia Iagellonica Press.

Bethmann, Carla. 2013. *"Clean, Friendly, Profitable." Tourism and the Tourism Industry in Varna, Bulgaria.* Berlin: LIT.

Binns, Christopher A. P. 1979–80. "The Changing Face of Power: Revolution and Accommodation in the Development of the Soviet Ceremonial System" *Man* 14 (4): 585–607 and 15 (1): 170–88.

Biskupski, Romuald. 1991a. *Ikony w zbiorach polskich*. Warsaw: Wydawnictwa Artystyczne i Filmowe.

———. 1991b *Ikony ze Zbiorów Muzeum Historycznego w Sanoku*. Warsaw: KSAT.

Bloch, Maurice. 1975. "Property and the End of Affinity." In *Marxist Analyses and Social Anthropology*, edited by Maurice Bloch, 203–28. London: Malaby Press.

Block, Fred, and Margaret R. Somers. 2014. *The Power of Market Fundamentalism: Karl Polanyi's Critique*. Cambridge: Harvard University Press.

Bociurkiw, Bohdan. 1996. *The Ukrainian Greek Catholic Church and the Soviet State, 1939–1950*. Edmonton: CIUS Press.

Bockman, Johanna. 2011. *Markets in the Name of Socialism. The Left-Wing Origins of Neo-Liberalism*. Stanford: Stanford University Press.

Bockman, Johanna, Ariane Fischer, and David Woodruff. 2016. "'Socialist Accounting' by Karl Polanyi: with preface 'Socialism and the Embedded Economy'." *Theory and Society* 45 (5): 385–427.

von Bogyay, Thomas. 1979. "Zum Stand der Sankt-Stephan-Forschung: Bemerkungen zu Györffys 'István király és müve'." *Südost-Forschungen* 38: 240–57.

Bohannan, Paul, and George Dalton, eds. 1961. *Markets in Africa*. Evanston: Northwestern Unversity Press.

Bohle, Dorothee. 2016. "East Central Europe in the European Union." In *The Palgrave Handbook of Critical International Political Economy*, edited by Alan Cafruny, Lela S. Talani, and Gonzalo P. Martin, 369–89. London: Palgrave McMillan.

Boldizsár, Iván. 1988. "The Past as Prologue." *New Hungarian Quarterly* 112: 3–7.

Brandtstädter, Susanne. 2001. "Re-defining Place in Southern Fujian: How Overseas Mansions and Ancestral Halls Re-appropriate the Land from the State." *Working Paper* No. 30, Halle/Saale: Max Planck Institute for Social Anthropology.

———. 2003. "The Moral Economy of Kinship and Property in Southern China." In *The Postsocialist Agrarian Question: Property Relations and the Rural Condition*, Chris Hann and the "Property Relations" Group, 419–37. Münster: LIT.

Bridger, Sue and Frances Pine, eds. 1998. *Surviving Post-Socialism: Local Strategies and regional responses in Eastern Europe and the Former Soviet Union*. London: Routledge.

Brie, Michael and Claus Thomasberger, eds. 2018. *Karl Polanyi's Vision of a Socialist Transformation*. Montreal: Black Rose Books.

Bringa, Tone. 1995. *Being Muslim the Bosnian Way: Identity and Community in a Central Bosnian Village*. Princeton: Princeton University Press.

Brock, Peter. 1969. "Polish Nationalism." In *Nationalism in Eastern Europe*, edited by Peter F. Sugar and Ivo J. Lederer, 310–72. Seattle: University of Washington Press.

Brown, Michael. 2003. *Who Owns Native Culture?* Cambridge, MA: Harvard University Press.

Brubaker, Rogers. 1996. *Nationalism Reframed: Nationhood and the National Question in the New Europe*. Cambridge: Cambridge University Press.

Brunnbauer, Ulf. 2003: "Descent or Territoriality: Inheritance and Family Forms in the Late Ottoman and Early Post-Ottoman Balkans." In *Distinct Inheritances: Property, Family and Community in a Changing Europe*, edited by Hannes Grandits, and Patrick Heady, 181–206. Münster: LIT.

Buchowski, Michał. 1997. *Reluctant Capitalists: Class and Culture in a Local Community in Western Poland*. Berlin: Centre Marc Bloch.

———. 2004. "Redefining work in a local community in Poland: 'Transformation' and class, culture and work." In *Workers and Narratives of Survival in Europe: The Management of Precariousness at the End of the Twentieth Century*, edited by Angela Procoli. New York: State University of New York Press.

———. 2008. "The enigma of the middle class: a case study of entrepreneurs in Poland." In *Changing Economies and Changing Identities in Postsocialist Eastern Europe*, edited by Ingo W. Schröder, and Asta Vonderau, 47–74. Berlin: LIT.

———. 2009. "Property relations, class, and labour in rural Poland." In *Postsocialist Europe. Anthropological Perspectives from Home*, edited by László Kürti, and Peter Skalník, 51–75. New York: Berghahn.

Bujak, Franciszek. 1929. "Historia osadnictwa ziem polskich w krótkim zarysie," In *Studia Historiczne i Społeczne Lwów-Warszawa*, edited by Franciszek Bujak, 59–103. Lwów: Ossolineum.

Busek, Erhard. 1996. "Europa 1989 bis 1995 – Was ist daraus geworden?" in *Nation, Ethnizität und Staat in Mitteleuropa*, edited by Urs Altermatt, 165–70. Wien: Böhlau.

Buxton, David. 1981. *The Wooden Churches of Eastern Europe*. Cambridge: Cambridge University Press.

Buzalka, Juraj. 2007. *Nation and Religion: The Politics of Commemoration in South-East Poland*. Berlin: LIT.

Cartwright, Andrew. 2001. *The Return of the Peasant: Land Reform in Post-Communist Romania*. Ashgate: Aldershot.

———. 2003. "Private Farming in Romania or What Are the Old People Going to Do with their Land?" In *The Postsocialist Agrarian Question: Property Relations and the Rural Condition,* Chris Hann, and the "Property Relations" Group, 171–188. Münster: LIT.

Cash, Jennifer. 2015. "Economy as ritual: The problems of paying in wine." In *Economy and Ritual: Studies of Postsocialist Transformations*, edited by Stephen Gudeman and Chris Hann, 31–51. New York: Berghahn.

Cellarius, Barbara. 2003. "Property Restitution and Natural Resource Use in the Rhodope Mountains, Bulgaria." In *The Postsocialist Agrarian Question: Property Relations and the Rural Condition,* Chris Hann, and the Property Relations Group, 189–218. Münster: LIT.

———. 2004. *In the Land of Orpheus: Rural Livelihoods and Nature Conservation in Postsocialist Bulgaria*. Madison: University of Wisconsin Press.

Chambers, Simone, and Will Kymlicka, eds. 2002. *Alternative Conceptions of Civil Society*. Princeton: Princeton University Press.

Chayanov, Alexander. 1986. *The Theory of Peasant Economy*. Manchester: Manchester University Press.

Chlewiński, Zdzisław. 1980. "Dystans społeczny wobec wyznawców innych religii oraz innych narodowości." *Przegląd Socjologiczny* 32 (1): 157–79.

Cohen, Abner. 1974. *Two Dimensional Man: An Essay on the Anthropology of Power and Symbolism*. London: Routledge.

Cole, John W. 1976. "Familial Dynamics in a Romanian Workers Village." *Dialectical Anthropology* 1 (3): 251–65.

Comisso, Ellen. 1991. "Property Rights, Liberalism, and the Transition from 'Actually Existing' Socialism." *Eastern European Politics and Societies* 5 (1): 162–88.

Conte, Édouard, and Christian Giordano. 1995. "Sentiers de la ruralité perdue: Réflexions sur le post-socialisme." In: *Études Rurales: Paysans au-delà du mur* (138–140): 11–33.

Coombe, Rosemary. 1998. *The Cultural Life of Intellectual Properties*. Durham: Duke University Press.

Creed, Gerald W. 1998. *Domesticating Revolution: From Socialist Reform to Ambivalent Transition in a Bulgarian Village*. Pennsylvania: State University Press.

———, ed. 2006. *The Seductions of Community: Emancipations, Oppressions, Quandaries*. Santa Fe: SAR Press.

———. 2011. *Masquerade and Postsocialism: Ritual and Cultural Dispossession in Bulgaria*. Bloomington: Indiana University Press.

Crouch, Colin. 2011. *The Strange Non-Death of Neoliberalism*. Cambridge: Polity.

Czakó, Ágnes, Johanna Giczi, and Endre Sik, eds. 2010. *Piachely, KGST-piac, Emberpiac*. Budapest: ELTE TáTK.

Czech, Miroslaw. 1992. "O tożsamość grekokatolików." In *O tożsamość grekokatolikow: Zbiór dokumentów z historii Cerkwi Grekokatolickiej w Polsce*, edited by Miroslaw Czech, 7–27. Warsaw: Zakład Wydawiniczy.

———, ed. 1993. *Ukraińcy w Polsce 1989–1993: Kalendarium, dokumenty, informacje*. Warszawa: Związek Ukraińców w Polsce.

Dale, Gareth. 2010. *Karl Polanyi: The Limits of the Market*. Cambridge: Polity.

———. 2016a. *Karl Polanyi: A Life on the Left*. New York: Columbia University Press.

———. 2016b. *Reconstructing Karl Polanyi*. London: Pluto.

Dalton, George. 1968. "Introduction." In *Primitive, Archaic and Modern Economies: Essays by Karl Polanyi*, edited by George Dalton, ix-liv. New York: Anchor Books.

Davis, John. 1984. "The Sexual Division of (religious) Labour in the Mediterranean." In *Religion, Power and Protest in Local Communities: The Northern Shore of the Mediterranean*, edited by Eric R. Wolf, 17–50. Berlin: De Gruyter.

Demsetz, Harold. 1967. "Towards a Theory of Property Rights." *American Economic Review* 57 (2): 347–59.

Dilley, Roy, ed. 1992. *Contesting Markets: Analyses of Ideology, Discourse and Practice*. Edinburgh: Edinburgh University Press.
Dragadze, Tamara. 1991. "Land Lease and Village Logic." Paper presented at a Georgian Studies Day, University of London, May 9.
Duć-Fajfer, Olena. 1993. "The Lemkos in Poland." In *The Persistence of Regional Cultures: Rusyns and Ukrainians in their Carpathian Homeland and Abroad*, edited by Paul Robert Magocsi, 83–104. New York: Columbia University Press.
Dumont, Louis. 1983. "Préface." In Karl Polanyi, *La Grande Transformation: Aux origines politiques et économiques de notre temps*, 7–23. Paris: Gallimard.
Dunn, Elizabeth. 2004. *Privatizing Poland: Baby Food, Big Business, and the Remaking of Labor*. Ithaca, NY: Cornell University Press.
Dziubina, Stefan. 1995. *Stwierdzi dilo ruk naszych.* Warszawa: Spohady.
Eibner, John V. 1988. "A New Primate: A New Policy." *Religion in Communist Lands* 16 (2): 164–68.
Eickelman, Dal F., and Jon W. Anderson, eds. 1999. *New Media in the Muslim World: The Emerging Public Sphere.* Bloomington: Indiana University Press.
Eidson, John. 2006. "Cooperative property at the limit." In *Changing Properties of Property*, edited by Franz von Benda Beckmann, Keebet von Benda-Beckmann, and Melanie Wiber, 147–69. Oxford: Berghahn.
Eidson, John and Gordon Milligan. 2003. "Cooperative Entrepreneurs? Collectivisation and Privatisation of Agriculture in Two East German Regions." In *The Postsocialist Agrarian Question: Property Relations and the Rural Condition,* Chris Hann, and the "Property Relations" Group, 47–92. Münster: LIT.
Elek, Sándor. 1991. "Part-time Farming in Hungary: An Instrument of Tacit Decollectivization." *Sociologia Ruralis* 31: 82–88.
Ellen, Roy, Ernest Gellner, Grażyna Kubica, und Janusz Mucha, eds. 1988. *Malinowski between Two Worlds: The Polish Roots of an Anthropological Tradition.* Cambridge: Cambridge University Press.
Elwert, Georg. 1989. "Nationalismus und Ethnizität: Über die Bildung von Wir-Gruppen." *Kölner Zeitschrift für Soziologie und Sozialpsychologie* 3: 440–64.
Emericus. 1984–85. "János, a király—avagy árad a kegyelem fénye reánk." *Hirmondó.*
Engel, Christoph. 2002. "Die soziale Funktion des Eigentums." In *Bericht zur Lage des Eigentums,* edited by Thomas Danwitz, Otto von Deppenheuer, and Christoph Engel, 9–107. Berlin: Springer.
Engels, Friedrich. 1972 (1884). *The Origin of the Family, Private Property and the State.* New York: Pathfinder Press.
Erdei, Ferenc. 1977 (1936). *Futóhomok.* Budapest: Akadémiai Kiadó.
Erlmann, Veit. 1999. *Music, Modernity, and the Global Imagination: South Africa and the West.* New York: Oxford University Press.
Fehérváry, Krisztina. 2013. *Politics in Color and Concrete: Socialist Materialities and the Middle Class in Hungary.* Bloomington: Indiana University Press.
Feischmidt, Margit. 2016. "Manipulált félelmek és dehumanizált idegenek." *Regio* 24 (4): 5–32.

Fél, Edit, and Tamás Hofer. 1969. *Proper Peasants: Traditional Life in a Hungarian Village*. Chicago: Aldine.

Fenczak, August S. and Stanisław Stępień. 1993. "Przemyśl jako regionalne centrum administracyjne – zarys dziejów." *Studia Przemyskie* 1: 9–48.

Fertő, Imre, Lénárt Zsolt, Maurer György, and Winkler Tamás. 1988. "Egy forma lehetőségei." *Gazdálkodás* 32 (12): 41–49.

Fertő, Imre, Lénárt Zsolt, Maurer György, and Winkler Tamás. 1990. "A siker titka: a magánerős modernizáció (Soltvadkert)." *Tér és Társadalom* 4: 77–88.

Figes, Orlando. 1987. "V.P. Danilov on the Analytical Distinction between Peasants and Farmers." In *Peasants and Peasant Societies*, edited by Teodor Shanin, 121–24. Oxford: Blackwell.

Firth, Raymond. 1965 (1939). *Primitive Polynesian Economy*. London: Routledge.

Follis, Karolina S. 2012. *Fortress Europe: The Polish-Ukrainian Frontier*. Philadelphia: University of Pennsylvania Press.

Franklin, Samuel Harvey. 1969. *The European Peasantry: The Final Phase*. London: Methuen.

Fraser, Nancy. 2014. "Can Society Be Commodities All the Way Down? Post-Polanyian Reflections on Capitalist Crisis." *Economy and Society* 43 (4): 541–58.

Friedman, Jonathan. 1994. *Cultural Identity and Global Process*. London: Sage.

Galbraith, Marysia. 2014. *Being and Becoming European: Self-Identity and European Integration in Poland*. London: Anthem Press.

Gałęski, Bogusław. 1972. *Basic Concepts of Rural Sociology*. Manchester: Manchester University Press.

Gambold Miller, Liesl L. and Patrick Heady. 2003. "Cooperation, Power and Community: Economy and Ideology in the Russian Countryside." In *The Postsocialist Agrarian Question: Property Relations and the Rural Condition*, edited by Chris Hann, 257–92. Münster: LIT.

Garton Ash, Timothy. 1989. *The Uses of Adversity: Essays on the Fate of Central Europe*. Cambridge: Granta Books.

Geertz, Clifford. 1963. *Agricultural Involution: The Processes of Ecological Change in Indonesia*. Berkeley: University of California Press.

———. 1980. *Negara: The Theatre State in Nineteenth-Century Bali*. Princeton: Princeton University Press.

Gellner, Ernest. 1959. *Words and Things: A Critical Account of Linguistic Philosophy and A Study in Ideology*. London: Gollancz.

———. 1964. *Thought and Change*. London: Weidenfeld and Nicolson.

———. 1983. *Nations and Nationalism*. Oxford: Blackwell.

———. 1994. *Conditions of Liberty: Civil Society and its Rivals*. London: Hamish Hamilton.

———. 1997. *Nationalism*. London: Weidenfeld and Nicolson.

———. 1998. *Language and Solitude: Wittgenstein, Malinowski and the Habsburg Dilemma*. Cambridge: Cambridge University Press.

Gergely, Jenő. 1988. *Eucharisztikus Világkongresszus Budapesten, 1938*. Budapest: Kossuth Könyvkiadó.

Gille, Zsuzsa. 2016. *Paprika, Foie Gras, and Red Mud: The Politics of Materiality in the European Union.* Bloomington: Indiana University Press.

Giordano, Christian. 2005. *Die postsozialistische Transition ist beendet, weil sie nie angefangen hat: zur Archäologie eines gescheiterten Entwicklungsmodells.* Braunschweig: Georg-Eckert-Institut für Internationale Schulbuchforschung.

Giordano, Christian, and Dobrinka Kostova. 2002. "The Social Production of Mistrust." In *Postsocialism: Ideals, Ideologies and Practices in Eurasia*, edited by Chris Hann, 74–91. London: Routledge.

Glasman, Maurice. 1996. *Unnecessary Suffering: Managing Market Utopia.* London: Verso.

Glatz, Ferenc. 1988. "Szent István 1038–1938–1988." In *István és kora*, edited by Ferenc Glatz, and József Kardos, 239–52. Budapest: MTA Történettudományi Intézet.

Gluckman, Max. 1943. *Essays on Lozi Land and Royal Property.* Livingstone: Rhodes-Livingstone Institute.

———. 1965. *The Ideas in Barotse Jurisprudence.* New Haven: Yale Univ. Press.

Goddard, Victoria, Josep R. Llobera, and Chris Shore, eds. 1994. *The Anthropology of Europe: Identity and Boundaries in Conflict.* Oxford: Berg.

Goodwin, Matthew and Caitlin Milazzo. 2017. "Taking Back Control? Investigating the Role of Immigration in the 2016 Vote for Brexit." *The British Journal of Politics and International Relations* 19 (3): 450–64.

Goody, Jack, ed. 1958. *The Developmental Cycle of the Domestic Group.* Cambridge: Cambridge University Press.

———. 1962. *Death, Property and the Ancestors: A Study of the Mortuary Customs of the LoDagaa of West Africa.* Stanford: Stanford University Press.

———. 1976. *Production and Reproduction: A Comparative Study of the Domestic Domain.* Cambridge: Cambridge University Press.

———. 1998. *Food and Love: A Cultural History of East and West.* London: Verso.

———. 2003. "Sorcery and Socialism." In *Distinct Inheritances: Property, Family and Community in a Changing Europe*, edited by Hannes Grandits and Patrick Heady, 391–406. Münster: LIT.

———. 2006. *The Theft of History.* Cambridge: Cambridge University Press.

———. 2010. *The Eurasian Miracle.* Cambridge: Polity.

Gossiaux, Jean-François. 2016. *Les débris épars du progress: Évolutionnisme vs anthropologie.* Paris: Maison des Sciences de l'Homme.

Graeber, David. 2001. *Toward an Anthropological Theory of Value: The False Coin of our own Dreams.* New York: Palgrave.

Grandits, Hannes, and Patrick Heady, eds. 2003. *Distinct Inheritances: Property, Family and Community in a Changing Europe.* Münster: LIT.

Gray, Patty. 2001. "The Obshchina in Chukotka: Land, Property and Local Autonomy." *Working Paper* No. 29. Halle/ Saale: Max Planck Institute for Social Anthropology.

———. 2003. "Volga Farmers and Arctic Herders: Common (Post)Socialist Experiences in Rural Russia." In *The Postsocialist Agrarian Question: Property Relations and the Rural Condition*, Chris Hann, and the "Property Relations" Group, 293–320. Münster: LIT.

———. 2005. *The Predicament of Chukotka's Indigenous Movement: Post-Soviet Activism in the Russian Far North*. Cambridge: Cambridge University Press.

Gregory, Chris. 2009. "Whatever Happened to Householding?" In *Market and Society: The Great Transformation Revisited*, edited by Chris Hann, and Keith Hart, 133–59. Cambridge: Cambridge University Press.

Gudeman, Stephen. 2001. *The Anthropology of Economy: Community, Market, and Culture*. Oxford: Blackwell.

———. 2006. "Trade's Reason." *Working Paper* Nr. 81, Halle/Saale: Max Planck Institute for Social Anthropology.

———. 2008. *Economy's Tension: The Dialectics of Community and Market*. New York: Berghahn.

Gudeman, Stephen, and Chris Hann, eds. 2015a. *Economy and Ritual: Studies of Postsocialist Transformations*. New York: Berghahn.

———. 2015b. *Oikos and Market: Explorations in Self-Sufficiency after Socialism*. New York: Berghahn.

Gyenis, János, ed. 1971. *Az egyszerűbb mezőgazdasagi szövetkezetek*. Budapest: Mezőgazdasági/Kossuth.

Györffy, György. 1973. *István király emlékezete*. Budapest: Magyar Helikon.

———. 1977. *István király és műve*. Budapest: Gondolat.

Halamska, Maria. 2011. "The Polish Countryside in the Process of Transformation, 1989–2009." *Polish Sociological Review* 173: 35–54.

Halecki, Oskar. 1958. *From Florence to Brest 1439–1596*. Rome: Fordham University Press.

Hall, John A., ed. 1998. *The State of the Nation: Ernest Gellner and the Theory of Nationalism*. Cambridge: Cambridge University Press.

———. 2010. *Ernest Gellner: An Intellectual Biography*. London: Verso.

Hankiss, Elemér. 1990. *East European Alternatives*. Oxford: Oxford University Press.

Hann, Chris. 1979. "A Frontier Community on the Great Plain." *New Hungarian Quarterly* 20 (74): 116–22.

———. 1980a. *Tázlár: A Village in Hungary*. Cambridge: Cambridge University Press.

———. 1980b. "Rural Social Change in Hungary and Poland." *Cambridge Anthropology* 6 (1–2): 142–60.

———. 1985. *A Village Without Solidarity: Polish Peasants in Years of Crisis*. New Haven: Yale University Press.

———. 1988. "Christianity's Internal Frontier: The Case of Uniates in South-East Poland." *Anthropology Today* 4 (3): 9–13.

———. 1990a. "Introduction." *Journal of Communist Studies* 6 (2): 1–20.

———. 1990b. "Second Economy and Civil Society." *Journal of Communist Studies* 6 (2): 21–44.

———, ed. 1990c *Market Economy and Civil Society in Hungary*. London: Frank Cass.

———.1990d "Socialism and King Stephen's Right Hand." *Religion in Communist Lands* 18 (1): 4–24.

———. 1992a. "Radical Functionalism: The Life and Work of Karl Polanyi." *Dialectical Anthropology* 17 (2): 141–66.

———. 1992b. "Civil Society at the Grassroots: A Reactionary View." In *Democracy and Civil Society in Eastern Europe*, edited by Paul G. Lewis, 152–65. London: Macmillan.

———. 1992c. "Market Principle, Market-place and the Transition in Eastern Europe." In *Contesting Markets: Analyses of Ideology, Discourse and Practice*, edited by Roy Dilley, 244–59. Edinburgh: Edinburgh University Press.

———. 1993a. "From Production to Property: Decollectivization and the Family-Land Relationship in Contemporary Hungary." *Man* 28 (2): 299–320.

———. 1993b. "Property Relations in the New Eastern Europe: The Case of Specialist Cooperatives in Hungary." In *The Curtain Rises: Rethinking Culture, Ideology and the State in Eastern Europe*, edited by Hermine G. De Soto, and David G. Anderson, 99–119. Atlantic Highlands, NJ: Humanities Press.

———. 1993c. "From Comrades to Lawyers: Continuity and Change in Local Political Culture in Rural Hungary." *Anthropological Journal on European Cultures* 2 (1): 75–104.

———. 1993d. "Religion and Nationality in Central Europe: The Case of the Uniates." *Ethnic Studies* 10 (1–3): 201–13.

———. 1995a. "Ferenc Erdei and Antal Vermes: The Struggle for Balance in Rural Hungary." In *East European Communities: The Struggle for Balance in Turbulent Times*, edited by David A. Kideckel, 101–14. Boulder, Col: Westview Press.

———. 1995b. "Philosophers' Models on the Carpathian Lowlands." In *Civil Society; Theory, History, Comparison*, edited by John A. Hall, 158–82. Cambridge: Polity.

———. 1995c. *The Skeleton at the Feast: Contributions to East European Anthropology*. Canterbury: Centre for Computing and Social Anthropology.

———. 1996a. "Introduction: Political Society and Civil Anthropology." In *Civil Society: Challenging Western Models*, edited by Chris Hann, and Elizabeth Dunn, 1–26. London: Routledge.

———. 1996b. "Ethnic Cleansing in Eastern Europe: Poles and Ukrainians Beside the Curzon Line." *Nations and Nationalism* 2: 389–406.

———. 1996c. "Land Tenure and Citizenship in Tázlár." In *After Socialism: Land Reform and Social Change in Eastern Europe*, edited by Ray Abrahams, 23–49. Oxford: Berghahn.

———. 1997. "Ethnicity in the New Civil Society: Lemko-Ukrainians in Poland." In *Beyond Borders: Remaking Cultural Identities in the New East and Central Europe*, edited by László Kürti, and Juliet Feldman, 17–38. Boulder, Col.: Westview Press.

———. 1998a. "Introduction: The Embeddedness of Property." In *Property Relations: Renewing the Anthropological Tradition*, edited by Chris Hann, 1–47. Cambridge, Cambridge University Press.

———, ed. 1998b. *Property Relations: Renewing the Anthropological Tradition*. Cambridge, Cambridge University Press.

———. 1998c. "Drama postkomunizmy." *Lyudina i Svit* 38 (4): 9–14.

———. 1998d. "Nationalism and Civil Society in Central Europe: From Ruritania to the Carpathian Euroregion." In *The State of the Nation. Ernest Gellner and the Theory of Nationalism*, edited by John A. Hall, 243–57. Cambridge: Cambridge University Press.

———. 1998e. "Postsocialist Nationalism: Rediscovering the Past in Southeast Poland." *Slavic Review* 57 (4): 840–63.

———. 1998f. "Religion, Trade and Trust in South-East Poland." *Religion, State and Society* 26 (3–4): 235–49.

———. 2000a "Culture and Civilization in Central Europe: A Critique of Huntington's Theses." In *Ein erweitertes Europa verstehen/Understanding an Enlarged Europe*, edited by Werner Konitzer, and Kristian Bosselmann-Cyran, 99–120. Frankfurt am Main: Peter Lang/Europa-Universität Viadrina.

———. 2000b "Zivilgesellschaft oder Citizenship? Skeptische Überlegungen eines Ethnologen." In *Europäische Zivilgesellschaft in Ost und West: Begriff, Geschichte, Chancen*, edited by Manfred Hildermeier, Jürgen Kocka, and Christoph Conrad, 85–109. Frankfurt am Main: Campus.

———. 2002. "The Development of Polish Civil Society and the Experience of the Greek Catholic Minority." In *Protecting the Human Rights of Religious Minorities in Eastern Europe*, edited by Peter G. Danchin, and Elizabeth A. Cole, 437–54. New York: Columbia University Press.

———. 2003a. "Civil Society: The Sickness, Not the Cure?" *Social Evolution & History* 2 (2): 34–54.

———. 2003b. "Creeds, Cultures and the Witchery of Music." *Journal of the Royal Anthropological Institute* 9 (2): 223–39.

———. 2004. "In the Church of Civil Society." In *Exploring Civil Society: Political and Cultural Contexts*, edited by Marlies Glasius, David Lewis, and Hakan Seckinelgin, 44–50. London: Routledge.

———. 2005a. "Between East and West: Greek Catholic Icons and Cultural Boundaries." In *Technology, Literacy and the Evolution of Society: Implications of the Work of Jack Goody*, edited by David Olson, and Michael Coleman, 73–100. Mahwah, NJ: Erlbaum.

———, ed. 2005b. *Property Relations: The Halle Focus Group 2000–2005.* Halle/Saale: Max Planck Institute for Social Anthropology.

———. 2006. *"Not the Horse We Wanted!" Postsocialism, Neoliberalism and Eurasia.* Münster: LIT.

———. 2007. "A New Double Movement? Anthropological Perspectives on Property in the Age of Neoliberalism." *Socio-Economic Review* 5 (2): 287–318.

———. 2009. "Does Ethnic Cleansing Work? The Case of Twentieth Century Poland." *Cambridge Anthropology* 29 (1): 1–25.

———. 2010a. "Class, Clans and the Moral Economy in Rural Eurasia." In *From Palermo to Penang: A Journey into Political Anthropology*, edited by François Ruegg, and Andrea Boscoboinik, 195–204. Berlin: LIT.

———. 2010b. "Moral Economy." In *The Human Economy: A Citizen's Guide*, edited by Keith Hart, Jean-Louis Laville, and Antonio David Cattani, 187–98. Cambridge: Polity.

———, ed. 2010c. *"Religion, Identities, Postsocialism": The Halle Focus Group, 2003–2010*. Halle: Max Planck Institute for Social Anthropology.

———. 2011. "Moral Dispossession." *InterDisciplines* 2 (2): 11–37 [and Reply to a comment by Stefan Merl, 46–51].

———. 2012. "The Europe Trap." *Lud* 96: 31–49.

———. 2013a. "Introduction: Nations and Nationalism, Societies and Socialism, Fields and Wars." In *The Anthropological Field on the Margins of Europe, 1945–1991*, edited by Chris Hann and Alexandar Bošković, 1–28. Berlin: LIT.

———. 2013b. "Still an Awkward Class: Central European Post-peasants at Home and Abroad in the Era of Neoliberalism." *Praktyka Teoretyczna* 3 (9): 177–98. http://www.praktykateoretyczna.pl/czasopismo/still-an-awkward-clas/

———. 2014a. "The Economistic Fallacy and Forms of Integration under and after Socialism." *Economy and Society* 43 (4): 626–49.

———. 2014b. "The Heart of the Matter: Christianity, Materiality, and Modernity." *Current Anthropology* [Supplement on *The Anthropology of Christianity: Unity, Diversity, New Directions*, edited by Joel Robbins, and Naomi Haynes] 55 (Supp. 10): 182–92.

———. 2014c. "Birds, Crowns and Christian Europe: The Ritual Symbolism of the Postsocialist Hungarian Nation-State." In *Kultura, tożsamość, integracja społeczna*, edited by Dariusz Niedźwiedzki, 71–84. Kraków: Nomos.

———. 2015a. "Backwardness Revisited: Time, Space, and Civilization in Rural Eastern Europe." *Comparative Studies in Society and History* 57 (4): 881–911.

———. 2015b. "Goody, Polanyi and Eurasia: An Unfinished Project in Comparative Historical Economic Anthropology." *History and Anthropology* 26 (3): 308–20.

———. 2015c. "Why Postimperial Trumps Postsocialist: Crying Back the National Past in Hungary." In *Anthropology and Nostalgia*, edited by Olivia Angé and David Berliner, 96–122. New York: Berghahn.

———. 2015d. "Property: Anthropological Aspects." In *International Encyclopedia of the Social & Behavioral Sciences*, (2nd edition), editor-in-chief James D. Wright, Vol. 19, 153–59. Oxford: Elsevier.

———. 2016a. "A Concept of Eurasia." *Current Anthropology* 57 (1): 1–27 (including symposium).

———. 2016b. "Cucumbers and Courgettes: Rural Workfare and the New Double Movement in Hungary." *Intersections* 2 (2): 38–56.

———. 2016c. "Overheated Underdogs: Civilizational Analysis and Migration on the Danube-Tisza Interfluve." *History and Anthropology* 27 (5): 602–16.

———. 2017. "Embeddedness and Effervescence: Political Economy and Community Sociality throughout a Century of Transformations in Rural Hungary." *Ethnologie française* 3 (167): 543–53.

———. 2018. "'Countryside—Soul of the Nation': Ideals and Realities in Contemporary Hungary." In *Über Land: Aktuelle literatur- und kulturwis-*

senschaftliche Perspektiven auf Dorf und Ländlichkeit, edited by Magdalena Marszałek, Werner Nell, Marc Weiland, 187–200. Bielefeld: transcript.
Hann, Chris, and the "Civil Religion" Group. 2006. *The Postsocialist Religious Question: Faith and Power in Central Asia and East-Central Europe*. Münster: LIT.
Hann, Chris, and Keith Hart, eds. 2009. *Market and Society: The Great Transformation Today*. Cambridge: Cambridge University Press.
———. 2011. *Economic Anthropology: History, Ethnography, Critique*. Cambridge: Polity.
Hann, Chris and László Kürti. 2015. "Agrarian Ideology and Local Governance: Continuities in Postsocialist Hungary." In *Knight from Komárov: To Petr Skalník for his 70th Birthday*, edited by Adam Bedřich and Tomáš Retka, 93–115. Prague: AntropoWeb.
Hann, Chris, and the "Property Relations" Group. 2003. *The Postsocialist Agrarian Question: Property Relations and the Rural Condition*. Münster: LIT.
Hann, Chris, and Mihály Sárkány. 2003. "The Great Transformation in Rural Hungary; Property, Life Strategies and Living Standards." In *The Postsocialist Agrarian Question: Property Relations and the Rural Condition,* Chris Hann, and the Property Relations Group, 117–42. Münster: LIT.
Hann, Chris, and Stanisław Stępień, eds. 2000. *Tradycja a tożsamość: Wywiady wśród mniejszości ukraińskiej w Przemyślu*. Przemyśl: Południowo-Wschodni Instytut Naukowy.
Harcsa, István and Imre Kovách. 1996. "Farmerek és mezőgazdasági vállalkozók." In *Társadalmi riport 1996*, edited by Rudolf Andorka, Tamás Kolosi and György Vukovich, 104–34. Budapest: TÁRKI Századvég.
Hardin, Garrett. 1968. "The tragedy of the commons." *Science* 162: 1243–48.
Hart, Keith. 2000. *The Memory Bank: Money in an Unequal World*. London: Profile Books.
———. 2013. "Manifesto for a Human Economy." *The Memory Bank*. http://thememorybank.co.uk/2013/01/20/object-methods-and-principles-of-human-economy/
———. n.d. "Intellectual property." Available at *The Memory Bank*, Accessed July 10, 2016. http://thememorybank.co.uk/papers/intellectual-property/.
Hart, Keith, Jean-Louis Laville and David Cattani, eds. 2010. *The Human Economy: A Citizen's Guide*. Cambridge: Polity.
Hauser, Leopold. 1991 [1883]. *Monografia miasta Przemyśla*. Przemyśl: Południowo-Wschodni Instytut Naukowy
Heady, Patrick. 2005. "Property and Kinship in Rural Russia—and Elsewhere." In *Property Relations: The Halle Focus Group 2000–2005*, edited by Chris Hann, 46–49. Halle/ Saale: Max Planck Institute for Social Anthropology.
Heller, Michael E. 1998. "The Tragedy of the Anticommons: Property in the Transition from Marx to Markets." *Harvard Law Review* 111 (3): 621–88.
Hertz, Robert. (1909) 1960. *Death and the Right Hand*. Aberdeen: Cohen and West.
Himka, John-Paul. 1984. "The Greek-Catholic Church and Nation-Building in Galicia, 1772–1918." *Harvard Ukrainian Studies* 8 (3–4): 426–52.

Hirschon, Renée, ed. 1984. *Women and Property, Women as Property*. London: Croom Helm.

Hobsbawm, Eric 1992. *Nations and Nationalism since 1780: Programme, Myth, Reality*. Cambridge: Cambridge University Press.

Hollos, Marida and Bela C. Maday, eds. 1983. *New Hungarian Peasants: An East Central European Experience with Collectivization*. New York: Brooklyn College Press.

Holmes, Leslie. 1997. *Post-Communism: An Introduction*. Cambridge: Polity.

Holtmann, Everhard. 2009. "Transition, Transformation, Posttransformation – zur Heuristik des Systemwandels in longitudinaler Perspektive." *Transition Transformation Posttransformation*. SFB 580 (Mitteilung 31): 21–37.

Hołuszko, Marek. 1993. "Mniejszości narodowe i etniczne w Polsce." *Społeczénstwo Otwarte* (2): i-xv.

Holy, Ladislav. 1992. "Culture, Market Ideology and Economic Reform in Czechoslovakia." In *Contesting Markets: Analyses of Ideology, Discourse and Practice*, edited by Roy Dilley, 231–43. Edinburgh: Edinburgh University Press.

Hosking, Geoffrey and George Schöpflin, eds. 1997. *Myths and Nationhood*. London: Taylor & Francis.

Hrytsak, Yaroslav 2006. "Historical Memory and Regional Identity among Galicia's Ukrainians." In *Galicia: a Multicultured Land*, edited by Christopher Hann and Paul Robert Magocsi, 185–209. Toronto: Toronto University Press.

Humphrey, Caroline. 1983. *Karl Marx Collective: Economy, Politics and Religion in a Siberian Collective Farm*. Cambridge: Cambridge University Press.

———. 2002a. *The Unmaking of the Soviet Live: Everyday Economies after Socialism*. Ithaca: Cornell University Press.

———. 2002b. "Rituals of Death as a Context for Understanding Personal Property in Socialist Mongolia." *Journal of the Royal Anthropological Institute* 8 (1): 65–87.

———. 2007. "New Subjects and Situated Interdependence: After Privatization in Ulan Ude." In *Urban Life in Post-Soviet Asia*, edited by Catherine Alexander, Viktor Buchli and Caroline Humphrey, 175–217. London: University College Press.

Humphrey, Caroline and David Sneath. 1999. *The End of Nomadism? Society, State, and the Environment in Inner Asia*. Knapwell: White Horse Press.

Hunt, Robert C. 1998. "Properties of Property: Conceptual Issues." In *Property in Economic Context*, edited by Hunt, R. C. and A. Gilman, 7–28. Lanham: University Press of America.

Hunt, Robert and A. Gilman, eds. 1998. *Property in Economic Context*. Lanham: University Press of America.

Huntington, Samuel P. 1996. *The Clash of Civilizations and the Remaking of World Order*. New York: Simon and Schuster.

Ignatieff, Michael. 1994. *Blood and Belonging: Journeys into the New Nationalism*. New York: Farrar, Straus, and Giroux.

Jakab, Attila. 2014. "Jó napom volt. Megírom." *Galamus Csoport*, January 16, http://www.galamuscsoport.hu/tartalom/cikk/351411_jo_napom_volt._megirom. Accessed June 3, 2016.

James, Deborah. 2006. "The Tragedy of the Private: Owners, Communities and the State in South Africa's Land Reform Programme." In *Changing Properties of Property*, edited by Franz von Benda-Beckmann, Keebet von Benda-Beckmann and Melanie Wiber, 243–68. Oxford: Berghahn.

Jasińska-Kania, Aleksandra. 1992. "Zmiany postaw Polaków wobec róznych narodów i panstw." In *Bliscy i dalecy: Studia nad postawami wobec innych narodów, ras i grup etnicznych*, edited by Aleksandra Jasińska-Kania, 219–46. Warsaw: Uniwersytet Warszawski Instytut Socjologii.

Jenkins, Robert. 1999. "The Role of the Hungarian Non-Profit Sector in Post-Communist Society." *East European Studies*. Newsletter, Woodrow Wilson International Center, Washington DC.

Jestal, Jerzy. 1994. "Stereotyp Ukraińca w świadomości młodzieży Polski południowo-wschodniej." *Fraza* 4 (5–6): 89–97.

Joó, Rudolf, ed. 1994. *The Hungarian Minority's Situation in Ceausescu's Romania*. Boulder: Social Science Monographs.

Juhász, Antal, ed. 1990. *Migráció és település a Duna-Tisza közén*. Szeged: Józef Attila Tudományegyetem.

Kalb, Don. 2009. "Conversations with a Polish Populist: Tracing Hidden Histories of Globalization, Class, and Dispossession in Postsocialism (and beyond)." *American Ethnologist* 36 (2): 207–23.

Kalb, Don and Csaba Halmai, eds. 2011. *Headlines of Nation, Subtexts of Class: Working-Class Populism and the Return of the Repressed in Neoliberal Europe*. New York: Berghahn Books.

Kamali, Masoud. 2001. "Civil Society and Islam: A Sociological Perspective." *Archives Européennes de Sociologie* 42 (3): 457–82.

Kaneff, Deema and Lale Yalçın-Heckmann. 2003. "Retreat to the Cooperative or to the Household? Agricultural Privatization in Ukraine and Azerbaijan." In *The Postsocialist Agrarian Question: Property Relations and the Rural Condition*, Chris Hann and the "Property Relations" Group, 219–56. Münster: LIT.

Karácsonyi, János. 1904. *Szent István királi Király Élete*. Budapest: Hermit Könyvkiadó Bt.

Karakasidou, Anastasia N. 1997. *Fields of Wheat, Hills of Blood: Passages to Nationhood in Greek Macedonia 1870–1990*. Chicago: University of Chicago Press.

Kasten, Erich. 2004a. "Ways of Owning and Sharing Cultural Property." In *Property of Culture – Culture as Property: Pathways to Reform in post-Soviet Siberia*, edited by Erich Kasten, 9–32. Berlin: Dietrich Reimer Verlag.

———. ed. 2004b. *Property of Culture – Culture as Property: Pathways to Reform in Post-Soviet Siberia*. Berlin: Dietrich Reimer Verlag.

Kearney, Michael. 1996. *Reconceptualizing the Peasantry: Anthropology in Global Perspective*. Boulder: Westview.

Keleher, Serge. 1993. *Passion and Resurrection: The Greek-Catholic Church in Soviet Ukraine 1939–1989.* L'viv: Stauropegion.

Kertzer, David. 1988. *Ritual, Politics and Power.* New Haven: Yale University Press.

Khazanov, Anatoly. 1995. *After the USSR: Ethnicity, Nationalism and Politics in the Commonwealth of Independent States.* Madison: University of Wisconsin Press.

Kideckel, David A. 1983. "Secular Ritual and Social Change: A Romanian Case." *Anthropological Quarterly* 56 (2): 69–75.

———. 1993. *The Solitude of Collectivism: Romanian Villagers to the Revolution and Beyond.* Ithaca: Cornell Univ. Press.

———, ed. 1995. *East European Communities: The Struggles for Balance in Turbulent Times.* Boulder: Westview Press.

King, Alexander. 2003. "Social Security in Kamchatka: Rural and Urban Comparisons." In *The Postsocialist Agrarian Question: Property Relations and the Rural Condition,* Chris Hann and the "Property Relations" Group, 391–418. Münster: LIT.

Klaniczay, Gábor. 1984. "Rockvázlat, történelmi háttérrel." *Filmvilág* 5: 17–19.

———. 1986. "From Sacral Kingship to Self-Representation. Hungarian and European Royal Saints in the 11th-13th centuries." In *Continuity and Change: Political Institutions and Literary Monuments in the Middle Ages,* edited by Elizabeth Vestergaard, 61–86. Odensee: Odense University Press.

———. 1988. "Szent István legendái a középkorban." In *Szent István és kora: A 950 éves hagyaték mai leltára,* edited by Ferenc Glatz and József Kardos, 185–96. Budapest: MTA Történettudományi Intézete.

Klosińska, Janina. 1966. *Ikonen aus Polen.* Recklinghausen: Ausstellungskatalog.

———. 1989. *Icons from Poland.* Warsaw: Arkady.

Kocka, Jürgen. 1997. "The Difficult Rise of a Civil Society; Societal History of Modern Germany." In *German History since 1800,* edited by Mary Fulbrook, 493–511. London: Oxford University Press.

Kolankiewicz, George. 1980. "The New 'Awkward Class': The Peasant-Worker in Poland." *Sociologia Ruralis* 20 (1–2): 28–43.

Koltay, Gábor. 1984. *István, a király.* Budapest: Ifjusági Lap és Könyvkiadó.

Konrád, George and Ivan Szelényi. 1979. *The Intellectuals on the Road to Class Power.* Brighton: Harvester Press.

Kornai, János. 1980. *Economics of Shortage.* Amsterdam: North Holland Press.

———. 1990. *The Road to a Free Economy: Shifting from a Socialist System: The Example of Hungary.* New York: W.W. Norton.

———. 1992. *The Socialist System: The Political Economy of Communism.* Oxford: Oxford University Press.

———. 2007. *By Force of Thought: Irregular Memoirs of an Intellectual Journey.* Cambridge, MA: MIT Press.

Korzec, Paweł. 1991. "The Ukrainian Problem in Interwar Poland." In *Ethnic Groups in International Relations,* edited by Paul Smith, 187–210. New York: New York University Press.

Kovách, Imre. 1988. *Termelők és vállalkozók: Mezőgazdasági kistermelők a magyar társadalomban, Rétegződés-modell vizsgálat (IX)*. Budapest: Társadalomtudományi Intézet.
Központi Statisztikai Hivatal. 2005. *Népszámlálás 2001. Vol. 28: A mezőgazdasági tevékenység jelentősége a foglalkoztatásban*. Budapest: KSH.
Krader, Lawrence, ed. 1972. *The Ethnological Notebooks of Karl Marx*. Assen: Van Gorcum.
Krajewski, Stanisław 2002. "Catholic-Jewish Dialogue in Poland: A Difficult Road to Tolerance." In *Protecting the Human Rights of Religious Minorities in Eastern Europe,* edited by Peter G. Danchin and Elizabeth A. Cole, 490–507. New York: Columbia University Press.
Kristóf, Luca. 2017. "Cultural Policy in an Illiberal State. A Case Study of Hungary after 2010." *Intersections* 3 (3): 126–47.
Kubik, Jan. 1994. *The Power of Symbols against the Symbols of Power: The Rise of Solidarity and the Fall of State Socialism in Poland.* Pennsylvania: Penn State University Press.
Kuper, Adam. 2003. "The Return of the Native." *Current Anthropology* 44 (3): 389–402.
Kürti, László. 2011. "The Politics of Festivals." In *Every Day's a Festival! Diversity on Show,* edited by Susanne Küchler, László Kürti and Hisham Elkadi, 53–82. Wantage: Sean Kingston Publishing.
———. 2015. "Neoshamanism, National Identity and the Holy Crown of Hungary." *Journal of Religion in Europe* 8 (2): 235–60.
Kürti, László and Peter Skalník, eds. 2009. *Postsocialist Europe: Anthropological Perspectives from Home.* New York: Berghahn.
Kwilecki, Andzej. 1974. *Łemkowie: Zagadnienie migracji i asymilacji.* Warszawa: Państwowe Wydawnictwo Naukowe.
Lampland, Martha. 1995. *The Object of Labor: Commodification in Socialist Hungary.* Chicago: University of Chicago Press.
———. 2002. "The Advantages of Being Collectivized: Cooperative Farm Managers in the Postsocialist Economy." In *Postsocialism: Ideals, Ideologies and Practices in Eurasia,* edited by Chris Hann, 31–56. London: Routledge.
Lane, Christel. 1981. *The Rites of Rulers: Ritual in Industrial Society—The Soviet Case.* Cambridge: Cambridge University Press.
László, Gyula and István Rácz. 1977. *A nagyszentmiklósi kincs.* Budapest: Corvina.
Latawski, Paul, ed. 1995. *Contemporary Nationalism in East Central Europe.* Basingstoke: Macmillan.
Layton, Robert. 2000. *Anthropology and History in Franche Compte: A Critique of Social Theory.* Oxford, Oxford University Press.
Leach, Edmund R. 1961. *Pul Eliya: A Village in Ceylon.* Cambridge: Cambridge University Press.
Ledeneva, Alena. 1998. *Russia's Economy of Favours: Blat, Networking and Informal Exchange.* Cambridge: Cambridge University Press.
Le Grand, Julian and Saul Estrin, eds. 1989. *Market Socialism.* Oxford: Oxford University Press.
Lendvai, Paul. 1988. *Hungary: The Art of Survival.* London: I.B. Tauris.

Lenin, Vladimir I. 1977 (1899). *The Development of Capitalism in Russia: The Process of the Formation of a Home-Market for Large-Scale Industry*. Moscow: Progress Publishers.

Leonard, Pamela and Deema Kaneff, eds. 2002. *Post-Socialist Peasant? Rural and Urban Constructions of Identity in Eastern Europe, East Asia and the Former Soviet Union*. Basingstoke: Palgrave.

Leutloff-Grandits, Carolin. 2006. *Claiming Ownership in Postwar Croatia: The Dynamics of Property Relations and Ethnic Conflict in the Knin Region*. Berlin: LIT.

Levitt, Kari Polanyi, ed. 1990. *The Life and Work of Karl Polanyi*. Montreal: Black Rose Books.

———. 2013. *From the Great Transformation to the Great Financialization: On Karl Polanyi and Other Essays*. London: Zed Books.

Lewicki, Anatol. 1994 (1880). *Obrazki najdawniejszych dziejów Przemyśla*. Przemyśl: Południowo-Wschodni Instytut Nauk.

Lockwood, William G. 1975. *European Moslems: Economy and Ethnicity in Western Bosnia*. New York: Academic Press.

Macfarlane, Alan. 1978. *The Origins of English Individualism*. Oxford: Blackwell.

———. 1987. *The Culture of Capitalism*. Oxford: Blackwell.

Mach, Zdzisław. 1993. *Symbols, Conflict, and Identity: Essays in Political Anthropology*. Albany, NY: State University of New York Press.

Macpherson, C. B. 1962. *The Political Theory of Possessive Individualism: Hobbes to Locke*. Oxford: Clarendon Press.

Magocsi, Paul Robert. 1987. "The Lemko Rusyns: Their Past and Present." *Carpatho-Rusyn American* 10 (1): 5–12.

———. 1988. "Religion and Identity in the Carpathians." *Cross Currents* 7: 87–107.

———. 1990. "Nation-Building or Nation Destroying? Lemkos, Poles and Ukrainians in Contemporary Poland." *Polish Review* 35 (3–4): 197–209.

———. 1993a. *Historical Atlas of East Central Europe*. Seattle: University of Washington Press.

———. 1993b. "Made or Re-made in America? Nationality and Identity Formation among Carpatho-Rusyn Immigrants and Their Descendants." In *The Persistence of Regional Cultures: Rusyns and Ukrainians in their Carpathian Homeland and Abroad*, edited by Robert Paul Magocsi, 163–78. New York: Columbia University Press.

———. 1993c. "Commentary." In *The Persistence of Regional Cultures: Rusyns and Ukrainians in their Carpathian Homeland and Abroad*, edited by Paul Robert Magocsi, 191–97. New York: Columbia University Press.

———. 1996. *A History of Ukraine: The Land and Its Peoples*. Toronto: University of Toronto Press.

———. 2015. *With Their Backs to the Mountains: A History of Carpathian Rus' and Carpatho-Rusyns*. Budapest: Central European University Press.

Magyar, Bálint. 2016. *Post-Communist Mafia State: The Case of Hungary*. Budapest: Central European University Press.

Mahieu, Stéphanie and Vlad Naumescu, eds. 2008. *Churches In-Between: Greek Catholic Churches in Postsocialist Europe*. Berlin: LIT Verlag.

Maine, Henri. 1861. *Ancient Law*. London: John Murray.

Makovicky, Nicolette. 2013. "'Work Pays': Slovak Neoliberalism as 'Authoritarian Populism.'" *Focaal* 67: 77–90.

———. 2014a. "Old Minorities in a New Europe: Enterprising Citizenship at the Polish-Czech Border." In *Neoliberalism, Personhood, and Postsocialism: Enterprising selves in changing economies*, edited by Nicolette Makovicky, 163–85. Farnham: Ashgate.

———, ed. 2014b. *Neoliberalism, Personhood, and Postsocialism: Enterprising Selves in Changing Economies*. Farnham: Ashgate.

Malewska-Szałgin, Anna. 2017. *Social Imaginaries of the State and Central Authority in Polish Highland Villages, 1999–2005*. Newcastle: Cambridge Scholars Publishing.

Malinowski, Bronislaw. 1966. *Coral Gardens and their Magic*. 2 vols. London: Allen and Unwin. First published in 1935.

Mandel, Ruth 2002. "Seeding Civil Society." In *Postsocialism: Ideals, Ideologies and Practices in Eurasia*, edited by Chris Hann, 279–96. London: Routledge.

Marshall, Thomas. 1977. *Class, Citizenship and Social Development*. Chicago: Doubleday & Company.

Maurer, Bill. 1999. "Forget Locke? From Proprietor to Risk-Bearer in New Logics of Finance." *Public Culture* 11 (2): 365–85.

Mauss, Marcel. 1990 (1925). *The Gift: The Form and Reason for Exchange in Archaic Societies*. London: Routledge.

McCay, Bonnie. J. 2001. "Environmental Anthropology at Sea." In *New Directions in Anthropology and Environment: Intersections*, edited by Carol. L. Crumley, 254–72. Walnut Creek: Alta Mira Press.

McCay, Bonnie J. and James Acheson, eds. 1987. *The Question of the Commons: The Culture and Ecology of Communal Resources*. Tucson: University of Arizona Press.

McNeill, William H. 1986. *Polyethnicity and National Unity in World History*. Toronto: University of Toronto Press.

Meek, Charles K., ed. 1946. *Land Law and Custom in the Colonies*. London: Oxford University Press.

van Meijl, Toon. 2006. "Who Owns the Fisheries? Changing Views of Property and its Redistribution in Post-Colonial Maori Society." In *Changing Properties of Property*, edited by von Benda-Beckmann, Franz, Keebet von Benda-Beckmann and Melanie Wiber, 170–93. Oxford: Berghahn.

Michna, Ewa. 1995. *Łemkowie: Grupa etniczna czy naród?* Kraków: Nomos.

Michnik, Adam. 1985. *Letters from Prison and Other Essays*. Berkeley: University of California Press.

———. 1995. "Nationalism." *Social Research* 58 (4): 757–63.

Miller, Daniel, ed. 1996. *Acknowledging Consumption: A Review of New Studies*. London: Routledge.

Minnich, Robert G. 1992. *Homesteaders and Citizens: An Ecology of Person and Self-Realisation among Slovene-Speaking Villagers on the Austro-Italian Frontier*. Bergen: University of Bergen.

Mokry, Włodzimierz, ed. 1997. *Problemy Ukrainców w Polsce po wysiedlenczej akcji "Wisła" 1947 roku*. Kraków: Wydawn/"Szwajpolt Fiol."

Molnár, István. 1995. *Vallási kisebbség és kisebbségi vallás: Görögkatolikusok a régi és a mai Lengyelországban*. Budapest: Balassi.

Moore, Jason W. 2015. *Capitalism in the Web of Life: Ecology and the Accumulation of Capital*. London: Verso.

Morgan, Lewis H. 1877. *Ancient Society*. New York: H. Holt.

Mucha, Janusz. 1988. "Malinowski and the Problems of Contemporary Civilisation." In *Malinowski Between Two Worlds: The Polish Roots of an Anthropological Tradition*, edited by Roy. F. Ellen, 149–63. Cambridge: Cambridge University Press.

———. 1989. "The Status of Unbelievers as a Group in Polish Society." *Journal of the Anthropological Society of Oxford* 20 (3): 209–18.

———. 1992. "Democratization and Cultural Minorities: The Polish Case of the 1980s/90s." *East European Quarterly* 25 (4): 463–82.

———. 1997a. "Cultural Minorities and the Dominant Group in Poland: A General Overview." In *Ethnic Minorities and Ethnic Majority,* edited by Marek S. Szczepanski, 83–94. Katowice: Uniwersytetu Śląskiego.

———. 1997b. "Mniejszości kulturowe a grupa dominująca w Polsce: Badania kulturowe z perspektywy zbiórowości mniejszościowych." In *Grupa etniczna, region, tożsamość kulturowa,* edited by Marek Dziewierski and Tomasz Nawrocki, 11–20. Katowice: Institut Socjologii Universitetu Śląskiego.

Müller, Birgit. 2007. *Disenchantment with Market Economics: East Germans and Western Capitalism*. Oxford: Berghahn Books.

Nagy, Terézia. 2009. "Being Locked Out and Locked In: The Culture of Homelessness in Hungary." In *Postsocialist Europe: Anthropological Perspectives from Home* edited by László Kürti and Peter Skalník, 206–26. New York: Berghahn.

Neale, Walter. 1962. *Economic Change in Rural India: Land Tenure and Reform in Uttar Pradesh, 1800–1955*. New Haven: Yale University Press.

Newbery, David M. 1991. *The Safety Net during Transformation: Hungary*. Working Paper, Department of Applied Economics, University of Cambridge.

Niedermüller, Peter. 1997. "Zeit, Geschichte, Vergangenheit: Zur kulturellen Logik des Nationalismus im Postsozialismus." *Historische Anthropologie: Kultur-Gesellschaft-Alltag* 5 (2): 245–67.

Niemiec, Agnieszka. 1998. "Akt adaptacji czy wyrok zniszczenia? Spóry o przebudowe przemyskiej katedry." *Architektura* (2): 68–69.

Nikulin, Alexander. 2011. "Misunderstanding and Confusion in Zemstvo and Post-Kolkhoz Budget Studies: Comparing Field Experiences." *Przegląd Wschodnioeuropejski* 2: 207–16.

North, Douglas. 1981. *Structure and Change in Economic History*. New York: Norton.

Nowak, Jacek. 1993. "Reconstruction of Ethnic Identity vs Inequalities: Lemkos in Poland." Paper presented at Amsterdam conference, The Anthropology of Ethnicity: A Critical review.

———. 1996. *Dynamika tożsamości Łemków wobec przemian w Europie Środkowej.* Ph.D. diss., Jagiellonian University, Kraków.

———. 2000. *Zaginiony świat? Nazywają ich Łemkami.* Kraków: Universitas.

Nowicka, Ewa. 1980. "Przyczynek do teorii etnicznych mniejszości" In *Założenia teorii asymilacji,* edited by Hieronim Kubiak and Andrzej Paluch, 105–26. Wrocław: Ossolineum.

Obrębski, Józef. 1976 (1936). *The Changing Peasantry of Eastern Europe.* Cambridge, MA: Schenkman Publishing Company Inc.

OECD. 1991. *Economic Surveys, Hungary.* Paris: OECD.

Offe, Claus. 2016. *Europe Entrapped.* Cambridge: Polity.

Offe, Claus and Jeremy Gaines. 1996. *The Varieties of Transition: The East European and East German Experience.* Cambridge: Polity Press.

Orwell, George 1970 (1947) "As I Please." In *The Collected Essays, Journalism and Letters of George Orwell, Volume 4, In Front of Your Nose 1945–1950,* edited by S. Orwell and I. Angus, 323–47. Harmondsworth: Penguin Books.

Ostrom, Elinor. 1990. *Governing the Commons: The Evolution of Institutions for Collective Action.* Cambridge: Cambridge University Press.

Pálsson, Gísli and Kristin Eerla Harðardóttir. 2002. "For Whom the Cell Tolls: Debates about Biomedicine." *Current Anthropology* 43 (2): 271–301.

Parry, Bronwyn. 2004. "Bodily Transactions: Regulating a New Space of Flows in 'Bio-Information.'" In *Property in Question: Value Transformation in the Global Economy,* edited by Katherine Verdery and Caroline Humphrey, 29–48. Oxford: Berg.

Parry, Jonathan and Maurice Bloch, eds. 1989. *Money and the Morality of Exchange.* Cambridge: Cambridge University Press.

Pasieka, Agnieszka. 2015. *Hierarchy and Pluralism: Living Religious Difference in Catholic Poland.* New York: Palgrave.

Pavlovits, Miklós. 1990. *A Tázlári Béke Mg. Szakszövetkezet harminc éve.* Tázlár: Béke Szakszövetkezet.

Paxson, Margaret. 2005. *Solovyovo: The Story of Memory in a Russian Village.* Washington DC and Bloomington: Woodrow Wilson Center Press and Indiana University Press.

Peters, Pauline Elaine. 1998. "The erosion of commons and the emergence of property: problems for social analysis." In *Property in Economic Context,* edited by Hunt, Robert C. and Antonio Gilman, 351–79. Lanham: University Press of America.

———. 2006. "Beyond Embeddedness: A Challenge Raised by a Comparison of the Struggles over Land in African and Post-Socialist Countries." In *Changing Properties of Property,* edited by von Benda-Beckmann, F., K. von Benda-Beckmann and M. Wiber, 84–105. Oxford: Berghahn.

Pieradzka, Krystyna. 1939. *Na Szlakach Łemkowszczyzny.* Kraków: Nakładem Komitetu do spraw szlachty zagrodowej na wschodzie Polski.

Piketty, Thomas. 2018. "2018, l'année de l'Europe." *Le blog de Thomas Piketty*, January 16, 2018, http://piketty.blog.lemonde.fr/2018/01/16/2018-lannee-de-leurope/. Accessed on October 12, 2018.

Pilichowska, Anastazija. 2008. "Changing Identities in the Polish Countryside? A Case Study from Lublin." In *Changing Economies and Changing Identities in Postsocialist Eastern Europe*, edited by Ingo W. Schröder and Asta Vonderau, 75–94. Berlin: LIT.

Pine, Frances. 1998. "Dealing With Fragmentation: The consequences of privatization for rural women in central and southern Poland." In *Surviving Post-Socialism: Local Strategies and regional responses in Eastern Europe and the Former Soviet Union*, edited by Sue Bridger and Frances Pine, 102–23. London: Routledge.

Pine, Frances, Deema Kaneff, and Haldis Haukanes, eds. 2004. *Memory, Politics and Religion: The Past Meets the Present in Europe.* Münster: LIT Verlag.

Pogátsa, Zoltán. 2016. *The Solution to Brexit Lies in Eastern Europe.* Social Europe blog, posted on July 1. https://www.socialeurope.eu/2016/07/solution-brexit-lies-eastern-europe/?utm_source=Viber&utm_medium=Chat&utm_campaign=Private

Polanyi, Karl. 1944. *The Great Transformation.* New York: Farrar and Rinehart.

———. 1957. "The Economy as Instituted Process." In *Trade and Market in the Early Empires*, edited by Karl Polanyi, Conrad Arensberg and Harry Pearson, 243–70. Glencoe: Free Press.

———. 1966. *Dahomey and the Slave Trade: An Analysis of an Archaic Economy.* Seattle: University of Washington Press.

———. 1971. "The Economy as Instituted Process." In *Trade and Market in the Early Empires: Economies in history and theory*, edited by Polanyi, Karl, Conrad Arensberg and Harry W. Pearson, 243–69. Chicago: Henry Regnery Company.

———. 1977. *The Livelihood of Man*, edited by Harry W. Pearson. New York: Academic Press.

———. 2014. *For a New West. Essays, 1919–1958*, edited by Giorgio Resta and Mariavittoria Catanzariti. Cambridge: Polity.

———. 2016. *The Hungarian Writings*, edited by Gareth Dale. Manchester: Manchester University Press.

Polanyi, Karl, Conrad Arensberg, and Harry W. Pearson, eds. 1957. *Trade and Market in the Early Empires.* Glencoe: Free Press.

Poliszczuk, Wiktor. 1993. *Gorzka Prawda: Zbrodniczość OUN-UPA.* Warsaw.

Potichnyj, Peter J., ed. 1980. *Poland and Ukraine: Past and Present.* Edmonton: CIUS Press.

Potter, Sulamith Heins and Jack M. Potter. 1990. *China's Peasants: The Anthropology of a Revolution.* Cambridge: Cambridge University Press.

Povinelli, Elisabeth. 2004. "At Home in the Violence of Recognition." In *Property in Question: Value Transformation in the Global Economy*, edited by Katherine Verdery and Caroline Humphrey, 185–206. Oxford: Berg.

Pryor, Frederic L. 1991. "When is Collectivization Reversible?" *Studies in Comparative Communism* 24: 3–24.

Pudło, Kazimierz. 1987. *Łemkowie: Proces wrastania w środowisko Dolnego Śląska 1947–1985*. Wrocław: Polskie Towarzystwo Ludoznawcze.

Pünkösti, Árpád. 1986. *Az elithez tartozni: A téeszelnökök kapcsolatrendszere*. Budapest: Tömegkommunikációs Kutató-központ.

Pusztai, Bertalan and Neill Martin, eds. 2007. *Feasts, Tourism and Local Identity: Fish Soup Cooking in Baja, Hungary*. Edinburgh, Szeged: University of Edinburgh & SzTE Néprajzi és Antropológiai Tanszék.

Rakowski, Tomasz. 2016. *Hunters, Gatherers, and Practitioners of Powerlessness: An Ethnography of the Degraded in Postsocialist Poland*. New York: Berghahn.

Ratzinger, Joseph. 1987. "Vatican Condemnation of Bulányi's Teachings." *Religion in Communist Lands* 15 (3): 346–50.

Reinfuss, Roman. 1948–49. "Łemkowie jako Grupa Etnograficzna." *Prace i Materiały Etnograficzne*, no. 7, 77–210. Lublin: Polskiego Towarzstwa Ludoznawczego.

Rifkin, Jeremy. 2001. *The Age of Access: The New Culture of Hypercapitalism, Where all of Life is a Paid-for Experience*. New York: TarcherPerigee.

Rivers, W. H. 1924. *Kinship and Social Organization*. London: Kegan Paul, Trench, Trubner.

Robertson, Roland. 1992. *Globalization: Social Theory and Social Culture*. London: Sage.

Rogan, Tim. 2017. *The Moral Economists: R. H. Tawney, Karl Polanyi, E. P. Thompson, and the Critique of Capitalism*. Princeton: Princeton University Press.

Roy, Olivier. 1999. "Kolkhoz and Civil Society in the Independent States of Central Asia." In *Civil Society in Central Asia*, edited by M. Holt Ruffin and Daniel Waugh, 109–21. Washington: Washington University Press.

Ruffy, Péter. 1988. *Magyar ereklyék, magyar jelképek*. Budapest: Kossuth.

Ryan, Alan. 1984. *Property and Political Theory*. Oxford: Blackwell.

Sahlins, Marshall. 1972. *Stone Age Economics*. London: Tavistock.

Salais, Robert. 2013. *Le viol d'Europe. Enquête sur la disparition d'une idée*. Paris: PUF.

Sampson, Steven. 2002. "Beyond Transition: Rethinking Elite Configurations in the Balkans." In *Postsocialism: Ideals, Ideologies and Practices in Eurasia*, edited by Chris Hann, 297–317. London: Routledge.

Sárkány, Mihály. 1983. "A lakodalom funkciójának megváltozása falun." *Ethnographia* 92: 279–85.

———. 2002. "Cultural and Social Anthropology in Central and eastern Europe." In *Three Social Science Disciplines in Central and Eastern Europe: Handbook on Economics, Political Science and Sociology (1989–2001)*, edited by Max Kaase, Vera Sparschuh, and Agnieszka Wenninger, 558–66. Bonn/Berlin and Budapest: Social Science Information Centre (IZ) and Collegium Budapest.

Schlicht, Ekkehart. 1998. *On Custom in the Economy*. Oxford: Clarendon Press.

Schneider, Deborah C. 2006. *Being Goral: Identity Politics and Globalization in Postsocialist Poland*. Albany, NY: State University of New York Press.

Schöpflin, George. 2016. "Political Lessons for Central Europe from Orbán's Hungary." *Aspen Review* 2. https://www.aspen.review/article/2017/political-lessons-for-central-europe-from-orbans-hungary/
Seddon, David, ed. 1978. *Relations of Production: Marxist Approaches to Economic Anthropology*. Brighton: Frank Cass.
Seeger, Anthony. 2004. "The Selective Protection of Musical Ideas: The 'Creators' and the Dispossessed." In *Property in Question: Value Transformation in the Global Economy*, edited by KatherineVerdery and Caroline Humphrey, 69–83. Oxford, Berg.
Sekeráková Búriková, Zuzana. 2014. "Earning Money, Learning the Language: Slovak au pairs and their passage to adulthood." In *Neoliberalism, Personhood, and Postsocialism. Enterprising Selves in Changing Economies*, edited by Nicolette Makovicky, 145–61. Farnham: Ashgate.
Seligman, Adam. 1992. *The Idea of a Civil Society*. Princeton: Princeton University Press.
Seredi, Jusztinián. 1988 (1938). *Emlékkönyv Szent lstván király halálának kilencszázadik évfordulóján.* Budapest: Szent István-Társulat.
Servet, Jean-Michel. 2010. *Le grand renversement: De la crise au renouveau solidaire.* Paris: Desclée de Brouwer.
———. 2013. "Le principe de réciprocité aujourd'hui. Un concept pour comprendre etconstruire l'économie solidaire." In *Socioéconomie et démocratie: L'actualité de Karl Polanyi,* edited by Isabelle Hillenkamp and Jean-Louis Laville, 187–213. Toulouse: Erès.
Shanin, Teodor. 1972. *The Awkward Class: Political Sociology of Peasantry in a Developing Society: Russia 1910–1925.* Oxford: Clarendon Press.
———. 1990. *Defining Peasants.* Oxford: Blackwell.
Shore, Cris. 1993. "Inventing the 'People's Europe': Critical Approaches to European Community 'Cultural Policy'." *Man* 28 (4): 779–800.
Siegrist, Hannes. 2003. "Geschichte und aktuelle Probleme des geistigen Eigentums 1600–2000." In *E-Merging Media: Kommunikation und Medienwirtschaft der Zukunft,* edited by Axel Zerdick, 313–32. Berlin: Springer.
———. 2006. "Die Propertisierung von Gesellschaft und Kultur. Konstruktion und Institutionalisierung des Eigentums in der Moderne." *Comparativ* 16 (5–6): 9–52.
Sik, Endre. 1988. "Reciprocal Exchange of Labour in Hungary." In *On Work: Historical, Comparative and Theoretical Approaches*, edited by Ray Pahl, 527–47. Oxford: Basil B1ackwell.
———. 1994. "From the Multicoloured to the Black and White Economy: The Hungarian Second Economy and the Transformation." *International Journal of Urban and Regional Research* 18 (1): 46–70.
Simó, Tibor, ed. 1987. *Szakszövetkezetek Bács-Kiskun megyében.* Kecskemét: Kiskunsági Mezőgazdsági Szövetkezetek Területi Szövetsége.
Skalník, Peter. 1993. "'Socialism is Dead' and Very Much Alive in Slovakia: Political Inertia in a Tatra Village." In *Socialism: Ideals, Ideologies and Local Practice*, edited by Chris Hann, 218–26. London: Routledge.

———. 2009. "Political Anthropology of the Postcommunist Czech Republic: Local-national and Rural-urban Scenes." In *Postsocialist Europe: Anthropological Perspectives from Home*, edited by László Kürti and Peter Skalník, 227–51. New York: Berghahn.

Skurnowicz, Joan S. 1981. *Romantic Nationalism and Liberalism: Joachim Lelewel and the Polish National Idea.* Boulder: East European Monographs.

Smigielska, Joanna. 1995. "A Rural Business Class in Transition: Observations from a Polish Region." In *East European Communities: The Struggle for Balance in Turbulent Times,* edited by David A. Kideckel, 237–48. Boulder: Westview Press.

Sneath, David. 2000. *Changing Inner Mongolia: Pastoral Mongolian Society and the Chinese State.* Oxford: Oxford University Press.

Sorabji, Cornelia. 1989. "Muslim Identity and Islamic Faith in Sarajevo." Unpublished PhD. Dissertation, University of Cambridge.

Sosnowska, Danuta. 1997. "Narodziny rezuna." *Gazeta Wyborcza,* June 6, 1997, 20–22.

Sreenivasan, Govind. 1991. "The Land-Family Bond at Earls Colne (Essex) 1550–1650." *Past & Present* 131: 3–37.

Stammler, Florian. 2005. *Reindeer Nomads Meet the Market: Culture, Property and Globalisation at the "End of the Land".* Münster: LIT.

Stammler, Florian and Aimar Ventsel. 2003. "Between Neoliberalism and Dirigisme: Approaches to Reindeer Herding in Yamal and Sakha." In *The Postsocialist Agrarian Question: Property Relations and the Rural Condition,* Chris Hann and the "Property Relations" Group, 321–62. Münster: LIT.

Standing, Guy. 2011. *The Precariat—The New Dangerous Class.* London: Bloomsbury.

Stark, David. 1989. "Coexisting Organizational Forms in Hungary's Emerging Mixed Economy." In *Remaking the Economic Institutions of Socialism: China and Eastern Europe,* edited by Victor Nee and David Stark, 137–92. Stanford: Stanford University Press.

———. 1990. "Privatization in Hungary—from Plan to Market or from Plan to Clan?" *Eastern European Politics and Societies* 4 (3): 351–92.

Stewart, Michael. 1990. "Gypsies, Work and Civil Society." In *Market Economy and Civil Society in Hungary,* edited by Chris Hann, 140–62. London: Frank Cass.

———, ed. 2012. *The Gypsy "Menace": Populism and the New Anti-Gypsy Politics.* London: Hurst.

Strathern, Marilyn. 1988. *The Gender of the Gift: Problems with Women and Problems with Society in Melanesia.* Berkeley: University of California Press.

———. 1999. *Property, Substance and Effect: Anthropological Essays on Persons and Things.* London: Athlone.

Streeck, Wolfgang. 2016. *How Will Capitalism End? Essays on a Failing System.* London: Verso.

———. 2017. *Buying Time. The Delayed Crisis of Democratic Capitalism.* (translated by Patrick Camiller) London: Verso.

Swain, Nigel. 1985. *Collective Farms Which Work?* Cambridge: Cambridge University Press.

———. 1992. *Hungary: The Rise and Fall of Feasible Socialism.* London: Verso.

———. 2013. *Green Barons, Force-of-Circumstance Entrepreneurs, Impotent Mayors: Rural Change in the Early Years of Post-Socialist Capitalist Democracy.* Budapest–New York: Central European University Press.

Swain, Geoffrey and Nigel Swain. 2018. *Eastern Europe since 1945.* (5th Edition) New York: Palgrave.

Szabadi, Pál. 1997. *Tázlár krónikája.* Tázlár: Önkormányzat.

Szajkowski, Bohdan. 1983. *Next to God . . . Poland. Politics and Religion in Contemporary Poland.* London: Frances Printer Publishers Ltd.

Szántó, Konrád. 1988. "A Szent Jobb tisztelete a középkorban." In *Szent István és kora,* edited by Ferenc Glatz and József Kardos, 173–79. Budapest: MTA Történettudományi Intézet.

Szász, Imre. 1985. *Vadászat.* Budapest: Szépirodalmi.

Szelenyi, Ivan. 1983. *Urban Inequalities under State Socialism.* Oxford: Oxford University Press.

———. 1988. *Socialist Entrepreneurs: Embourgeoisement in Rural Hungary.* Madison: University of Wisconsin Press.

———. 1989. "Eastern Europe in an Epoch of Transition: Toward a Socialist Mixed Economy?" In *Remaking the Economic Institutions of Socialism: China and Eastern Europe,* edited by Victor Nee and David Stark with Mark Selden, 208–32. Stanford, CA: Stanford University Press.

Szikra, Dorottya. 2014. "Democracy and welfare in hard times: The social policy of the Orbán Government in Hungary between 2010 and 2014." *Journal of European Social Policy* 24 (5): 486–500.

Szőke, Alexandra. 2012. *Rescaling States—Rescaling Insecurities. Rural Citizenship at the Edge of the Hungarian State.* Doctoral Dissertation, Central European University, Budapest.

Sztompka, Piotr. 1996. "Trust and Emerging Democracy: Lessons from Poland." *International Sociology* 11 (1): 37–62.

Szűcs, Jenő. 1988. "Saint Stephen's Exhortations: King Stephen's State." *New Hungarian Quarterly,* 29 (4): 89–98.

Tarnovschi, Daniela. 2003. "Roma Civil Society Romania." Paper presented at the Conference Intercultural Relations, Citizenship and Human Rights in the Context of Central and Eastern Europe. Coppet, Switzerland, June 26–29, 2003.

Taylor, Mary. 2008. "Does Folk Dancing Make Hungarians? Táncház, Folk Dance as Mother Tongue, and Folk National Cultivation." *Hungarian Studies* 22 (1–2): 9–29.

Thelen, Tatjana. 2003a. *Privatisierung und soziale Ungleichheit in der osteuropäischen Landwirtschaft: Zwei Fallstudien aus Ungarn und Rumänien.* Frankfurt: Campus.

———. 2003b. "Are the kuláks back? Inherited Capital and Social Continuity in Mesterszállás, Hungary." In *Distinct Inheritances: Property, Family and*

Community in a Changing Europe, edited by Grandits, Hannes and Patrick Heady, 329–46. Münster: LIT.

———. 2011. "Shortage, Fuzzy Property and Other Dead Ends in the Anthropological Analysis of (Post)socialism." *Critique of Anthropology* 31 (1): 43–61.

Thomas, William I. and Florian W. Znaniecki. 1918–19. *The Polish Peasant in Europe and America.* Chicago: University of Chicago Press.

Thomasberger, Claus. 2018. "Freedom, Responsibility and the Recognition of the Reality of Society." In *Karl Polanyi's Vision of a Socialist Transformation,* edited by Michael Brie and Claus Thomasberger. Montreal: Black Rose Books.

Thornton, Robert and Peter Skalník, eds. 1993. *The Early Writings of Bronislaw Malinowski.* Cambridge: Cambridge University Press.

Todorova, Maria and Zsuzsa Gille, eds. 2012. *Post-Communist Nostalgia.* New York: Berghahn.

Tomaszewski, Jerzy. 1985. *Ojczyzna nie tylko Polaków: Mniejszości narodowe w Polsce w latach 1918–1939.* Warsaw: Młodzieżowa Agencja Wydawnicza.

———. 1993. "The National Question in Poland in the Twentieth Century." In *The National Question in Europe in Historical Context,* edited by Mikulas Teich and Roy Porter, 293–316. Cambridge: Cambridge University Press.

Torsello, Davide. 2003a. *Trust, Property and Social Change in a Southern Slovakian Village.* Münster: LIT.

———. 2003b. "History, Trust and Property in the Relation between Villagers and the Agricultural Cooperative. The Case of Királyfa, Southern Slovakia." In *The Postsocialist Agrarian Question: Property Relations and the Rural Condition,* Chris Hann and the "Property Relations" Group, 93–116. Münster: LIT.

Trevisani, Tommaso. 2010. *Land and Power in Khorezm: Farmers, Communities and the State in Uzbekistan's Decollectivisation.* Berlin: LIT.

Uherek, Zdenek. 2009. "Immigrants from Ukraine in the Czech Republic: Foreigners in the Border Zone." In *Postsocialist Europe: Anthropological Perspectives from Home,* edited by László Kürti and Peter Skalník, 270–94. New York: Berghahn.

Váradi, Monika M. 2016. "Értékteremtő közfoglalkoztatás periferikus vidéki terekben." *Esély,* 27 (1): 30–56.

Vasary, Ildiko. 1987. *Beyond the Plan: Social Change in a Hungarian Village.* Boulder: Westview Press.

Végh, Zsuzsanna. 2018. "The Power of the Visegrad Cooperation." In *Understanding Central Europe,* edited by Marcin Moskalewicz and Wojciech Przybylski, 441–49. New York: Routledge.

Ventsel, Aimar. 2005. *Reindeer,* Rodina *and Reciprocity: Kinship and Property Relations in a Siberian Village.* Münster: LIT.

Verdery, Katherine. 1983. *Transylvanian Villagers: Three Centuries of Political, Economic and Ethnic Change, 1700–1980.* Berkeley: University of California Press.

———. 1991a. *National Ideology under Socialism: Identity and Cultural Politics in Ceauçescu's Romania.* Berkeley: University of California Press.

———. 1991b. "Theorizing Socialism: A Prologue to the 'Transition'." *American Ethnologist* 18 (3): 419–39.
———. 1996. *What Was Socialism and What Comes Next?* Princeton: Princeton University Press.
———. 1999. "Fuzzy Property: Rights, Power, and Identity in Transylvania's Decollectivization." In *Uncertain Transition: Ethnographies of Change in the Postsocialist World*, edited by Michael Burawoy and Katherine Verdery, 53–82. Lanham: Rowman & Littlefield.
———. 2003. *The Vanishing Hectare: Property and Value in Postsocialist Transylvania*. Ithaca, NY: Cornell University Press.
Verdery, Katherine and Caroline Humphrey, eds. 2004. *Property in Question: Value Transformation in the Global Economy*. Oxford: Berg.
Vidacs, Bea. 2015. "The Ideal of Self-Sufficiency and the Reality of Dependence: A Hungarian Case." In *Oikos and Market: Explorations of Self-Sufficiency after Socialism*, edited by Stephen Gudeman and Chris Hann, 24–46. New York: Berghahn.
Visser, Oane. 2003. "Family Farms, Community and the Decline of the Former Kolkhozy in Russia." In *Distinct Inheritances: Property, Family and Community in a Changing Europe*, edited by Hannes Grandits and Patrick Heady, 313–28. Münster: LIT.
———. 2006. "Property, Labour Relations and Social Obligations in Russia's Privatized Farm Enterprises." In *Changing Properties of Property*, edited by von Benda-Beckmann, Franz, Keebet von Benda-Beckmann and Melanie Wiber, 126–46. Oxford: Berghahn.
Walker Bynum, Caroline, Stevan Harrell, and Paula Richman, eds. 1986. *Gender and Religion: On the Complexity of Symbols*. Boston: Beacon.
Wall, Caleb. 2007. "Peasant Resistance in Khorezm? The Difficulties of Classifying Non-Compliance in Rural Uzbekistan." In *Patterns of Transformation In and Around Uzbekistan*, edited by Paolo Sartori and Tommaso Trevisani, 217–40. Reggio Emilia: Edizione Diabasis.
Warriner, Doreen 1939. *The Economics of Peasant Farming*. London: Oxford University Press.
Watson, James L., ed. 1997. *Golden Arches East: McDonald's in East Asia*. Stanford: Stanford University Press.
Wedel, Janine R. 1998. *Collision and Collusion: The Strange Case of Western Aid to Eastern Europe 1989–1998*. New York: St Martins Press.
Wegren, Stephen K, Valeri V. Patsiorkovski and David J. O'Brien. 2006. "Beyond Stratification: The Emerging Class Structure in Rural Russia." *Journal of Agrarian Change* 6 (3): 372–99.
Wiatr, Jerzy Józef 1977. "Polish society." In *Poland: A Handbook*, 126–45. Warsaw: Interpress.
Wiber, Melanie. 2000. "Fishing Rights as an Example of the Economic Rhetoric of Privatization: Calling for an Implicated Economics" *Canadian Review of Sociology and Anthropology* 37: 267–88.
———. 2006. "Cultural Property, Repatriation and Relative Publics: Which Public? Whose Culture?" In *Changing Properties of Property*, edited by

Franz von Benda-Beckmann, Keebet von Benda-Beckmann, and Melanie Wiber, 330–48. Oxford: Berghahn.

Widlok, Thomas. 2001. "Living on Ethnography and Comparison: What difference do Hai//om 'Bushmen' make to anthropology (and vice versa)?" *Anthropos* 96: 359–78.

Wilson, Stephen. 1983. "Introduction." In *Saints and Their Cults: Studies in Religious Sociology, Folklore and History*, edited by Stephen Wilson, 1–51. Cambridge: Cambridge University Press.

Yalçın-Heckmann, Lale. 2010. *The Return of Private Property: Rural Life after Agrarian Reforms in the Republic of Azerbaijan.* Berlin: LIT Verlag.

Zięba, Andrzej. 1988. "The Lemko Question in the Polish Press 1980–86." *Carpatho-Rusyn American* 11 (1): 9–11.

Ziker, John P. 2002. *Peoples of the Tundra: Northern Siberians in the Post-Communist Transition.* Prospect Heights, IL: Waveland Press.

———. 2003. "Horseradish is No Sweeter than Turnips: Entitlements and Sustainability in the Taimyr Autonomous Region, Northern Russia." In *The Postsocialist Agrarian Question: Property Relations and Rural Condition*, Chris Hann and the Property Relations Group, 363–90. Münster: LIT.

Index

F

N

R